FOCUS ON SUCCESS

The new edition

Ausgabe Baden-Württemberg

David Clarke

Michael Macfarlane

in Zusammenarbeit mit
Philipp Fehrenbach
und der Verlagsredaktion

Cornelsen

Focus on Success – The new edition: Ausgabe Baden-Württemberg wurde geplant und entwickelt von der Redaktion Moderne Fremdsprachen des Cornelsen Verlags, Berlin.

Verfasser:	David Clarke, Witten Michael Macfarlane, Oxford
Berater/innen:	Rolf Bastian, Wetzlar; Philipp Fehrenbach, Nürtingen; Elke Uthoff, Osnabrück; Sibylle Vogel, Erfurt; Sybille Weiß, Mönchengladbach; Kathrin Wendling, Kamenz
Projektleitung:	Jim Austin
Verlagsredaktion:	Kieran Breen, Andreas Goebel
Außenredaktion:	James Abram, Christine House
Redaktionelle Mitarbeit:	Leah Holroyd, Laura Spratling, Lauren Chexal Yovana Gruissem, Fritz Preuss, Oliver Gascoigne (Wörterverzeichnisse)
Bildredaktion:	Kieran Breen, Jürgen Frey, Gertha Maly
Layout und technische Umsetzung:	Petra Eberhard Grafik Design, Berlin; Oxana Rödel, Absatz DTP-Service, Berlin
Umschlaggestaltung:	werkstatt für gebrauchsgrafik, Berlin
Illustrationen:	Marcin Nowakowski, Mariusz Zabdyr, Oxford Designers & Illustrators, Thomas Malangeri, Berlin

Erhältlich sind auch:

Workbook (zur Ausgabe Baden-Württemberg)	978-3-06-450652-7
Handreichungen für den Unterricht (zur Ausgabe Baden-Württemberg) mit CD-ROM und Audio-CDs	978-3-06-450653-4
Vocabulary Practice Book (zu allen Ausgaben)	978-3-06-020279-9

www.cornelsen.de

Die Links zu externen Webseiten Dritter, die in diesem Lehrwerk angegeben sind, wurden vor Drucklegung sorgfältig auf ihre Aktualität geprüft. Der Verlag übernimmt keine Gewähr für die Aktualität und den Inhalt dieser Seiten oder solcher, die mit ihnen verlinkt sind.

1. Auflage, 1. Druck 2011

Alle Drucke dieser Auflage sind inhaltlich unverändert und können im Unterricht nebeneinander verwendet werden.

Druck: CS-Druck CornelsenStürtz, Berlin

ISBN 978-3-06-450631-2

Inhalt gedruckt auf säurefreiem Papier aus nachhaltiger Forstwirtschaft.

VORWORT

Liebe Lehrerinnen und Lehrer,

Focus on Success – The new edition: Ausgabe Baden-Württemberg ist konzipiert für Lernende an Berufskollegs. Es setzt Englischkenntnisse auf dem Niveau des mittleren Abschlusses voraus und bereitet auf die zentrale Klassenarbeit Hörverstehen und die neue zentrale schriftliche Prüfung zur Erlangung der Fachhochschulreife vor. Das Lehrwerk führt zur Stufe B2 des Gemeinsamen europäischen Referenzrahmens.

Focus on Success – The new edition: Ausgabe Baden-Württemberg bietet neue, interessante Texte, aktuelle Themen und einen auf den Lehrplan und die Prüfung abgestimmten Aufgabenapparat. Die bewährte Struktur wurde beibehalten:

Auf den *Refresher Course* folgen 12 *Main Course*-Units, die einheitlich aufgebaut sind:

> Focus: Der Einstieg ins Thema

> Text A: *Personal perspectives*

> Text B: *The bigger picture*

> *Further options:* Zusatzmaterialien

Die Übungen, die auf die Texte folgen, schulen eine Vielzahl von *Skills* und trainieren darüber hinaus gezielt alle Aufgabentypen, die in der Abschlussprüfung vorkommen.

Die Grammatik befindet sich am Ende jeder Unit in einem *Grammar checkpoint*.

Der Anhang bietet neben einer *Grammar summary* umfangreiche Wörterverzeichnisse, einen Leitfaden zu Lernstrategien (*Skills*) sowie Tipps für die zentrale Abschlussprüfung (*Exam preparation*).

Liebe Schülerinnen und Schüler,

Focus on Success – The new edition: Ausgabe Baden-Württemberg ist Ihr neuer Begleiter auf dem Weg zur Fachhochschulreife.

Verschaffen Sie sich einen kurzen Überblick über das Buch, und Sie werden darin alles finden, was Sie für einen erfolgreichen Englischunterricht benötigen.

Sie möchten ...

> eine grammatische Form nachschlagen?
Dann schauen Sie einfach hinten in der *Grammar summary* oder der Liste der *Irregular verbs* nach.

> Tipps und Hilfen für den Umgang mit schwierigen Texten und kniffligen Aufgaben bekommen?
Dann werden Sie in dem Teil *Skills* im Anhang fündig – hier finden Sie zahlreiche Tipps, die Ihnen helfen, das Lernen effektiver zu gestalten.

> sich gezielt auf die zentrale Abschlussprüfung und die Hörverstehensklausur vorbereiten?
Jede Unit enthält eine Vielzahl an Aufgaben, die genau das üben, was in der Abschlussprüfung und der Klausur verlangt wird. Im Anhang *Exam preparation* finden Sie auch Tipps für die Abschlussprüfung und die Klausur.

> Vokabeln so lernen, dass Sie sie nicht gleich wieder vergessen?
In der *Unit word list* im Anhang ist der Lerneffekt gleich doppelt: Neben der deutschen Übersetzung lernen Sie auch Wörter mit gleicher oder gegensätzlicher Bedeutung, kurze und bündige Umschreibungen usw.

Viel Spaß und Erfolg mit dem Buch!

Autoren und Redaktion

CONTENTS

Refresher Course

Page	Unit	Title and texts	Grammar
6	A	**Free-time activities**	Subject and object pronouns Simple present Present progressive
12	B	**Girls fight for their rights**	Simple past
16	C	**You are what you eat**	Possessive adjectives Countable and uncountable nouns Unspecified quantities
22	D	**Time out**	Future
26	E	**Shopping**	Adjectives and adverbs Position of adverbs
30	F	**Ready for a job?**	Present perfect

Main Course

Page	Unit	Title and texts	Exam preparation	Grammar	Further options
35	1	**City lights** > Moving to NY > A Bite of the Big Apple	Mediation Textaussagen Materialgest. Aufsatz Hörverstehen	Comparison of adjectives Comparatives and superlatives	Planning a day out
45	2	**Advertising** > Dream destinations > Focus Forum: 'We're swimming in a sea of advertising'	Mediation Textaussagen Bildbeschreibung Hörverstehen	Past progressive and simple past Relative clauses	Analyzing and constructing an advertise-ment
55	3	**Media madness** > Big Bother hits Big Brother > Great medium, but what about your message?	Materialgest. Aufsatz Hörverstehen	Modal verbs and their substitutes	1984 (extract)
65	4	**On the move** > On the roads: four views > Satellite road pricing is on the way / The road to zero emissions	Textaussagen Bildbeschreibung Materialgest. Aufsatz Hörverstehen	*If*-sentences types 1 and 2	Looking at the car of the future

Page	Unit	Title and texts	Exam preparation	Grammar	Further options
75	5	**Green enough?** > Going green: the final report > News from the future	Mediation Textaussagen Bildbeschreibung Materialgest. Aufsatz Hörverstehen	Past perfect *If*-sentences type 3	Activities to help the environment
85	6	**Modern ways to work** > Routes to the modern workplace: complex but flexible > A contract too good to be true?	Mediation Materialgest. Aufsatz Hörverstehen	Present perfect progressive and present perfect General revision of tenses	Aptitude tests
95	7	**Going global** > Globalization – good or bad? > Let's be fair about trade	Mediation Textaussagen Materialgest. Aufsatz Hörverstehen	Passive Passive with modal verbs	A big journey for a small apple Role-play: Should the factory close?
105	8	**Finding a job in the EU** > An internship in the UK > Now it's your turn: Britain and the EU	Bildbeschreibung Hörverstehen	Gerunds and infinitives	Personality test
115	9	**Social challenges** > What's in a family? > Changing society	Textaussagen Materialgest. Aufsatz Hörverstehen	Participles	Dress sense
125	10	**Multiculturalism** > My Son the Fanatic > The New Face of America	Mediation Textaussagen Bildbeschreibung Materialgest. Aufsatz Hörverstehen	Reported speech	Immigration in Germany
135	11	**Crime** > A step too far? > A stitch in time saves nine	Mediation Bildbeschreibung Materialgest. Aufsatz Hörverstehen	Word order	Three case studies: school shootings
145	12	**Future life, future living** > British supermarkets call for a boycott of 'cloned' meat and milk > Gene technology	Mediation Textaussagen Bildbeschreibung Materialgest. Aufsatz Hörverstehen	Grammar quiz	Project: Visions of the future

Appendix

155	Files	176	Grammar summary	237	A–Z word list
160	Skills	191	Basic word list	250	Geographical names
171	Exam preparation	198	Unit word list	252	Irregular verbs

A Free-time activities

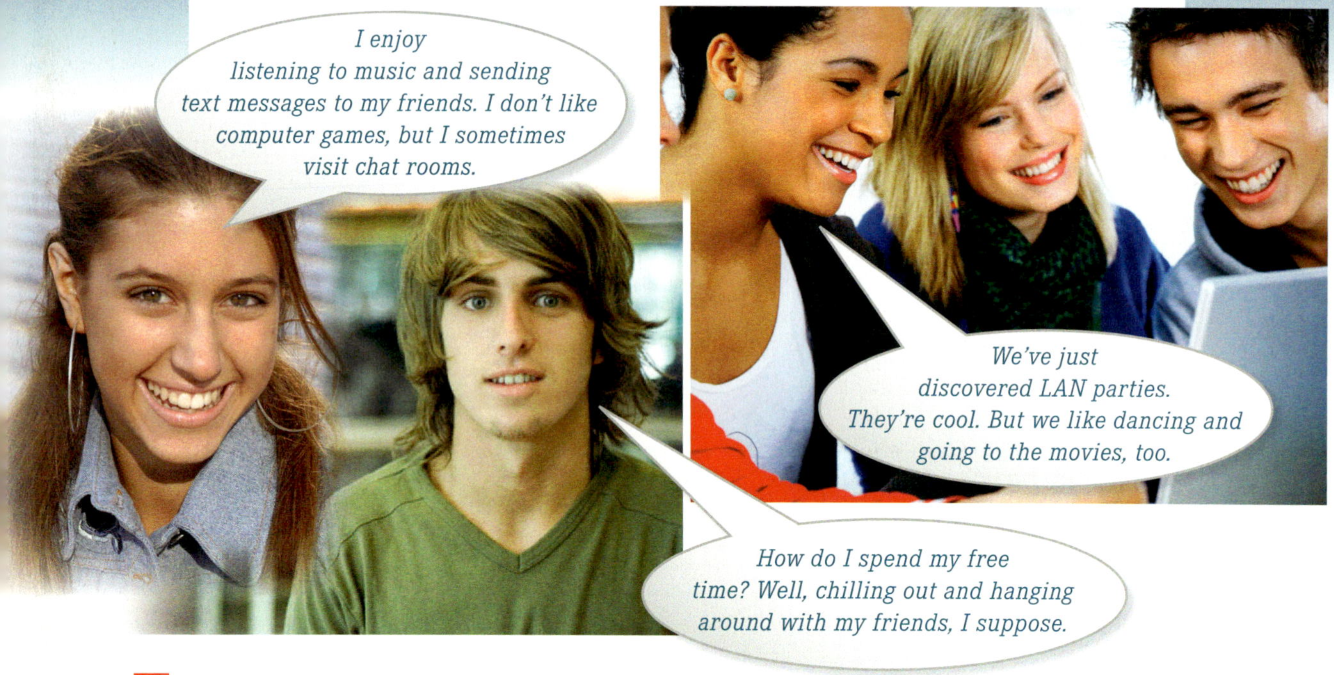

1 TALKING ABOUT YOURSELF

How do you spend your free time? Just chilling out, or doing something more active like sport? Use the language in the speech bubbles and the ideas in the box to talk about what you do.

chilling out | clubbing | dancing | doing sport | fishing | going to LAN parties | going to the movies | hanging around with friends | listening to music | making/mixing music | playing computer/video games | playing online poker | reading | riding | sending text messages / images with a mobile | shopping | surfing the net | phoning friends | visiting chat rooms | watching TV/DVDs

2 CARRYING OUT A SURVEY

A Ask other people what they like – or don't like – doing in their free time.

What's your favourite free-time activity?
What do you like doing most, ... or ...?
Which (activity) do you prefer, ... or ...?
Do you enjoy reading / doing a sport / ...?
Do you belong to a sports club?
How much time do you spend playing computer games / ... every day/week?

B Now carry out a survey. Which are the three most popular activities in your class?

According to the media, young people today spend too much of their free time just sitting in front of televisions or computers. But is this true? We asked four young people to describe their free-time activities. Read what they had to say.

DANA ***I spend most of my free time working for the Red Cross.*** *I really feel that I'm doing something worthwhile, not just sitting in front of the box! This week we're working with the homeless. That may not sound like fun, but I get a lot out of it. My brother Lee says I should enjoy life while I'm young, but he doesn't know what he's talking about. I'm sure that I'm having more fun than he is at the moment!*

LUCY ***Free time? Are you joking?*** *I work three evenings a week and all day Saturday too – I don't have much time for anything else. And then there's my mum. She says I can only have a job if my schoolwork doesn't suffer. So when I get home after work I usually do my homework and go to bed. When I go out, I enjoy looking round the shops with my friends. But that doesn't happen very often, I'm afraid.*

RAVI ***I'm playing in the first team of my football club*** *this season, so that takes up most of my free time. We train twice a week, you see, and then I usually have matches at the weekend. When I'm not playing football, I hang around with my friends or just chill out. I really like clubbing, but that's difficult in the football season. The coach expects us to keep fit and I don't want him to take me off the team.*

SAM ***What do I do in my free time?*** *Well, I enjoy playing computer games most, I suppose, but I don't like the violent stuff. I prefer the games that test your skill against other players. I often network with other players online or go to LAN parties. They're really cool. I make a lot of new friends that way. At the moment, we're planning a big international LAN party. People are coming to it from all over the place.*

3 LOOKING AT THE TEXT

Join the beginnings (1–6) to the endings (a–f) to make sentences about the texts.

1 An international LAN party could
2 The four people all have
3 One of the four people doesn't have
4 Dana's voluntary work with the Red Cross
5 Competitive computer games have the
6 Some parents say that part-time jobs

a can have a bad effect on schoolwork.
b makes her feel good about herself.
c much free time because she has a job.
d advantage of bringing people together.
e be a great way to make new friends.
f very different interests.

4 WORKING WITH WORDS

A Find words/expressions in the texts above to fit the definitions.

DANA
1 adjective: useful, valuable
2 people without a permanent home
3 certain

RAVI
4 noun: time of year during which something happens
5 noun: competitive game
6 verb: relax by doing nothing

LUCY
7 opposite of 'being serious'
8 verb: become worse
9 another expression for 'I'm sorry to say'

SAM
10 verb: like one thing more than another
11 noun: ability to do sth
12 verb: English for German *vernetzen*

B Complete the sentences with six of the words/expressions from exercise A. They are not necessarily in the same order. Sometimes you must change the form.

1 My team has an important ... today.
2 A lot of employers say social ... are as important as qualifications.
3 Can you call back later, please? ... Ms Barton is in a meeting at the moment.
4 When parents work too hard, family life always ...
5 DVDs are OK, I suppose, but I ... to see films at the cinema.
6 Can't you do something ... instead of just watching TV all the time?
7 Petrol prices always go up during the holiday ...
8 You're ...! You don't really expect me to work all weekend, do you?

C Say who or what the circled words refer to in the texts.

EXAMPLE > I don't want him to take me off the team. (*Ravi*)
> *'Him' refers to Ravi's football coach.*

1 ... but I get a lot out of it. (*Dana*)
2 ... he doesn't know what he's talking about. (*Dana*)
3 I usually have matches at the weekend. (*Ravi*)
4 The coach expects us to keep fit. (*Ravi*)
5 She says I can only have a job if ... (*Lucy*)
6 But that doesn't happen very often, I'm afraid. (*Lucy*)
7 They're really cool. (*Sam*)
8 At the moment, we're planning a big international LAN party. (*Sam*)

5 LOOKING AT GRAMMAR: SUBJECT AND OBJECT PRONOUNS

Subjektform	Objektform
I	me
you	you
he/she/it	him/her/it
we	us
you	you
they	them

A Replace the underlined words with suitable subject pronouns.

1 John and Ann often go cycling at the weekend.
2 Does Jack belong to a sports club?
3 Sharon spends too much time in chat rooms.
4 Paul scored the goal from a distance of 30 metres.

B Now use object pronouns.

5 A lot of people enjoy going to LAN parties.
6 I'm lucky. My parents pay for my mobile.
7 Jack phones Sharon five or six times a day.
8 We meet Joshua in town every Friday.

6 LOOKING AT GRAMMAR: SIMPLE PRESENT

Form

Lucy and her friends ***enjoy*** *shopping.* *Sam* ***plays*** *computer games.*	wie der Infinitiv, außer in der 3. Person Singular (*he, she, it*), die auf *-s* endet
Lucy ***wishes*** *she had more free time.* *Ravi* ***tries*** *to keep fit.* *Dana* ***has*** *more fun than her brother* ***does****.*	Besonderheiten der 3. Person Singular: > endet das Verb auf *-ch, -sh, -s, -x*, folgt *-es* > endet das Verb auf Konsonant + *-y*, wird die Endung zu *-ies* Sonderformen: *do* – ***does****, go* – ***goes****,* *have* – ***has****, be* – ***am/are/is***
I ***do not / don't want*** *to lose my place on the first team.* *Sam* ***does not / doesn't like*** *violent games.*	**Verneinung:** *do not / don't* bzw. *does not / doesn't* (3. Person)
How ***do*** *you* ***spend*** *your free time?* ***Does*** *Lucy* ***work*** *on Saturdays?*	**Fragen:** *do* bzw. *does*

Gebrauch

I'm still at school and I also ***have*** *a job.* *Sam often* ***goes*** *to LAN parties.*	für Dauerzustände und wiederholte, oft regelmäßige Ereignisse bzw. Handlungen

> Das *simple present* steht häufig mit den folgenden Zeitangaben:
- *always, often, sometimes, rarely/seldom* (selten), *never*
- *generally* (im Allgemeinen), *normally, regularly, usually* (gewöhnlich)
- *every day/week/month/..., every morning/afternoon/...*
- *on Mondays/Tuesdays/...*
- *on weekdays / during the week, at weekends / the weekend / ...*

> Kurze Adverbien der Häufigkeit wie *often, never* usw. stehen unmittelbar vor dem Vollverb.
Lucy ***never*** *goes out during the week.*

A Put the verbs into the correct form of the simple present. Be careful about negatives and questions.

1 My mate Josh ...[1] (*spend*) a lot of time playing online poker, but he ...[2] (*not play*) for money.

2 A ...[1] (*Lucy/meet*) her friends in town every day?
B No, of course she ...[2] (*not meet*) them every day. She usually ...[3] (*meet*) them on Tuesdays and Fridays, I ...[4] (*think*).

3 A ...[1] (*you/watch*) much TV?
B Well, I ...[2] (*not watch*) TV at all during the week, but I ...[3] (*enjoy*) watching a good film at weekends.

4 I ...[1] (*belong*) to a football club but I ...[2] (*not play*) in the first team because I just ...[3] (*not have*) the time to train twice a week.

5 A What ...[1] (*Frank/do*) in his free time? ...[2] (*you/know*)?
B He ...[3] (*play*) the drums in a rock band and so he ...[4] (*not do*) anything else really.

6 Girls ...[1] (*not surf*) the net as much as boys. ...[2] (*you/think*) that ...[3] (*be*) the reason why girls' marks ...[4] (*be*) often better than boys' marks at school?

B **Work with a partner. Use the ideas below and the activities on page 6 to tell your partner what you normally/often/sometimes/never/... do or don't do and when.**

argue with my parents/brother/sister | catch the bus | come home late | do homework | email friends | get up | go clubbing/dancing/shopping | go to school / to the cinema / to the pub / to bed | leave for school / leave the house

EXAMPLES
- > I **usually go** to bed at about 11 o'clock **on weekdays**.
- > My mate and I **often go** to LAN parties **at the weekend**.
- > I **don't watch** / **never watch** TV **during the week**.

C **Now ask your partner about what he/she does or does not do. Add other activities if you wish.**

EXAMPLES
- > **When** do you leave for school?
- > **How often** do you work?
- > **Where** do you go shopping?
- > **Do** you **go** to LAN parties?

D **Report back to the class. Say what your partner does and when.**

Bernd usually goes clubbing on Saturdays.

Kathrin and her sister often play computer games.

7 LOOKING AT GRAMMAR: PRESENT PROGRESSIVE

Form

*I **am** / **I'm playing** in the first team this season.* *At the moment, we **are** / **we're planning** a LAN party.*	*am / is / are* + *-ing*-Form des Vollverbs
*When I **am** / **I'm not working**, I'm sleeping.* *You **are** / You'**re not** just **sitting** in front of the box.*	**Verneinung:** *not* unmittelbar nach *am / is / are*
***Are you** helping homeless people, Dana?* ***Is Ravi** training at the moment?*	**Fragen:** Austausch von Subjekt und *am / is / are*

Gebrauch

*I **am working** at a supermarket.* *We **are helping** homeless people.*	für Situationen und Ereignisse, die im Moment des Sprechens bzw. Schreibens tatsächlich im Gange sind

- > Das *present progressive* steht häufig mit den folgenden Zeitangaben: *at present, at the moment, currently, now*
- > Normalerweise haben folgende Verben keine Verlaufsform: *be, believe, dislike, hate, know, like, love, mean, notice, see, seem, think* (= meinen), *understand, want, wish*

A Put the verbs into the correct form of the present progressive.

1 The players ... (*have*) a shower at the moment.
2 Wait a minute, please. I ... (*talk*) to a customer.
3 Dana ...[1] (*not work*) with old people. She ...[2] (*help*) the homeless at present.
4 A What ...[1] (*you/do*), Sam? B I ...[2] (*try*) to organize a LAN party.
5 A Why ...[1] (*Lucy/cry*)? B She ...[2] (*not cry*). She has a cold, that's all.
6 A Can you two help me, please? B Can't it wait? We ... (*serve*) meals.
7 Jack ...[1] (*not ride*) an ordinary bike. He ...[2] (*use*) an exercise bike.
8 Lucy's mum is very angry. Lucy ... (*work*) so many hours at the moment that she doesn't have time for her schoolwork.

B Use the present progressive to ask each other questions with *what* and *who*.

EXAMPLES
> What is Tom doing/practising?
> Who is practising penalties?
> Tom is (practising penalties).

cycle to the shops | do keep-fit exercises | get money from a cash machine | meet friends at the pub | play poker | practise penalties | surf the internet | take the dog for a walk | try on some shoes | wash the car

1 Tom

2 Mary + Julie

3 Brian + Sam

4 Tracey

5 Dick + Ella

6 Josh + Becky

7 Kate

8 Lee + Vera

9 Helen

10 Janna

8 MANAGING SITUATIONS

Sie möchten jemandem auf Englisch sagen, dass ...

1 ... Peter Drexler nicht mehr für Ihren Club spielt. Jetzt spielt er irgendwo in Norddeutschland, aber seinen neuen Club kennen Sie nicht.
2 ... Sie sich für Online-Poker interessieren und viel Freizeit damit verbringen.
3 ... Markus mit einem Freund gerade ein Computerprogramm schreibt.
4 ... Jasmin in der Woche meist zu Hause bleibt, da sie viel für die Schule tun muss.
5 ... Sie zurzeit Geld sparen, da Sie ein Auto kaufen wollen.
6 ... Sie einen neuen Job bei einer Pizzeria haben, Ihre Eltern aber wegen der Schule dagegen sind.
7 ... Ihr Bruder im Moment zu viel Zeit vor dem Fernseher verbringt.
8 ... die meisten Leute gar keine Freizeitbeschäftigung ausüben.

B

Refresher Course

Girls fight for their rights

'Title IX' is a law that bans sex discrimination in US public schools[1]. One requirement of this law is that girls must have exactly the same chance to do sports as boys. The result? Girls have to join boys' teams if there are not enough girls to make up a team of their own. Read on to find out more.

Last March, Ashley Moore, 18, faced an awesome challenge[2]. She walked on to a wrestling mat to fight against her school's biggest wrestling rival. As he looked at her with hard, unblinking[3] eyes, Ashley felt a shiver of fear. Was she crazy? She was about to wrestle a hulk of a guy[4].

Four minutes later, however, Ashley walked off the mat a winner - and the hulk left on a stretcher. "He was big and strong, but he was slow," says Ashley of Edison High School, Richmond, Virginia. "He always tried the same hold. Then I took his arm and twisted it behind his back. When I did that, I pulled his back muscles. I didn't want to injure him. That's not what wrestling is about."

Ashley Moore is one of a growing number of American high school girls who play on boys' sports teams. While that can be tough, fighting stereotypes can be even tougher. But Ashley and girls like her are showing week after week that girls can compete against boys - and win.

Ashley had to fight hard to earn the respect of her male teammates. At the first training session, they greeted her with funny looks and nasty jokes. "Some of my teammates didn't say a word. They just looked at me," says Ashley. "Other boys said stuff like 'Hi sweetie, the volleyball team's next door. Aren't you at the wrong training session?'"

But Ashley didn't listen to the jokes and set to work - and soon she really impressed her teammates. "When they couldn't beat me in training," she says, "they soon backed off."

However, Ashley, who is called Xena after the TV warrior princess by her fans, doesn't want guys to back off. In fact, when she's on the mat, she wants to be their equal in every way.

1 **public school (AE) = state school (BE)** *staatliche Schule*
2 **awesome challenge** *überwältigende Herausforderung*
3 **unblinking** *unbewegt*
4 **hulk of a guy** *Kerl wie ein Baum*

1 LOOKING AT THE TEXT

Read the speech bubbles and the list of people in the box. Then decide who said each statement.

a female ice-hockey player ❙ a first aider ❙ Ashley ❙ Ashley's mother ❙ Ashley's opponent ❙ one of Ashley's fans ❙ one of Ashley's teammates ❙ the wrestling coach at Edison High

1 *At first I said Ashley should do something, well, more 'feminine'. But now I'm so proud of her!*

2 *I had to take her because of Title IX. There's no girls' wrestling team at Edison High, you see.*

3 *I thought, "No problem, she's just a girl", but she taught me a lesson. I won't be able to wrestle again this season.*

4 *Ashley doesn't look like Xena, but she's our warrior princess. We never miss a match.*

5 *Ashley's hard to beat – very fast, very clever. We're all glad she's on the team now.*

6 *Ashley's right. I had problems at the beginning too, but after a couple of games the boys accepted me.*

7 *My partner said, "Let's go and get the girl off the mat." Then we realized it was the boy.*

8 *Well, I watch a lot of wrestling on TV with my dad. I thought, "Why not?"*

2 WORKING WITH WORDS

A Find words in the text and introduction that fit the definitions below.

1 verb: synonym for '(to) forbid' (*introduction*)
2 adjective: opposite of 'private' (*introduction*)
3 adverb: synonym for 'precisely' (*introduction*)
4 verb: synonym for '(to) put together' (*introduction*)
5 adjective: 'difficult or frightening' (*ll. 1-4*)
6 adjective: synonym for 'mad' (*ll. 1-4*)
7 noun: opposite of 'loser' (*ll. 5-10*)
8 adjective: opposite of 'weak' (*ll. 5-10*)
9 adjective: synonym for 'increasing' (*ll. 11-18*)
10 adjective: synonym for 'very difficult' (*ll. 11-18*)
11 noun: 'member of the same team' (*ll. 19-25*)
12 adjective: opposite of 'nice', 'pleasant' (*ll. 19-25*)

B Now write six sentences of your own about sport, using words you found in exercise A.

C Copy the table and fill in the missing forms from the text.

	Verb	*Noun*
1	...	*ban*
2	*(to) discriminate*	...
3	*(to) require*	...
4	*(to) challenge*	...
5	*(to) rival*	...
6	...	*wrestler*
7	*(to) win*	...
8	...	*injury*
9	...	*competition*
10	...	*impression*

D **Complete the sentences using words from the table on page 13. Sometimes you must change the form.**

1 Many EU countries have a ... on smoking in pubs.
2 It is harder for women to play sport because there is so much ... against them.
3 Ashley took part in an important wrestling ... in Charlotteville yesterday.
4 Ashley's biggest ... has challenged her to fight him again when he's fit.
5 When she beat them in training, Ashley's skill ... her teammates.
6 A lot of people were surprised when Ashley left the mat as the ...

3 LOOKING AT GRAMMAR: SIMPLE PAST

Form

*Ashley **walked** off the mat a winner.* *I **took** his arm and twisted it behind his back.*	**regelmäßig:** Infinitiv + *-ed* **unregelmäßig:** Sonderform, siehe S. 252
*Some of my teammates **didn't say** a word.*	**Verneinung:** *did not / didn't* + Infinitiv
***Did I win** just because I'm a girl?*	**Fragen:** *did* + Subjekt + Infinitiv

Gebrauch

*Ashley **faced** an awesome challenge last March.* *This big guy **backed off** at a match last week.*	für Handlungen/Situationen, die in der Vergangenheit abgeschlossen wurden

Signalwörter

yesterday, the day before yesterday
two/three/... days/weeks/months/years ago
last week/month/year/summer/Christmas/...
the week/month before last
in 1973/2007/...
at that time / in those days
when he/she was a child / at school / ...

1 4 **A** **Complete the report with the simple past forms of the verbs in the box. Then listen to the CD to check your answers.**

agree | give | grow up | hear | kick | live | not be | not do | not even have | not go | promise | talk

Otis Shipley ...[1] in the poorest part of Perryton, a small town in Texas. He ...[2] with his mother and four brothers and sisters. Otis didn't know his father and sometimes the family ...[3] enough money to buy food. But Otis had one thing going for him: his skill as a football player. Nobody could run as fast as Otis and nobody ...[4] the ball as far as Otis.

It ...[5] long before Duane Tyler, the football coach at Robert E. Lee High School in Abilene, ...[6] about Otis's phenomenal talent. Tyler went to Perryton and ...[7] to Mrs Shipley. He ...[8] her that she would have money, a nice house and a future for her children. How could she say no? Mrs Shipley soon ...[9] to move to Abilene.

And Otis didn't disappoint her. Although he ...[10] anything except play football and often ...[11] to his classes, his teachers still ...[12] him very good grades.

B This is a page from Ellie Brown's weekly planner. Use the simple past to say what Ellie and her friends did last week. Add any further details if necessary.

EXAMPLES
> Ellie rang Ben and Annie about tennis at lunchtime on Monday.
> Ben and Annie had a phone call from Ellie about tennis on Monday.

MARCH		
14	Monday	*lunchtime: ring Ben & Annie (tennis)* *evening: do ironing!!*
15	Tuesday	*8:00 a.m. take bike to Apex Bikes* *3:15 p.m. hairdresser's* ✕ *on way home: bank, pay garage bill*
16	Wednesday	*late afternoon: pick up bike (Apex)*
17	Thursday	*5:30 p.m. meet Mandy, Annie (Virgin Media) buy birthday present (Sam)*
18	Friday	*6–8 p.m. training, swimming competition* *9:30 p.m.–11:00 p.m. record film, BBC2*
19	Saturday	*10 a.m. meet Mandy (power walking, Mousehold Heath)*
20	Sunday	*visit Kate (hospital, Ward 4)* *GET BOOK – NO FRUIT, NO FLOWERS!!*

C Work with a partner. Use the words in the box and the simple past to ask your partner what he or she did *yesterday / last night / last weekend / last summer / last Christmas / …*. Swap roles at least once.

go riding/camping/dancing/swimming/shopping/… | go to a disco / the gym / the leisure centre / the movies / a party / the pub / … | go on holiday / a trip / a cycle tour to … | go on a date | meet sb | play basketball/cards / computer games / football / …

EXAMPLES
> Did you go to the pub last Friday?
> Yes, I did. / No, I didn't. I went to a party at Paula's.

> What did you do last weekend?
> We went shopping on Saturday, but I stayed at home on Sunday.

4 MANAGING SITUATIONS

Sie möchten jemandem auf Englisch sagen, dass …

1 … Ihr Fußballverein gestern den Pokal gegen eine holländische Mannschaft gewonnen hat.
2 … es Donnerstag Abend kein Training gab, da der Trainer krank war.
3 … Sie und Ihr Bruder am Sonntag eine 60-km-Radtour gemacht haben.
4 … Sie vor zwei Monaten Golf ausprobiert haben, aber das Spiel äußerst langweilig fanden.
5 … Sie und Ihre Familie letztes Jahr einen Campingurlaub in Italien gemacht haben.
6 … Ihr Kanuverein letzten Samstag eine tolle Saisonabschlussfeier (*end-of-season party*) hatte.

C

Refresher Course

You are what you eat

BEFORE YOU READ

1 5 **What do you think the text might be about?**

A case study: **Maddy Johnson's double life**

A lot of people eat too much food or spend too much time sitting in front of the TV. That's OK because if they eat less and do more exercise, they can become healthy. But some people have a genuine problem. They have a compulsive eating disorder like anorexia[1] or bulimia[2]. Read on to find out more ...

Maddy Johnson is charming, attractive and successful. She's popular, too - at school, in her part-time job and in her community. Everybody loves Maddy. But the reality is different. Maddy is leading a double life - the public one and a secret one that nobody sees. Maddy is ill. She suffers from bulimia.

The poster outside the fast-food restaurant showed a double-decker cheeseburger with an XXL packet of fries, two little tubs of sauce and a big can of coke. 'Today's Special!' it screamed. 'Buy two cheeseburgers and get free fries!'

Maddy looked at the poster and had that familiar, tingling feeling. It was like sex. "No!" she said to herself. "Just walk away! You don't want it! You don't need it!" But that was the problem, wasn't it? Maddy couldn't 'just walk away'. It was as if she had lost control over her own body.

Maddy went into the restaurant and bought two cheeseburgers with free fries. She walked to an empty table and sat down with her back to the room. She didn't want people to see how she stuffed the burgers greedily into her mouth. In no time, she was back at the counter. She ordered a dessert: an XL tub of ice cream with caramel sauce and two cream donuts. The guy behind the counter looked at her. "Hungry, are we?" he said with a cheeky grin. "He knows," thought Maddy. She wanted to sink through the floor.

Maddy finished her meal and went into the toilets. The tingling had stopped, but she hated herself. She felt dirty and so guilty. She went into a cubicle, bent over the toilet pan and threw up.

When she came out of the cubicle, a woman was washing her hands. "Are you all right?" she asked. "That sounded ... Well, I couldn't help hearing. I'm so sorry." The woman offered Maddy a card. 'Ellen Anderson, National Association for Eating Disorders', it said. It gave the number of a free hotline and Ellen's email address. "Will you let me help you?" Ellen asked. Maddy looked at her. "It's OK," she said. "What do you mean 'help me'? I'm fine. Really. I just felt sick, that's all. I don't need ... Well, I mean, ..." "You don't have to explain, dear. I've been down that road as well. I *know*. You just can't beat this illness alone. Please ring that number, day or night."

1 anorexia: refusal to eat for fear of putting on weight *Magersucht*
2 bulimia: addiction to food and vomiting to lose weight *Ess-Brech-Sucht*

1 LOOKING AT THE TEXT

A Do the following tasks.

1 Compare Maddy's public and secret lives.
2 Describe how Maddy felt a) outside the restaurant and b) when she went into the toilets.
3 Find evidence to show that Maddy felt embarrassed and ashamed of herself in the restaurant.
4 Describe Maddy's reaction to Ellen Anderson's offer of help. What does it tell us about Maddy's attitude to her illness?
5 Explain how we know that Ellen Anderson really understood Maddy's problem.

B Read the speech bubbles and say which opinion about eating disorders you agree or disagree with most. Give reasons for your choice.

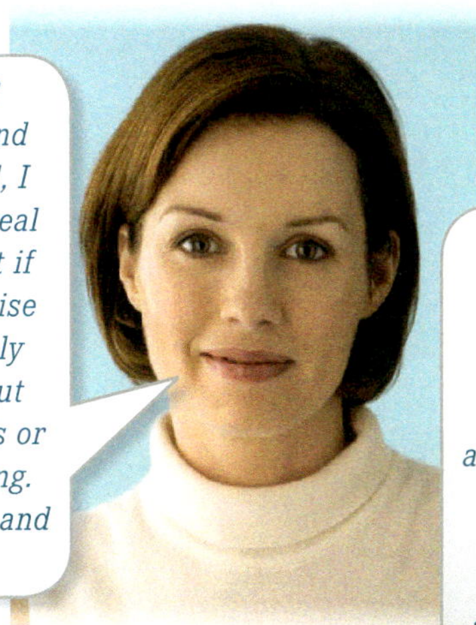

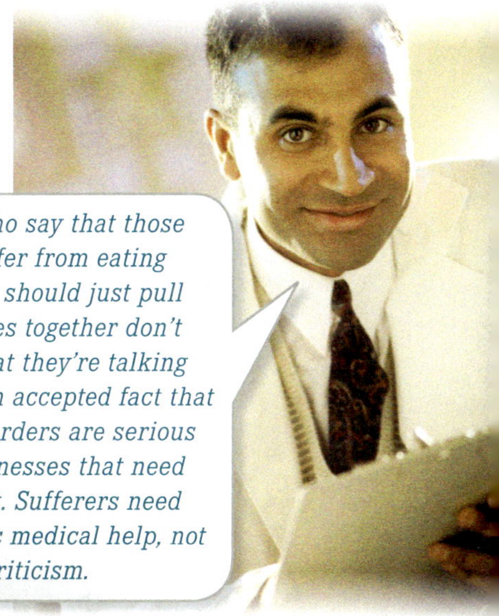

2 WORKING WITH WORDS

A Read the introduction and the case study again. Complete the table with the missing verbs.

verb + noun / noun phrase					
1	*(to) eat*	*too much food*	*6*	*(to) ...*	*free fries*
2	*(to) ...*	*an eating disorder*	*7*	*(to) ...*	*food into one's mouth*
3	*(to) ...*	*a double life*	*8*	*(to) ...*	*a dessert*
4	*(to) ...*	*from bulimia*	*9*	*(to) ...*	*a meal*
5	*(to) ...*	*a cheeseburger*	*10*	*(to) ...*	*an illness*

B Complete the sentences with verbs from exercise A. Make sure the verbs are in the right form.

1 I'm sure Alice can ... bulimia if she gets help from a doctor.
2 I always ... too much chocolate at Easter.
3 Two years ago Sally was very thin because she ... anorexia.
4 At this restaurant you ... a free dessert with every meal.
5 George must be hungry – he is ... that cake into his mouth!
6 I ... chicken but the waiter brought me fish.

C Replace the <u>underlined</u> words with a synonym from the introduction and text. They are in the same order.

1 <u>Many</u> burger bars attract customers with special offers. *A lot of*
2 People who drink too much alcohol <u>get</u> drunk.
3 Do you have a <u>real</u> reason for not doing any exercise today?
4 The <u>difficulty</u> is that 'natural food' is too expensive for most people.
5 Everybody knows that <u>good-looking</u> people have an easier life.
6 I live in a mixed <u>neighbourhood</u> with people from all over the place.
7 The <u>truth</u> of most people's lives is far from what you see in TV ads.
8 The driver of the car was so angry that she <u>shouted</u> at me.
9 The film was really disgusting. Afterwards I <u>was sick</u>.
10 It is almost impossible to <u>overcome</u> an eating disorder without help.

3 WRITING

Imagine you are Maddy. Use your answers from exercise 1 A to write an email to Ellen Anderson asking for her help.

Email

Hi Ellen

Thanks for giving me your email address. I think you are right – yes, I have a problem and I just don't know what to do about it. I feel so …

4 LOOKING AT GRAMMAR: POSSESSIVE ADJECTIVES

> *Possessive adjectives* zeigen an, wem irgendetwas gehört. Sie stehen – wie andere Adjektive – unmittelbar vor dem Nomen.

I	*Maddy is* ***my*** *sister.*	
you	*Can you tell me* ***your*** *name, please?*	
he	*What is* ***his*** *job?*	
she	*Is Joshua* ***her*** *brother?*	
it	*Wales is in the UK.* ***Its*** *capital is Cardiff.*	⚠ *it's* = *it is*
we	*There are 1,500 students at* ***our*** *school.*	
you	*Please open* ***your*** *books at page 23.*	
they	***Their*** *home is in London.*	⚠ ***there*** = da, dort

Complete these sentences with the English equivalent of the words in brackets.

1 What's *your name* (*dein Name*), please?
2 He's walking home because ... (*sein Rad*) is broken.
3 Maddy is writing ... (*ihrer Freundin*) an email.
4 Unfortunately the students have to buy ... (*ihre Bücher*) themselves.
5 The trainer asked me for ... (*meinem Gewicht*).
6 This table is too small for ... (*unsere Gruppe*).
7 The doctor thinks ... (*ihre Krankheit*) is curable.
8 You shouldn't give ... (*Ihren Kindern*) so much fatty food.
9 (*Ihr Name*) ... is Madison, but she calls herself 'Maddy'.
10 Look at that poor bird. What's the matter with ... (*seinem Bein*)?

5 LOOKING AT GRAMMAR: COUNTABLE AND UNCOUNTABLE NOUNS

*Maddy ordered **a dessert**. She had **an ice cream** and **two donuts**.*	*dessert, ice cream, donuts* usw. = zählbare Nomen (Pluralform möglich, können mit Zahlwörtern oder *a/an* verwendet werden)
*I'd like **cheese** and **mayonnaise** on my burger, please.*	*cheese, mayonnaise* usw. = nicht zählbare Nomen (keine Pluralform, keine Verwendung mit Zahlwörtern oder *a/an*)
*Oliver had **two cups of tea, a plate of ham and eggs** and **a bowl of corn pops** for breakfast.*	bei nicht zählbaren Nomen: Pluralbildung durch Hinzufügen eines zählbaren Nomens wie *two cups of ..., a plate of ..., a bowl of ...*
***Research** shows that bulimia is a serious illness. Ellen gave Maddy **some advice** about bulimia. Two recent **pieces of news** showed that exercise is very important.*	nicht zählbare Sammelbegriffe: *luggage, furniture, hardware/software* sowie *advice, evidence, information, knowledge, news* und *research* stehen mit Verben im Singular; Pluralbildung mit *pieces of ...* (formell) bzw. *bits of ...* (weniger formell)

⚠ Beachten Sie, dass wir die Nomen *people* und *police* nur im Plural verwenden können. Wollen wir sie im Singular gebrauchen, benutzen wir ***person*** für *people* und ***police officer*** für *police*.

> *The **people** in the café **were** drinking coffee. Only **one person was** drinking wine.*
> ***A police officer** said that **the police were** on their way.*

A **In your exercise book, draw a table for countable and uncountable nouns like the one below. Put the nouns in box A into the correct column.**

B **Give the plural form of the countable nouns. Add a suitable countable expression from box B to the uncountables so that you can use them in the plural.**

A

box | bread | bus | car | cheese | child | chocolate | coffee | evidence | family | fish | glass | house | kiss | knife | life | meat | mustard | news | oil | paint | water | woman | yoghurt

B

bars/pieces of | bits/pieces of | bottles/glasses of | cans/tins of | cups of | loaves/slices of | tubs of | tubes/jars of

Countable		Uncountable	
Singular	Plural	Base form	Qualified form
box	*boxes*	*bread*	*loaves/slices of bread*

C **Now write five sentences using some of the expressions from exercise B. Be careful with singular/plural verbs.**

6 LOOKING AT GRAMMAR: UNSPECIFIED QUANTITIES

> ***Some, any*** **und ihre Zusammensetzungen**

*Please add **some** salt to the potatoes.*	**bejahte Aussagen:** *some*
*We don't have **any** butter. Use olive oil.* *Did you put **any** salt on the potatoes?*	**verneinte Aussagen** und **Fragen:** *any*
*May I have **some** salt, please?* *Can I get you **some** orange juice, Maddy?*	**Bitten** und **Angebote,** die wahrscheinlich mit ja beantwortet werden: *some*
*There is **something** wrong with the toaster.* *I didn't see **anybody** I knew at the pub.* *Have you seen the cookbook **anywhere**?*	Zusammensetzungen von *some / any* werden genauso verwendet

A Complete the sentences with *some* or *any*.

1 Do you have *any* mustard, please?
2 We don't need ... bread.
3 There is ... butter in the kitchen.
4 It was awful. ... men had too much to drink and started a fight.
5 Would you like ...[1] more fries? You can have ...[2] of mine. I don't want ...[3] more.
6 The party was a bit boring because there wasn't ... music.
7 Don't forget to buy ...[1] drinking chocolate or we won't have ...[2] for breakfast.
8 We can't invite ...[1] more people to the party. We don't have ...[2] room.

B Complete the sentences with *somebody / anybody*, *something / anything* or *somewhere / anywhere*.

1 A Listen! I think there's *somebody*[1] at the door.
B I didn't hear *anything*[2]. I don't think there's ...[3] there.
2 I can't find the shopping list. Have you seen it ...[1]? It must be here ...[2]
3 A Did you buy ...[1] to drink?
B Well, I bought some mineral water, but I expect you'd like ...[2] stronger.
4 I need ...[1] to help with the barbecue on Saturday. Can you think of ...[2] we could ask?
5 We need some more coke. If you're not doing ..., could you go and buy some?
6 Do you know ... who can mix cocktails, Janna?

> ***Much, many, a lot of*** **und** ***plenty of***

*We don't need **many steaks**.* *How **many tomatoes** do we need?* *I don't use **much salt** in my cooking.* *How **much butter** do we have?*	**verneinte Aussagen** und **Fragen:** *many* mit zählbaren und *much* mit nicht zählbaren Nomen
***A lot of / Lots of children** are too fat.* *Maddy eats **a lot of food** and then she makes herself sick.*	**bejahte Aussagen:** *a lot of* oder *lots of* (weniger formell) bei zählbaren und nicht zählbaren Nomen
*Drink **as much water** as you like.* *We bought far **too many steaks**.*	Beachten Sie: *much / many* nach *as, how, so, too* und *very* auch in bejahten Aussagen
*There's **plenty of bread** in the freezer.*	„viel" in der Bedeutung „mehr als genug": *plenty of* statt *a lot of / lots of*

C Complete the sentences with *much, many, a lot of* or *plenty of.*

1 There weren't *many*[1] people at the supermarket. I think *a lot of*[2] people are away on holiday at the moment.

2 A Hurry up! We don't have ...[1] time.
B Don't panic. We have ...[2] time. The shops don't close until 10 o'clock.
A Really? I thought they closed ...[3] earlier than that.

3 A How ...[1] people are coming to the barbecue on Saturday?
B Not ...[2]. Six, I think.
A Only six? Why on earth did you buy so ...[3] meat then?

4 You needn't go shopping. We have ...[1] food in the freezer and we won't need ...[2] drink. ...[3] people are driving.

5 ...[1] women work in supermarkets but not ...[2] of them have a top job.

6 A John eats ...[1] chocolate, doesn't he?
B Yes. He eats far too ...[2] sweets and he shouldn't drink so ...[3] coke, either.

> **(A) little, (a) few**

*Add **a little water** if necessary.* (ein wenig) *Jake has **little interest** in food.* (nur wenig)	**nicht zählbare Nomen:** *(a) little*
*You need **a few carrots**, too.* (ein paar) ***Few cooks** are as good as she is.* (nur wenig)	**zählbare Nomen:** *(a) few*

D Complete the sentences with *(a) little* or *(a) few.*

1 A Can I give you *a few*[1] more fries?
B No, thanks, but I'd like *a little*[2] more bread, please.

2 A Why did you buy so much beer?
B Because we only have ... cans in the fridge.

3 A Nobody gets fat at Brenda's parties. You only get ...[1] bread.
B Be fair. Last time we got ...[2] bits of cheese, too.

4 A Most doctors say that you should only use ...[1] salt.
B Sure, but only ...[2] doctors follow their own advice.

5 A There's ...[1] point in saying anything. The boss never listens to us.
B I know, but I have ...[2] questions I want to ask him.

6 A Shops can open on Sundays in the UK but only ...[1] do so.
B That's understandable. People want ...[2] time off.

7 MANAGING SITUATIONS

Sie möchten jemandem auf Englisch sagen, dass ...

1 ... Sie eine gute Nachricht haben. Die Polizei hat das Kind gefunden.
2 ... Sie nur wenig Zeit haben, da Sie noch viel Arbeit zu erledigen haben.
3 ... die medizinischen Beweise eindeutig (*conclusive*) sind. Essstörungen sind eine psychische Erkrankung. Viele junge Mädchen leiden unter Essstörungen.
4 ... Sie auf der Party viel Fisch und Käse aber nur wenig Fleisch anbieten wollen.
5 ... viel zu viele Leute Fast Food essen, weil sie keine Zeit haben, etwas gesundes zu kochen.
6 ... es dieses Jahr so viel Obst gibt, dass die Bauern nur wenig Geld verdienen. Viele lassen das Obst an den Bäumen.

D

Time out

Many young people now choose to spend some time abroad after they leave school. Holly Morris wants to do exactly that – but she can't decide where to go. So she writes an email to a magazine, asking for help with her problem.

Hi Jala

I hope other readers will help me with my problem. It's like this: I'm leaving school next July and then I'm taking time out, six months or so, to spend time abroad. I'd really like to go somewhere like Brazil or maybe India that I won't have a chance to see again. But my parents, who are going to help me financially, are totally against these 'exotic destinations'. They want me to go to a rich English-speaking country like Australia or Canada.

As I am going to work some of the time, they say it'll be easier for me to find a 'proper job' there and 'people are more like us'. But what's the point in going somewhere like that? I want to see new places and meet new people. But what can I do? My dad says that there's no way that he's going to pay for me to get myself killed!

Do you or your readers have any bright ideas?

Holly Morris

OK, Holly, so you're going to pay for some of your time out as you go – but how? Are you going to pick fruit or work in a bar, for example? If so, your dad's absolutely right. You can forget places like South America and India – and safety really is a problem, especially for girls. Please believe this, Holly, or I can see that you're going to have a lot of very nasty surprises.

1 LISTENING

1 6 **Work with a partner. Complete the email with suitable words. Then listen to the CD to check your answers.**

Hi

Look, this may sound totally uncool, Holly, but I *agree*[1] with your dad. You will find it very ...[2] to find a job in a country like Brazil, where millions of people are out of ...[3]. And even if you do find one, what are you going to do about language difficulties? Or do you ...[4] Portuguese? Come on! Let's get real!

Here's my advice. Go to a richer, English-speaking ...[5] like the USA or Australia, where you speak the ...[6] and will be able to find a job. Please remember that you won't just want to earn enough for your ordinary living expenses, either. You'll also want to save some ...[7] to travel around while you're there. Otherwise, what's the ...[8] in going?

Now, here's a tip. You will find it very difficult to organize a trip like this yourself. You need expert ...[9]. As a first step, why not visit a ...[10] like bunac.org and ...[11] the country you want to go to, America, for example? There you will find all the information, advice and job offers you need.

Good ...[12], Holly, and have lots of fun!

Casey

2 LOOKING AT THE TEXTS

A **Draw a table like the one below in your exercise book. Then complete it with information from the emails.**

Holly	Holly's parents	Jala + Casey
– is leaving school in July	*– are going to help financially*	*– agree with Holly's parents*

B **Holly is telling a friend about her plans. Use information from your table to complete the conversation.**

3 WORKING WITH WORDS

Complete the sentences with words from the emails. They are not necessarily in the same order.

1 So many tourists go to 'exotic ...' that they are no longer exotic.
2 You won't have any language ... because everyone in Australia speaks English.
3 The USA is the biggest English-speaking ... in the world.
4 My dad wants me to get a '... job', but how? I'm only here for a month or so.
5 Spending time ... can be a great way to find out about life in another country.
6 We had a nasty ... when we got home. Somebody had broken into the house.
7 You can pick ..., but you will not earn very much money.
8 Holly will have to work some of the time to pay her living ...
9 How can she find a job in Canada? Do you have any ... ideas?
10 If you've never worked in Brazil before, you should get expert ... before you leave.

4 LOOKING AT GRAMMAR: FUTURE

> Das *will future*

Form

*You **will be able to** find a job in the USA.*	*will* + Infinitiv für alle Personen
*I **will not / won't have** a chance to go there again.*	**Verneinung:** *not* unmittelbar nach *will* ⚠ Kurzform: *won't*
***Will Holly** be safer in the USA?*	**Fragen:** Austausch von Subjekt und *will*

Gebrauch

*I think you **will have** problems finding a job.* *I **won't have** a chance to go there again.* *I hope Holly **will follow** Jala's advice.*	Vorhersagen/Vermutungen/Hoffnungen über die Zukunft
*I've missed my bus. – Don't worry. I'**ll give** you a lift.*	spontane Entscheidungen
***Will** you **help** me complete this form, please?*	Bitten

> Das *going to future*

Form

*My parents **are going to help** me.*	*am/is/are going to* + Infinitiv
*We **are/'re not going to help** you get yourself killed!*	**Verneinung:** *not* unmittelbar nach *am/is/are*
***Are you** going to work in a bar, for example?*	**Fragen:** Austausch von Subjekt und *am/is/are*

Gebrauch

*Holly **is going to take** time out in the USA.*	Absichten und Pläne
*I can see that you **are going to have** a lot of nasty surprises.*	unmittelbar bevorstehende Ereignisse, für die es schon Anzeichen gibt

A Use the correct form of the *will* or *going to* future.

1 I'm sure Holly *will enjoy* (*enjoy*) her time out in Georgia.
2 Holly's parents ... (*visit*) her in the USA.
3 The weatherman on TV thinks it ... (*rain*) tomorrow.
4 Watch out! Can't you see that child ... (*run*) across the road?
5 Is it true? ... (*Casey/help*) Holly find a job?
6 We ... (*do*) our best, but I don't think your visa ... (*be*) ready by Friday.
7 Let me know what flight you're on and I ... (*meet*) you at the airport, OK?
8 Hey, Dad, ... (*you/help*) me with my luggage, please?

> Das *present progressive* und *simple present* mit zukünftiger Bedeutung

*I **am leaving** school **next July**.* *Holly **is flying** to Atlanta **at 7:30 this evening**.*	für Termine und fest geplante Vorhaben, mit Zeitangabe
*Holly's plane **takes off** at 10:30 tomorrow.* *The film **starts** at 8 o'clock on Sundays.*	für Flugpläne, Fahrpläne usw. für Kinoprogramme usw.

B Make sentences with the *going to* future or the present progressive. Only use the present progressive when there is an adverb of future time. Add any missing words.

EXAMPLES
> several school-leavers | take time out | Australia
> *Several school-leavers* ***are going to take*** *time out in Australia.*

> I | fly | Cologne next Saturday
> *I* ***am flying*** *to Cologne next Saturday.*

1 we + meet | 7 or 7:30 tomorrow?
2 we | get a job | pay for our holiday
3 you + come | Holly's farewell party | Friday?
4 Casey + work | the USA?
5 I | start work | six | and I | finish | two | next week
6 A What are your plans for the summer?
  B we | look for | a job on a farm in France
7 they + sell | their car | internet?
8 we | not have | holiday | next summer | | we | stay at home

C Put the verbs into the correct form: *will* future, *going to* future, present progressive or simple present.

1 A What time ...[1] (*you/go*) into town tomorrow, Ann?
  B Well, I ...[2] (*meet*) Ellie in the pub at 7. Jack and Sarah ...[3] (*come*), too. Why don't you come? I'm sure they ...[4] (*be*) really pleased to see you again.
  A Great. I ...[5] (*definitely* + *be*) there. It ...[6] (*be*) nice to see Jack and Sarah again.

2 A Is it true that Holly ...[1] (*not come*) back home at the end of her time out?
  B Who told you that? She ...[2] (*come*) home in August and then she ...[3] (*start*) college in October.

3 A The TV programme ...[1] (*start*) at 8:15 so I want to get the bus that ...[2] (*leave*) at 7:50.
  B But that bus ...[3] (*not get to*) Oak Street until about 8:10. We ...[4] (*only* + *have*) five minutes to walk home. Let's take the bus that ...[5] (*go*) at 7:30.

4 A We ...[1] (*not go*) away on holiday at all next summer. We ...[2] (*spend*) the whole time at home.
  B Good idea. They say we ...[3] (*have*) a very hot summer. I'm sure you ...[4] (*be*) much more comfortable at home.
  A True – and we ...[5] (*save*) a lot of money, too!

5 MANAGING SITUATIONS

Sie möchten jemandem auf Englisch sagen, dass ...

1 ... es morgen sonnig sein soll.
2 ... Ihre Schwester am 10. Juli in die USA fliegt, um ihren Job in New Orleans anzufangen.
3 ... Ihre Eltern Sie während Ihrer Zeit im Ausland finanziell unterstützen werden.
4 ... Sie wissen wollen, ob Tom vorhat, eine neue Stelle zu suchen.
5 ... Mary bestimmt ein Jahr in Australien verbringen wird.
6 ... Sie am Donnerstag nicht zu Hause sind, da Sie am Mittwoch in den Urlaub nach Italien fliegen.

Shopping

Shopping online certainly has its advantages: no parking problems, no queues, no pushy sales staff, no carrying shopping home. Plus credit cards make it so easy to pay – too easy, perhaps. Read on to find out what that can mean.

1 7

Sharon Miller's virtual world of online shopping

Clothes and fashion are important to me. When I was a child, my mum had mail-order catalogues. I liked to look at them and make long lists of the clothes I wanted. Of course, my mum didn't buy them. She couldn't. She didn't have the money.

When I got older, I started buying my own clothes. I spent happy hours at the bargain counters of big department stores in Manchester. Then, when I was 16, I discovered a 'nearly-new' shop in King Street. My first purchase there was a fabulous blouse in the latest fashion colours for just £30.

After that, I went there every week. The clothes were cheaper than in ordinary shops and often much better quality. You see, a lot of rich, fashion-conscious women sometimes wear really expensive clothes only once. And I wanted to be like those women. I wanted the coolest and smartest and most fashionable clothes, you know, exclusive Italian designer labels like Versace, Armani and Gucci – and I wanted my wardrobe to be full of them.

When I was 18, I discovered the thrill of eBay. I always thought eBay was just for techno freaks, but how wrong I was! Once I bought a lovely Armani cocktail dress in pure silk for just £4.99!

Soon I was doing all my shopping online – not just on eBay, but at top designer sites as well. But I spent more money than I had – much, much more money. With a credit card, it was so easy. I just clicked the mouse – click, click, click into the virtual shopping trolley. But in the meantime I've run up debts of over £4,500. And they aren't virtual, they're real.

1 LOOKING AT THE TEXT

Choose the right answer to complete the statements.

1 Sharon discovered her interest in clothes by ...
  a visiting exclusive boutiques.
  b looking through mail-order catalogues.
  c searching for special offers.

2 At first, Sharon bought her clothes at ...
  a bargain counters in big stores.
  b second-hand shops.
  c exclusive designer boutiques.

3 When she was 16, Sharon ...
  a heard about bargains on eBay.
  b bought fashionable clothes from rich women.
  c found a nearly-new shop in Manchester.

4 Sharon wanted to be like ...
  a her friends who wore the latest fashions.
  b smart women who wore expensive clothes just once.
  c the other customers at the nearly-new shop.

5 Sharon thought that eBay was ...
  a only for techno freaks.
  b an internet auction site that sold everything.
  c an online clothes shop.

6 On eBay, Sharon once bought a ...
  a blouse in the latest fashion colours.
  b wardrobe full of designer clothes.
  c silk cocktail dress.

7 Soon Sharon was doing all her clothes shopping ...
  a in online shops and on eBay.
  b on eBay.
  c in ordinary shops.

8 Sharon got into debt because she ...
  a used a credit card.
  b spent much more money than she had.
  c did a lot of online shopping.

2 WORKING WITH WORDS

A Link the nouns in the box on the left with a noun from the box on the right to form compounds.

1 bargain	5 designer	9 shopping
2 cocktail	6 fashion	10 techno
3 credit	7 mail-order	
4 department	8 sales	

card | catalogue | colour | counter | dress | freak | label | staff | store | trolley

B Complete the sentences with the English equivalent of the German words or phrases in brackets. Be careful to use the correct form.

1 There are many ...[1] (*Vorteil*) in shopping online. ...[2] (*Inzwischen*) more and more people have ...[3] (*entdecken*) how easy shopping from home is.
2 Many people prefer to order goods from a ...[1] (*Versandhauskatalog*) because they don't like ...[2] (*aufdringlich*) sales assistants.
3 ...[1] (*modebewusst*) women don't like to wear the same ...[2] (*Kleidungsstück*) too often.
4 It's a crime to ... (*Schulden zusammenkommen lassen*) that you know you won't be able to pay.
5 I didn't ...[1] (*ausgeben*) much at the supermarket yesterday. In fact, I didn't even use a ...[2] (*Einkaufswagen*) as I only needed two things.
6 Clothes at the new boutique are not as ...[1] (*teuer*) as at the ...[2] (*Warenhaus*) next door.

C First read the five golden rules. Then complete them with words from the box.

The Five Golden Rules

1 Know how much ...[1] you have. Be ...[2] and **never** just 'hope for the best'.
2 Buying for ...[1] is **always** much, much cheaper than buying ...[2].
3 Be very sceptical about ...[1]. In the end, nothing is ...[2].
4 If you ignore ...[1], it doesn't go away. It just gets worse – and ...[2].
5 Keep in touch with your ...[1]. Describe your problem honestly and say how you plan to ...[2] the debt.

cash I creditors I debt I free I free offers I money I on credit I realistic I repay I worse

3 LOOKING AT GRAMMAR: ADJECTIVES AND ADVERBS

*Sharon spent **happy** hours in boutiques.* *Shopping online is **quick** and **convenient**.*	Adjektive beschreiben Nomen Stellung: entweder unmittelbar vor dem Nomen oder nach einer Form von *be/become*
*Think about your needs **honestly**.* *All the clothes in this shop are **nearly** new.*	Adverbien beschreiben Verben oder Adjektive
*Sharon ran up debts **quickly**.*	Form: weitaus die meisten Adverbien enden auf *-ly*
*We must do two things **fast**.*	wichtige unregelmäßige Adverbien: *good – **well**, fast – **fast**, hard – **hard***
*Sharon **looks awful** in that dress.*	*(to) feel, (to) look, (to) sound, (to) taste* stehen mit Adjektiven

Choose the correct form of the underlined words to complete this text.

The man walked into the phone shop and went over to the display of mobile phones. He walked slow/slowly[1] along the rows of elegant/elegantly[2] phones, stopping occasional/occasionally[3] to look at a phone more close/closely[4]. But he couldn't look at them proper/properly[5]. They were all fixed firm/firmly[6] in anti-theft pads with little red lights that glowed bright/brightly[7].

An assistant came over. "Can I help you at all?" she asked polite/politely[8]. "Sure," said the man. "I need a new phone. This one looks good/well[9]." "The 6131? Well, you can't go wrong there. It's a very reliable/reliably[10] model." "Yes, but it's not cheap/cheaply[11], is it?" "You're right there," said the assistant. She smiled pleasant/pleasantly[12] at the customer. "But it's fantastic/fantastically[13] good value for money, you know. It's got every possible/possibly[14] modern feature. Let me show you." The assistant switched off the alarm and removed the phone careful/carefully[15] from its pad. "This way, please, sir," she said.

4 LOOKING AT GRAMMAR: POSITION OF ADVERBS

Satzadverbien	
Of course, *Mum didn't buy the clothes.*	**Satzanfang:** *(un)fortunately, actually, in fact, (un)luckily, maybe, perhaps, naturally, obviously*
Art und Weise	
Think about your needs ***honestly.***	**Satzende**
Ort und Zeit	
The shop is ***in King Street.*** *Mum comes home* ***at 6 o'clock.*** *The train leaves* ***Manchester at 10:30.*** *Ashley was* ***great in the match last night.***	**Satzende:** Reihenfolge bei mehreren Adverbien: Ort – Zeit Art und Weise – Ort – Zeit
Häufigkeit	
We ***often*** *go shopping in King Street.* *Sharon is* ***sometimes*** *irresponsible.* *We go shopping* ***every Saturday.*** *We only go shopping* ***once a week.***	**Satzmitte:** unbestimmte Häufigkeit – vor Vollverben, nach *be* **Satzende:** bestimmte Häufigkeit sowie zusammengesetzte Häufigkeitsangaben wie *from time to time, (every) now and then*

A Say where you would put the adverbs of frequency: position A or B.

1 Retailers A say B that shoplifting is getting worse. (*often*)
2 Tough punishment A stops a shoplifter B. (*seldom*)
3 Modern technology is A catching more and more shoplifters B. (*every year*)
4 Some shoplifters are so clever that they A get caught B. (*never*)
5 Other shoppers A see people shoplifting B. (*now and then*)
6 But they don't A do B anything about it. (*usually*)

B Rewrite the sentences with the adverbs in the correct position.

1 The coat was in the sale. (*luckily*)
2 Before buying on credit, you should think about your financial situation. (*realistically*)
3 Fashionable women wear expensive clothes only once. (*sometimes*)
4 I am very tired after doing the shopping. (*always*)
5 Sharon visits the eBay site. (*several times a week*)
6 I didn't buy anything because the shop assistant spoke to me. (*rudely*)
7 The Brad Pitt film is on TV this evening. (*at 9:30, on Channel 4*)
8 I think you acted very well – congratulations! (*in the play, last night*)

5 MANAGING SITUATIONS

Sie möchten jemandem auf Englisch sagen, dass ...

1 ... nächste Woche ein neues Kaufhaus in der Stadt eröffnet.
2 ... viele Produkte online billiger sind.
3 ... man leicht Schulden macht, wenn man immer online kauft.
4 ... riesige Supermärkte viele kleinere Geschäfte ruinieren (*ruin*).
5 ... Sie versuchen so oft wie möglich in kleineren Geschäften einzukaufen.
6 ... Stadtzentren in der Zukunft ganz anders aussehen werden.

F

Ready for a job?

Have you ever thought of working in your spare time? If so, this questionnaire will help you to find out if you're ready to take on a part-time job as well as school.

1 DOING A QUESTIONNAIRE

Do the questionnaire by choosing the answer for each question that fits you best. Use the table opposite to work out your score and then read what your score means.

1 ***Why do you want a part-time job?***

A I've just seen a really cool new MP3 player and I have to buy it!
B I want to earn some money so I don't have to keep asking my parents to buy stuff for me.
C To get some work experience – I think it will help me find a good job when I leave college.

2 ***How much time do you spend doing your homework?***

A Some nights I stay up late working, some nights I watch TV instead.
B I usually spend an hour every evening working. That way I get all my work done and have time for other things.
C Sometimes I get home from school and start watching a DVD or texting my friends and forget all about my homework.

3 ***How often do you do out-of-school activities?***

A I do loads of stuff after school – I'm always busy!
B I'm quite lazy. When I get home from school, I just want to sit and watch TV.
C I go to one or two after-school clubs but I'm free most evenings.

4 ***How much time do you plan to spend doing your part-time job?***

A My schoolwork and my social life are important, so maybe 15 hours a week.
B As much as I can! Just think of all the money ...
C That depends on what job I get.

5 ***Are you ever late for school?***

A I always get to school on time – with my homework ready to be handed in.
B If my mum didn't wake me up every morning, I'd probably never get out of bed.
C I've missed the bus a couple of times, but I usually get to school on time.

6 ***How well do you work with other people?***

A I hate being told what to do.
B I work quite well in a group. But sometimes I just sit back and let the others do the work.
C I like meeting new people and I'm always happy to help someone out.

Scoring

Question	Answer	Points
1	A	2
	B	4
	C	6
2	A	4
	B	6
	C	2

Question	Answer	Points
3	A	2
	B	4
	C	6
4	A	6
	B	2
	C	4

Question	Answer	Points
5	A	6
	B	2
	C	4
6	A	2
	B	4
	C	6

What your score means

29–36 Congratulations! You are organized, motivated and have a really positive attitude to work – all things that employers think are really important! Getting a part-time job should be no problem for you.

21–28 You seem to be ready for a part-time job. Just make sure you don't do too much – leave enough time for doing your schoolwork and having fun.

12–20 You're not ready for a part-time job yet. You should learn to organize your time better. Forget about looking for a job and concentrate on getting your schoolwork done on time! You need to be more sensible with money too.

2 LISTENING

1 8 **Reporter Clare Harris is interviewing careers adviser Bob Jackson. Work with a partner. Read the interview and try to fill the gaps with suitable words. The words are all linked to the theme of school and work. Then listen to the CD to check your answers.**

CLARE Good morning, Bob, and thanks for seeing me.

BOB Don't mention it.

CLARE Over the last few years, more and more teenagers have taken a part-time ...[1] while they're still at school. But is that a good thing? Shouldn't they concentrate on their ...[2]?

BOB Well, Clare, that depends on the person. Some people do part-time work and do well at ...[3] too. But others find schoolwork more difficult and might need more time for it.

CLARE But some people don't have a choice, do they? Lots of young people say they have to work just to get by – they have to earn ...[4] to buy the things they need.

BOB I'm not sure that's true, Clare. What do they need the money for? For food or for a new mobile phone? But you're right, part-time ...[5] among the over-16s has increased a lot since the 1990s and, in most cases, I think that's a good thing.

CLARE Really? But don't young people nowadays have much more stress in their lives because they have jobs?

BOB No, not really. People have been working their way through school for generations. Many people think it's right that students help to ...[6] for their education.

CLARE Sure, I understand that. But I still think people who have to work while they're at school are at a disadvantage.

BOB Well, most American ...[7] are looking for someone with experience. They think working while you're at school helps young people to learn important job-related skills.

CLARE Oh, come on, Bob! Filling supermarket shelves and cooking burgers are skills, are they?

BOB That's not what I meant. I'm talking about real ...[8] that are important for all jobs. Things like getting to work on time – I mean, if you can't organize your ...[9] then you're not ready to work yet. Part-time jobs teach you how to work well with other ...[10] too.

3 LOOKING AT THE TEXT

Do the following tasks.

1 List three objections that Clare has to school students taking part-time jobs.
2 Say why Bob is sceptical about Clare's point that some young people have to take a job just to live.
3 Explain why American employers think that working your way through school or college is an advantage.
4 Describe the misunderstanding that Clare and Bob have about 'job-related skills'.

4 WORKING WITH WORDS

A Find the English equivalents of these German phrases in the interview in exercise 2. They are in the same order.

1 Keine Ursache!
2 darauf ankommen
3 über die Runden kommen
4 recht haben
5 Wirklich?
6 eigentlich nicht
7 Ich bitte dich!
8 nicht so weit sein

B Use two of the English words or expressions you found in exercise A to complete these cartoons.

C Complete Susan Barton's description of her job with words from the box.

afternoons ı brochures ı busy ı careless ı customers ı interesting ı main job ı parents ı pay ı part-time ı plenty ı work

Hi. My name's Susan Barton and I'm 17. I'm still at school, but I have a ...[1] job at a travel agency in the town centre. I ...[2] there for three hours on Wednesday, Thursday and Friday ...[3], and four hours on Saturday mornings, from 8:30 to 12:30. That makes 13 hours in all, which my ...[4] say is more than enough.
My ...[5] is to make sure that there are always enough ...[6] in the racks, and that they are all correctly sorted. That doesn't sound much, but in fact there's ...[7] to do. Some people are so ...[8]. They often look at brochures and then put them back in the wrong rack – if they put them back at all, that is! Now that I have been there for a few months, I also sometimes help the assistants to deal with ...[9] and answer the phone when we're ...[10]. As I like people, I find that more ...[11] than just looking after brochures, of course. And the ...[12] is good – £5.50 an hour! I certainly can't complain about that, can I?

5 SPEAKING

A Work with a partner. Take it in turns to ask each other questions about your part-time jobs. Use the language below to help you.

Do you have a part-time job?	*Yes, I do. / No, I don't.*
What do you do?	*I'm a bartender/cashier/shelf-stacker/waiter/...* *I give private tuition.* *I help in an old people's home / at a filling station / ...*
How long have you had it?	*I've had it for (+* Zeitraum: *six weeks, three months).* *I've had it since (+* Zeitpunkt: *last February, summer 2008).*

B Now discuss someone you know who has a part-time job.

Does ... have a job?	
What does he/she do?	*He's/She's a ...*
How long has he/she had it?	

6 LOOKING AT GRAMMAR: PRESENT PERFECT

Form

Your boss ***has asked*** *you to clean the floor.* *A lot of students* ***have taken*** *part-time jobs.*	*have/has* + 3. Form **regelmäßig:** *have/has* + 3. Form auf *-ed* **unregelmäßig:** *have/has* + unregelmäßige 3. Form: siehe S. 252
Ellie ***has not / hasn't found*** *a job yet.*	**Verneinung:** *not* unmittelbar hinter *have/has*
Have you *answered the questions honestly?*	**Fragen:** Austausch von Subjekt und *have/has*

Gebrauch

I can't come to work. I ***have hurt*** *my hand.* *Jane isn't here. She****'s gone*** *to the bank.*	ohne Zeitangabe für Situationen/Ereignisse, die noch andauern oder deren Auswirkungen noch in der Gegenwart spürbar sind
Have *you* ***ever been*** *to the USA, Holly?* *I****'ve never had*** *a part-time job.* *Casey* ***hasn't answered*** *my email* ***yet****.* *Part-time work among the over-16s* ***has increased*** *a lot* ***since the 1990s****.* *Maddy* ***hasn't stopped*** *eating* ***all day****.*	mit Zeitangaben für die ganze Zeit bis jetzt wie *ever* (jemals), *never, yet, still, for* (+ Zeitraum), *since* (+ Zeitpunkt)
Ellie ***has just found*** *a job at a boutique.* *I****'ve been*** *to the cinema a lot* ***recently****.*	mit Zeitangaben für die (aller)letzte Zeit wie *just, recently*

⚠ Beachten Sie die Stellung der Adverbien:
The film has ***just*** *started.*
The bus has ***already*** *left.*
I have ***never*** *been to New York.*
They ***(still)*** *have* ***not*** *finished the job* ***yet****.* ⚠ (immer) noch nicht

A Put the verbs into the correct form of the present perfect. Be careful about negatives and questions.

1 The students *have already arrived*[1] (*already* + *arrive*). In fact, they ...[2] (*already* + *be*) here for an hour.
2 The mechanic ...[1] (*repair*) the car and he ...[2] (*wash*) it as well.
3 The men ...[1] (*not start*) work yet. ...[2] (*you/tell*) them what to do yet?
4 I ...[1] (*not see*) Ben since yesterday. I hope he ...[2] (*not take*) the day off again.
5 The boss ...[1] (*ask*) me twice if we ...[2] (*finish*) this job yet.
6 I ...[1] (*not be*) here long. I ...[2] (*only* + *live*) in Atlanta for two weeks.
7 ...[1] (*Benny/clean*) the floor yet? I ...[2] (*ask*) him to do it several times.
8 ...[1] (*you/meet*) our new part-timer yet? He ...[2] (*just* + *start*) here.

B Complete the sentences with *for* (period of time: *for two years*) or *since* (point in time: *since 3 o'clock*).

1 I haven't watched TV ... last weekend.
2 I haven't seen Sharon ... months.
3 Have you seen Carey ... she got back from Georgia?
4 Jack hasn't spent any time with his family ... years.
5 Amy has worked here ever ... we opened.
6 Holly has worked here ... a month now.
7 I haven't seen Ann ... she started her part-time job.
8 Kenny has only lived in England ... a few weeks.

C Look at the pictures. Use the present perfect to say what has *just* happened.

1 finish
The film *has just finished*.

2 leave
Mum and Dad ... for work.

3 send
Ed ... a text message.

4 switch on
Susan ...

5 clean
The boys ...

6 begin
The news ...

7 MANAGING SITUATIONS

Sie möchten jemandem auf Englisch sagen, dass ...

1 ... Sie seit sechs Monaten einen Nachmittagsjob haben.
2 ... Sie gerade eine E-Mail geschrieben haben.
3 ... Holly nie für Geld gearbeitet hat.
4 ... Familie Carter seit zwei Jahren in Deutschland wohnt.
5 ... Sie seit drei Wochen in einem Computergeschäft arbeiten.
6 ... ein Freund gerade angerufen hat, um Ihnen seine Ankunftszeit (*time of arrival*) zu sagen.

1 City lights

FOCUS

1 Read the quotation. Explain how this statement could be true.

'The strange thing about New York City is that you feel as though you've been there before, even if you've never set foot in the US.' Simon Gage, Introduction to *Out Around New York*

2 Look at photos A–F and match them to places 1–6.

1 Brooklyn Bridge
2 Central Park
3 Grand Central Terminal
4 the Chrysler Building
5 the Empire State Building
6 the Statue of Liberty

A

B

C

D

E

F

3 Work with a partner. Think of films that show some of these places. Use the ideas below to help you talk about the films.

A	*I think the Empire State Building*	*features appears*	*in King Kong.*
B	*Oh, you mean that (famous)*	*scene, sequence,*	*don't you? The one where King Kong climbs to the top and catches planes in his hand.*

4 Say which place in New York you would most like to visit and why. Use the list from exercise 2 or your own ideas.

A Personal perspectives

BEFORE YOU READ

A Compare and contrast the two photos opposite. Use the language below to help you.

One photo shows a country scene, whereas the other one ...		
In the picture on the right,	*there are a lot of* *we can see lots of*	*cars, while in the ...*

B Scan the emails quickly and find out who they are to and from.

> Lesen schwieriger Texte: S. 160

1 LOOKING AT THE TEXTS

A Read the emails and do these activities.

> Lesen schwieriger Texte: S. 160

1 Put emails A–D in order from 1 to 4.
2 Name the places in the photos. Match the writer and reader of the emails to the photos.
3 Find the state of Oregon and the city of New York on the map at the back of the book. Say roughly how far Ricky and his family travelled when they moved.

B Decide whether the following statements are true or false and explain your reasons in German.

> EXAM PREPARATION Beurteilen von Textaussagen (S. 172)

1 Ricky wrote his first email about a week after the move from Silver Creek to New York.
2 The family made the move because Ricky's parents say New York is the most exciting place in the world.
3 After his quiet life in Silver Creek, Ricky quickly started to enjoy the fast, loud life of New York.
4 Ricky checked air flight prices so that Sue could fly to New York and be with Ricky.
5 The family moved into their new apartment between Ricky's second and third emails.
6 They moved into an apartment at street level, close to Central Park.

C Say what you think.

1 Compare the endings of the emails.
2 Work out what is probably happening with Ricky and Lucy.
3 What are your views on this kind of change in this particular situation?

2 COMPOSITION

> EXAM PREPARATION Materialgestützter Aufsatz (S. 173)

Use the pictures and text on the opposite page to compare and contrast rural and urban life. Use these phrases and adjectives to help you.

In the photo of a rural scene on the left, we see ... *As we learn from Ricky's emails to Sue, rural life is ...*	*On the other hand, urban life is ...* *However, there are also very positive things to say about ...*

beautiful | busy | calm | enjoyable | exciting | fast | friendly | fun | intense | interesting | noisy | pleasant | quiet | relaxed | slow

1 9

A

Dear Sue

I still miss you as much as ever – more, in fact! I've been checking out flight prices on the internet, and they're less expensive than I thought. Pretty soon, I promise, I'll be back in Silver Creek with you.
I still can't get used to this city. It's just too fast, too loud. The people too. Out on the street, they seem like they're always power-walking – except when they stop to yell at each other!
Yesterday, we went up the Empire State Building, and the view was really something. The downtown Manhattan skyline just blows you away.
Must run. We're going to check out some places to live.

Lots of love
Ricky

B

Dear Sue

Well, I'm starting to like New York a lot more than before. They say it's the most exciting place in the world, and maybe it really is. Music, sport, movie theaters, festivals – you name it, New York's got it!
I start at John F Kennedy High next week, and that's scary. But I met a girl called Lucy in the elevator – she lives two floors down – and we got talking. Turns out Lucy's at JFK, and she's going to be a senior too. She's going to introduce me to everyone, and that's great.
There's a lot more to tell you, but I have to stop now. I'm going to a party with Lucy.

Best wishes
Ricky

C

Dear Sue

Sorry I didn't write last week, but life was busy. We finally got our new apartment, and last week we moved in.
It's much smaller than our old place, but I guess that's because there's no space to waste in this city. (After all, it's the city of skyscrapers, isn't it?) Anyway, it's big enough, and we've got great views of Central Park. It's huge, it's green and it's right in the middle of Manhattan. Amazing.
I'm beginning to get to know NY now, and it's OK. But it would be a whole lot better if you could be here too.

Love
Ricky

D

Dear Sue

I still can't believe what's happening. A week ago, I was still in the best place in Oregon, with the best girl in the world.
And now what? The forest and waterfalls are gone, and I'm stuck in this non-stop nightmare of noise. Even up here on the 17th floor of our hotel, you still hear the traffic 24-7. What were Mom and Dad thinking of, coming to work in New York?
All I want is to get back home to see you. I miss you more than anything in the world. Write soon.

I love you so much! XXX
Ricky

(438 words)

3 WORKING WITH WORDS

A Explain the words and expressions from their context.

1 ... the view was **really something**. (*email A, line 12*)
2 The downtown Manhattan skyline just **blows you away**. (*email A, line 13*)
3 ... – **you name it**, and it's here. (*email B, line 6*)
4 ... you still hear the traffic **24-7**. (*email D, line 6*)

B Find words and phrases in the emails that mean the same as the following.

Email A	Email B	Email C	Email D
1 shout	4 frightening	6 suppose	9 never-ending
2 city-centre (adjective)	5 lift	7 exactly	10 day and night, all week
3 have a look at		8 much	

C Now use some of the words from exercise B to complete these sentences.

1 We have a ... apartment ... opposite the new shopping mall.
2 I once got stuck in the ... of a skyscraper – it was really ...
3 I ... we could ... the new art exhibition tonight – we have no other plans.

4 LISTENING

1 10
A Beantworten Sie die folgenden Fragen zum Text auf Deutsch.

> ZENTRALE KLASSENARBEIT
Hörverstehen (S. 175)

1 Warum ist New York für Europäer trotz der großen Entfernung gut erreichbar?
2 Was ist das Besondere an den Restaurants in New York?
3 Um welche Sehenswürdigkeiten soll es in der Sendung in erster Linie gehen?

1 11
B Ergänzen Sie auf Deutsch das Raster mit Informationen aus dem zweiten Hörtext.

Sehenswürdigkeit/Aktivität	*Ort*	*Preis*	*Zeit*
Wolkenkratzer	*Empire State Building*	...	...
...	*Broadway*	*billige Karten*	...
Fahrrad oder Boot mieten	...	*relativ billig*	...
...	*South Ferry*	...	*5 Minuten*
Statue of Liberty	...	*gratis*	...

5 WRITING

Write Sue's reply to Ricky's last email.

1 Start with your greeting: *Dear ...*
2 Paragraph 1: Refer to Ricky's email, and say how you felt when you received it.
Well, I got your email. And when I read it, I have to say I felt ...
3 Paragraph 2: Say how you feel about the relationship and what has happened to it.
Thinking about our relationship now, it seems to me that ...
4 Paragraph 3: Say what you think should happen now.
I'll tell you what I think should happen now. I think ...
5 Use one of Ricky's endings.

B The bigger picture

BEFORE YOU READ

A Look at the map. Do these activities.

1. Try to match the six famous places shown in Focus to numbers 1–6 on the map.
2. Say how a) a German immigrant in 1900 and b) a German tourist today might reach the centre of New York.

B The main title of the text on page 40 is 'A Bite of the Big Apple'. Say what you think the text might be about.

C Look at the sub-headings. Which of the following could the text be from?

an encyclopedia entry on New York
a novel about life in New York
a tourist guidebook about New York

A Bite of the Big Apple

Coming to New York

When you come from the airport on a sunny day, the distant towers of Manhattan shine magically. Closer, as you cross the river, the great skyline still takes your breath away, even though you know it from a thousand films.

As you begin exploring 'the Big Apple', you soon realize that it is many cities in one. For a start, New York is far more than Manhattan. Famous though this is, it is only one of five boroughs. There are also the Bronx, Brooklyn, Queens and Staten Island. Together, they cover the shores and islands of the Hudson and East Rivers and New York Bay.

Every borough has a different look and feel to it, and within each there are neighbourhoods, all with their own characteristics and sense of community.

The melting pot

Much of the city's variety comes from its many cultural and ethnic traditions. In the 19th century, the city drew millions of Irish, German, Italian, Jewish and other immigrants from Europe. And since then the waves of immigration have never stopped. After World War II, they came from Latin America and the Caribbean, and then from eastern Europe and Asia. In fact, 36% of today's New Yorkers were born abroad.

New York has also always attracted Americans from all over the country - people who want to make it in the big city.

The effects are everywhere. There are street festivals for everything from Chinese New Year to St Patrick's Day. In Queens, for example, you will hear a hundred different languages. As for food, you will find every dish under the sun in New York City.

The city that never sleeps

By the late nineteenth century, Manhattan was becoming quite crowded. With typical energy, New York began to use the newly-invented steel-frame construction to build streets to the sky. The skyscraper was born.

This energy is famous and has made New York the city that never sleeps. It has also made it a world leader in many areas, including finance, fashion, advertising, media and the arts. And, of course, NYC is the shopping capital of the world!

However, there have been hard times, too. The worst was in the 1970s. Drugs and crime were taking over, taxpayers were moving out and the city was nearly bankrupt. But, as always, the city came back stronger than ever.

The terrorist attacks of 9/11 of course brought more hard times, and another bad period of business failure and unemployment followed. The huge new 'Freedom Tower' will soon replace the former World Trade Center as a symbol of the city's recovery. (443 words)

1 LOOKING AT THE TEXT

A **Copy the mind map and add to it from the text, the map and what you know.**

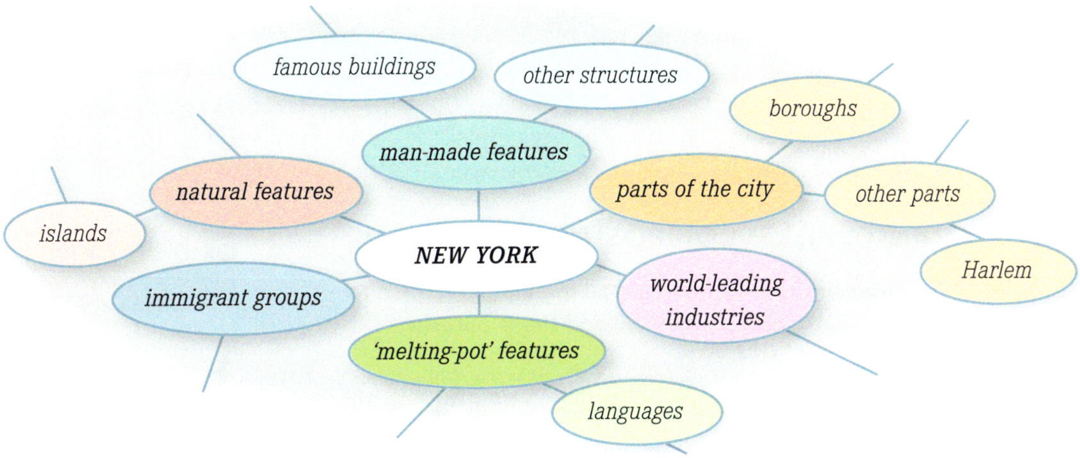

B **Complete the sentence beginnings 1–6 by adding a sentence part from the first box and an ending from the second.**

> Lesen schwieriger Texte: S. 160

1 Manhattan is the most famous part of New York, ...
2 The city has many cultural traditions ...
3 It has always attracted not just people from around the world, ...
4 When construction with steel became possible, ...
5 Through its huge energy, ...

... this soon led to the birth of ...
... because of the non-stop ...
... but also people from ...
... but it is only one of ...
... the city now leads the world ...

... every part of America itself.
... in many aspects of life.
... the skyscraper in crowded Manhattan.
... the five city boroughs.
... waves of immigrants.

2 MEDIATION

> EXAM PREPARATION
Mediation (S. 171)

Sie arbeiten an einem Projekt zum Thema New York. Ihre Aufgabe besteht darin, in einem kurzen Text über die kulturelle Vielfalt der Stadt zu berichten. Entnehmen Sie dem Text auf Seite 40 die relevanten Informationen.

3 WORKING WITH WORDS

Copy and complete the table with a) words from the text and b) other words that you know. (Check your dictionary if necessary.)

> TIP
When you collect words like this, you get two, three or even more words for the price of one.

Verb	*Noun*	*Adjective*
differ	*difference*	...
immigrate	...	
...	*attraction*	...
...	...	*sleepy*
...	...	*leading*
...	...	*informative*
strengthen	...	...

4 USING YOUR OWN WORDS

Rewrite the sentences using the words in brackets in the correct form – see exercise 3.

1 One great attraction to visitors is the city's huge energy. (*attract*) *One thing that greatly …*
2 Many parts of NY differ amazingly. (*difference*) *There are amazing …*
3 NY leads the financial centres of the world. (*leading*) *NY is the …*
4 This book has a lot of information about NY's history. (*informative*) *This book is …*
5 Over the last two centuries, large numbers of people have continued to immigrate to America. (*immigration*) *Over the last two centuries, large-scale …*

5 BUILDING SKILLS: COMPOSITION

> EXAM PREPARATION
> Materialgestützter Aufsatz (S. 173)

Write a composition about rising urban populations. Use the materials below, the text on page 40 and these phrases.

First, we should look at some basic urban population facts …
According to the chart, … risen from … to … between … and …
Today, more than half …
Now let us ask why more and more people …

The China fact file gives us one very clear reason …
There are other reasons, too.
To take New York as an example, the text tells us that …
I think that the urban population is growing for many reasons …

Latest figures prove that …
Statistics tell/show us that …
According to the graph …
If we look at the graph/chart …

China fact file

Annual income per person		Annual increase
Urban areas	$2,515	+8.8%
Rural areas	$755	+0.6%

(Adapted from: China Daily, 16 Feb 2011)

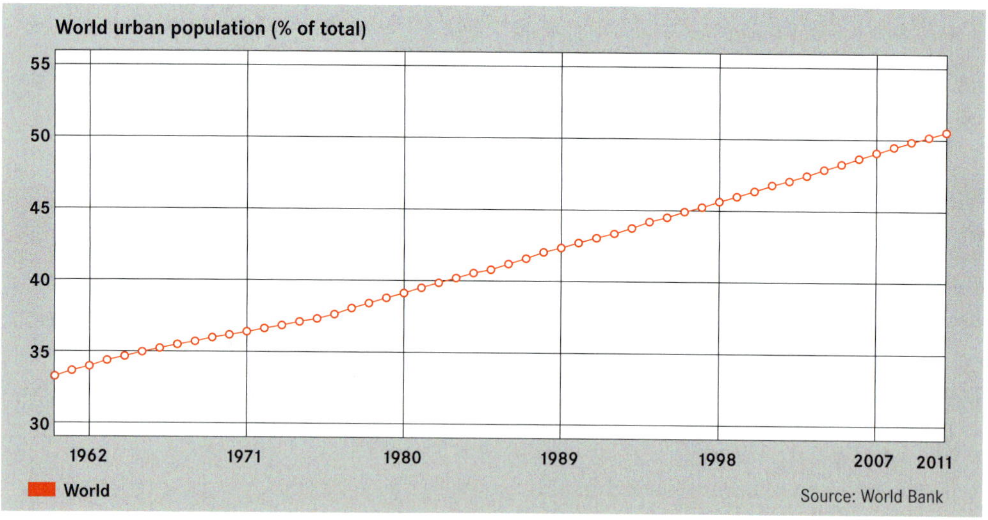

> **TIP**
> Read as many articles as you can in English newspapers or on the Internet about topics that could appear in the exam. The more you read, the more words you will have in your active vocabulary. This will help you to express your ideas clearly when you are writing an essay.

C Further options

1 PLANNING A DAY OUT

Students Martin and Kristal have just one free day in New York – Sunday, November 18 – and they want to do all of these things:

> go to a 'ball game' and see one of NY's great baseball teams;
> take in a big Broadway show – something with lots of music;
> experience some really American music, which could be jazz, country, gospel or blues.

Do these tasks.

1 Work out a plan for the day which allows Martin and Kristal to do everything.
2 Shows are expensive in NY, so find out how they can get cheap tickets.

The Baseball lineup

Home / Away

	Thu 15	Fri 16	Sat 17	Sun 18	Mon 19	Tue 20	Wed 21
ny	No game	No game	No game	Lions 1pm Fox	No game	No game	No game
JETS	No game	No game	No game	Steelers 4:05pm CBS	No game	No game	No game
	No game	Islanders 7pm FSNY	Flyers 7pm FSNY				Penguins
NY Islanders	Penguins 7:30pm FSNY	Devils 7pm FSNY	No game				

Seats for a song

Rush tickets to Broadway and Off Broadway shows for as little as $20 apiece. Go to the theater's box office on the day of the performance (most open at noon) and wait in line. Some sell rush tickets early, others an hour before curtain. Many shows also offer discounted rates for students and seniors.

Discount tickets available for same-day performances through the Theater Development Fund/TKTS on W 46th St between Broadway and Eighth Ave – Mon–Sat 3–8 p.m.; Wed, Sat 11 a.m.–6 p.m.; Sun 11 a.m.–4 p.m.

The Farnsworth Invention *Music Box Theater, W 45th St between Broadway and Eighth Ave $51.50 – $201.50. Tue 7 p.m.; Wed 2 p.m., 8 p.m.; Thu, Fri 8 p.m.; Sat 2 p.m., 8 p.m.; Sun 3 p.m.* Television heavyweight Aaron Sorkin *(The West Wing)* returns to the stage, but with his eye still fixed on the small screen. His new period drama concerns the 1928 invention of the electronic television by high-school boy genius Philo T. Farnsworth.

♫ ***Mamma Mia!*** *Winter Garden Theater, 1634 Broadway at 50th St. $62.75 – $251.50. Wed 2 p.m., 8 p.m.; Thu, Fri 8 p.m.; Sat, Sun 2 p.m., 8 p.m. 2 hrs 30 mins. One intermission.* Almost two dozen hits from the '70s pop sensation ABBA form the spine of this worldwide smash. As a delivery system for pop-

2 WRITING AN EMAIL

Write to an old English friend. Follow these steps.

1 Paragraph 1: Ask how your friend is and thank him/her for the last email/postcard/letter and for all the news. Apologize for taking a while to reply.
2 Paragraph 2: Begin with: *Guess what!* Say that you have won a competition and that the prize is a two-day trip to New York.
3 Paragraph 3: Describe your plans for the trip. (Include the big 'sights' and some events above – or anything else you like.)
4 Paragraph 4: Write a short closing paragraph. (See Ricky's emails on page 37 for ideas.)

D Grammar checkpoint

1 COMPARISON OF ADJECTIVES

> Grammar summary S. 187

A Work with a partner. Choose a city from below and find it on the map at the back of your book. Do not tell your partner the name of your city!

City	Approx population	City	Approx population	City	Approx population
New York	8.0 million	Houston	2.0 million	Seattle	570,000
Los Angeles	4.0 million	Phoenix	1.4 million	Washington D.C.	560,000
Chicago	3.0 million	San Francisco	750,000	Miami	380,000

B Give your partner some clues about your city. Which one is it? Can he/she guess?

A It's bigger than ..., but it isn't as big as ...
B That means you're talking about either ... or ...
A And it's farther south than ..., but it isn't as far south as ...
B Well, in that case, you mean ..., don't you?
A That's right. Now it's your turn. | No, sorry. You'd better try again.

2 COMPARATIVES AND SUPERLATIVES

> Grammar summary S. 187

A Look at *Top Holiday* magazine's survey of New York bus tours. Then read the junior reporter's comments and correct his five mistakes.

Tour details

	Length of tour	Cost	Departures
Big Apple Tours	2hr 50min	$25.00	Every 30 minutes
City Sights	1hr 50min	$22.00	Every hour
Central Experience	2hr 40min	$30.00	Every two hours

Visitors' opinions

	How interesting?	How helpful?	Value for money
Big Apple Tours	*****	**	****
City Sights	**	*	**
Central Experience	****	***	***

City offers the shortest tour of the three companies. At $22.00, the tour is cheaper than Big Apple's but more expensive than Central's. With departures every hour, it provides the least frequent service of all. Visitors feel that the tour itself is more interesting than Big Apple's and less interesting than Central's. They also say that the company is the most helpful of the three. Overall, they feel that the City tour is better value for money than the Central tour.

B Now write a similar paragraph to compare Big Apple Tours with City Sights and Central Experience.

2

Main Course

Advertising

FOCUS

1 **Advertising never leaves us alone. Where have you seen or heard advertisements in the last 24 hours? What sorts of advertising were they?**

brochures | classified, full-page or panel adverts in magazines/newspapers | leaflets | online pop-up/banner ads | posters | product placements (in TV programmes or films) | radio/TV commercials | sponsorship advertising (on football shirts, etc.)

A

B

C

D

E

F

2 **What do you think of the adverts above? Use adjectives like these.**

annoying | boring | clever | disgusting | funny | glamorous | shocking | silly | strange

3 **The aims of advertising vary – for example, to present products, promote brands or to make the public think. What do the adverts above do?**

A Personal perspectives

BEFORE YOU READ

Look at the photo and the title of the magazine article. Say which of the following you think it is not about, and why.
a) Places to go on holiday, b) planning for a happy old age or c) finding a great career.

1 13

DREAM destinations

Every week, DO IT! magazine's Ben Starr talks to young people in great jobs who have great futures. This week, Ben meets Lisa Scott at the fast-growing advertising agency *iMAGE iMPACT*.

BEN *Lisa, what brought you to iMAGE iMPACT's online advertising team?*

LISA *Well, while I was studying ICT at college, I designed a website for the volleyball team I played for. We were doing well in the national league, so we had lots of hits on the site. We also had a sponsor – SportStyle. They got their name on our shirts, and we got financial help. Then I added a simple game to the website. Visitors to our website pressed number keys to make a player jump and return the ball. Of course, SportStyle's name was on the player's shirt. They loved the whole website – and we got extra money.*

BEN *What happened then?*

LISA *After college, I became a freelance website developer, but I wanted something more. One day, I was looking at job ads on the internet when I saw that 'something'. iMAGE iMPACT were expanding their online team, and they wanted someone like me.*

BEN *So you applied for the job. And I guess the interview went well.*

LISA *Yes, and the volleyball website also helped, of course, so here I am. We're still only a small group in the Creative Design Department, but online advertising is the part of the whole business that's now growing the fastest.*

BEN *Where does Creative Design fit in?*

LISA *Well, let's start at the beginning. A potential client needs a campaign for a new product and invites several agencies, including us, to 'pitch' for the contract. One of our account managers visits the client to discuss their needs and then becomes the bridge between the client and us. Together, we and the account manager work out the key campaign concept. Then we, the 'creatives', produce the magic words and images that will sell the product.*

BEN *Let's say you win the pitch. What happens then?*

LISA *We get the green light to develop the concept into a full campaign. That's when the media planners also become very important. They're the people who decide exactly what media to use when, and how much. We could launch the campaign with a first run of TV commercials, for example, followed by online advertising.*

BEN *And what are you working on at the moment?*

LISA *Right now, I'm having real fun with a campaign for a new online travel agency. I'm using characters from the TV commercials to create a travel game that takes you on journeys to dream destinations right round the world.*

BEN *Well, thank you, Lisa. It's clear that this job really suits you – it's your own dream destination!*

(457 words)

1 LOOKING AT THE TEXT

> **EXAM PREPARATION**
> Beurteilen von Textaussagen (S. 172)

A Decide whether the following statements are true or false and explain your reasons in German.

1 Every week Ben Starr interviews young people who are in good jobs with a future.
2 Lisa Scott works in the online team of a successful advertising agency.
3 First, Ben asks Lisa why she wanted a job in advertising.
4 Lisa tells Ben that she designed her first website when she was still at school.
5 The volleyball team got extra money from a sponsor because Lisa put a game on the website.
6 Lisa found her job with iMAGE iMPACT in a national newspaper.
7 According to Lisa, online advertising is now the fastest-growing sector in the advertising industry.
8 Media planners are the 'bridge' between the client and the advertising agency.
9 The team that wins the pitch turns the basic advertising concept into a real advertising campaign.
10 At the moment, Lisa is making a game for TV commercials.

B This flow chart shows how an advertising campaign is set up. Copy and complete it with information from the text. Use the simple present, and leave out unnecessary words, e.g. *a, an, the*.

STEP 1	→	*STEP 2*	→	*STEP 3*	→	*STEP 4*	→	*STEP 5*	→	*STEP 6*	→	*STEP 7*
Potential client invites agencies to pitch.		...		...		...		...		...		*Agency launches campaign.*

C Which of these typical agency jobs – if any – might be right for you? Why? Discuss with a partner using the words and phrases below.

account manager | creative | IT support staff member | media booker (booking commercial slots, e.g. TV) | media planner | PA (personal assistant) to a senior manager

(I think) I'd find *I'd (probably) find*	*being a (creative)* *the job of (account manager)*	*(very) enjoyable.* *(quite) stressful.*
That's (probably) because *(I think) that's due to the fact that*	*I (don't) like ...* *I'm (quite/not very) good at ...*	

2 DESCRIBING A PROCESS

Look back to exercise 1B. Now write a summary of the process in full sentences. Use these connectors.

First (of all), ... | Then ... | Next, ... | After that, ... | Following that, ... | Finally, ...

3 WORKING WITH WORDS

A **Copy and complete the table.**

B **Complete the *iMAGE iMPACT* advert that Lisa saw. Use words from the table.**

	Verb	Noun (thing)	Noun (person)
1	...	design	...
2	...	development	...
3	...	interview	...
4	...	management	...
5	sponsor	sponsorship	...
6	supply	supply	...

http://www.

iMAGE iMPACT is a fast-developing, London-based advertising agency. We are expanding our online team and urgently require an innovative ...[1].
Please visit our website at www.imageimpact.co.uk for further information and an application form, or call Human Resources ...[2] Helen Troy on 020-1946583. The closing date for applications is 28th February, and we expect to ...[3] candidates between 10th and 14th March. All shortlisted candidates will be asked to ...[4] examples of their work.

4 CULTURE CHECK: FORMS OF ADDRESS

Email

Dear Ms Scott,
Thank you for your application for the new position in our online team. I am pleased to invite you for an interview on 12 March at 2 p.m. Please confirm that you are able to attend on this date and bring some recent examples of your work with you.
I look forward to meeting you.
Best wishes,
Mandy Carr

Email

Dear Lisa,
I am very pleased to offer you the position in our online team. Please reply by 28 March to confirm whether you would like to accept the post. Then we can organize contracts, etc.
I look forward to working with you!
Best regards,
Mandy Carr
P.S. Please do call me Mandy – we are pretty informal here!

Read the correspondence between Mandy Carr and Lisa Scott. Decide the following:

1 When and why were these emails written?
2 What rules does the writer follow? Who can/cannot suggest using first names?
3 In the same situations in Germany, what forms of address would people use?

> INFO

1 *Mr*, *Mrs* and *Ms* are the usual formal titles used when dealing with clients, customers and senior colleagues. *Ms* is used for all women, whether they are married or not.
2 In many companies, staff use first names with each other, even between junior and senior staff. This may seem very informal, but it is not and has nothing like the closeness of the German 'du'.
3 As in Germany, changing from formal style to first names must come from the senior person, e.g. here, from Mandy Carr to Lisa Scott.

5 SPEAKING

Discuss things that you should and should not do before and during an interview.

B The bigger picture

BEFORE YOU READ

Look at the heading. Say what you understand by the word 'Forum'.

http://www.

1 14

FOCUS Forum

JOIN TODAY'S DISCUSSION: 'We're swimming in a sea of advertising'

Rob, London, UK

Dear FOCUS Forum
It's more true to say that we're drowning in a sea of advertising! And what's so terrible is that it tries to control our minds. And what about the 'frustration problem'? Ads create unrealistic desires that most people can only dream about.
We just have to ignore all the thousands of adverts around us as much as we can. For example, when commercial breaks come on, it's time to make coffee. Even better, I often record programmes and my DVD recorder automatically cuts the commercials.

Lucy, Melbourne, Australia

Dear FOCUS Forum
Rob is far too negative. We live in a very rich society that offers lots of choices. And advertising tells us about those choices. Think of it as a public information service! Personally, I also love ads. They're lively and fun. So lighten up, Rob!

Julia, Seattle, United States

Dear FOCUS Forum
Like Rob I hate living in a sea of advertising, but I know that we can't escape from the advertisers so easily. Just think of the branded entertainment on our screens. With all that product placement, programmes like House Wars are really extended commercials! For example, the families always go to the same store for their building supplies.
And then there's online viral advertising, too. This often comes as a game, and it passes from friend to friend by email. And then the product appears on every screen. It spreads around the world like a virus.
'Word of mouth' agencies that pay people to talk up a product at parties or in online chatroom discussions are just another sort of viral advertising.
So while I really dislike traditional advertising, I prefer it to the new methods. At least you know it when you see it, and you can always change channel or turn the page. Viral advertising is often harder to recognize.

Peter, Johannesburg, South Africa

Dear FOCUS Forum
Unlike Julia, I think viral advertising is good because it's cheaper than traditional forms of advertising. I must admit, I do worry about those billions of dollars that traditional advertisers spend. What's more, advertising makes us buy more than we need, so we're using global resources more wastefully than ever. We should spend the money on something more useful – more hospitals, for example.

Sally, Toronto, Canada

Dear FOCUS Forum
Poor Peter! He just doesn't understand. Advertising adds a bit to costs, but it helps keep the whole global economy going. Without it, sales drop, companies collapse, jobs disappear, the economy fails, and we all go back to the Middle Ages! Is that what we want? Are we mad enough to do that?

(422 words)

1 LOOKING AT THE TEXT

> **EXAM PREPARATION**
> Mediation (S. 171)

A **Sie müssen zur Schülerzeitung einen kurzen Artikel zum Thema Werbung beitragen. Ihr Anliegen ist es, Ihren Mitschülern über die unterschiedlichen Formen der Werbung Auskunft zu geben und zu erklären, welche Methoden 'hard sell' und 'soft sell' sind. Entnehmen Sie dem Text auf Seite 49 die relevanten Informationen. Übersetzen Sie dabei nicht Wort für Wort.**

B **Use the information from the forum to decide which person made each comment. Read the speech bubbles 1–5 and match them to the photographs A–E.**

1 *I enjoy watching ads on TV! And I often buy things that I see in adverts.*

2 *Yes, advertising makes products a bit more expensive, but we would have so many problems without it.*

3 *People don't understand how much advertising there is around them – it's everywhere. We just can't escape from it!*

4 *I don't let advertising influence me. I do everything I can to avoid it. People should make their own choices.*

5 *What about the impact on the environment? Just think of all the raw materials that are used up to produce the things we buy.*

A Rob, 17

B Lucy, 15

C Julia, 20

D Peter, 18

E Sally, 20

C **Explain one point of disagreement between each pair, using these connectors.**

| but | whereas | while | By contrast | However | On the other hand |

1 Rob and Lucy **2** Rob and Julia **3** Julia and Peter **4** Peter and Sally

EXAMPLE *Rob says that there is far too much ..., while Lucy feels that advertising ...*

D **Say what you think.**

1. Name some adverts that you like or dislike and say why.
2. In FOCUS Forum there are five different opinions on advertising. Which do you agree/disagree with? Use these phrases:
   I totally/partly agree/disagree with ... when he/she says/suggests that ...
   Personally, I think that ... is exaggerating.
   It seems to me that ... is giving a one-sided view.
   In my opinion, ... has got it about right.

2 CARTOON ANALYSIS

> **EXAM PREPARATION**
> Bildbeschreibung mit Analyse (S. 172)

Describe what you can see in the cartoon. Explain the message and relate it back to Rob's comment on page 49.

in the foreground/background there is a ... watching ... / looking through ... at ...
on the left/right you see ...
the thought bubble ...
the man doesn't realize ...
The cartoon is satirizing / making fun of ...
The cartoon illustrates Rob's opinion in the following way ...

> **TIP**
> Note down your first reaction to the cartoon as long as it is fresh in your memory. Look at the cartoon closely and mention as many details as possible in your text. There is no 'correct' answer as your personal interpretation is required. Don't be afraid to express your own opinion or to use your own imagination.

3 LISTENING

> **ZENTRALE KLASSENARBEIT**
> Hörverstehen (S. 175)

1 15 **A Vervollständigen Sie auf Deutsch die unten stehenden Aussagen mit Informationen aus dem ersten Hörtext.**

1 Die Gastrednerin, Mandy Carr, ist eine Führungspersönlichkeit aus ... .
2 Sie arbeitet für eine Werbeagentur aus ... .
3 Sie wird den Studenten einige ... vorstellen.
4 Die Studenten werden wahrscheinlich gut zuhören, weil viele von ihnen ... .

1 16 **B Beantworten Sie auf Deutsch die unten stehenden Fragen zum zweiten Hörtext in ganzen Sätzen.**

1 Wie lautet die Grundformel der Werbung?
2 Wo hat Mandy Carr ihr Beispiel gefunden?
3 Welche Aspekte der Anzeige erweckt die Aufmerksamkeit der Leser?
4 Wie erweckt die Anzeige das Interesse der Leser?
5 Mit welchem Angebot wird das Verlangen der Leser erweckt?
6 Wo kann man sich mehr darüber informieren?
7 Welche Verkaufsstrategie steckt hinter dem Sonderangebot?

4 BUILDING SKILLS: ANALYZING CHARTS

> Interpretation von Grafiken, Diagrammen und Tabellen S. 169

A Match the chart types a–c to their names 1–3.

a

b
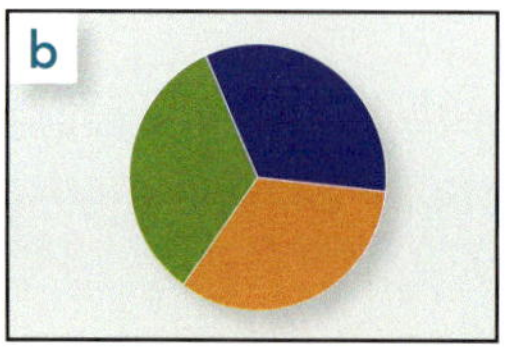

c
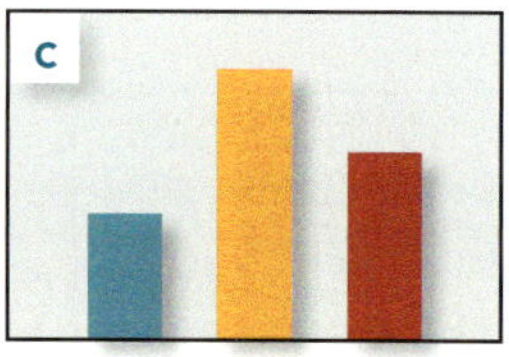

1 bar chart
2 line graph
3 pie chart

> **TIP**
>
> Charts show statistical information in a way that is easy to understand. When you give presentations, try to use suitable charts to support your explanations.

B Here are some useful words for describing graphs and statistics.
Use them to describe what is happening in A–F.

verb +	*adverb*
rise	*rapidly*
increase	*sharply*
grow	*steadily*
fall	*gradually*
decrease	*slowly*
decline	*slightly*

adjective +	*noun*
rapid	*rise*
sharp	*increase*
steady	*growth*
gradual	*fall*
slow	*decrease*
slight	*decline*

verb +	*adjective*
be	*flat*
remain	*steady*

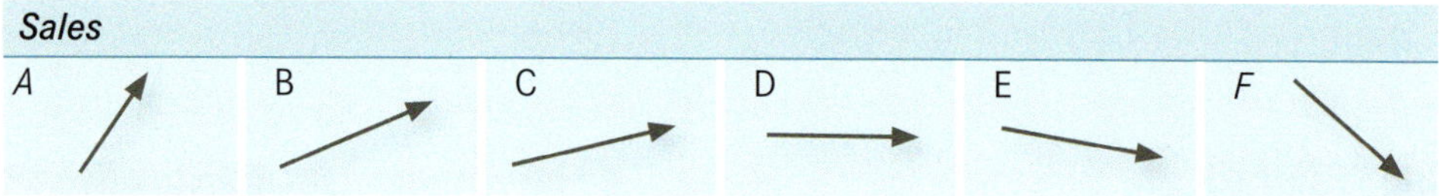

EXAMPLES *In A, sales increased sharply. / In A, there was a rapid rise in sales.*

C Read and do the activities.

Tony Lee, *iMAGE iMPACT*'s Finance Director, is describing some company sales trends.

1 Look at the chart, read what Tony Lee says, and decide whether he is talking about total sales or TV sales.
2 Say which five years he is talking about.

In the first year of this period, sales were flat, but in the next year they increased steadily, and in the year after that, they rose slightly again. However, in the following year, sales were flat again, and in the final year of the period they fell very sharply.

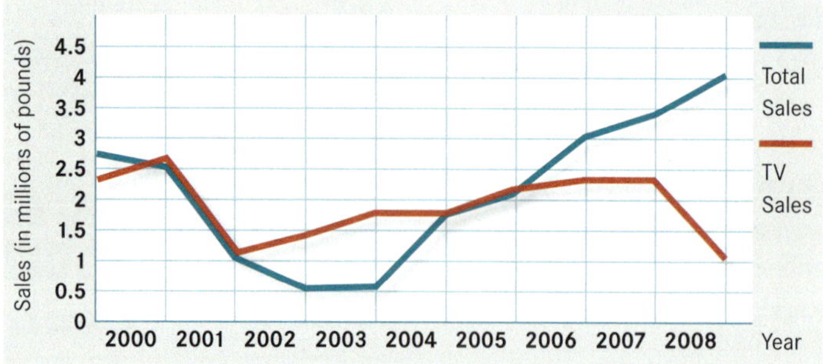

C Further options

1 ANALYZING AN ADVERTISEMENT

With a partner analyze an advert. Find a good advert – in English or German – that uses the AIDA formula. Your analysis should explain the following:

> what the advert is for
> where it comes from
> who it is aimed at (the target audience)
> how it works (using the AIDA formula – see exercise 3B, page 51)
> how well it works, particularly with its target audience and why you both like it

2 ANALYZING THE CONSTRUCTION OF ADVERTISEMENTS

Work with a partner, and analyze the advert on the right. Think about:

> what first draws the eye to the advert
> the arrangement of images, colours and words
> the message that the advertiser wants to get over to you
> how the images, colours and words support that message

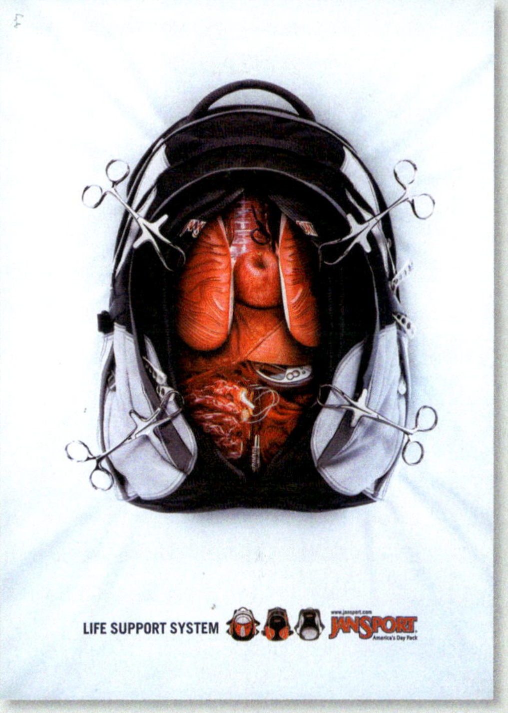

3 CONSTRUCTING AN ADVERTISEMENT

Work with a partner. As creatives, work out an advertising concept for a new product.

> Choose a product, e.g. a new high-tech mobile phone, a glamorous range of fashion accessories or a special event.
> Agree on your target audience.
> Work out a message that will attract that audience.
> Develop the images, colours and words that will support that message.

4 PRESENTING YOUR PITCH

Work with another pair – they are your agency's clients. Take turns to pitch to each other.

Explain your concept and your choice of image and words. Try to persuade them that your ideas would make a great campaign.

5 WRITING A COMMENT ABOUT ADVERTISING

> Eine Stellungnahme (*comment*) schreiben S. 165

In exercise 1D (page 50) you discussed other comments in FOCUS Forum. Now write your own comment about advertising in today's world.

D Grammar checkpoint

1 PAST PROGRESSIVE

> Grammar summary S. 177

At 6 p.m. everybody at *iMAGE iMPACT* was still working. Use the past progressive to say what they were doing. Add any missing words.

1 Lisa Scott (*test*) | new online game | SkyTravel.com.
Lisa Scott was testing her new online game for SkyTravel.com.
2 Mandy Carr (*prepare*) business plan | next year.
3 Tony Lee and his assistant (*study*) | latest sales figures.
4 Media planners (*discuss*) | new campaign.
5 Carrie, the senior account executive, (*call*) | client | America.

2 PAST PROGRESSIVE AND SIMPLE PAST

> Grammar summary S. 177

Fill in the gaps with the past progressive or simple past. (Use the past progressive when both tenses are possible.)

Lisa has worked very long hours for months now, without any holidays. Yesterday, for example, she *was still working*[1] (*still work*) at 7.00, and she *finally finished*[2] (*finally finish*) at nearly 7.30.

While she …[3] (*walk*) past an electrical store on her way to the bus stop, something on the TV screens in the window …[4] (*catch*) her eye. They …[5] (*show*) the new SkyTravel commercial! Then she …[6] (*remember*): this …[7] (*be*) the first day of the campaign.

At home, Lisa …[8] (*put*) a curry in the microwave and …[9] (*turn on*) the TV. She …[10] (*see*) the commercial again. The people in it …[11] (*have*) a wonderful time on a golden beach under a blue sky. 'And why not me, too?' Lisa …[12] (*ask*) herself. The company owes me two weeks' holiday!'

While she …[13] (*eat*) her curry, Lisa …[14] (*log on*) to SkyTravel. She …[15] (*get*) really excited when she …[16] (*find*) cheap holidays available in Ibiza. Two minutes later, she …[17] (*talk*) on the phone to her friend Alice about dates. Later, she …[18] (*think*), 'Our commercial must be pretty good: it even worked on me!'

3 RELATIVE CLAUSES

> Grammar summary S. 188

Form complete sentences by putting together one line from 1–5 and one from a–e. Make them into one sentence by adding *who*, *which* or *that*.

1 Rob (*be*) the person
Rob is the person who tries to ignore and avoid advertising.
2 Lucy and Sally (*be*) the ones
3 Viral advertising (*be*) a new type of advertising
4 Rob (*use*) a DVD recorder
5 There (*be*) programmes like *House Wars*

a It (*cut*) the commercials.
b They clearly (*support*) advertising.
c They (*be*) really just long commercials.
d ~~He (*try*) to ignore and avoid advertising.~~
e It (*work*) by spreading from person to person, often by email.

4 RELATIVE CLAUSES AND CONTACT CLAUSES

> Grammar summary S. 188

Copy and complete the slogans. Add *who*, *which* or *that* where necessary. If not, write *X*.

1 STARWAYS – a film *X* you'll never forget
2 AIR-WISE – the people … get you there
3 HOME GYM – for a personal trainer … you can trust
4 PRO-VIT – the vitamins … doctors recommend
5 LOOKS – for fashion … won't break the bank
6 RANGER XF – the car … the whole world's waiting for
7 SAT-PAK – the satnav system … beats them all

3 Media madness

FOCUS

> **> TIP**
> Word fields and networks are great ways of collecting and learning new vocabulary.

1 Think about the ways you keep in contact with the world.

A Copy and complete the network with the ideas below.

B Say which of these ways of communicating you use most and least. Say why.

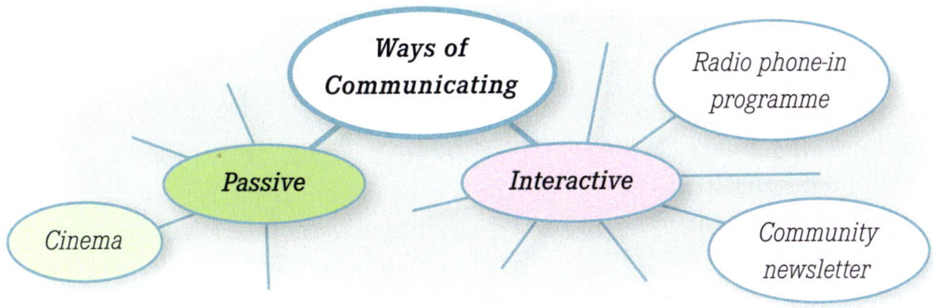

Blog

Celebrity magazine

Face-to-face contact

Mobile phone

Newspaper

Social networking site

Television

Text message

2 Decide how you would react in these situations.

1. Hurricane Zoe has just hit Florida. Your cousin is on holiday there, so you want to find out the latest news - and fast. How?
2. Your school is organizing a public event to raise money for the charity 'Children in Need'. Which forms of communication could help, and how?
3. For a presentation about refugees in the EU, you want to understand the background better. Which forms of communication might help most - or would you go to the library?
4. You suddenly realize that you missed the last Spiderman film when it was on at the local multiplex! What can you do about it?
5. You want to chat with a friend. What might you do?
6. You want to meet new people. What could you do?

A Personal perspectives

BEFORE YOU READ

A **Explain what you understand by 'reality TV'.**

B **Give examples of reality TV programmes in Germany at the moment, and say what you like/dislike about them.**

1 17

http://www.

THE BIRMINGHAM HERALD

Big Bother hits Big Brother

The long-running UK reality show Big Brother began screening its new series – Celebrity Big Brother – in January. But yesterday, the whole story finally came to a sorry end. This was when BB's producers had to apologize very publicly for their mistakes.

As usual, the series brought together a group of people – this time they were all well-known celebrities – in the Big Brother House. And, as usual, TV cameras followed every action and every word, and then the most 'entertaining' parts went out to millions of viewers. Every week they voted by phone or text to throw out the least popular member of the group.

The trouble began when Jade Goody (and others) launched into a series of racist attacks on the Indian Bollywood actress Shilpa Shetty. Thousands of viewers complained, and the popular press quickly joined the protest. Soon, Goody could no longer stay: millions of the audience had voted her out.

Then the press attacked the programme makers. After all, they had encouraged and exploited the situation. Before long, the BB series was no longer able to continue.

(179 words)

Readers' comments

The programmes did get out of control and the abuse Shilpa Shetty suffered was terrible. But I don't think you can blame the show's producers. Reality TV producers have to choose people with different psychological profiles to create personality clashes. That produces popular TV, which brings the advertisers and the big profits.

If we really disagree with these shows, we needn't watch them, need we? After all, they can't survive without an audience. The problem is that so many people are addicted to these shows and simply can't turn them off. *Lisa Sanchez* (92 words)

Why do people agree to appear on programmes like Big Brother? They know the world will see them in embarrassing or stressful situations. I suppose some of them want to test themselves or win the big prize, but I think lots of them just want their 'fifteen minutes of fame'. As for celebrities like Jade Goody and Shilpa Shetty, perhaps they want to keep themselves in the public eye and have fifteen more minutes of fame. *Mark Romano* (76 words)

I wonder about the psychology of reality TV viewers. What makes us want to watch these shows? With Big Brother, I suppose we enjoy seeing people behaving badly towards each other. And on other reality TV programmes the contestants have to do really painful and grotesque tests. It seems that we actually enjoy watching people suffer. Are these shows making us all a little mad?

Perhaps we aren't very different from the Romans – they loved watching people die for sport.
Jean O'Hanlon (81 words)

1 LOOKING AT THE TEXT

A Put statements a–f in the correct order to summarize the newspaper article.

a And as usual, the viewers voted one of these people out every week.
b The press also attacked the producers for encouraging the situation and forced the whole series to stop.
c But then, one of the *Big Brother* housemates began to make racist remarks against another housemate.
d Yesterday, the producers of TV's *Big Brother* had to apologize to the public.
e This brought huge protests from viewers and the press, and the viewers quickly voted the abusive housemate out.
f During the latest *Big Brother* series, cameras filmed the lives of a group of people in the BB House in the usual way.

B Pick out the readers' points on the weakness of human nature.

One reader says that ... *Another reader notes that ...* *A third reader suggests that ...*

C Say what you think.

1 Why do you think people appear on reality TV shows?
2 Would you agree to appear on any of the German reality TV shows? Give reasons.

2 WORKING WITH WORDS

A Collect opposites. You can use your dictionary if you need to.

1 The words in the box below are all from page 56. Copy the table and complete columns 1–3 with opposite forms.

able | agree | appear | behave | encourage | popular | understand | usual

1	*2*	*3*	*4*
un~	*dis~*	*mis~*	*in~ il~ ir~ im~*

2 Now add some more words that you already know to columns 1–3.
3 Put the opposites of these words in column 4.

accurate | complete | correct | legal | legible | logical | moral | perfect | possible | regular | relevant | responsible

4 What do you notice about all the opposites with the forms *il~* and *ir~*?
5 Add more words to column 4.

B Use the adjectives above or their opposites to complete the following sentences.

1 Jade Goody became very ... because of her racist attacks on Shilpa Shetty.
2 A lot of people felt that the producers were ... because they let the situation develop.
3 Following the press attacks, *Big Brother* was ... to continue.
4 Goody later apologized for her behaviour, but she said she was not a racist, and she believed that people had ... her.
5 A lot of people were pleased that BB had ... from the TV screen.
6 But, after a year with no *Big Brother*, the TV producers finally decided that, with some changes, it would be ... to bring it back.

3 LISTENING

A Before you listen, think about different film genres.

1 Look at this list of film genres and give examples of each.

action comedy | action movie | comedy | documentary | road movie | romantic comedy | satire | sci-fi movie | spy movie

2 List some more film genres. Then give examples of films in these genres that you have enjoyed and explain why.

1 18 **B Vervollständigen Sie auf Deutsch die unten stehenden Aussagen mit Informationen aus dem ersten Hörtext.**

> ZENTRALE KLASSENARBEIT
Hörverstehen (S. 175)

1 Dave hat gestern seine ... bestanden.
2 Um heute Abend ins Kino zu fahren, darf er ... .
3 Dave fragt Steve, ob er und Claire mit ihm und Debbie ... .
4 Er schlägt vor, dass sie sich ..., während er und Debbie zu ihnen unterwegs sind.
5 Er möchte auch ... im Greenside Center essen.
6 Er schätzt, dass sie in ... bei Steve und Claire sein werden.

1 19 **C Ergänzen Sie das Raster mit Informationen aus dem zweiten Hörtext.**

Kino	*Film*	*Genre*	*Abend Anfangszeiten*
1	...	*action comedy*	*5.30 – ... – ...*
2	*Journey to the Stars*	...	*... – ... – 9.30*
3	...	...	*... – 7.30 – ...*

4 DOING A ROLE-PLAY

Do the following role-play.

1 Work in groups of four and choose a role each.
2 Put forward your point of view. Use some of these phrases.

Roles

Debbie > File 3, page 155
Dave > File 13, page 158
Claire > File 5, page 156
Steve > File 18, page 159

I (don't) think we should / ought to ... *I think we'd better (not) ...*	*We can / could ... first, and then ...* *We might (not) be able to ...*	*I wish we could ...* *It's a pity we can't ...* *Whatever we do, we must(n't) ...*

3 Report your group's decisions to the class.
4 Compare different groups' plans. Has everyone made the same decisions? If not, try to say why not.

B The bigger picture

BEFORE YOU READ

What personal information would you (not) put on a social networking site (e.g. MySpace, Facebook)? Say why.

Great medium, but what about your message?

Jenny has tried several different drugs, has two piercings and also a butterfly tattoo on her arm. She earns $23,000 a year, and hasn't seen her parents for two years. I know her address, but they don't.

Altogether, I know a lot about Jenny, although I've never met her and probably never will. This is strange really. A few years ago, I'm sure hardly anyone in her circle of friends knew as much about her as I, a complete stranger, do today.

Not that this is unusual. Consider the enormous numbers who now share very personal details with others on social networking sites. As of January 2011, there were more than 500 million active Facebook users, 175 million users of Twitter, over 100 million on MySpace and more than 80 million on LinkedIn. Everyone knows the dangers to children if they put personal information on the internet. But what about the dangers to the rest of us? Shouldn't Jenny - and many millions more adults like her - be a lot more careful too?

The US National Association of Colleges and Employers recently discovered that 27% of employers search Google and other sites such as MySpace for profiles of their job applicants. And they may find information that those applicants do not want them to have.

On the face of it, the difference between behaviour online and offline makes no sense. In their ordinary lives, people do not easily give strangers personal details such as their phone number or date of birth. It is simply not sensible. Why then do the same people offer these things freely when they go on the internet? It is because both the social network providers and the users know that they need to give quite a lot of information in order to make the system work. After all, it is hard for people to start communicating if they know very little about each other. The trouble is that when private information gets out there, it can become very public, and it may also remain out there forever.

We are starting to hear about people who have lost jobs or college places because of things they said about themselves online. And it is not just jobs and college places at risk. Many people are worried that social networking sites could also be used by identity thieves. Even a little personal information may be enough for others to learn - and then to use! - your bank details. As for chatrooms, you can never be absolutely sure who you're talking to, and this can be dangerous. Perhaps we should think more carefully about the risks we run when we share information online.

Some students in the USA now have to take a 1st-semester class in social networking so that they clearly understand the risks. Internet researcher Steve Jones of the University of Illinois goes further. He says, 'If you put something on MySpace or Facebook, ask yourself whether you'd be comfortable shouting it out at a family reunion. If the answer is no, then don't put it up.'

(507 words)

Heavily abridged and adapted from *Things you wouldn't tell your mother, Alison George, New Scientist 16/09/06 p. 50*

1 LOOKING AT THE TEXT

A Scan the text for these numbers. Then read further and explain what the numbers refer to in the text.

$23,000 27% 1st

B Copy and complete the statements. As far as possible, use your own words.

1 It is sad for Jenny's parents that ...
2 We all know that children should not put personal information on the internet, but adults should ...
3 Employers often search the internet in order to ...
4 People do not usually give personal information to people they have just met, so it is strange that ...
5 A good general rule is that you should only put information on the internet that ...

C Use words from the text to complete this summary.

Large numbers of people use social ...1 sites like MySpace to share their ...2 details. They often share information online that they would never share ...3. The more information they give, the easier it is to begin ...4 with similar people. This is the system the social networking ...5 have created. And if this private information becomes ...6, people could lose their job or their place at university. ...7 thieves are another danger. There is also a risk that when you talk to someone in an internet ...8, they might be lying about who they are.

D Say what you think.

What are the dangers of meeting people through the internet? What should you do to make sure that you stay safe?

2 WORKING WITH WORDS

A Match the words from each box to form word pairs and expressions from the text.

personal I job I date of I social I circle of I family	applicant I birth I details I friends I networking I reunion

B Use word pairs from exercise A to complete the following sentences.

1 All my cousins are coming to our ... next month.
2 We're asking all the ... to come for interviews on March 28th.
3 ... websites like MySpace and Facebook are becoming more and more popular.
4 Susie is at a different party every weekend! She has a very large ...
5 People's ... can be very useful for identity thieves. Make sure that you keep yours safe!

3 SPEAKING

Work with a partner. Talk about your own experiences with social networking sites.

1 Ask each other questions about the sites you have heard of and what you think of them.
2 If you are a member of a networking site, explain why you use it and whether you have had any bad experiences with the site.

4 COMPOSITION

> EXAM PREPARATION
> Materialgestützter Aufsatz (S. 173)

Read and study the following. Use ideas from at least three sources to write two paragraphs on this topic. Use the language shown to start each paragraph.

The internet: the bad – and the good

Paragraph 1:
It is certainly true that there are many problems and dangers on the internet. For example, ... Then again, ... It is also a fact that ...

Paragraph 2:
On the other hand, it is very important to say that the internet allows us to do things that we could not do before. To give one example, ... In addition, ... Finally, ...

1

"What shall I do? She wants to meet for coffee."

2

MARKET MONITOR — February 02, 20..

US online sales reach $173 billion last year, up 19%

3

RADIO 3

PRESENTER Welcome to Radio 3, David Klein. Now, you have recently completed a study of online activities by young people, haven't you?

KLEIN That's right, it's a study of 2,000 young Britons aged 14 to 21 – and the results are very worrying. The information people put up is often an open door to identity thieves.

PRESENTER How do you mean?

KLEIN Let me give you some examples. Nearly two-thirds put up their date of birth, a quarter give their job title and almost one in ten post their home address. And people also often give details that they also use as passwords: 23% give the name of a brother or sister and a quarter of all girls give a pet's name, for example. When you put all that information together, it's often all those thieves need.

4

http://www.OneWorld/Discussion forum/Living/Internet/Good_or_bad?

OneWorld Forum — SUBJECT: The internet: is it good or bad?

California Dreamer	*Fri May 15 10.47* The internet is amazing! Whatever you need to know, you'll find something somewhere out there on the internet. In fact, you'll find a whole lot more.
Essenengel	*Fri May 15 20.23* That's the trouble. There's too much out there, and it's hard to find what you want. To start with, lots of websites are rubbish. Others are OK, but they don't tell you what you want. It can take ages to find the stuff you need.
Free2BMe	*Sat May 16 09.38* Actually, a lot of websites aren't just useless: they're really bad. For instance they may say things that are untrue or racist. And the trouble is that there's no one to stop people saying these things. And of course, there are also those identity thieves. They can take all your money before you realize there's anything wrong.
Typhoon Takeo	*Sun May 17 21.06* Oh, come on! I think we're all sensible enough to avoid the bad websites. Anyway, for me the great thing is that I can email my friends at any time, or we can chat to each other on Facebook at any time we want. It still seems amazing that I can communicate with people on the other side of the world so easily – just like we're doing now!

5 CULTURE CHECK: NETIQUETTE

Many young people in English-speaking countries like Britain and America use internet forums to have discussions online. These forums allow English speakers from around the world to talk about a wide range of topics, from politics and religion, to music and computer games. English speakers are careful to sound polite in a face-to-face conversation and this is just as important in an online discussion. Most forums have their own rules but here are some general points on how to behave in an internet forum.

> Keep to the point - only write about the topic that is being discussed.
> Don't write everything in CAPITAL LETTERS. This is considered 'shouting' and is difficult to read. If you want to emphasize a word, you can use **bold** or <u>underline</u> it.
> Use capital letters for names, places and so on - otherwise you will seem lazy.
> Check your spelling and grammar and avoid using too many abbreviations, as other people may not understand them.
> Be polite to other users and do not be rude about them or their ideas.
> Use normal punctuation - don't write '!!!!' or '????' to emphasize a point, this is just unnecessary.
> avoid using too many *abbreviations, as other people may not understand them.

* These are some abbreviations that many people understand and use.

u - you	OTT - over the top	PLS - please
r - are	ATM - at the moment	TBH - to be honest
2 - to	BTW - by the way	THX - thanks
1 - (e.g. sum 1 = someone)	FYI - for your information	TMI - too much information
ur - you're/your	IMO - in my opinion	TTYL - talk to you later
	LOL - laughing out loud	BRB - be right back

Read this discussion and say which users are not showing good 'netiquette' and why.

http://www.

forum

we should do more to protect children who use the internet!!!! my brother jack is only 8 and i don't think he should go online. what do you think???? David

SHUT UP. That's STUPID. Kids can have so much FUN online. If you don't like the internet, why are you here? Ed

I think David is rite, we hav 2 b careful that kids don't spend 2 much time online. There r lots of things they can do instead of sittin in front of a computer all day! Georgia

PLS can we talk about something else? Did any1 c the football match on TV last night? Ben

Ben, if you want to talk about that, you can find a football forum. I think it's important to talk about this - if children use the internet, we need to make sure that they are safe. Laura

C Further options

1 READING LITERATURE

In 1949 George Orwell published his most famous novel *1984*. *1984* is about living in a fictional surveillance society. The extract comes from the start of Orwell's book.

Before you read, say what you understand by the term 'surveillance society'.

1984 (extract) *by George Orwell*

It was a bright cold day in April, and the clocks were striking thirteen. Winston Smith, his chin nuzzled into his breast in an effort to escape the vile wind, slipped quickly through the glass doors of Victory Mansions, though not quickly enough to prevent a swirl of gritty dust from entering along with him. The hallway smelt of boiled cabbage and old rag mats. At one end of it a coloured poster, too large for indoor display, had been tacked to the wall. It depicted simply an enormous face, more than a metre wide: the face of a man of about forty-five, with a heavy black moustache and ruggedly handsome features.

... On each landing, the poster with the enormous face gazed from the wall. It was one of those pictures which are so contrived that the eyes follow you about when you move. BIG BROTHER IS WATCHING YOU, the caption beneath it ran. Inside the flat a fruity voice was reading out a list of figures which had something to do with the production of pig-iron. The voice came from an oblong metal plaque like a dulled mirror which formed part of the surface of the right-hand wall. Winston turned a switch and the voice sank somewhat, though the words were still distinguishable. The instrument (the telescreen, it was called) could be dimmed, but there was no way of shutting it off completely ...

... Outside, even through the shut window-pane, the world looked cold. Down in the street little eddies of wind were whirling dust and torn paper into spirals, and though the sun was shining and the sky a harsh blue, there seemed to be no colour in anything, except the posters that were plastered everywhere. The black-moustachio'd face gazed down from every commanding corner. There was one on the house-front immediately opposite. BIG BROTHER IS WATCHING YOU, the caption said, while the dark eyes looked deep into Winston's own ...

... The telescreen received and transmitted simultaneously. Any sound that Winston made, above the level of a very low whisper, would be picked up by it; moreover, so long as he remained within the field of vision which the metal plaque commanded, he could be seen as well as heard.

There was of course no way of knowing whether you were being watched at any given moment. How often, or on what system, the Thought Police plugged in on any individual wire was guesswork. It was even conceivable that they watched everybody all the time.

But at any rate they could plug in your wire whenever they wanted to. You had to live – did live, from habit that became instinct – in the assumption that every sound you made was overheard, and, except in darkness, every movement scrutinised.

(463 words)

3 nuzzle *drücken, schmiegen*
4 vile *garstig*
6 swirl *Schwall*; gritty *sandig*
8 rag *Lumpen*
14 rugged *rau*
18 contrived *ausgeklügelt*
22 fruity *voll/herzhaft*
24 pig-iron *Roheisen*
25 oblong *rechteckig*; plaque *Tafel*; dulled *trübe*
28 somewhat *ein wenig*
31 dim *abblenden, verdunkeln*
35 eddy *Windstoß*; whirling *wirbeln*
39 plaster *ankleben, bepflastern*
40 moustachio'd *hier: schnauzbärtig*
41 commanding *Respekt einflößend, beherrschend*
55 given *gegeben*
56 plug in *sich verbinden*
57 wire *Leitung*
58 conceivable *denkbar*
63 assumption *Annahme*
65 scrutinise *überprüfen*

2 THINKING ABOUT THE TEXT

Now answer these questions on the text.

1. How does Orwell show us that the world in *1984* is organized very differently from ours?
2. Orwell used the term 'Big Brother' long before the TV series was invented. What are the similarities and differences between our world and the one that Orwell describes in *1984*?

D Grammar checkpoint

1 MODAL VERBS

Grammar summary S. 180

A Your school is planning a fundraising event. Write full sentences to make suggestions for the event.

EXAMPLES *All of us should put up posters around town.*
Somebody ought to invite the TV news to film us.

I *We* *Somebody* *One of us* *Some of us* *All of us*	*can* *could* *should* *ought to* *must*	*put up posters around town.* *invite the TV News to film us.* *get an interview on local radio.* *ask local shops to sell tickets for us.* *put a special page on the school website.* *ask all the local bands to come and play.* *hire a bouncy castle for the children.* *have a barbecue and sell soft drinks.* *organize a car park for visitors.*

B Think about how you can stay in touch with the world. Talk about good ways and ways that do not seem so good.

EXAMPLES *I could go on the internet to do research for school projects.*
I shouldn't call friends on my mobile so much.

Use these ideas.

call friends on my mobile | email my friends | go on the internet to do research for school projects | read celebrity magazines | send friends text messages | watch TV during the week

2 *MUST, MUST NOT* AND *NEED NOT*

Grammar summary S. 180

Complete the exchanges with *must*, *must not* and *need not*.

1 A My sister's getting her exam results today, so I ... get home and call her.
B You ... wait till then. You can use my mobile to call her.

2 A We ... tell anybody about what has happened.
B I agree. Sarah ... never hear about it, or she'll be really angry!

3 A Quick, turn on the TV! I ... miss the news.
B But you've already heard the news on the radio, so surely you ... watch it as well!

4 A ... I really pay over the internet? It doesn't feel safe.
B You ... worry: it's a secure website. And in fact, you ... pay this way, or they won't send you the goods!

5 A Come on! Hurry! We ... miss the big film, and that means we ... be at the cinema by 3.30.
B But we ... watch it then because they're showing the film again at 6.00. So stop panicking!

4 On the move

FOCUS

1 Talk about the cartoons.

Today, we are free to travel where we want and when we want. Or are we? What do these cartoons say about various forms of transport?

1

"The salesman said that this was the ideal car for life in the fast lane."

2

"The flight is only 99p ... but it will be another £120 if you want to sit inside the plane!"

3

2 Think about it.

To what extent do these British and American cartoons also show the reality of travel in Germany?

3 Talk about your own travel experiences. Use words from the box.

1 Have you ever had any bad experiences while travelling at home or abroad? What happened? How did you feel?
2 What about good experiences? What happened? How did you feel?

amazed | angry | annoyed | anxious | delighted | depressed | disappointed | embarrassed | excited | exhausted | frightened | frustrated | nervous | pleased | relaxed | shocked | surprised | terrified | upset | worried

A Personal perspectives

BEFORE YOU READ

1 22 **Look at the photo. How do you think the people in this traffic jam probably feel?**

TONY ASH green campaigner

Twenty years ago, there were 22 million cars on Britain's roads. Now there are over 30 million. And soon there will be 40 million if we don't take urgent action. Think of the pollution, and the environmental and health damage from the exhaust fumes. The world's choking to death on its tailbacks and gridlocks. And when you look up and down a traffic jam, 90% of those cars contain one driver and no passengers. It's mad, and it has to stop!

RUTH ROSS working mother

I'm a working mum, and I have to drive. If public transport could get me everywhere I need to go, I'd use it. But can it get me to the nursery after work to pick up my little girl? And to the supermarket or the dry-cleaner's? No. There isn't enough of it, and it's also far too expensive. Plus we pay a fortune to drive our cars! Surely, if the government spent all our road and fuel taxes on more and cheaper public transport, things would be better.

LAURA SMITH government transport minister

More roads aren't the answer. If we build one to reduce congestion on another, what happens? In five years, they're both congested. So, if we try to build our way out of road chaos, we will just build our way into more road chaos. As for public transport, this is improving, but it's a long and expensive job. And much of the money has to come from drivers, so the cost of driving can only increase. What we need is a better balance. People who must drive should be able to drive efficiently. Others must change to public transport. If that happens, life will be much better for everyone and CO_2 emissions will be much lower.

WAYNE SIMPSON office worker

OK, so I spend too much time in tailbacks, but I wouldn't give up my car even if you paid me. It says who I am. It means freedom and flexibility. I can go where I want when I want. It also means privacy. I've got my own space, and I can listen to the music I like. Cars give people the freedom to live and work where they want.

(412 words)

1 LOOKING AT THE TEXTS

A Make notes from the texts.

Give five reasons why the drivers do not want to change to public transport.

B Say what you think.

You and your partner live in the suburbs, and you both drive to work in the city centre.

1 Discuss the options below to save money. Talk about the pros and cons, e.g. costs, savings, flexibility, time and impact on the environment.
2 Decide what to do. Give reasons for your choice.

- Drive to work with friends/colleagues (= car sharing).
- Sell one or both cars and use public transport.
- Sell both cars; use bikes to get to work. Use public transport or hire a car for longer trips.

2 WORKING WITH WORDS

Find idiomatic expressions in Tony Ash's comments to complete the following sentences.

1 With everyone trying to leave the city, there was soon total ... on every road: nothing could move for hours!
2 Just look at the ... from that truck: emissions like that are illegal! (*word pair*)
3 If we don't take action to cut emissions, the world will ... (*idiom*)
4 After the accident, there was a ten-mile ... on the motorway.

3 LISTENING

A Think about it.

Distance and travel are the themes of many songs. Can you think of any? Brainstorm some ideas with a partner.

1 23

B Beantworten Sie auf Deutsch die unten stehenden Fragen zum Lied *Route 66* in ganzen Sätzen.

> ZENTRALE KLASSENARBEIT
Hörverstehen (S. 175)

1 In welcher Richtung durch die Vereinigten Staaten führt die Route 66?
2 Welche zwei Städte sind am Anfang und am Ende der Route 66?
3 Wie lang ist die Straße insgesamt?
4 Wie beschreibt der Sänger die Stadt Oklahoma?
5 Was empfiehlt der Sänger den Zuhörern?

C Say what you think.

What differences are there between the image of travel in the song *Route 66* and the real situation that most commuters experience every day? Think about cartoon 1 on page 65.

4 BUILDING SKILLS: TEXT-BASED CARTOON ANALYSIS

> EXAM PREPARATION
> Bildbeschreibung mit Analyse (S. 172)

A Describe the cartoon and its message. Then relate it to the text below.

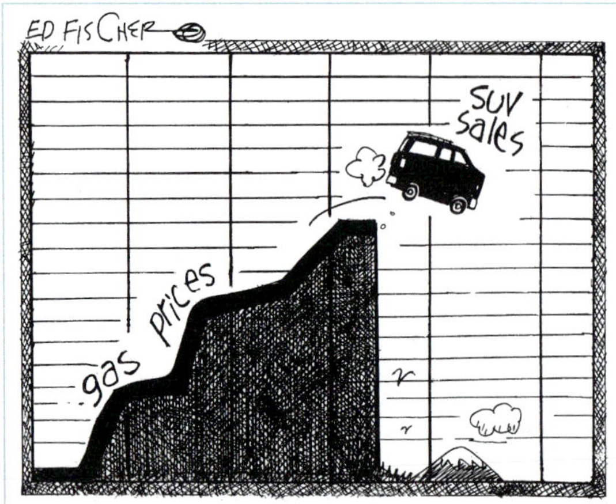

According to ...
Looking at ... one sees that ...
It is/seems clear from ... that ...
On the one hand ..., but on the other hand ...
It is necessary to make a distinction between ... and ...
In contrast to ... , ...
There seems to be conflicting figures for ...

Even advanced SUVs like the Mercedes GL consume over 12 litres of fuel per 100 kilometres. The Hummer - based on the Humvee, a US Army vehicle - disappeared from the showrooms in 2006 partly because it consumed nearly twice that amount.

When the Hummer went out of production, many observers thought that this marked the end of SUVs. They claimed that in times of rising fuel prices and increased ecological awareness, there was obviously no longer a market for these environmental disasters on wheels.

But as so often with things that 'simply must be true', the facts tell a very different story. While it is true that sales of downmarket big SUVs dipped for a year or two in the middle of the 2000s, sales of upmarket models remained more or less constant - and even in the worst years, sales of smaller SUVs like the VW Tiguan and crossovers like the Toyota RAV4 actually increased.

The Hummer SUV

In November 2008, wsoctv.com, a North Carolina news site, was able to report that 'falling gas prices jump start GM SUV sales.' And just two months later, in January 2009, science20.com complained that 'SUV sales rise sharply while hybrid sales fall' and asked 'Will Americans ever learn?'

> TIP

Structure your composition like this:
Introduction: The message of the cartoon
Main part 1: Information in the text that supports this message (pro)
Main part 2: Information that opposes the cartoon (contra)

B Choose and describe one of the cartoons on page 65. Then relate it to one or two of the texts on page 66.

In my opinion, the first/... cartoon reflects Tony's/...'s views.
It is clear from what Wayne/... says that he/... agrees with the suggestion in ...
The first/... cartoon does not (really) relate to ...
Laura's/... opinions are not (really) expressed in the first/... cartoon / in any of the cartoons.

B The bigger picture

BEFORE YOU READ

If you were the German minister for transport, how would you try to reduce a) traffic congestion and b) vehicle emissions?

1 24

Satellite road pricing is on the way

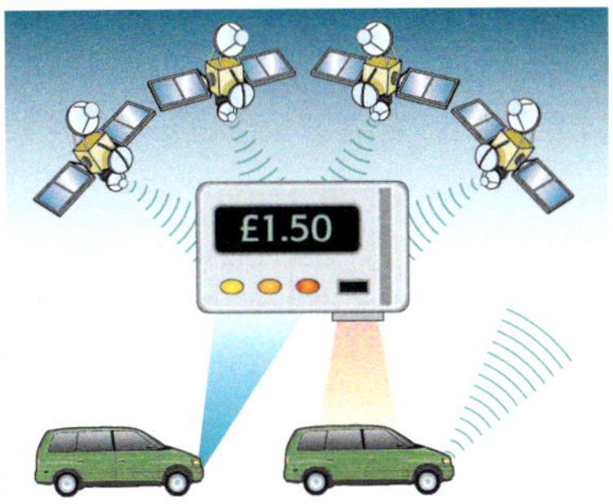

Transport Minister Laura Smith has given new details of our future road tax system: road pricing.

If you drive in a road-pricing zone, you are charged according to where, when and how far you drive. On a quiet road in the country at night you will pay just 2p per mile. However, on a busy main road in the rush hour you can expect to pay £1.34 per mile. 'Unless we do this,' Smith says, 'there will be national gridlock by 2020.'

The technology is quite similar to the 'satnav' (satellite navigation) systems in many modern cars. In each case, satellites and a 'black box' in the vehicle communicate to record location, time and distance travelled. Your bill will arrive monthly.

For some people, this means a 'Big Brother' society, and they hate the idea. 'But,' Smith argues, 'as long as you've nothing to hide from the police, what's the problem?' Road hauliers say that the cost will destroy their businesses, but Smith believes that costs will balance – provided that hauliers avoid rush hour on the busiest roads. City commuters say their lives will be impossible. However, Smith says that people will turn to public transport and car sharing. 'Road use will become more efficient, and we estimate that traffic congestion will fall by 50%.'

(214 words)

1 25

THE ROAD TO ZERO EMISSIONS

Fuel prices have increased hugely, and CO_2 emissions have to decrease hugely. At last, car owners and environmentalists want the same thing – a car that does not 'cost the earth' to run. Engineers using several different technologies are racing to provide that car.

Some city dwellers are choosing electric vehicles like the tiny, zero-emission 'G-Wiz'. Joanna Page, actress, Londoner and G-Wiz owner, says: 'We've saved a small fortune in petrol.' Costing 40p (50 cents) to charge at night, it has a range of 80 kilometres. 'That's enough to drive round town all day.' The problem? The electricity comes from a traditional power station.

Hybrid petrol-electric vehicles like Toyota's best-selling Prius cleverly turn energy from the car's movement into electricity. The electric motor then supports the petrol engine, for example on hills. The technology is complicated and expensive, but these cars give something like petrol-engine performance with much greater fuel efficiency.

Long in development, zero-emission fuel-cell technology finally entered commercial car production in 2008. The Honda FCX Clarity is the result. It combines hydrogen and oxygen to produce power – and the only waste is water. Amazing. But remember: we still have to manufacture the hydrogen. If, though, we can do this with renewable energy sources one day, we will finally have an environmentally friendly car with low running costs.

(217 words)

1 LOOKING AT THE TEXTS

> **EXAM PREPARATION**
> Beurteilen von Textaussagen (S. 172)

A Decide whether these statements about the texts on page 69 are true or false and explain your choices in German.

Satellite road pricing is on the way

1 Satellite road pricing is still a long way off.
2 In a road-pricing zone drivers pay according to the time of the day and the distance they drive.
3 Drivers will pay 2p a mile on a quiet country road at night.
4 The transport minister says that without road-pricing the UK will have national gridlock by 2020.
5 Some people hate the idea of satellite road pricing because of privacy issues.

The road to zero emissions

6 Engineers are working with several technologies to develop a zero-emission car.
7 Small electric cars like the G-Wiz are a complete answer to environmental pollution.
8 The fact is that hybrids are not much more fuel-efficient than conventional cars.
9 Fuel cells only produce water but the production of the hydrogen they need is an environmental problem.
10 It is very doubtful if we will ever have an environmentally friendly car with low running costs.

B Say what you think.

Dad – why can't we have a proper car?

2 WORKING WITH WORDS

A There are several word pairs in the texts. Find partner words for 1–8.

Text 1			*Text 2*		
1	*Paragraph 1:*	*... tax*	*5*	*Paragraph 1:*	*... prices*
2	*Paragraph 1:*	*road ...*	*6*	*Paragraph 1:*	*... emissions*
3	*Paragraph 2:*	*... road*	*7*	*Paragraph 4:*	*... production*
4	*Paragraph 4:*	*traffic ...*	*8*	*Paragraph 4:*	*... sources*

B The same words can have other partners. Find more using the words in the box.

country | diesel | electricity | haulier | income | jam | lights | oil | power | side

3 SPEAKING

A Follow these steps to prepare a role-play.

1 Read the following information about congestion charging.

London started congestion charging several years ago, and many other cities want to do the same. All vehicles (except public transport, taxis and 'green' cars like the G-Wiz) have to pay a daily charge if they enter the city centre. The aim is to reduce congestion as much as possible.

Positive results:

a) 30% congestion reduction in the central zone;

b) bus travel up by 38%;

c) 65% of charges go towards better public transport.

Negative results:

a) much more traffic now on roads around the zone: new areas of congestion;

b) reduced sales for 65% of small businesses in and close to the zone: many have considered moving away;

c) a lot of anger among people negatively affected.

Source: Times Online, Oct 29, 2006: Focus: How to get gridlock Britain moving again

2 As a class, choose a city near you which could benefit from congestion charging.

3 Imagine you are at a meeting on congestion charging. Work in groups of four and choose a role each.

Roles

Businessperson	> File 2, page 155
City councillor	> File 7, page 157
Road commuter	> File 12, page 158
Government transport official	> File 14, page 159

B Do the role-play.

1 Put forward your point of view and try to persuade the others. Use these phrases:
If we do/don't ..., ... will/won't ...
Provided ...
As long as ...
Unless ...

2 Agree what to do.

3 Compare your decision with the other groups. Take a class vote to choose the best one.

4 COMPOSITION

> EXAM PREPARATION
> Materialgestützter Aufsatz (S. 173)

Use the photos and information in the texts below and the first text on page 69 to write a composition about the pros and cons of road-pricing. Start like this:

Congestion on our roads is a serious problem for our environment. One of the solutions that have been suggested is a road-pricing system which charges people ...

1

2 Big impact for road-pricing

For the fans of road-pricing, building and maintaining roads is a service just like everything else – and it has to be paid for by users. They say that road-pricing would help to pay for the road network and subsidize public transport. But they claim that it also has one further huge advantage: depending on the road and the time of day, it would limit car-use to essential journeys and persuade people to make greater use of public transport, and this would obviously be much better for the environment.

3

Koalition streitet über Pkw-Maut — *FOCUS online*

Wirbel um Pkw-Maut — *Süddeutsche Zeitung*

Jeder Dritte befürwortet Pkw-Maut — *B4b Schwaben*

4 Mautgegner: „Big Brother" fährt mit

Trotz allem, was für die Maut spricht, sind ihre Kritiker alles andere als überzeugt. Zum einen argumentieren sie, dass viele Menschen die mautpflichtigen Straßen einfach umfahren werden, was leicht zu einem Verkehrskollaps auf Nebenstraßen und auch zu Problemen der Verkehrssicherheit führen könnte. Zum anderen weisen sie darauf hin, dass die Mauterhebungstechnologie erhebliche Datensicherheitsprobleme aufweist, da sie Regierungen in die Lage versetzt, Menschen verfolgen zu können. Und würden nicht Mauten die Benutzung von Hauptverkehrsstraßen und Autobahnen so teuer machen, dass ärmere Personen sie sich nicht leisten könnten? Ist es das, was wir in einer Demokratie wirklich wollen?

5 DISCUSSION

> Diskussionen führen S. 170

In small groups, discuss the possible effects of an oil crisis.

Imagine a major oil and gas crisis during the winter. Both oil and gas are almost completely unavailable and extremely expensive. How would a crisis like this affect you personally? How might it affect the whole community? Use phrases like these:

If we had a crisis like that,	*it might*	*mean ...ing ...*
If something like that happened,	*it could*	*make me / us ...*

C Further options

LOOKING AT THE CAR OF THE FUTURE

Look at some of the features which most new cars will have in the future. Then do the tasks.

1 Read and rank the new features from *1) Most useful* to *8) Least useful.*

2 Work with a partner. Compare your lists. Note differences and explain your different choices to each other.

Safe, clean and green

the technologies that will soon change the way we drive

Safety systems
A monitor will see when the driver starts to fall asleep, and an alarm will sound. A disabler will stop the car from starting if the driver smells of alcohol.

Stay-in-lane technology
Sensors will detect white lines on the road and will warn the driver if the car starts to move from side to side.

'No hands' technology
These will allow the driver to control sound systems, air conditioning and heating just with hand movements. It will not be necessary to touch controls.

Fuel sources
These will include hydrogen and electricity.

Radar
This will detect dangers ahead faster than the driver can and start to slow the car down.

Further satellite communications technologies
In addition to satellite navigation systems, two-way communications will provide information on e.g. dangers and traffic jams ahead and will direct the driver to available parking spaces. The road pricing system will monitor the car's route and automatically charge the driver. The driver's insurance company will also check his/her driving and charge higher premiums if he/she drives badly.

Moving lights
The lights will automatically turn as the car turns in order to prevent 'blind spots' to the left or right.

Automatic braking
Roadside sensors will detect a speeding car and send a signal to override the driver and slow down.

(215 words)

Heavily adapted and abridged from "Zero emissions, zero deaths, total choice", *Sunday Times*, 19th June 2005

D Grammar checkpoint

1 *IF*-SENTENCES TYPE 1

> Grammar summary S. 184

A Tomas, a student in London, has to travel to Paris. Use the table to help him decide how to get there. Use *if*-sentences type 1 and add information from the table where required.

Travel between London and Paris

	Cost	Time
By plane	£122 return	1 hr 20 min (+ about 3 hours travel/waiting time)
By train & Eurostar	£159 return	2 hr 30 min
By car & ferry	£135 return	about 9 hr

TOMAS What's the best way to get to Paris?
YOU If you *go*[1] (*go*) by plane, it *will be*[2] (*be*) cheaper than by train or ferry.
TOMAS Will it be faster to fly too?
YOU Well, yes and no. If you ...[3] (*count*) just the flight time, it ...[4] (*take*) less time.
TOMAS So why do you say 'yes and no'?
YOU Because it ...[5] (*take*) longer if you ...[6] (*also allow*) time for travel to and from the airport.
TOMAS Really? So if I ...[7] (*travel*) by plane, how much ...[8] (*it/cost*) and how long ...[9] (*it/take*)?
YOU It ...[10] (*cost*) ...[11], and it ...[12] (*take*) about ...[13] altogether.
TOMAS What about the train? How long ...[14] (*it/take*) if I ...[15] (*go*) by train?
YOU Just ...[16] from the UK straight to Paris. But then there's also the cheaper ferry option. If you ...[17] (*take*) your car, it ...[18] (*cost*) ...[19]. Of course, the journey time is longer – about ...[20].
TOMAS Well, I like ships and the sea, so perhaps I'll take the ferry. Thanks for your help.

B Work with a partner. Practise the dialogue together.

2 *IF*-SENTENCES TYPE 2

> Grammar summary S. 184

A Make *If*-sentences type 2 with the verbs in the right forms and the correct punctuation.

1 Wayne Simpson: the government (*build*) more roads | we (*not have*) road congestion | And | we (*not have*) congestion | everybody (*be able to*) get around faster
If the government built more roads, we would not have congestion. And if we did not have congestion, everybody would be able to get around faster.
2 Tony Ash: car drivers (*carry*) more passengers | traffic jams (*disappear*) | And | traffic jams (*disappear*) | everybody (*be*) much healthier
3 Ruth Ross: transport services (*become*) cheaper | more people (*use*) them | And | more people (*use*) them | they (*expand*) and (*get*) better
4 Laura Smith: the government (*do*) nothing about transport | the situation (*go*) from bad to worse | And | that (*happen*) | the government (*lose*) the next election

B Imagine you are in London and in the following situations. Look at the table in exercise 1A again, and make statements using *If*-sentences type 2.

1 You need your car for a holiday in France.
 a How would you go?
 If I needed my car for ..., I would go by ...
 b Cost?
 If I went by ..., it ...
2 You have to get to Paris urgently.
 a How would you travel?
 b Time?
3 You need to connect with a flight from Paris to Tokyo.
 a How would you go?
 b Cost and time?

5 Green enough?

FOCUS

1 Compare the past and the present.

Thinking about the environment ...

> how are things worse now than, say, 50 years ago?

> could some things actually be better now than 50 years ago?

2 Work with a partner. Discuss some Hollywood views of the future.

a Look at pictures 1–4 and match them to titles a–d.

a Waterworld
b 28 Days Later
c The Day after Tomorrow
d Armageddon

2

1

4

3

b All of these films imagine future disasters. Are the disasters a) natural, b) man-made or c) a mixture of both?

c Briefly discuss what each film is about. The following words may be helpful.

asteroid | catastrophe | destruction | disaster | epidemic | flood | hurricane | ice age | tsunami

A *Armageddon is set in the (near/distant) future, and it's about (an asteroid which is going to hit Earth).*

B *That's right. And they have to (find a way of stopping it).*

A Personal perspectives

BEFORE YOU READ

A **Look at the pictures and say what is happening in each.**

B **Read the title of the text. Try to link the pictures to the title.**

Going green: the final report

By Julie Price

A

B

C

D

We started our 'green year' exactly twelve months ago – on January 1st last year. Now, we have finished, and it is time to look back on the experience.

Like a lot of people, Paul and I had already made ourselves a little greener. For example, we had started recycling more carefully, and we had fitted low-energy light bulbs around the house.

But last year was a very different matter, and this is how it all began. As a journalist, I had written an article in December called *How to save the planet*. My boss had then asked me to turn my fine words into action for a year – and write monthly progress reports. Oh, dear! My boss is a woman you do not refuse.

Fortunately, Paul agreed, and so our new way of life began. First, we simply turned down the heating. That was not too difficult: we just suggested that visiting friends should wear sweaters! And we immediately started saving both energy and money.

We also considered changing to alternative energy sources. Should we put a wind turbine on the roof perhaps? No. Wind strength in a city crowded with buildings is too weak and unreliable. Well, then, what about solar power? Surely even under grey north European skies we could meet many of our energy needs. Well, yes, but the cost was far too high. In the end, we spent our limited budget on more roof insulation. This simple, sensible step has already paid for itself.

After we had done this, we faced our first hard decision. We loved our car, but we decided it had to go. Once we had finally sold it, things slowly got easier. After all, we live in a city, so we could walk, cycle and use public transport. Sometimes it took longer, but we learned to allow extra time. As for the money we got from selling the car, we decided to use it to finish double-glazing the house. (We had done most of the house previously but had run out of cash.)

The other difficult thing was the summer holiday. We had always loved going somewhere warm and exotic, especially India, but last year no. Instead, we took the train to Wales and had a walking holiday. We got wet but very fit, and we also discovered beautiful places we had never heard of in our own country. And, by avoiding those flights, we saved two tonnes of CO_2 emissions – the amount that two average cars produce in a whole year!

What about the future? Well, we're used to our new lifestyle now, and we aim to continue. The only thing is this: somehow we *must* find a way to travel the world again.

(454 words)

1 LOOKING AT THE TEXT

A Read the text quickly to match pictures A–D to different paragraphs.

B Copy and complete the tables using information from the text.

Timeline		*Events*
December, the year before last *January 1st last year* *Today, a year later*	→	*1 JP wrote 'How to save the planet'.* *2 ...*

Actions taken last year		*Benefits mentioned in the text*
1 Turned down ... 3 ... *2 ... 4 ...*	→	*1 Saved energy & ...* *2 ...*

Actions not taken		*Reasons mentioned*
1 Put a ... 2 ...	→	*1 ...*

Plans/Hopes for the future
1 ... 2 ...

C Use your notes to give a spoken summary. You can use these ideas.

In December the year before last, Julie Price wrote ..., and her boss then ... And so, on January ..., ... Today, a year ..., ...
Julie and her husband took a number of actions last year. First of all, they ..., and this immediately saved energy and ... Then they ... They also ... Finally, they ...
There were other actions that they considered but did not take. For one thing, they thought about putting a ..., but they ... because ... For another, they wondered about ..., but ...
As for the future, they plan to ... However, they really want to ...

2 MEDIATION

> **EXAM PREPARATION**
> Mediation (S. 171)

Ein deutscher Freund schreibt Ihnen in einer E-Mail, dass seine Familie gerade nach Möglichkeiten sucht, Heiz- und Energiekosten im Haushalt zu sparen. Sie erinnern sich an den Text auf S. 76. Schlagen Sie ihm in einer E-Mail zwei Dinge vor, die seine Familie unbedingt tun sollte, und zwei, die sie lieber nicht tun sollte.

3 SPEAKING

Say what you think.

In my family, we couldn't do any of those things – except maybe put in more insulation.

At home, we've already done some of those things, but we would never get rid of our car. That would be going too far!

4 WORKING WITH WORDS

A Find words or expressions in the text that have similar meanings to these expressions.

1 every month (*lines 15–20*)
2 at once (*lines 20–25*)
3 finally (*lines 26–41*)
4 got used to (*lines 43–56*)
5 before that (*lines 43–56*)
6 particularly (*lines 57–69*)
7 quantity (*lines 57–69*)
8 way of life (*lines 70–74*)

B Rewrite the sentences with the words and phrases from the box below and your own words.

1 We started our 'green year' on January 1st last year.
2 My boss had asked me to write monthly progress reports.
3 We suggested that visiting friends should wear sweaters.
4 We also considered changing energy sources.
5 We learned to allow extra time.

advised | every month | got used to | in addition | was the start of

> **TIP**
>
> When you use information from a text to write a comment or summary, you need to change the original words and phrases as much as possible. But be careful: changing a word might mean you need to change other parts of the sentence too, like the word order.

C Read the dictionary section below on phrasal verbs with the verb *turn*. Then do the following tasks.

1 Complete the following sentences from the text with the correct phrasal verbs.
  a My boss had then asked me to ... my fine words ... action for a year.
  b First, we simply ... ... the heating.

2 Complete the following with phrasal verbs from the dictionary section.
  a Every month last year, a lot of readers used to ... ... page 8 to read Julie Price's latest monthly report on her green year.
  b Her husband Paul was very interested in her project, and the many difficult changes to their way of life did not ... him ...
  c They quickly learned to ... ... all lights and appliances that they were not using.
  d They also used to ... ... the hot water system for fewer hours a day.
  e They were quite worried about going on holiday to Wales, but everything ... ... very well, and they loved their time there.
  f One cloudy day, they walked about two kilometres along a valley, and then ... ... the road and climbed a steep mountain path.
  g They nearly ... ... when it started raining heavily, but they kept going and came to a beautiful lake – just as the sun started shining again!

turn back to go back in the same direction as you came: *The weather became so bad that they had to turn back.*
turn sb/sth down to refuse an offer or request, or the person that makes it: *Why did you turn that job down? · He asked her to marry him, but she turned him down.*
turn off sth to leave one road and and go on another: *We turn off the motorway at junction 10.*
turn (sb) off to lose or make sb lose interest; to make sb feel bored or disgusted: *Men with beards turn me off.*
turn sth off to move the switch, etc. on a piece of machinery, etc. to stop it working: *He turned the TV off.*
turn sth on to move the switch, etc. on a piece of machinery, etc. to start it working: *Turn the lights on!*
turn out (to be sth) to be sth in the end: *The weather turned out fine. · The house that they had promised us turned out to be a tiny flat.*
turn to sth to find a page in a book: *Turn to page 45.*

B The bigger picture

BEFORE YOU READ

Fifty years from now, do you expect the environmental situation to be better, worse or the same? Give reasons. Then read to find out whether either article matches your ideas.

News from the future 1

January 2, 2060

Yesterday, entering the 2060s, we heard the news we desperately did not want to hear. Around the world, the airwaves were full of it: we have passed the figure of 560 parts per million of CO_2 in the Earth's atmosphere, twice the level it was before the Industrial Revolution. More importantly, 99% of scientists agree that it is also the point of no return for climate change. We have just passed the last red danger light at high speed.

What will happen now? The answer is: a lot. Here in Europe, summers will get hotter and hotter and winters ever wetter. Sudden violent storms will become more and more common. And we are the lucky ones. In other parts of the world, life has already become impossible because of climate change. Hurricanes are forcing people away from Central America and the USA's south-eastern coasts. In Asia, cyclones are doing the same from China to India. Africa's deserts are expanding fast. Thousands are dying. Millions more are refugees. These regions are falling into chaos.

Moreover, the Greenland and Antarctic ice sheets are melting and sea levels are rising a centimetre a year. Many low-lying islands have disappeared, and soon great coastal cities from Shanghai to Alexandria to New York will drown.

Scientists were warning the world about this 60 years ago. If people had acted quickly back then, they would have prevented today's disasters. But they did nothing. Why? (238 words)

News from the future 2

January 2, 2060

Yesterday, entering the 2060s, we heard the news we were hoping for. Champagne has become a rare luxury these days, but people happily paid €1,000 for a bottle to celebrate. For the world has again held atmospheric CO_2 at 450 ppm. Moreover, the level will fall slightly this year – even though the world economy will continue growing by 4%.

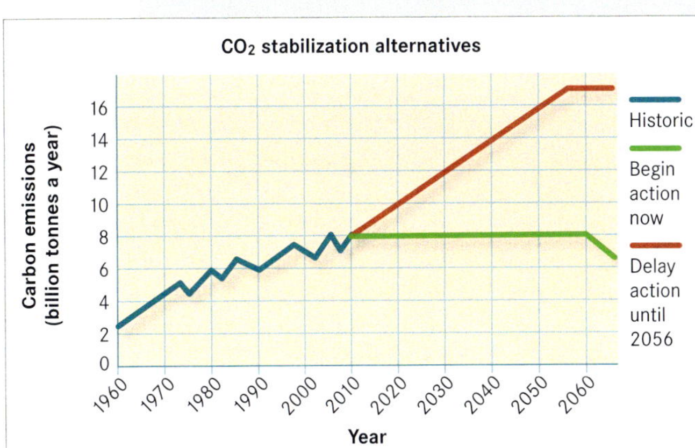

There are many reasons for this success, and here are just a few. First, we have reduced our use of oil, gas and coal by nearly 80% over the last 50 years, and it is these fossil fuels that produce most of the CO_2 emissions. We have replaced them with various alternative forms of energy, including 'renewables' such as solar, wind, tidal and hydroelectric power. There is also fuel cell technology. Today this runs the world's three billion vehicles, and it produces no CO_2 at all – nor any other sort of pollution. Then there is nuclear fusion, the safe, cheap nuclear technology that EU members first began developing 80 years ago.

These and other changes have happened thanks to the strength and vision of our grandparents' generation. Their governments understood the need to fight global warming. If they had not started – and continued – the fight to control CO_2 emissions then, severe climate change would have begun by now. Our world would have fallen into chaos if those wise leaders had not been there. Today we owe them a big thank you as we emerge from human history's greatest crisis. (248 words)

1 LOOKING AT THE TEXTS

> **EXAM PREPARATION**
> Beurteilen von Textaussagen (S. 172)

Decide whether the following statements about the articles on page 79 are true or false and explain your choices in German.

According to the first newspaper article ...

1 there was twice as much atmospheric CO_2 before the Industrial Revolution as in 2060.
2 the effects are bad in Europe, but they are much worse in other parts of the world.
3 people in the early 21st century did not know anything about climate change.

According to the second article ...

4 the world in 2060 uses only about a third of the fossil-fuel energy that it used half a century ago.
5 fossil fuels are still used in 2060 to power some of the world's vehicles.
6 the nuclear technology developed in the mid-twentieth century is still an important energy source.

2 WORKING WITH WORDS

A Use fractions and percentages from the box to complete the statements.

a fifth (1/5) | half (1/2) | three-fifths (3/5) | 20% | 60% | 100%

1 According to the first report, CO_2 levels before the Industrial Revolution used to be ... of the 2060 figure of 560 ppm. In other words, they have risen by ... %.
2 Turning to the second report, we can say that if the pre-industrial CO_2 level was 280 ppm, then that was about ... of the 2060 figure of 450 ppm that this report notes. That is to say, the level of CO_2 shows an increase of roughly ... %.
3 The second report goes on to say that today's use of fossil fuels is roughly ... of the 2010 total, i.e. the use of fossil fuels now is only about ... % of what it was.

B Practise saying fractions and percentages. Read out the statements in exercise A.

3 LISTENING

> **ZENTRALE KLASSENARBEIT**
> Hörverstehen (S. 175)

2 5

A Vervollständigen Sie auf Deutsch die unten stehenden Aussagen mit Informationen aus dem Hörtext. Hören Sie den Text nur einmal.

1 Der Studiogast, Dr Tom Parry, ist ein bekannter ... .
2 Bis zum Jahre ... müssen alle westliche Industrieländer den Ausstoß von CO_2 erheblich reduzieren.
3 Der CO_2-Ausstoß im Westen muss unbedingt reduziert werden, weil der Ausstoß von Treibhausgasen in den Entwicklungsländern ... .
4 2000 betrug der Ausstoß von Treibhausgasen 5,2 Tonnen pro Jahr für ... in den Industrieländern.
5 Wenn man den CO_2-Ausstoß mitberechnen würde, der durch die Herstellung von Waren und Dienstleistungen verursacht wird, würde man auf ... pro Kopf pro Jahr kommen.
6 Ab dem Jahr 2030 wird es ... sein, ausreichende Möglichkeiten zu finden, den CO_2-Ausstoß weiter zu reduzieren.

B Hören Sie den Text jetzt ein zweites Mal. Eine Freundin muss ein Referat über den Klimawandel halten, aber sie hat diese interessante Radiosendung leider verpasst. Schreiben Sie ihr eine E-Mail, die die wesentlichen Aussagen von Dr Parry kurz zusammenfasst. Sie müssen dabei nicht alle Zahlen nennen.

4 IMAGE ANALYSIS

> **EXAM PREPARATION**
> Bildbeschreibung mit Analyse (S. 172)

Describe the picture. Relate it to the texts on page 79 and explain the message. Use these phrases.

On the left, we see a world that is ...
On the right, by contrast, we have a very different view. Here, ...
These two very different visions of the future relate back to the two ...
The one on the left-hand side is the world that ... describes. The right-hand one is ...
The message of this powerful image is that we, today, must choose ...
If, on the one hand, we decide to ... If, on the other hand, we decide to ...

5 BUILDING SKILLS: COMPOSITION

> EXAM PREPARATION
> Materialgestützter Aufsatz (S. 173)

Read the following materials and use three of them to answer the question: *Does the world need nuclear power?* Use the phrases below to help you.

> **TIP**
>
> In a composition you often need to contrast arguments for and against a particular issue, e.g. nuclear power. In this case, each of your main paragraphs should present contrasting arguments about one aspect of the problem, e.g. safety.

1

World Energy Consumption 1990–2035

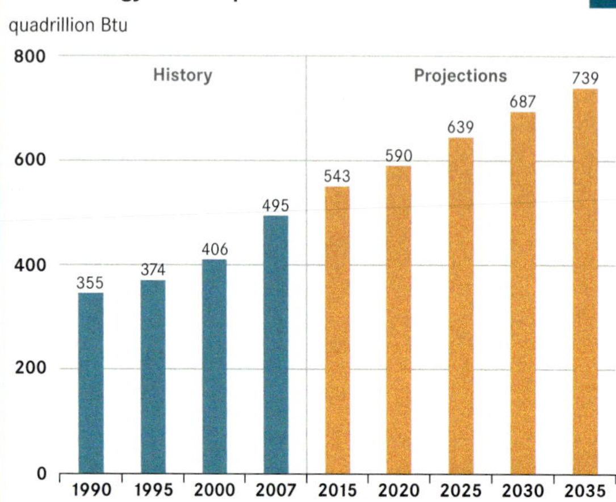

Source: U.S. Energy Information Administration

2

Leserbrief an die *Westfälischen Nachrichten*

Nach der Katastrophe in Japan müssen wir endlich einsehen, dass die Technologie der Atomkraftwerke gescheitert ist. Die Risiken sind viel zu groß, und, besonders bei einer Katastrophe wie einem Erdbeben oder Tsunami, nicht vorhersehbar.

Wir wissen alle, dass wir dringend neue Energiequellen brauchen, die weniger Treibhausgase in die Atmosphäre ausstoßen. Aber Atomkraft ist keine Lösung. Zuerst müssen wir unsere enorme Energieverschwendung reduzieren – besonders in den USA, aber auch in den anderen Industriestaaten. Gleichzeitig müssen wir jede erdenkliche Art der erneuerbaren Energie – Sonnen-, Gezeiten-, Windenergie und Wasserkraftwerke – nutzen. Diese Technologien sind im Kampf gegen den drohenden Klimawandel die einzige Chance unseres Planeten.

Dieter Schumacher

3

Since 2000 renewable energy has increased to 10% of Germany's total energy needs

4

A letter to the Editor of the *Daily Herald*:

Compare the media storm that followed Chernobyl (56 direct deaths) to the very slight attention that the 1989 USSR train disaster (over 500 deaths) received. The difference? The word 'nuclear' puts fear in our hearts.

But consider the reality. Nuclear power has produced nearly 20% of the world's energy for many years, and it is actually far safer than every other energy source. Even wind turbines have caused around 50 deaths – and they produce just 0.1% of the world's energy!

Looking forward, we see energy demand rising, while we still depend on fossil fuels for 70% of our energy. Meantime, only around 10% comes from renewable energy sources.

So, yes, build and operate nuclear power stations carefully. But turn our backs on nuclear? No. Turn off nuclear and you turn out the lights all over the world. It is hardly surprising that around 30 countries are now planning to build new nuclear power stations.

Karen Rees

Introduction:

The recent disaster at Fukushima in Japan makes us consider yet again the arguments ...

Arguments:

On the issue of safety, it is certainly true that ... For example, ... However, ... The reality is that ...

On the other hand, others say that ...

Introducing examples and facts:

For example, ... For instance, ... To give an/another example, ...

To put matters into perspective, ... The reality, however, is that ...

Conclusion:

The arguments for and against nuclear power are complex, but it seems that ...

C Further options

1 THINKING A LITTLE GREENER

Read the texts, work with a partner and do the following activities.

1 Say what purpose all the texts have.
2 Agree on an overall title for the texts.
3 Discuss which numbers or other pieces of information surprise you most.
4 Say whether you would like to try any of these ways of helping to save the planet.

2 6

http://www.

Have a bath with someone you love

If you really must have a bath instead of a shower, well, it's too good not to share. And when you consider an average bath uses 65 litres of water, you'll not only feel good in the bath but feel good afterwards too. Just get out before everything becomes too wrinkly and make sure you don't get the end where the taps are.

Turn off appliances at the mains

The average TV is left on standby for 17.5 hours a day, and secondary TVs average 21.5 hours per day. This means that over the course of a year every household with two TVs will waste a whopping 35 kWh/year.

If everybody in the UK turned off their TV overnight, it would save more than £66 million (€100 million) worth of electricity each year, which would be enough to power floodlights for 250,000 Premiership* football matches.

* the top professional league, with the largest stadiums

Turn off the tap while you brush your teeth

Fancy saving the world while brushing your teeth?

Most people keep the tap running all the time they're brushing their teeth. This wastes huge amounts of water and is a bit stupid – it's like having the toilet flush the whole time you're on it.

In fact, it adds up to quite a few litres a day. And families in the developing world exist on just that to survive each day.

So why not turn off the tap while you clean your teeth?

Find out where your lunch has come from

Did you know that the average kiwi fruit flown in from New Zealand travels 12,000 miles to be part of your lunch?

And, according to the experts, that kiwi fruit creates five times its own weight in greenhouse gases in getting here.

'How on earth does it do that?' you might ask. Well, think of the fuel needed to get that little fruit from there to here. And then think of the emissions which that fuel produces as it burns.

Adapted from www.wearewhatwedo.org

2 DOING YOUR BIT TO SAVE THE PLANET

Go to www.wearewhatwedo.org and do the following activities.

1 Skim through the 100 simple suggestions (including the ones above) to help save the planet.
2 Read the ones that interest you.
3 If you wish, you can commit yourself to following one or more of the suggestions.
4 If you do, add yourself to the number at the top right of each suggestion. This is the number of people who have already made the same commitment.

D Grammar checkpoint

1 PAST PERFECT

> Grammar summary S. 178

Make one sentence from each pair of sentences using the expression in brackets. Put one clause in the past perfect. Add a comma if necessary.

1 Julie and Paul changed to low-energy light bulbs. She wrote 'How to save the planet'. (*before*)
Julie and Paul had changed to low-energy light bulbs before she wrote 'How to save the planet'.

2 Julie produced this piece for the *Daily News*. She and Paul also started recycling. (*before*)
3 Life began to change much, much more dramatically. She wrote about saving the planet. (*after*)
4 Julie's newspaper never said much about green issues. She wrote her article. (*until*)
5 Julie's boss Karen read the article. She began thinking hard about Julie's ideas. (*when*)
6 Karen decided that the *Daily News* should go green. She saw all the letters from readers. (*once*)
7 Karen made this decision. She picked up the phone and called Julie to her office. (*as soon as*)
8 Julie left Karen's office 30 minutes later. She agreed to live a 'green year' and write about it. (*by the time*)
9 Paul accepted the idea. He and Julie discussed it carefully that evening. (*once*)
10 They decided to begin their new lifestyle. They immediately took the first step and turned down the heating. (*after*)

2 *IF*-SENTENCES TYPE 3

> Grammar summary S. 184

Put the verbs in the right forms to make *if*-sentences type 3. (The *if* part may be in first or second position.) Add a comma if necessary.

1 Julie (*not write*) her article on 'How to save the planet' / her boss (*not ask*) her to go green for a year
If Julie had not written her article on 'How to save the planet', her boss would not have asked her to go green for a year.

2 Paul (*not agree*) to go green for a year / Julie (*say*) no to her boss.
If Paul hadn't agreed ...

3 Julie and Paul (*not be able to*) pay for efficient roof insulation / they (*spend*) their money on wind or solar power instead
Julie and Paul would not have been able to ...

4 they (*keep*) their car / they (*not learn*) to get around the city in other ways
5 they (*not make*) some money from selling the car / they (*not be able to*) finish double glazing their house
6 they (*fly*) to India for their summer holiday / they (*add*) two tonnes of CO_2 emissions to the atmosphere
7 they (*not go*) to Wales instead / they (*not discover*) lots of beautiful places that were new to them

6 Modern ways to work

FOCUS

Holiday Club International operates ski and seaside resorts across Europe. Members buy points when they join, and these points allow them to use the resorts where and when they want.
Like other organizations, HCI needs a variety of staff and skills. Here are some of them.

1 accountant
2 bookings clerk
3 customer relations officer
4 IT technician
5 receptionist
6 publicity assistant
7 resort activities officer
8 salesperson
9 ski instructor
10 waiter

1 **Match the people in the photos (A–F) to six of the jobs (1–10).**

2 **Say which of employees 1–10 you think said the following. Explain why.**

My job is temporary because it's seasonal and it's not well paid. In high season, I have to work long, irregular hours. So it can be stressful. But I meet lots of people, and the job is fun. I love working outdoors, helping people to learn a new skill. I always have to be friendly and helpful, but that's me anyway. And I decide how to do things. I just love being independent.

My work is office-based and, with its regular routines, I suppose it's rather repetitive and not very challenging. But it's a responsible job and I have to be accurate. It's secure, permanent, full-time, and I like the regular hours. There's a reasonable salary with good fringe benefits. I work with numbers and don't have any customer contact, but I have to be a good team player in our small group.

3 **Imagine you have a choice of jobs 1–10 at Holiday Club International. Say which you would or would not choose and why, using the highlighted vocabulary above.**

I'd try the job of ... I think *I wouldn't try ... I don't think*	*it would be good* *I would enjoy it / be good at it* *I would like it / be good at it*	*because ...*

A Personal perspectives

BEFORE YOU READ

A student from another country asks you this question: 'After Class 10 in Germany, what routes can you take to get a good, permanent job by your early 20s?' How would you answer?

Routes to the modern workplace: complex but flexible

ANNA Haven't we met somewhere before? It's Ed, isn't it?

ED That's right. You were at Oxford CFE, weren't you?

ANNA Yes, I finished there a year ago, last July.

ED Me too. I was there for two years.

ANNA So was I. It's strange we didn't get to know each other.

ED Well, it's a big place, and we were on different courses. I did the one-year IT Diploma. And you did Business Studies, didn't you?

ANNA Not in the first year. When I came over from Germany, I joined the International Study Programme.

ED That sounds very grand!

ANNA Well, it included lots of English – and some IT and basic Business Studies. It was a bridge to my second year.

ED So what brought you over from Germany?

ANNA Well, after I left school, I did a one-year secretarial course in Dortmund. But then I found out I could get a business qualification over here for free, thanks to the EU. And I wanted to get some international work experience too.

ED Is that what you're doing now?

ANNA Yes, I scanned the internet for suitable job adverts, sent out loads of CVs and letters of application towards the end of my course, and I got some interviews – and a job offer from Mediscan. I've been there for a year now, and they're a good employer. The hours are a bit longer than at home, but the salary's reasonable and there are good benefits. I'm training in Export Sales now, and it's quite challenging. I'll probably stay for several years.

ED Great! Actually, your first year at CFE reminds me a bit of mine. I was on an 'access' programme.

ANNA What's that exactly?

ED It's for people who want to get back into education – and need some help getting there.

ANNA So what were you doing before that then?

ED It was stupid really. I left school and just drifted into a temporary job at a local factory that made car seats for Honda in Swindon. They put me in stock control as I'd done some ICT at school. It was a boring, dead-end job, but the pay was OK.

ANNA What happened then?

ED Well, after three years, the company decided to move production to Bulgaria and make us all redundant. Two months later, the factory was gone and so were 140 jobs! We were out of work!

ANNA Was that when you decided to go to CFE?

ED Yes, it was hard, but my redundancy pay helped, and I got a part-time job too. I upgraded my skills, and it worked. BSG, the solar heating company, were hiring as I was finishing. I applied for an IT job, and I got it. I'm finally in full-time, permanent work at last, the salary is good and I'm going to stay.

ANNA Let's hope BSG doesn't decide to move to Bulgaria too!

(462 words)

> **INFO**

CFE = college of further education: a local college that offers full-time and part-time vocational and school examination classes. Access courses are available for people who need to raise their basic educational level before joining other classes. Similarly, there may also be international study programmes, which are free to full-time students from other EU countries.
CV = curriculum vitae (AE: resume): a document giving personal details and details of qualifications and past employment. Often required by an employer as part of a job application. For more on CVs and resumes, see Unit 8.
ICT = information and communications technology: the school subject that used to be known as information technology.

1 MEDIATION

> **EXAM PREPARATION**
> Mediation (S. 171)

Sie nehmen an einer Berufsorientierungsstunde teil und besprechen die verschiedenen Wege in den Arbeitsmarkt. Andere erkundigen sich nach den Jobaussichten im Ausland und Sie erinnern sich an die Geschichten von Ed und Anna, die Sie auf Englisch gelesen haben. Fassen Sie die wichtigsten Punkte ihres Gesprächs für Ihre Mitschüler auf Deutsch schriftlich als Info-Blatt zusammen.

2 LOOKING AT THE TEXT

A Compare and contrast Ed's and Anna's routes to their jobs today.

1 Contrast what they did after they left school.
2 Outline the college training that they each did in Oxford.
3 Compare their experiences since they finished their courses.

B Say what you think.

1 Who do you think was clearer and more organized at the beginning – Ed or Anna?
2 Do you think this mattered much?
3 Which person are you more like – Ed or Anna – and why?

3 BUILDING SKILLS: TAKING NOTES FROM READING

> **TIP**

When you take notes, organize them with sub-headings or dates (see below). Leave out unnecessary words such as pronouns and articles. Use abbreviations and symbols such as: *e.g., km, =, etc.*

Copy and complete the notes about Ed and Anna from the past to now and to their future plans. (To work out dates in the past, work backwards from this year.)

1

Ed	
Summer 20..:	*Left school, got job at ...*
Summer 20..:	*Lost ...*
...	...
...	...
Future plans:	...

2

Anna	
Summer 20..:	*Left school., started a ...*
Summer 20..:	...
...	...
...	...
Future plans:	...

4 WORKING WITH WORDS

A Copy and complete the lists with 'employment' vocabulary from pages 85–86. Then add other words that you know.

Employment

Getting a job	*Things an employer wants*	*Pay and conditions*
job advertisement (advert/ad)	*experience*	*wages*
…	…	…
…	…	…

Describing work	*Types of employment*	*Being out of a job*
stressful	*permanent*	*redundancy pay*
…	…	…
…	…	…

B Rewrite the sentences using the words in brackets (all from pages 85–86) instead of the underlined words.

1. I had a lot of pressure in my old job. (*stressful*)
   My old job was very stressful.
2. Susie is paid very well. (*salary*)
3. Tina works full-time now. (*job*)
4. Tony has responsibility for all export sales. (*responsible*)
5. Helping people is part of my job. (*helpful*)
6. Jo doesn't meet many customers in her work. (*customer contact*)
7. They closed the factory and put everybody out of work. (*redundant*)

5 BUILDING SKILLS: TAKING NOTES FROM LISTENING

> Das Hörverständnis üben S. 163

2 8 **A Listen for general understanding. Listen to Part 1 and answer these questions.**

1. Who is speaking?
2. Use your notes from exercise 2A to say when this phone conversation happened.
3. What do you think the speakers are going to talk about in Part 2?

> **TIP**
> This is harder than taking notes from reading because you can easily fall behind as you write. But don't panic! Speakers often make false starts and repeat themselves.

2 9 **B Listen for detail. Listen to Part 2 and do the following:**

1. Listen once. Try to remember as many details as you can, but do not write notes.
2. Briefly, report details that you remember to the class. Do you all remember the same?
3. Prepare headings, referring to exercise 3A for help. Start like this:
   Job: Assistant IT …, Marketing Support …
   Type of employment: full-time, …
4. Listen again and take notes.
5. Work with a partner. Take turns to talk about the job from your notes. Make sure that you have both noted the important information fully and accurately. Add to or change your notes as necessary.

B The bigger picture

BEFORE YOU READ

A **What benefits beyond pay may temporary jobs in Germany offer?**

B **What further benefits do you expect when you get a permanent job?**

2 10

A contract too good to be true?

The aptitude tests and the interview were over: after several false starts, Steve finally had the 'right' job. The starting salary was not great, but his career prospects were good. Who could tell? After many years of commitment, Steve might even become a director.

In return, the company was also making big commitments. When Steve showed his family his new contract of employment, his long-retired grandad could hardly believe his eyes. The overall terms and conditions of service were generous and the fringe benefits excellent. 'We didn't have all this when I was your age,' he said.

He recognized cheap cafeteria prices, but subsidized travel, the rise from two weeks' paid holidays to five and the long-term sick pay were new to him. So were the free private healthcare, travel insurance and gym membership.

Then there was the flexitime system to help employees create a good work-life balance. There was also generous paid maternity and paternity leave, and subsidized creche facilities encouraged mothers to return to part-time or full-time work when they were ready.

Such employee benefits have developed over many years. Some have been due to union pressure, and some to government and EU laws. Others have come from business itself. A modern employer invests a lot of money in training its employees. In return, it wants to keep them – and to keep them working hard. It knows that a happy worker is a harder worker. Its workforce is its most valuable resource.

'But how can they afford all these benefits?' Grandad finally asked.

In today's competitive world of work, this is a very good question, and many European business leaders and politicians are asking it.

The big problem is this: business in rich, expensive Europe has to compete globally, most of all with low-cost East Asia. There, working hours are long, pay is low and benefits are few. In order to compete, European business has been taking tough action. First, it has sent manufacturing and now also many white-collar clerical and IT jobs to East Asia and other low-cost regions. It has also been taking away some of its generous benefits. For example, Europe's short, 35-hour week is dying. British business never accepted it. German firms have forced employees to accept longer hours. Now the French are starting to work longer hours too.

* * * * *

After an increasingly hard working life, Steve may one day have to answer his grandad's question like this: 'They really *couldn't* afford all those benefits – at least not for very long.'

(416 words)

1 LOOKING AT THE TEXT

A Read quickly to find information.

1 List the fringe benefits that the photos on page 89 illustrate.
2 List the benefits Steve's grandad had when he was young and those he did not.

B Copy and complete the notes on the text.

1 *Aspects of Steve's new job – good and bad:*
a starting salary: not great
b career: …
c …
d …

2 *Examples of benefits:*
a …
b …
c …

3 *Better benefits have come from:*
a …
b …
c …

4 *Global pressure on European business means:*
a …
b …

5 *Conclusion:*
…

2 COMPOSITION

> EXAM PREPARATION
> Materialgestützter Aufsatz (S. 173)

Look at the job advertisement, the cartoon and the text on page 89. Write a composition on how the workplace has changed.

3 LISTENING

2 11 **A Listen for general understanding. Listen to conversations 1–4 from Anna's first day at Mediscan. Match them to pictures A–D.**

A

B

C

D

B Hören Sie die ersten zwei Gespräche noch einmal an. Beantworten Sie auf Deutsch die unten stehenden Fragen in ganzen Sätzen.

> ZENTRALE KLASSENARBEIT
Hörverstehen (S. 175)

Conversation 1

1 Warum fragt Anna den Portier nach dem Weg zur Marketingabteilung? (2 Gründe)
2 Was braucht der Portier, bevor er sie ins Gebäude lassen darf?

Conversation 2

3 Die Managerin bittet Anna etwas zu tun. Was?
4 Was bietet sie ihr danach an?

C Hören Sie die letzten zwei Gespräche noch einmal an. Entscheiden Sie, ob diese Aussagen richtig oder falsch sind. Begründen Sie Ihre Entscheidung auf Deutsch.

Conversation 3

1 Anna's colleague knows that she is German.
2 He suggests that she moves her desk closer to the window.

Conversation 4

3 Anna asks her colleague if she can go with her to the staff canteen.
4 Anna has to quickly send an email before she can stop for lunch.

4 CULTURE CHECK: POLITE EXPRESSIONS

Germans can often sound too direct, and even rude, to English speakers – especially the British. On the other hand, English speakers' politeness and indirectness can sound absurd to Germans. However, polite expressions are very important to English speakers, so use them!

please | thank you | certainly | of course | I'm afraid (that) ... | I'm sorry, but ... |

Polite expressions for asking, requesting and offering are also very important. Try not to answer requests or questions with only 'Yes' or 'No'. Fuller replies are more friendly and polite.

May/Can I ask ... | If you don't mind me asking ... | Perhaps you could tell me ... | Could you/I (possibly) ... | Would you mind if ... | I wonder if you/I could ... | Do you think you/I could ... | Would you like (me) to ... | Shall I ... for you?

A Work with a partner. Practise offering and requesting in these situations.

1 The room is very hot.
2 An elderly man is standing on the bus.
3 Your boss has given your colleague a lot of work.
4 You are carrying a heavy parcel.
5 You have forgotten to bring some money for lunch.

B Work with a partner and act out the situations in exercise 3. You can vary the language from what you heard on the CD, but try to use expressions from exercises 3 and 4.

5 DISCUSSION

> Diskussionen führen S. 174

Work in a group. Use the questions to guide your discussion.

1 What sort of work have you done up to now, and when did you do it?
2 What did you enjoy, and what did you not like so much?
3 Are you going to look for a job in the summer?
4 What sort of job would you like to have ten years from now?
5 What steps will you need to take to get there?

C Further options

1 DOING APTITUDE TESTS

Try the following tests. Always note one answer for each test – A, B, C, D or E. Work fast!

Numerical Test 1

Select the number which best completes each series.

						A	B	C	D	E
1	1.5	8.5	15.5	?	29.5	A 17	B 23.5	C 21	D 22.5	E 20.5
2	3	6	?	24	48	A 20	B 12	C 18	D 9	E 21

Numerical Test 2

Use the figures in the table to answer questions 3 and 4.

3 Bennett Ltd produces units that sell for £12.00 each. What is the maximum gross profit per unit?

A £4.65 **B** £7.48 **C** £4.52 **D** £7.44 **E** £7.35

4 Labour costs £15.00 per hour at the moment, but this may soon rise to £18.00 per hour. At a production rate of 6 units per hour, what will be the new total cost per unit?

A £7.56 **B** £5.02 **C** £7.52 **D** £4.65 **E** £5.06

Bennett Ltd, Factory Production Costs

Units produced per hour	Total cost per unit
5	£4.65
6	£4.56
7	£4.52
8	£4.53

Coded Instructions

In the questions below, there are figures on the left in boxes. There are also instructions in circles. Read the instruction codes in the table to see how the figures in boxes must change. Choose the correct changes – A, B, C, D or E.

TABLE: INSTRUCTION CODES	
Code 1	Turn the figure clockwise through 90 degrees.
Code 2	Add the figure to the box above.
Code 3	Remove the figure from the box.

5
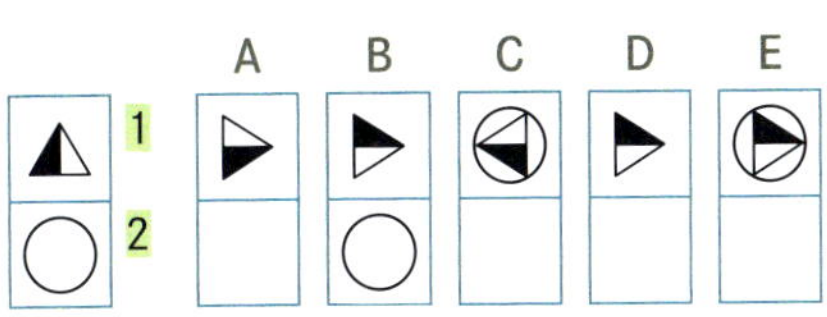

6
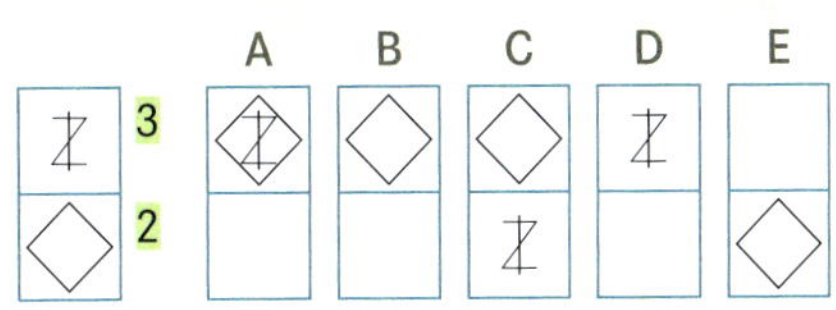

Diagrammatic Test

On the left there is a line of diagrams in a logical order, but one is missing. Choose A, B, C, D or E on the right to complete the line logically.

7
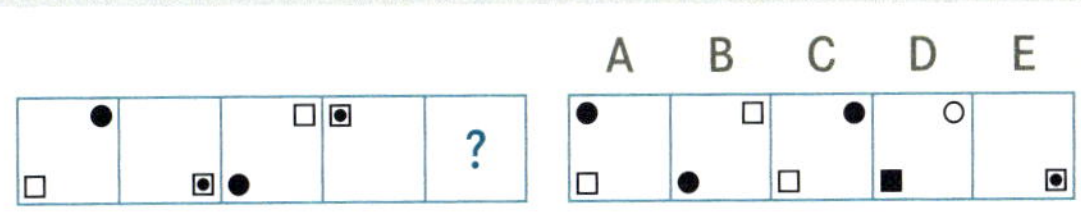

8
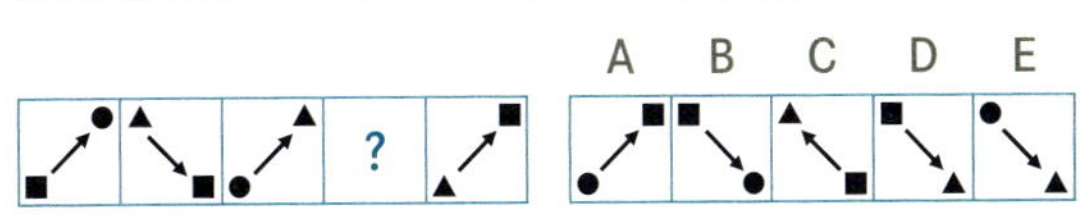

Answers > File 11, page 158

2 DRAWING CONCLUSIONS

Check your answers and think about what they mean.

1 First discuss your answers with a partner. Then look at the back of the book.
2 Think about your results and suggest jobs that might be suitable for you.

D Grammar checkpoint

1 PRESENT PERFECT PROGRESSIVE

> Grammar summary S. 178

Write replies to the questions. Use the words in brackets and the present perfect progressive.

1 A Clara started her training course about two months ago, didn't she? (*do*)
B *Yes, she has been doing her training course for about two months now.*

2 A Alex joined Altman GmbH about a year ago, didn't he? (*work for*)
B *Yes, ...*

3 A Maria and Nick began studying German around ten weeks ago, didn't they? (*learn*)
B ...

4 A Eva and her sister moved into the apartment roughly a month ago, didn't they? (*share*)
...

5 A Tomas started looking for a new job nearly a month ago, didn't he? (*search*)
B ...

6 A Jenny asked for a college application form over a week ago, didn't she? (*wait for*)
B ...

2 PRESENT PERFECT PROGRESSIVE AND PRESENT PERFECT

Complete the dialogue. Sometimes more than one tense is possible.

> Grammar summary S. 178

TONY Hi, Emma! How are you?
EMMA Oh, hi, Tony! Fine, thanks. And how *have you been keeping*?[1] (*you/keep*)
TONY Really well. I ...[2] (*not see*) you for ages.
EMMA No, we ...[3] (*not meet*) since Lucy's party last summer. What ...[4] (*you/do*) since then?
TONY I ...[5] (*travel*) in South America. What about you?
EMMA Oh, I ...[6] (*not do*) anything as exciting as that. I ...[7] (*take*) a business studies course at college.
TONY ...[8] (*it/go*) well?
EMMA Yes, and I ...[9] (*just finish*) the first year. And guess what! I ...[10] (*pass*) with top grades! I found out this morning.
TONY That's really great! Let's go and celebrate!

3 GENERAL REVISION OF TENSES

> Grammar summary S. 176–180

It is 10th December, and Stefanie is in Ireland to study English. Use appropriate tenses to describe Stefanie's year.
Start like this: *In late May, after she had ...*

late May	*finish her final school exams, decide to study English in Ireland for a year*
June – Sept	*take a holiday job and save as much as possible*
	do this job, book a place at the Language Centre in Dublin
10th Sept	*fly to Ireland to start her course*
then – now	*go to classes five days a week*
every morning	*study at the Centre for three hours*
this morning	*different – meet some friends to do some Christmas shopping*
Christmas	*plan to visit her family in Dortmund and stay for 10 days*
Easter	*if have enough money, travel round Ireland*
June	*take her English exam and then travel home via London*
autumn	*want to go to college*

7 Going global

FOCUS

Perhaps you have a laptop like this at home. If so, how did it get there? How was it made? This laptop and the products that run on it are the work of many people in many places.

1 Read the introduction above, and then make sentences like the one below.

The hardware was designed in Japan, and it was ...

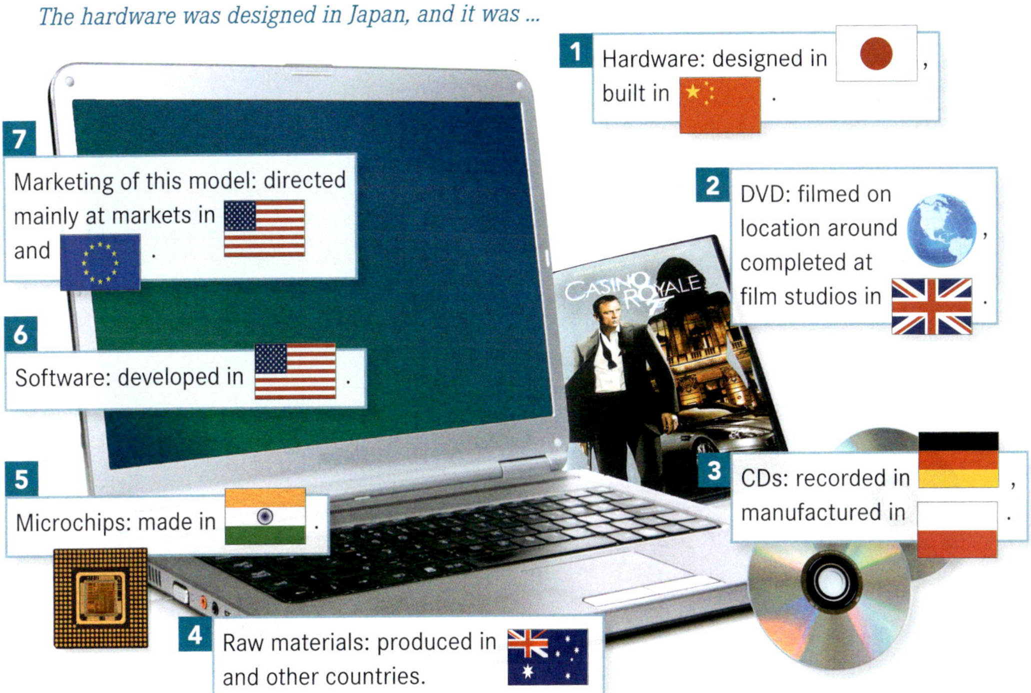

Key to flags > File 16, page 159

2 Discuss things that you have at home.

1 Use this checklist and note your 'Top 5' favourite things.

Accessories: e.g. bags, hats, shoes
Clothes: e.g. jeans, trainers,
Electronic goods: e.g. laptop, mobile phone, sound system, TV
Sports equipment: e.g. fitness machine, sports shoes
Transport: e.g. car, motorbike, scooter

2 Also note the brand name of each item, and where you think the following took place: development, design, production.

3 Work with a partner. Take turns to talk about things on your list like this:
(First) on my list is my ... It's a (brand name), and I think it was (produced) in ...

3 When you get home, check the labels on your favourite things. Were they made where you thought?

A Personal perspectives

BEFORE YOU READ

2 12 **You see lots of goods from around the world in the shops. What other effects of globalization can you also see?**

MONEY MATTERS

Globalization – good or bad?

WITH LISA HALL

They say globalization is good. But how good is it for ordinary people? Let's start by hearing from some ordinary people.

1 ARAND KRISHNAN senior software programmer, InfoXL, India

Here in Bangalore, India's IT capital, we support the team in Houston, Texas. At the end of their working day, they send us problems, ready for our working day here. We process the material and send back solutions, ready for their next day.

Lots of western companies do this. It works well because we have good English and IT skills, and because data transmission is very cheap. But it's not all foreign companies here now. India is developing fast, and many local IT companies are being set up. In fact, I've been asked to help set one up now. It's a big risk, but a big opportunity too. (108 words)

2 NICK BELL ex-furniture factory worker, Galax, Virginia, USA

One day, we had our jobs, the next we were told production was going offshore to Indonesia. Two months later we were made redundant.

Our factory was the main employer in town, and since it closed every other business has been hit hard. So there are no other jobs for us, and people are leaving to find work somewhere else.

They say globalization puts cheap goods in the shops from places like China, but it's also taken my job away. If I could just get it back, I'd give up cheap goods tomorrow. What good are they if you don't have a paycheck? They're still too expensive! (112 words)

3 MALIKA AL-MAGRABI textile worker, Tangier, Morocco

When I started here at 15, I was glad to find full-time work. But now it's terrible. Before, we were given 14 days to fill orders, but now we usually only get five. We're often required to work 16 hours a day, and we're sometimes forced to work through the night. People get ill, but that isn't allowed. I nearly lost my job when I was off sick for a day.

They're supposed to pay overtime for all the extra hours, but they never do. But what can we do? When my friend Fatima asked for her money, she was sacked immediately. We're just slaves. (105 words)

4 BORIS STEIN production engineer, BMW, Oxford, UK

I was one of many BMW staff sent to Britain to help rescue the Mini, a famous 1960s car that had never been brought up to date properly. It has been completely redeveloped by British and German engineers, and now the reborn Mini is as popular as ever. We're working flat out, and nearly 250,000 are being produced every year.

The Mini certainly isn't cheap, so price is not the main competitive advantage. Instead, it wins hearts and minds because it's fantastic to drive, it's beautifully made with cutting-edge technology, and it's one of the world's great brands. It shows that we can still win the globalization game right here in Europe. (121 words)

1 LOOKING AT THE TEXTS

A Decide whether the following statements are true or false and explain your choices in German.

> EXAM PREPARATION
> Beurteilen von Textaussagen (S. 172)

1 InfoXL has its main IT team in Bangalore, India.
2 Western companies like InfoXL often choose to set up an IT branch in Bangalore because India is developing fast.
3 Arand Krishnan is both excited and worried about the chance he now has to help set up a new local company for InfoXL.
4 Nick Bell thinks it is better to pay more in the shops if that means jobs like his can remain in the USA.
5 Boris Stein was sent to Oxford to work at BMW's Mini factory there.
6 Around 250,000 Minis are still being produced every year, using the designs that were developed about half a century ago.

B Sie arbeiten für *Unsere Welt*, eine Nachrichten-Webseite, und berichten über schlechte Arbeitsbedingungen in Nordafrika. Indem Sie die Situation Malika Al-Magrabis (Text 3) schildern, möchten Sie Ihre Leserschaft auf mangelhafte Standards in Fabriken aufmerksam machen, in denen ihre Kleidung hergestellt wird. Übersetzen Sie nicht Wort für Wort.

> EXAM PREPARATION
> Mediation (S. 171)

C Compare and contrast Boris Stein's experience with that of Nick Bell.

Find one similarity and several differences between them. Use this language:
Both of them have ... However, ... while ...
Concerning their recent experiences at work, ... but ...
Looking at the future, ... whereas ...

D Say what you think.

Our cutting edge technology means German jobs are safe.

Don't you believe it! Plenty of German jobs have gone abroad.

2 WORKING WITH WORDS

A Find opposites of these words in the text.

Text 1	Text 2	Text 4
1 problems (*lines 1-7*)	4 earlier (*lines 1-5*)	6 out of date (*lines 1-9*)
2 expensive (*lines 8-14*)	5 employee (*lines 6-9*)	7 loses (*lines 10-16*)
3 close down (*lines 8-14*)		

B Use pairs of opposites from exercise A in the correct form to complete the following.

1 In countries such as Morocco, most ... do not allow their ... to join unions.
2 This IT equipment is ten years old, so it's completely .... If we want to stay in business, we'll have to buy equipment that's ....
3 All sorts of electronic equipment used to be much more ... than it is now. It is amazing to see how ... today's very powerful computers are.
4 Sadly, European manufacturers have ... a lot of business to Chinese producers. However, they can still ... new customers in world markets when they offer excellent quality.
5 Because of global competition, older, less efficient European industries have had to .... At the same time though, new high-tech industries have continued to ... successfully.

3 CULTURE CHECK: BODY LANGUAGE AND PERSONAL SPACE

Globalization is bringing together more and more people from different parts of the world. However, different cultures have different ideas about such basic things as body language and personal space. Something acceptable in one culture may be unacceptable in another.

You have probably already noticed some of the differences, for example through meeting people from other cultures, and you have certainly seen different cultural behaviours in films and on TV.

So try this quiz and see how culturally sensitive you are. Decide who you think is making each point.

EA = an East Asian, LA = a Latin American, NA = a North American, NE = a northern European, SE = a southern European

We don't like making too much eye contact when we talk. We feel that's quite rude and 'pushy'. If somebody does that while speaking, we feel that person is trying to dominate or control the listener.

A EA | LA

It's just natural to touch the other person's arm or shoulder when we're talking. It shows the warmth that we feel towards each other.

B EA | LA

When I meet somebody new, I like to shake hands firmly to show that I want to have a warm, friendly relationship with that person.

C NA | EA

I don't feel comfortable with somebody who doesn't look me in the eye when we talk. Rightly or wrongly, I feel there's something dishonest about that person – something that I can't quite trust.

D EA | NA

It's not polite in our culture to stand too close when we talk. We need to give each other as much personal space as possible. That's at least 80 centimetres.

E SE | EA

Answers > File 17, page 159

4 DISCUSSION

> Diskussionen führen S. 170

Discuss these questions in small groups.

1 Whatever the activists say, do you think any government can or should try to stop or slow down globalization?
2 How might globalization affect you in the future? Are you more likely to be a 'winner' or a 'loser' in the globalization process?

B The bigger picture

BEFORE YOU READ

Have you seen products in the shops with a FAIRTRADE label on them? What do you think it means?

Let's be fair about trade by Sally Pearson

The not-so-fair trading

We are told that free trade is a good thing. But is it? For many people it is not, and they are some of the poorest in the world.

'Always low prices' promises Walmart, America's – and the world's – largest retailer. Consumers like this, of course, and so sales rise. But the big retailers do not cut their own profits to reduce prices. They pass those 'low prices' along the supply chain to the producers, who are forced to compete with each other globally to be the cheapest. The producers are 'free' only to pass on the cost pressures to their workers.

It happens all over the world, in factories and on farms, and the results are the opposite of freedom.

'We used to be well paid for meeting our targets,' Chandrika, a Sri Lankan textile worker reports. 'But now the targets they give us just cannot be met, so the bonus is never paid.'

'As a casual worker, I don't get a bonus, paid holidays or redundancy pay,' says Ragel, a fruit picker from South Africa.

Supply chain pressures create precarious employment

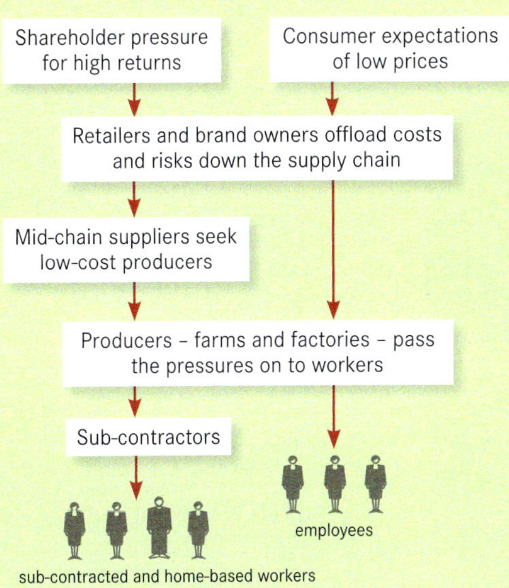

Ana, a Bolivian factory worker, despairs: 'We have buried our dreams. Our only concern for the future is to make sure that the same thing doesn't happen to our children.'

The FAIRTRADE way

For many of the world's poor, however, change is coming in the form of FAIRTRADE. This is an independent international organization that aims to develop fair trade between poorer and richer countries. Members of FAIRTRADE pay poor producers more than they can normally get, which means prices that are a little higher than normal in western shops. However, this is not hurting sales. Far from it, as sales are now expanding rapidly in Europe and North America. Bringing hope instead of despair, it seems that FAIRTRADE is here to stay. Coordinator Jack Carson explains how the system works:

'We visit potential suppliers to look at their products and their business strengths and weaknesses. If we are happy about these things, we develop an action plan. They may need design or technical support, for example, to get their products right for western markets. We also agree to buy directly and pay a fair, guaranteed price – and some of this immediately. This helps workers with things like paying for their children's education.

We later offer training in marketing and other skills so that producers can gradually become independent.

As for the products, these range from food produce like coffee and bananas to crafts and fashion clothing. They are sold through our own shops and increasing numbers of other stores, including big supermarket chains. Sales are growing by nearly 50% per year. Consumers recognize the FAIRTRADE label and know that it promises quality products at competitive prices – and help for the producers. Instead of rising profits for middlemen, FAIRTRADE brings rising living standards to some of the world's poorest people.' (479 words)

1 LOOKING AT THE TEXT

A Decide whether the following statements are true or false and explain your choices in German.

> EXAM PREPARATION
> Beurteilen von Textaussagen (S. 172)

1 Walmart sells more than any other retail business in the world.
2 Big retailers like Walmart accept that they need to cut their profits in order to give consumers the low prices that they want.
3 The three workers who speak about their problems all work in factories.
4 FAIRTRADE helps its suppliers to pay for their children's education.
5 More and more people are buying FAIRTRADE products because they are cheaper than normal supermarket goods.

B Read the text again and do these activities.

1 Explain the 'word play' in the title of the text.
2 Find one similarity between each of the workers who speak in the text and Malika's situation - see page 96.
3 Identify the three sentences that relate to the diagram on page 99.
4 In your own words, explain the process that the diagram in the text illustrates.
5 Find the sentence that the photos represent.
6 Copy and complete the diagram on the right.
7 Cover the diagram and describe the process it illustrates.

C Zu Ihrem Bedauern stellen Sie fest, dass Ihr Supermarkt keine FAIRTRADE-Produkte auf Lager hat. Schreiben Sie einen Beschwerdebrief an den Filialleiter. Erklären Sie ihm mithilfe des Artikels, wie FAIRTRADE funktioniert und welche Vorteile das System für Produzenten, Händler und Konsumenten hat. Übersetzen Sie nicht Wort für Wort.

> EXAM PREPARATION
> Mediation (S. 171)

D Say what you think.

So, we just need to start growing coffee and then we join FAIRTRADE. What do you think?

FAIRTRADE SALES
UP AND UP

MILK PRICES
DROP AGAIN

2 WORKING WITH WORDS

A Match words from the box to 1–12 to form word pairs. Then look for the expressions in the text to check your answers.

1 free (*paragraph 1*)
2 supply (*paragraph 2*)
3 cost (*paragraph 2*)
4 paid (*paragraph 5*)
5 redundancy (*paragraph 5*)
6 fruit (*paragraph 5*)
7 factory (*paragraph 6*)
8 action (*paragraph 8*)
9 food (*paragraph 10*)
10 fashion (*paragraph 10*)
11 supermarket (*paragraph 10*)
12 living (*paragraph 10*)

chain | chains | clothing | holidays | pay | picker | plan | pressures | produce | standards | trade | worker

B Complete the following sentences with word pairs from exercise A. Use plural forms where necessary.

1 Every good employer should offer its employees good pay and conditions, including … … and, if jobs have to be cut, fair … … .
2 The big … … like Walmart sell fresh … … as well as thousands of products in cans, packets and bottles.
3 The problems of poor working conditions apply to … … making trainers in Indonesia as well as to … … who gather oranges and lemons in countries around the Mediterranean.
4 Thanks to today's … … between different countries, there are huge … … that bring products to us from right around the world.

3 LISTENING

2 14 **A The journalist Sally Pearson visited Guatemala with Jack Carson, the FAIRTRADE coordinator. Listen to her interview with a farmer, Felipe Castro, and complete her notes.**

Felipe Castro: *age 48; wife & 3 children*
Farm: *1) _____ a hectare; 2) _____ coffee trees*
Co-operative – Manos Campesinas (= 'Workers' Hands'):
3) _____ members; 4) started in _____
What it does: *5) sells to _____*
6) gives _____
7) offers _____
Higher earnings allow farmers to build a new coffee mill:
What it will do: *8) add _____*
9) create _____
Higher earnings are also changing people's daily lives:
Farmers can now: *10) install _____*
11) keep _____
Felipe hopes to: *12) send _____*

B Sie möchten, dass FAIRTRADE-Produkte auch in der Schulcaféteria verkauft werden. Schreiben Sie einen Artikel für die Schülerzeitung, in dem Sie die konkreten Vorteile von FAIRTRADE für die Bauern in den Entwicklungsländern schildern. Benutzen Sie die Informationen aus dem Interview mit Felipe Castro.

> ZENTRALE KLASSENARBEIT
Hörverstehen (S. 175)

4 BUILDING SKILLS: COMPOSITION

> EXAM PREPARATION
> Materialgestützter Aufsatz (S. 173)

Refer to at least three of the materials below. Write about the following: *What is globalization doing to us in the Western economies?* Use the phrases below to help you.

Introduction:
When we start to consider globalization, we soon realize that it is a powerful force in today's world, and that it has a huge effect on ...
Arguments:
In some ways, globalization has brought us great benefits. For example, it has ... Then again, ...
However, globalization has also created many problems for ...
In the first place, ... In the second place, ... In addition, ...
People can now see the direct effects of ... on their own lives, and they feel ...
As a result, they are ... such as the one in ... on ... , which was against ...
Conclusion:
From all this, we can see that ... Therefore we can conclude that ...

> TIP

You have to use at least three of the sources, so choose those that best help to express your ideas. Start with your own first thoughts about the composition title. Then look through all the sources quickly to find ones that match and perhaps add to your ideas.

1

'Before you've finished breakfast this morning, you'll have relied on half the world.'

Martin Luther King

2

3

I do not underestimate the scale of the challenges we now face. ... On growth, the cause of the problem is global imbalances. Some countries, like Britain, have large deficits and must take tough, hard-headed decisions to cut back and restore sound public finances. But other countries have big surpluses. We need these countries to do the opposite: consume more and save less. ... Unless we address global imbalances, we won't fundamentally solve the problem of how to achieve strong, balanced and sustainable growth.

David Cameron, British Prime Minister
in The World in 2011,
published by *The Economist* in 2010

underestimate *unterschätzen* • scale *Ausmaß* • imbalance *gestörtes Gleichgewicht* • cut back *kürzen* • restore *wiederherstellen* • sound *gesund* • surplus *Überschuss* • sustainable *nachhaltig*

Erneute Proteste gegen Globalisierung

4

Bei der Demonstration gegen den G8-Gipfel in Rostock ist es am Nachmittag zu massiven Ausschreitungen gekommen. Mehrere hundert Polizisten gingen gegen rund 500 Autonome vor.

Ein Polizeisprecher sagte, aus den Reihen der Autonomen seien Molotow-Cocktails, Feuerwerkskörper und Steine geworfen worden, Polizisten seien von Demonstranten eingekesselt worden.

Augenzeugen berichteten von verletzten Demonstranten. Die Auseinandersetzungen fanden am Rande der weitgehend friedlichen Demonstration mit rund 20 000 Teilnehmern statt.

Quelle: www.stern.de

C Further options

1 ANALYZING EXPORT ECONOMICS

Do the following tasks to analyze how apples are exported from South Africa to the UK.

1 Put a–h in order to describe the journey of a South African apple to a UK retailer.

A big journey for a small apple

It all starts on a large fruit farm near Cape Town in South Africa.

a Next, there are expenses in getting a consignment of apples from the farm to the ship that will carry it to Europe. The cost of transport and customs comes to around 6% of the retail value.

b Finally, we come to the last and single largest part of the final cost of an apple. This is the enormous 42% that the supermarket itself makes.

c After it reaches its destination port, UK handling takes another 11% of the retail price. This is the cost of getting the consignment off the ship and through the distribution system.

d Growing apples and then packaging them there is not cheap: non-labour farm costs are 17% of the price of an apple in the UK supermarket.

e In addition to this direct cost of transport, we have to add another 7% for customs duty and importer's commission.

f The farm owner has to make money, too, and farm income is about another 5% of the cost of the apple. So, in total, the money that the grower receives is around 26% of the supermarket price.

g Then there are wages to pay to the farm workers, and farm labour makes up another (surprisingly low) 4% of the final cost of every apple.

h The consignment now begins its long, 12,000-kilometre journey by sea to Britain. Not surprisingly, the cost of shipping is quite a large part of the sale price – roughly 12%.

2 Create a graphic to present the above information in a clear visual manner. Label the parts of your graphic with the underlined information in a–h above.

3 Work with a partner. Use your diagram to describe the apple's journey to the UK retailer.

2 DOING A ROLE-PLAY

Work in a group. Read the information, then do a role-play: *Should the factory close?*

Background information on the Gold Star scandal

- Gold Star, the biggest local employer in the town of San Bernardo in the Philippines, makes trainers for a large fashion retail chain, Now Look.
- Recently, foreign journalists have reported to the world that Gold Star breaks various national and international laws on employment.
- Gold Star's offences include: unpaid compulsory overtime, unfair sacking, no holiday rights or sickness benefits, no right to join a union, employment of under-age girls.
- This is a big international scandal, and a big problem for Now Look, Gold Star and San Bernardo. Something has to be done: the present situation cannot continue.

Roles

The Director of International Public Relations, Now Look > File 8, page 157

The owner of Gold Star > File 9, page 158

The Mayor of San Bernardo > File 15, page 159

A national union official > File 4, page 156

D Grammar checkpoint

1 THE PASSIVE: MIXED TENSES

> Grammar summary S. 183

Jack Carson often interviews and writes reports about possible new FAIRTRADE suppliers. Write part of his report on 'Fruits of Africa' for him.

> Put the underlined sections into the passive.
> Use *by* + agent only where necessary.
> Think carefully about word order.

Start like this: *'Fruits of Africa' was started by Mr James Kasozi and some ...*

JACK Mr Kasozi, thanks for seeing me.
JAMES You're very welcome, but please call me James.
JACK Fine, well, when did you begin this project?
JAMES Some other fruit farmers and I started 'Fruits of Africa' five years ago.
JACK What made you do that?
JAMES Well, before that, we always lost our fresh fruit if we did not sell it quickly at the local market.
JACK And now?
JAMES Now we don't waste these valuable mangos, bananas and pineapples – we dry them instead in very cheap, simple dryers.
JACK Who supplies the dryers?
JAMES Our own organization is now making and selling these dryers as cheaply as possible.
JACK Do they run on electricity?
JAMES No, they don't use electricity. The natural heat of the sun does the drying.
JACK Are they popular?
JAMES Yes, farmers in the local area have already bought hundreds of the dryers. And we are now also receiving orders from all over the country.
JACK So what about the future?
JAMES If FAIRTRADE accepts our dried-fruit products, it will help a lot of poor farmers in this very poor part of Africa towards a much better life.

2 THE PASSIVE WITH MODAL VERBS

> Grammar summary S. 183

Jack and a colleague are summing up their ideas on another project. Use the underlined points and the passive to complete Jack's email to his boss.

JACK So let's sum up our ideas on the 'Baskets of Bengal' project.
LISA Right. First, they must improve their production quality control.
JACK And to help them do that, we should send our Technical Support Officer, Stephen Carter.
LISA Good idea. We could ask him to visit them early next month.
JACK Next, they have to supply a sample order so that we can test the market here.
LISA Right, and the next thing: we may need further basket designs at a later date.
JACK If so, we might supply a specialist product designer to work with them.
LISA And finally, about payment: we can make an immediate 30% payment with our first order, and we'll pay the rest 60 days after receipt of order.

Email

Dear Margaret

Lisa and I have reached the following conclusions re. 'Baskets of Bengal':

1 Their production quality control must be improved.

8

Finding a job in the EU

FOCUS

1 **Work with a partner or in a small group. Answer the questions and then check your score.**

A quiz about the EU

1 How many countries signed the original Treaty of Rome on 25 March 1957?
A 4 **B** 6 **C** 9

2 Where is the headquarters of the European Commission?
A Brussels **B** Luxemburg **C** Strasbourg

3 When was the euro introduced?
A 2000 **B** 2001 **C** 2002

4 The voters of which two countries rejected the EU constitution in 2005?
A Britain and Sweden **B** France and the Netherlands **C** France and Italy

5 Which country is not a member of the EU?
A Belgium **B** Norway **C** Sweden

6 How many members does the EU have?
A 25 **B** 27 **C** over 27

7 What is the Schengen Agreement about?
A Cross-border policing **B** Open frontiers **C** The introduction of the euro

8 Who wrote the music to the 'European anthem'?
A Edward Elgar **B** Guiseppe Verdi **C** Ludwig van Beethoven

Answers > File 10, page 158

2 **What is your own attitude to the EU? Choose the statement you agree with most and then do a class survey.**

I don't have an 'attitude'. The EU means nothing to me.

The EU has brought peace and prosperity to Europe, but I think that's enough. I don't want a United States of Europe with Brussels as its capital.

I'd like the EU to become like the USA. At the moment, national governments have more say than the people of Europe and that's a real problem.

A Personal perspectives

BEFORE YOU READ

What do you think applying for a six-month internship at a tourist information office involves?

An internship in the UK

Lisa Bach, 20, from Münster is studying tourism in Bremen. As part of her studies, she has to do six months' practical training as an intern in an English-speaking country. Lisa decides to look for an internship in the UK. She contacts a German online agency, SEC, that specializes in arranging internships abroad, and finds this offer:

Tourism internship

Location	Norwich, Norfolk, UK
Sector	tourism
Duties	dealing with enquiries, incl. accommodation; general office duties; occasional 'meeting & greeting' duties
Length	6 months, 1 April to 30 September 20..
Qualifications	18 or over; fluent English, one other major European language; MS Office; car driving licence; friendly, outgoing personality; ability to work well in a team
Remuneration	no salary; accommodation arranged; contribution towards travel/living expenses (by negotiation)
Application	email application, CV as attachment; host's name/email address and job reference number provided by SEC; phone interview will be arranged by email

Lisa fills in the SEC form, pays a fee and receives further details, including the name/email address and the job reference number.

Email

Betreff:	Application for tourism internship
Von:	Lisa Bach <lisa.bach@okipost.de>
Datum:	10 November 20.. 21:32
An:	Norwich City Council <human-resources@norwich.gov.uk>

Dear Sir or Madam

I refer to your offer of a tourism internship on SEC's website, reference ncc-tic-2064.
As you will see from my CV, I am studying Tourism Management at the University of Applied Sciences in Bremen, Germany. Students on this course are required to have a minimum of six months' practical work experience in an English-speaking country.
I am hoping to find an internship next year and would like to apply for the post you are offering. The dates 1 April to 30 September are fine, as are the duties you list in the job description. I worked for two months at the tourist office in Münster this summer, where I gained experience of similar work.
As requested, I attach my CV. If you have any further queries, please contact me by phone or email.
If you are interested in my application, I look forward to arranging a phone interview.

Yours faithfully

Lisa Bach

1 LOOKING AT THE TEXTS

A Do the following tasks.

1 What is Lisa's reason for applying for an internship?
2 Find information in the ad and email to show why Lisa chose this internship.
3 Say whether you think Lisa got a phone interview and explain your answer.

B Say what you think.

1 Could you imagine doing an internship abroad like Lisa? Say why / why not.
2 How would you feel about doing an unpaid internship?

2 WORKING WITH WORDS

A Find words or expressions in the ad (1–3) or email (4–6) to fit these definitions.

1 period of training – often unpaid
2 friendliness, enthusiasm for meeting new people
3 discussion to reach an agreement
4 department responsible for employees
5 opposite of 'theoretical'
6 summary of applicant's personal details, qualifications and work experience

B Write four sentences using some of the words and phrases from exercise A.

LISA BACH

	Personal details
Name:	Lisa Bach
Address:	Kreuzstraße 15, 48142 Münster, Germany
Date and place of birth:	28 May 1989, Münster
Nationality:	German
Daytime phone number:	+49-2571-547821
Email address:	lisa.bach@okipost.de
	Education
10/2007–present	Fachhochschule Bremen (University of Applied Sciences); 7-semester course, Touristik (Tourism Management)
08/2004–06/2007	Adolf-Kolping-Berufskolleg, Münster (vocational school); 3-year course, Hotelfachfrau (Hotel Administration); grade average: 1.9 on 6-point scale from 1 (very good) to 6 (very unsatisfactory)
08/1999–07/2004	Realschule im Kreuzviertel, Münster (secondary school); school-leaving certificate (equivalent of GCSE); grade average 2.1
	Work experience
2003	Altenzentrum St. Josef; assistant carer in home for the elderly
2002	Presto Supermarkt, Münster; sales assistant
	Paid employment
Summer 2009	vacation job, Verkehrsverein Münster; assistant in tourist information office
Summer 2008	vacation job, Hotel am Stadtgarten, Münster; assistant receptionist
	Interests and skills
Languages	English, advanced (some knowledge of business English)
IT skills	MS Office (Word, Excel, PowerPoint); HSTeam 2006 (hotel software); eComBot Travel (e-Tourism software)
Other	driving licence, EU class C
References	references can be supplied on request

3 LOOKING AT THE CV

Which part of a CV contains this information? Be careful: some information is not given in a CV at all.

1 ability to speak a foreign language
2 applicant's grade at end of Year 10
3 details of driving licence
4 details of unpaid jobs
5 how long an applicant went to primary school
6 information about paid holiday jobs
7 job applicant's email address
8 job applicant's name and address
9 names and addresses of referees
10 information regarding marital status and number of children

4 WORKING WITH WORDS

A Find the English equivalents of the following German words and expressions in the CV. They are not necessarily in the same order.

1 *Abschlusszeugnis*
2 *auf Wunsch*
3 *Berufserfahrung*
4 *bezahlte Beschäftigung*
5 *Empfangsassistentin*
6 *Ferienjob*
7 *fortgeschritten*
8 *Führerschein*
9 *Notendurchschnitt*
10 *Computerkenntnisse*

B Use some of the words and expressions from exercise A to explain the following in English.

Sie möchten jemandem sagen, dass ...
1 Sie etwas Berufserfahrung in der Touristikbranche haben.
2 Ihr Ferienjob als Empfangsassistentin Ihnen gut gefallen hat.
3 Sie nach einer bezahlten Beschäftigung suchen, bei der Sie Ihre Computerkenntnisse einsetzen können.
4 auf Wunsch Empfehlungsschreiben eingereicht werden können.
5 Sie fortgeschrittene Englischkenntnisse besitzen.
6 Sie seit zwei Jahren einen Führerschein haben.

5 GIVING AN OPINION

Work with a partner.

You work in the human resources department at Norwich City Council. Your boss refers you to Lisa's CV and to the email on page 106 and asks you to give your opinion about Lisa's application. Would you offer Lisa an internship?

6 WRITING

Write an English letter of application and CV based on your personal profile.

Imagine you are applying for a three-month internship in any country or field of your choice. Write the letter of application and your CV in English. Include information about your school career, work experience, skills, etc.

7 LISTENING

3 2 **A Listen for general understanding. Read the email and then listen to the extract from the telephone interview. How did the interview go: *well*, *badly* or *all right*?**

Email

Subject:	Application for tourism internship
Date:	21 November 20.. 10:12
From:	Norwich City Council <human-resources@norwich.gov.uk>
To:	Lisa Bach <lisa.bach@okipost.de>

Dear Lisa Bach

Further to your application for an internship, I would like to arrange a date and time for a telephone interview. This should take place during our office hours, which are 9:00 a.m. to 6:00 p.m. (local time), Monday to Friday.

Could you please let me have a date and time this week when I can reach you on a landline phone? Thank you and I look forward to hearing from you.

With regards
Ruth Morgan

B Ergänzen Sie auf Deutsch das Raster mit Informationen aus dem Hörtext.

> ZENTRALE KLASSENARBEIT
Hörverstehen (S. 175)

Lisa Bach, Ferienarbeit	
Ort:	...
Hauptaufgabe:	...
Telefonanfragen zu folgenden Themen:	... / ...
Probleme/Sonderwünsche der Anrufer:	*barrierefreier Zugang für ...* *Familien mit ... / ...*
Artikel, die im Laden verkauft werden:	*(Rad-)Wanderkarten* *... / ...* *Outdoor-Kleidung/ ...*

8 ROLE-PLAY

Work with a partner. Read the suggestions below and add any ideas or information of your own to complete the interview. Then act out the interview together.

Ruth asks:
... about Lisa's knowledge of French.
... what Lisa hopes to get out of her internship.
... what Lisa thinks she can offer the tourist information centre in Norwich.
... how Lisa got on with co-workers/managers in Münster.
... how Lisa handled difficult customers/callers.

Lisa asks:
... about her accommodation in Norwich.
... what she will be expected to do on a typical day.
... if she will be allowed to deal with callers herself.

B The bigger picture

BEFORE YOU READ

In this extract from *Now it's your turn*, a radio phone-in show, Helen Wood is asking callers about Britain and the EU. What opinions do you expect to hear?

HELEN Is the EU good or bad for Britain? Or is it a mixture of both? That is the topic of our programme this evening. And my first caller is John Harris from Bristol. John, now it's your turn.

JOHN Hello. Uhm ... Yes, well, first I want to say that I'm certainly not anti-European, but I'm totally against the EU.

HELEN Oh yes. Why's that, John?

JOHN Well, I think the EU's a waste of time and money – just corruption, bureaucracy and interference in our affairs. What right has Brussels to tell us what to do? And it's so undemocratic. Just a bunch of unelected foreign bureaucrats. And who pays for it all? We do! I say we should leave tomorrow!

HELEN Phew! Well, we've certainly got off with a bang. Now our next caller is ... Oh, yes. Jane Garner from Hull, right?

JANE That's right, Helen. Good evening.

HELEN Hi. And what's your opinion, Jane?

JANE Well, my brother works for the EU in Brussels, and I think your last caller was very unfair – what he said was misleading, frankly.

HELEN Oh? And what makes you say that?

JANE Well, for example, the so-called 'Brussels bureaucracy'. Believe it or not, the EU is run by fewer people[1] than it takes to run a medium-sized city like Leeds[2].

HELEN Really? So why do so many people say that the EU is too bureaucratic, then?

JANE Well, it's all a question of perception. The trouble is that a lot of people blame Brussels for things that national governments do. The fact is that the European Commission can't pass laws at all. It can only inform, advise and recommend. The rest is up to the Council of Ministers.

HELEN In other words, national governments, right?

JANE Right – and I'm afraid that national politicians just defend their own selfish interests, that's the problem. The UK is particularly bad there, I'm sorry to say.

HELEN Well, thank you for that, Jane. And now my next caller is Dr Peter Brown from Manchester University. What's your take on this, Peter?

PETER Well, we've been doing research into corruption in Europe, and our findings show that the EU is much less corrupt than many national governments. In fact, it's relatively clean.

HELEN Yes, but the media is full of stories about corruption, isn't it, Peter? They can't all be wrong, can they?

PETER Well, it's like the last caller said – the EU is often blamed for the corruption of its members. You see, the EU doesn't pay out any money directly, to farmers, say. The member states do that, and there you really do find some corruption.

HELEN OK. Thanks, Peter. And now a caller from Europe is on the line. Beate König from Aachen in Germany. What would you like to say, Beate?

BEATE Good evening everybody. Well, I think the EU is much more than just trade and so on. It's open frontiers, a common currency, the freedom to live, work and study where we want. And it's peace, stability and a European identity, too. I value those things a lot, that's all.

HELEN Fine. So you have no problem with Brussels interfering in German affairs?

BEATE Well, no, I don't. I think that in our globalized world, 'national sovereignty' doesn't mean much anyhow. That's why it's so bad when national politicians act only in their own selfish national interest.

HELEN Oh yes. Why's that?

BEATE Well, what about global threats like climate change, scarcity of raw materials, terrorism, mass migration, cross-border crime and so on? No country can fight those alone. We must all pull on the same rope in the same direction. We have no choice. We must integrate to survive.

(635 words)

[1] The EU has just over 23,000 employees (2007) [2] Leeds City Council employs about 33,000 people (2008)

1 LOOKING AT THE TEXT

A Do the assignments.

1 List arguments the callers give for and against the EU.

2 Explain why many people have a negative view of the EU.

B Describe what you can see in the cartoon. Explain its message and relate it back to the text on page 110.

> EXAM PREPARATION
> Bildbeschreibung mit Analyse (S. 172)

C Say what you think.

1 Say which opinion is closest to your own, John Harris's or Beate König's, and why.

2 Which of the statements (a, b or c) do you agree with most? Give reasons for your choice.

I would like to see ...

a a further widening of the EU to include all European countries.

b no further widening but greater integration of the present members.

c the EU remain as it is at the moment – no further widening, no further integration.

2 WORKING WITH WORDS

A Complete the table with the missing forms from the phone-in.

	verb	*noun*	*adjective*
1	*mix*	…	*mixed*
2	*corrupt*	…	…
3	…	…	*interfering*
4	*perceive*	…	*perceptive*
5	…	*advice, adviser*	*advisory*
6	…	*recommendation*	*recommended*
7		*responsibility*	…
8	*threaten*	…	*threatening*

B Complete the sentences with some of the words that you found in exercise A.

1 You'll find that all opinion is based on a …[1] of fact and …[2]
2 Ask Jane Baker. She's … for European affairs.
3 Unfortunately, where there's money, there's …
4 I'm sorry. I can't help you. I strongly … that you find a good lawyer.
5 Government …[1] in our private lives is getting worse because of the …[2] of terrorist attacks.

C Explain these sentences or phrases from the phone-in.

1 '… we've certainly got off with a bang.' (*line 17*)
2 '… what he said was misleading, frankly.' (*line 24*)
3 'The rest is up to the Council of Ministers.' (*line 37*)
4 'What's your take on this …?' (*line 47*)
5 'In actual fact, it's relatively clean.' (*line 52*)

3 WRITING

> Eine Stellungnahme schreiben S. 165

Use these ideas to write a comment evaluating arguments for and against a fully united Europe.

For:
> balance power of USA/Russia/China
> threats now global, not national (climate change, terrorism, etc.)
> federal system more democratic
> more efficient/effective single market

Against:
> member states too diverse to unite
> differences in size/economies too great
> no official language
> too much power to bigger countries
> people prefer nation states

Use these expressions to emphasize or moderate what you say:

Emphasizing expressions
> it is clear that …
> there can be no/little doubt that …
> no matter how …
> to begin/start with …
> on top of that …

Moderating expressions
> as far as I can see …
> on the one hand …, on the other (hand) …
> perhaps/maybe …
> it seems to me …
> most would perhaps admit …

C Further options

1 DOING A PERSONALITY TEST

This personality test is designed to give employers a better picture of their employees and job applicants. Do the test yourself to find out what kind of person you are.

QUESTIONS

1 You feel at your best ...
- a in the morning.
- b in the afternoon / early evening.
- c late at night.

2 You usually walk ...
- a quite fast with long steps.
- b quite fast with short steps.
- c less fast with head up.
- d less fast with head down.
- e very slowly.

3 When talking to people, you ...
- a stand with your arms folded.
- b have your hands clasped.
- c have one or both your hands on your hips.
- d sometimes touch the other person.
- e play with your ear, touch your chin or smooth your hair.

4 When relaxing, you sit with ...
- a your knees and legs neatly together.
- b your legs crossed.
- c your legs stretched out.
- d one leg curled under you.

5 If something is funny, do you ...
- a open your mouth wide and laugh loudly?
- b open your mouth a bit and laugh less loudly?
- c chuckle quietly?
- d just smile?

6 At party, do you make a ...
- a noisy entrance so everybody knows you're there?
- b quiet entrance, looking around for somebody you know?
- c very quiet entrance, hoping that nobody notices you?

7 You're concentrating on something and somebody interrupts you. Do you ...
- a welcome the break?
- b feel very annoyed?
- c move between these two extremes according to who it is?

8 Your favourite colour is ...
- a red or orange.
- b black.
- c yellow or light blue.
- d green.
- e dark blue or purple.
- f white.
- g brown or grey.

9 In the last few moments before you go to sleep, you lie ...
- a stretched out on your back.
- b stretched out on your stomach.
- c on one side with your knees slightly bent.
- d with your head on one arm.
- e with your head under the covers.

10 When you are asleep, do you ...
- a often dream you are falling?
- b often dream you are fighting against something?
- c often dream you are looking for something / somebody?
- d often dream you are flying or floating in the air?
- e usually have a dreamless sleep?
- f always have sweet dreams?

Results > File 1, page 155

When you have finished, work out your score and find out what it means.

2 ANALYZING THE RESULTS

What do you think of your own or your partner's score? Are there any surprises?

3 INTERPRETING PERSONALITY TYPES

Match the six categories in the results to jobs in the box. Give reasons for your choice.

electrician | handball coach | lab assistant | museum assistant | photographer | plumber | police officer | racing driver | security guard | software engineer | soldier | teacher

D Grammar checkpoint

1 GERUND OR INFINITIVE?

> Grammar summary S. 185

Choose the correct form, a) or b).

1 We really enjoy a) travelling | b) to travel [1] within the Eurozone because we dislike a) having to | b) to have to [2] change money all the time. In fact, I think the UK should consider a) giving up | b) to give up [3] the pound and a) adopting | b) to adopt [4] the euro.

2 We chose a) joining | b) to join [1] the EU, didn't we? In my opinion, we should stop a) opting out | b) to opt out [2] of everything and start a) playing | b) to play [3] a full role in the union. If we don't, we risk a) becoming | b) to become [4] isolated on the edge of Europe. We really must avoid a) letting | b) to let [5] that happen.

3 My sister wants a) studying | b) to study [1] German so my dad suggested a) applying | b) to apply [2] to a university in a German-speaking country. Anyhow, she decided a) going | b) to go [3] to Dresden and she plans a) moving | b) to move [4] there in August.

4 Both Austria and France have promised a) holding | b) to hold [1] a referendum about Turkey joining the EU. If they do, I can't imagine Turkey a) winning | b) to win [2] the vote. Personally, I would like a) avoiding | b) to avoid [3] a referendum at any cost. I would prefer Turkey a) stopping | b) to stop [4] negotiations to join the union before that happened. Just think about it! It could mean a) closing | b) to close [5] the door to Europe in Turkey's face!

5 I will never forget a) visiting | b) to visit [1] the EU headquarters in Brussels for the first time. I had read so much about the 'gigantic EU bureaucracy' that I expected a) seeing | b) to see [2] huge office blocks and so on. I remember a) being | b) to be [3] very surprised at what I found. In fact, the EU building did not seem a) being | b) to be [4] any bigger than that of many big international firms. But when I tried a) telling | b) to tell [5] people back home, many of them simply refused a) believing | b) to believe [6] me. Some even told me to stop a) talking | b) to talk [7] such nonsense.

2 GERUND OR INFINITIVE?

> Grammar summary S. 185

Use the infinitive or *-ing* form to complete this dialogue.

A radio producer, Nick West, is talking to a reporter, Sue Green, about a request from a listener.

NICK Hi, Sue. Look, do you remember ... [1] (*interview*) that guy about opening an office in Germany?

SUE Yes, of course. Greg Cox. Nice man but he just couldn't stop ... [2] (*talk*). He's trying ... [3] (*find*) an agent in the Ruhrgebiet, I think.

NICK Well, this email is from a guy called Lothar Moers in Bochum. He'd like ... [4] (*get*) in touch with Greg Cox but he says he forgot ... [5] (*note*) down his address. I meant ... [6] (*deal*) with it yesterday, but I just didn't manage ... [7] (*do*) it, I'm afraid. And I can't stop ... [8] (*reply*) to it now. Do you think you could answer it for me?

SUE Sure. I'll stop ... [9] (*work*) on this report and do it immediately.

NICK Thanks, a lot, Sue. I suppose it just means ... [10] (*tell*) Greg Cox Mr Moer's email address and then he can take it from there. I don't want ... [11] (*do*) it the other way round.

SUE Of course not. We always avoid ... [12] (*give*) other people somebody's address. Anyhow, luckily, I decided ... [13] (*keep*) Greg's contact details just in case anybody got in touch. I'll try his mobile number first and if I have no luck, I'll try ... [14] (*get*) him on his office number.

Social challenges

FOCUS

1 Do awareness activity 1: *Who are you?*

1. Work with a partner – someone you do not know well. Copy the chart below. Add extra writing space in columns 2–4.
2. Silently, fill in column 2 about yourself. Then guess your partner's answers and fill in column 3.
3. Next take turns to ask the questions and fill in column 4.
4. Discuss differences between your column 3 and 4 answers.

Who are you?	Myself	Partner (my guesses)	Partner (his/her answers)
1 What is your father's cultural heritage? (e.g. national / regional / ethnic / religious background)			
2 What is your mother's cultural heritage?			
3 Where were you born?			
4 What's your favourite school subject?			
5 What's your favourite sport?			
6 Who's your favourite musician / band?			
7 What's your favourite food?			
8 What's your biggest fear?			
9 What do you consider your best quality?			
10 How do you see yourself in ten years' time?			

2 Do awareness activity 2: *How does society help make me who I am?*

1. Use the diagram below to help you organize your thoughts. Think how different parts of society can benefit, control and influence you.

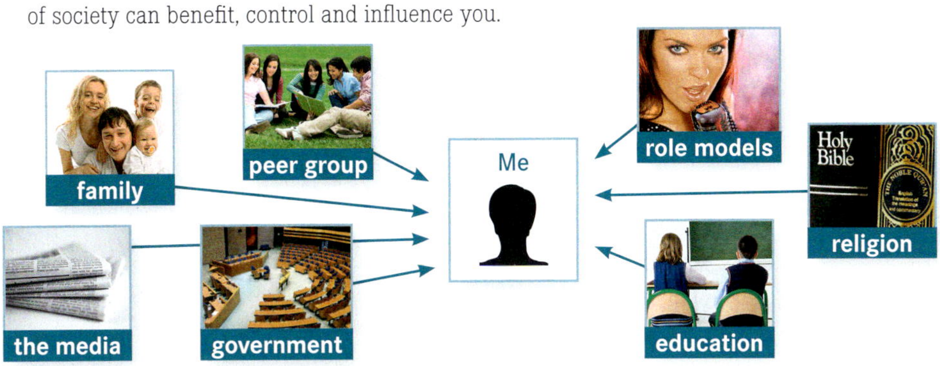

2. Work with a partner. Present your ideas to each other and discuss any differences.

A Personal perspectives

BEFORE YOU READ

3 4 **The first picture is from an old advert. What view of family life does it show? Is this your view?**

What's in a family?

Do you remember the 'perfect' family? You know, the one with the happy husband going off to his steady job in his clean, white shirt. And the happy wife looking after the perfect home while bringing up the perfect children.

Perhaps that family only ever existed in 1960s washing powder ads. Certainly, life today is much less tidy. The pressures on families are often huge. Few fathers have a steady job for life, and quite often there is no father. And the mother often works. Who then polishes the home and the children?

In fact, quite often there is no father *or* mother: in America about 4.5 million young people live with grandparents, and many more live with other relatives.

So can the family still do its traditional job for children? Can it still provide the steady structure, rules and role models that socialize the young, bringing them up to be responsible members of adult society? Every day the media seem to prove that street gangs have taken over – have become the only 'family' many teenagers have.

But there is better news too. When families break down, alternative arrangements with relatives can work well, as the stories of Brittany Hicks and Arianna Bianco show. Both have fathers they have never known. Brittany's mother could not look after her because of emotional problems. Arianna's mother had a drug addiction, making childcare impossible.

You might expect Brittany and Arianna to feel abandoned and angry. But both girls say they don't feel that way. 'I just deal with it,' says Arianna. 'I don't get mad at my mom. Being addicted to drugs was obviously a thing she couldn't stop.'

Brittany says she used to feel rejected by her mother, but, 'As I grew up, I came to realize that she loved me a lot. She told me, "I never abandoned you. I always knew where the best place was for you." And now I believe her.'

Brittany and Arianna both agree that they have to live by a tougher set of rules than kids in traditional families. 'My aunt is definitely stricter,' says Arianna. 'All my friends agree.' Brittany says her grand-parents check her activities more closely than she thinks they need to. 'I guess it's because they don't want me to run into the same problems my mom did.'

Talking about life outside the traditional family structure, Brittany speaks for both girls when she says, 'People think it's really different, but it's not. You're living with people who love you and want you to have a good life – just like any family.'

(426 words)

Brittany, who lives with her grandparents

Arianna, whose aunt and uncle care for her

1 LOOKING AT THE TEXT

> **EXAM PREPARATION**
> Beurteilen von Textaussagen (S. 172)

A Decide whether the following statements are true or false and explain your choices in German.

1 The writer suggests that 1960s washing powder ads showed what life was actually like for normal families in those days.
2 Under a million young people live with their grandparents in America.
3 The writer considers such alternative arrangements to be a good idea.
4 Brittany is in contact with her father and visits him regularly.
5 Arianna's mother was unable to look after her because her drug addiction made her reject her daughter.
6 Brittany lives with her grandparents, and Arianna's home is with her aunt.
7 Both girls are no longer angry with their mothers for abandoning them.
8 Brittany and Arianna are both more free to do what they want than their friends who are being brought up in traditional families.

B Say what you think.

"The only way I could get him to take any notice of me was to put myself on DVD."

"Couldn't you at least wait until half-time so we could discuss our communication problem?"

2 WORKING WITH WORDS

A Use the correct form of these phrasal verbs from the text to complete the story below.

break down | bring up | deal with | go off | grow up | look after | run into | take over

When Tony was three and his younger sister Lucy just two, their parents' marriage … …[1] big problems, and it … …[2] so badly that one day their father just disappeared. Years later, the family learned that he had … …[3] to start a new life in Australia.

For the next three years, their mother seemed to be able to … …[4] the situation. A childminder … …[5] the children every day while she went to work. In the end, though, the problems of … …[6] two small children as a single mother were too much for her, and she had a nervous breakdown. Social Services then … …[7] from her, and the children were taken into care for several months. Then, after recovering, their mother was able to take them back again. She also met a new partner who soon became a real father to the children. So, in the end, Tony and Lucy … …[8] quite normally and happily.

B Find words or expressions in the text to express the underlined parts of the sentences below more efficiently.

The old ways and the new

1 It has gradually become clear to people that the old ways of family and working life have changed forever. (*paragraph 7*)
People *have come to realize* that the old ways of family and working life have changed forever.
2 For example, people often change jobs these days, and nobody expects to find a job that will continue until one retires at the age of 65. (*paragraph 2*)

Becoming a member of society

3 It is essential for every community to bring up its young people to become good members of that community. (*paragraph 4*)
4 Young people need to learn to do things according to the rules and customs of their community. (*paragraph 8*)

Helping a boy called Sam

5 It is clear that Sam's mother, Carrie, has severe psychiatric problems and that looking after her child has become impossible for her. (*paragraph 5*)
6 Carrie's illness is a big problem and Sam's father has lost contact with the family, and so we have been trying to make other plans for dealing with the situation. (*paragraph 5*)
7 Although his situtation is very bad, I can tell you something more positive. It seems that his aunt and uncle are happy to give him a home. (*paragraph 5*)

3 LISTENING

> ZENTRALE KLASSENARBEIT
Hörverstehen (S. 175)

3 5 **Vervollständigen Sie auf Deutsch die unten stehenden Aussagen mit Informationen aus dem Hörtext.**

1 Der Sprecher ist ... Vater einer ... Tochter.
2 Manchmal wenn er von der Arbeit nach Hause kommt, möchte er ... .
3 Wenn sie die Zeit zusammen verbringen, ...
4 Er geht davon aus, dass ihre Freunde ihr helfen werden, ...
5 Obwohl er möchte, dass sie aufgeklärt wird, ...
6 Seiner Meinung nach, ist seine wichtigste Aufgabe, ...
7 Seine Tochter ist viel härter im Nehmen ... .
8 Er ist jetzt schon so lange allein, dass er es ... .

4 WRITING

Imagine yourself as the girl in exercise 3 thinking back at the age of 18. What would you say to 'your' father about his efforts? Write your thoughts in the form of a letter to him. Use these ideas:

When I look back at those years after Mum left us, I (sometimes/often) feel ...
I (often/always) remember that (I/we/you) used to ...
I'm sure it was very (hard/depressing/tiring) for you to ...
I wish (you/we/I) (had/hadn't) ...
Finally, I'd just like to say ...

B The bigger picture

BEFORE YOU READ

Say whether you think it is important for you to vote in elections. Explain why.

Changing society

In a recent survey, Britons showed that the people they trust least are politicians (and journalists). Membership of political parties has dropped to record low levels, and numbers voting in elections have fallen. In a recent national election, only 55% of voters took part and just 42% of these voted for the winning party. The new government was chosen by roughly a quarter of the adult population!

Election numbers are falling across most of the western world. And, worryingly, the people who are least likely to vote are the young. Does this mean that young people have turned away from politics? For many the answer is yes but for others, no. The thing that these young people have turned away from is traditional party politics. Political parties work by bringing together many shades of opinion, and then uniting these into policies covering all areas of government. But these young people have a narrower focus – the environment, for example, or animal rights.

'There is nothing so powerful as an idea whose time has come,' Victor Hugo said, and this is true of some single-issue campaigns. Think of the suffragette movement that won women's right to vote in the early 20th century. Think of the Civil Rights movement in the 1950s and 1960s, finally bringing Black Americans their full freedom. Think of the students' movement of the late 1960s, which gave the voice of the young new power. Finally, think of the recent popular movements across the Arab world, with millions of young people using social networks to help organize huge protests against old and undemocratic governments forever standing against freedom. All these campaigns have changed history in different and important ways.

They live in the world of single-issue politics, and they see their particular issue as one requiring urgent action. They want to force the government to understand it and to act. This often means direct action to get public opinion on their side. They organize campaigns that may include demonstrations, marches and other ways of attracting attention. They may use non-violent acts of civil disobedience that lead to arrest by the police. Sometimes, they might even use violence – although this very often actually reduces rather than increases sympathy for their cause.

Not every battle shakes the world though: smaller successes are possible too. Take the case of Julia Butterfly Hill, for example. Aged 23, she climbed a 180-foot, 1,000-year-old redwood tree in Stafford, California with the aim of preventing further logging in the area. She stayed there month after month, her friends supplying her with food by rope. After remaining in the tree for two years, she won. The loggers signed an agreement promising to save the tree and the surrounding forest forever.

Can traditional politicians attract people like Julia to join them? Sadly for mainstream politics they usually cannot.

(470 words)

1 LOOKING AT THE TEXT

> EXAM PREPARATION
> Beurteilen von Textaussagen (S. 172)

A Decide whether the following statements are true or false and explain your choices in German.

1 British people prefer to believe politicians rather than people in business.
2 In an election not long ago, approximately 25% of the British population voted for the new government.
3 Many young people have lost interest in politics, and this is the reason why numbers voting in elections across the western world are falling.
4 Young people are often more interested in single-issue politics than in traditional party politics.
5 Activists believe that the support of the public will help their cause.
6 The Civil Rights movement won equal rights for Black Americans.
7 Of the different social and political movements that the text mentions, we can only say for sure that young people played a large part in the students' movement towards the end of the 1960s.
8 Julia Butterfly Hill achieved nothing when she went to live up a tree.

B Say what you think.

1 Are politicians the only ones who can influence and change society? Are they even the main influencers and changers? Are there other groups in society that you think can influence and change society?
2 Do you agree with these statements?

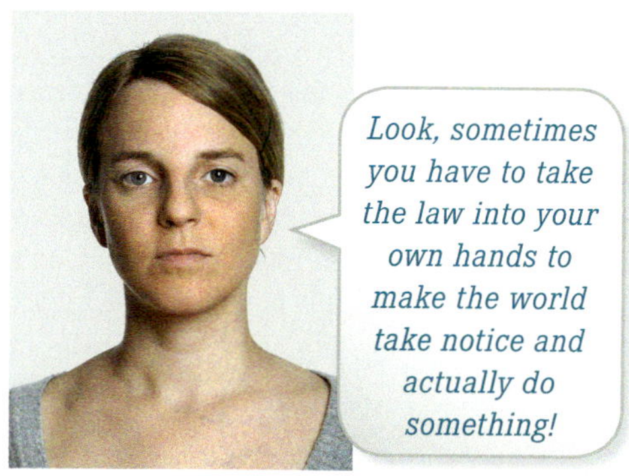

2 WORKING WITH WORDS

A Form adjectival compounds from the highlighted words.

1 Julia climbed a tree that was 180 feet tall.
Julia climbed a 180-foot tree.
2 She climbed a tree that was 1,000 years old.
3 She was a student who was 23 years old.
4 She began a protest that lasted for two years.
5 She was a good example of an activist who is concerned with a single issue.
6 In 1918, the suffragettes finally won the women's vote after a battle that had lasted 29 years.
7 The suffragettes and the Civil Rights movement were both important forces for change in the twentieth century.

> **TIP**
> - When plural nouns are used adjectivally, e.g. *a 180-foot tree*, they usually become singular, e.g. *feet* > *foot*.
> - Adjectives disappear if the meaning is obvious, e.g. *tall* when talking about the height of a tree.

B Find words or expressions in the text to express the underlined parts of the sentences below more efficiently.

1. Membership of political parties has recently fallen to the smallest numbers that there have ever been. (*paragraph 1*)
   Membership of political parties has recently fallen to record low levels.
2. Our festival is a great community event, and everybody in the village has a role to play in the various activities. (*paragraph 1*)
3. Our party is a very broad political group, and in it you can find lots of slightly different ideas. (*paragraph 2*)
4. Barbara is not interested in traditional political parties. She believes that fighting for just one political cause is the only way to change anything. (*paragraph 3*)
5. We believe that our new party is one that the world is now ready to listen to and follow. (*paragraph 4*)
6. The Civil Rights movement in America in the 1950s and 1960s was one that deeply affected everybody everywhere. (*paragraph 4*)

C Make statements from the notes. Use language from the table to turn the percentages into appropriate expressions of proportion.

Some statistics from the recent city elections:

1. Population registered to vote: 79%
   Just under four-fifths of the population were registered to vote.
   Or:
   Approximately four out of five of the population were registered to vote.
2. Electorate who actually voted: 62%
3. Those over 50 who took part in the election: 76%
4. Voters aged 18-30 who voted: 25%
5. Those in the age range 30-40 who took part: 34%
6. Votes for the winning candidate, Sally Driscoll: 42%
7. Electors voting for the runner-up, David May: 39%
8. Votes going to the other five candidates: 19%

fewer than *just under* *a little under* *nearly* *almost*	*(one) out of (five)* *(three) out of (eight)* *(seven) out of (ten)*
exactly *about* *around* *roughly* *approximately*	*half* *a third* *a quarter* *a tenth*
just over *a little over* *more than* *well over*	*(two) thirds* *(three) quarters* *(four) fifths* *(five) sixths* *(six) sevenths* *(seven) eighths* *(nine) tenths*

3 LISTENING

> ZENTRALE KLASSENARBEIT Hörverstehen (S. 175)

3 7 **Beantworten Sie auf Deutsch die unten stehenden Fragen zum Hörtext in ganzen Sätzen.**

1. Was wird für den Londoner Flughafen Heathrow geplant?
2. Warum behauptet Terry, dass die Regierung nicht auf die normalen Bürger hört?
3. Mit welchen Argumenten unterstützt die Regierung laut Julie den Ausbau des Flughafens?
4. Warum ist der Flughafen so gefährlich?
5. Mit welcher Begründung glaubt Julie, dass der Ausbau unmöglich ist?
6. Welchen Vorschlag hat Julie für den Flughafen?

4 COMPOSITION

> EXAM PREPARATION
> Materialgestützter Aufsatz (S. 173)

Refer to at least three of the following: the text on page 119, the comments in 1B on page 120, the materials below, and write about the following: *Is violence ever acceptable as a form of protest?* Use the phrases below.

1 *"An eye for an eye makes the whole world blind." "There are many causes that I am prepared to die for but no causes that I am prepared to kill for."*

Mahatma Gandhi, leader of the non-violent protest movement that helped end British rule in India in 1947

Paul Watson's Wild Mission to Save the Oceans

2

The Sea Shepherd Conservation Society is a non-governmental direct action environmental organization founded by Paul Watson over thirty years ago to protect the world's sea life. Since then he has been 'hunting' whaling and fishing ships at sea and attacking them with his own private army of followers.

When Watson is at sea, he does what he thinks is right, even if it means using violence or destroying property. If rules interfere with his goals, then to hell with rules! This is particularly true when whales are at issue. Watson believes that the killing of whales is the equivalent of murder. Within the animal-rights community, Watson is considered to be a hero by many.

Those who speak badly of Watson are just as firm in their opinions. Officials in many countries have criticized his methods and some have even called him a terrorist. He has been banned from meetings of the International Whaling Commission since

1986, when the Sea Shepherd sank two whaling ships in Reykjavik. Many believe that this attack negatively influenced Icelandic opinion of the cause of saving whales. Sidney Holt, a sea life expert, believes Watsons's involvement is "an absolute disaster" and has done more to damage progress than to end whaling.

Adapted from an article by Raffi Khatchadourian in *The New Yorker*, November 5, 2007

whaling *Walfang* • interfere *behindern* • firm *dezidiert* • cause *Sache*

Stuttgart-21-Gegner randalieren am Hauptbahnhof

3

28.03.11

Stuttgart - Wenige Stunden nach dem historischen Wahldebakel von Schwarz-Gelb in Baden-Württemberg ist es am Stuttgarter Hauptbahnhof zu Ausschreitungen gekommen. Mehrere Dutzend Gegner des umstrittenen Bahnprojekts „Stuttgart 21“ rissen am Sonntagabend Bauzäune am Nordflügel des Bahnhofs um. Nach Polizeiangaben wurden bei der spontanen Protestaktion mindestens zwei Beamte und ein Passant verletzt.

Source: dapd

Introduction:
Recent violent protests against Stuttgart 21 make us think again about the role of violence when expressing an opinion ...

Arguments:
Many people believe that ...
However, there are also many people who support ...
For example, ... For instance, ... To give an/another example, ...
Moreover, it is important to say that ... Again, we should remember that ...
Against that, it needs to be said that ... On the other hand, we must not forget that ...

Conclusion:
The arguments for and against violent protest are complex, but all in all it seems clear that ...
So, to summarize, ...

C Further options

1 DISCUSSING A POEM

A Discuss the poem and its ideas.

1 Say in one sentence what the poem is about.
2 Imagine what is happening between the verses.

B Talk about your own experiences.

Discuss any experience of generational conflict in your own life (or the lives of people that you know).

2 DOING A ROLE-PLAY

Work with a partner and do the following activities.

1 Work out what the girl is probably saying between the verses in the poem. Write down your ideas.
2 Take turns to be the girl and the speaker in the poem. Act out the argument.

Dress Sense *by David Kitchen* 3 8

You're not going out in that, are you?
I've never seen anything
More ridiculous in my whole life.
You look like you've been dragged
Through a hedge backwards
And lost half your dress along the way.

What's wrong with it?
You're asking me what's wrong with it?
Everything: that's what.
It's loud, it's common,
It reveals far too much of your ...
Your ... well your 'what you shouldn't be revealing'.

No, I'm not going to explain;
You know very well what I mean, young lady
But you choose to ignore
Every single piece of reasonable helpful advice
That you are offered.

It's not just the neckline I'm talking about
- And you can hardly describe it as a neckline,
More like a navel-line
If you bother to observe the way that it plunges.
Have you taken a look at the back?
(What little there is of it.)
Have you?

Boys are only going to think
One thing
When they see you in that outfit.
Where on earth did you get it?
And don't tell me that my money paid for it
Whatever you do.

You found it where?

Well, it probably looked different on her
And, anyway, you shouldn't be going through
Your mother's old clothes.

dress sense *Sinn für Kleidung*
3 ridiculous *lächerlich*
4 drag *schleifen*
5 hedge *Hecke*
10 loud *grell, schreiend*
10 common *gewöhnlich, ordinär*
11 reveal *zeigen*
16 reasonable *vernünftig*
18 neckline *Ausschnitt*
19 hardly *wohl kaum*
20 navel *Bauchnabel*
21 bother *sich die Mühe machen*
21 observe *sich ansehen*
21 plunge *tief fallen*

D Grammar checkpoint

1 PARTICIPLE CLAUSES 1

> Grammar summary S. 188

Join the pairs of sentences. Use the word in brackets with the correct sentence and change the following verb into an *ing* participle.

1 Joey first got high on medical drugs at the age of 13. He grew up in a small town in Vermont. (*while*)
Joey first got high on medical drugs at the age of 13 while growing up in a small town in Vermont.
2 He had used these drugs for two years. He finally allowed peer-group pressure to push him into trying heroin. (*after*)
3 He took this dangerous step. He had always been determined to avoid heroin because of all the frightening stories about it. (*before*)
4 He took the powerful new drug. He quickly found himself 'on the clouds'. (*on*)
5 He began selling heroin to pay for his $400-a-day habit. He moved from 'snorting' to using a needle. (*after*)
6 He studied at the University of Vermont. He knew he was reaching 'the bottom' and decided to visit the university's drug treatment centre. (*while*)
7 Soon after that, he realized that he really must break his addiction. He saw his best friend die of a drug overdose. (*on*)
8 He finally got clear of heroin ten months ago. He looks back on the whole experience now and says, 'I wouldn't wish it on my worst enemy.' (*after*)

2 PARTICIPLE CLAUSES 2

> Grammar summary S. 188

Change the relative clauses (starting with *who*, *which*, *that*) to *ing* or *ed* participle clauses. See the example below.

Sheena Alston, social worker

Sheena Alston is an experienced social worker who works for Redbridge Social Services and who is employed in the Children's Services Department.

For many years her job was to find suitable homes for children who had been taken into care from broken homes and from families which had a history of violence. She had special responsibility for children who came from ethnic backgrounds, and it was her job to find 'foster' families which offered these children similar ethnic backgrounds.

More recently, she has taken over a newly created section that is called 'Friends and Family' and that is tasked with the job of placing children with relatives or with family friends. The children who are brought into the system often have serious psychological problems, and their successful placement is a job which requires hard work and great care both by Sheena and by the new families. However, a good result also brings great happiness to the child, to the family – and of course to Sheena herself.

*Sheena Alston is an experienced social worker **working** for Redbridge Social Services and **employed** in the Children's Services Department.*

10 Multiculturalism

FOCUS

1 **Look at the picture of a typical London market scene. Use the words in the box to talk about the ethnic minorities you can see.**

> Afro-Caribbean | black | British Asian | Indian | Pakistani | white
> +
> bindi (red spot) | hijab (headscarf) | sari | turban

2 **Which different cultures live in your region or neighbourhood? Which do you belong to?**

3 **Do you have social contact with people of other cultures? Where? When?**

A Personal perspectives

BEFORE YOU READ

A Read the title and say what the story could be about.

B How would you expect a 'fanatic' to behave?

My Son the Fanatic

Hanif Kureishi's short story is set in East London. Parvez, a 40-year-old Pakistani taxi driver, has been living in England for almost 20 years. He is worried about his son, Ali, who is behaving strangely. Now, Parvez has taken a night off to take Ali out for a meal. In this extract he is telling Bettina, his friend and confidant, about that evening ...

This time Parvez was trembling. Bettina put her arms around him.

"What's happened?"

"I've just had the worst experience of my life."

As Bettina rubbed his head Parvez told her that the previous evening he and Ali had gone to a restaurant. As they studied the menu, the waiter, whom Parvez knew, brought him his usual whisky and water. Parvez had been so nervous he had even prepared a question. He was going to ask Ali if he was worried about his imminent exams. But first, wanting to relax, he loosened his tie, crunched a popadom and took a long drink.

Before Parvez could speak, Ali made a face.

"Don't you know it's wrong to drink alcohol?" he said.

"He spoke to me very harshly," Parvez told Bettina. "I was about to castigate the boy for being insolent, but managed to control myself."

He had explained patiently to Ali that for years he had worked more than ten hours a day, that he had few enjoyments or hobbies and never went on holiday. Surely it wasn't a crime to have a drink when he wanted one?

"But it is forbidden," the boy said.

Parvez shrugged, "I know."

"And so is gambling, isn't it?"

"Yes. But surely we are only human?"

Each time Parvez took a drink, the boy winced, or made a fastidious face as an accompaniment. This made Parvez drink more quickly. The waiter, wanting to please his friend, brought another glass of whisky. Parvez knew he was getting drunk, but he couldn't stop himself. Ali had a horrible look on his face, full of disgust and censure. It was as if he hated his father.

Halfway through the meal Parvez suddenly lost his temper and threw a plate on the floor. He had felt like ripping the cloth from the table, but the waiters and other customers were staring at him. Yet he wouldn't stand for his own son telling him the difference between right and wrong. He knew he wasn't a bad man. He had a conscience. There were a few things of which he was ashamed, but on the whole he had lived a decent life. "When have I had time to be wicked?" he asked Ali.

In a low monotonous voice the boy explained that Parvez had not, in fact, lived a good life. He had broken countless rules of the Koran.

"For instance?" Parvez demanded.

7 imminent *bevorstehend*
8 crunch *kauen, im Mund zerbrechen*
popadom *Papadam (knuspriger dünner Fladen)*
11 castigate *züchtigen*
12 insolent *unverschämt*
17 shrug *mit den Schultern zucken*
20 wince *zusammenzucken*
fastidious *nörgelnd*
26 rip *reißen*
30 decent *anständig*
wicked *böse, gottlos*

Ali hadn't needed time to think. As if he had been waiting for this moment, he asked his father if he didn't relish pork pies.

"Well ..."

Parvez

Parvez couldn't deny that he loved crispy bacon smothered with mushrooms and mustard and sandwiched between slices of fried bread. In fact, he ate this for breakfast every morning.

Ali then reminded Parvez that he had ordered his own wife to cook pork sausages, saying to her, "You're not in the village now, this is England. We have to fit in!"

Parvez was so annoyed and perplexed by this attack that he called for more drink.

"The problem is this," the boy said. He leaned across the table. For the first time that night his eyes were alive. "You are too implicated in Western civilisation."

Parvez burped; he thought he was going to choke.

"Implicated!" he said. "But we live here!"

"The Western materialists hate us," Ali said. "Papa, how can you love something which hates you?"

"What is the answer then?" Parvez said miserably. "According to you."

Ali addressed his father fluently, as if Parvez were a rowdy crowd that had to be quelled and convinced. The Law of Islam would rule the world; the skin of the infidel would burn off again and again; the Jews and Christians would be routed. The West was a sink of hypocrites, adulterers, homosexuals, drug takers and prostitutes.

As Ali talked, Parvez looked out of the window as if to check that they were still in London.

Parvez' son Ali

"My people have taken enough. If the persecution doesn't stop there will be *jihad*. I, and millions of others, will gladly give our lives for the cause."

"But why, why?" Parvez said.

"For us the reward will be in paradise."

"Paradise!"

Finally, as Parvez's eyes filled with tears, the boy urged him to mend his ways.

"How is that possible?" Parvez asked.

"Pray," Ali said. "Pray beside me."

Parvez called for the bill and ushered his boy out of the restaurant as soon as he was able. He couldn't take any more. Ali sounded as if he'd swallowed someone else's voice.

On the way home the boy sat in the back of the taxi, as if he were a customer. "What has made you like this?" Parvez asked him, afraid that somehow he was to blame for all this. "Is there a particular event which has influenced you?"

"Living in this country."

"But I love England," Parvez said, watching his boy in the mirror. "They let you do almost anything here."

"That is the problem," he replied. (830 words)

35 relish *genießen*
37 smother *bedecken*
42 be implicated in *Teil von etw sein*
43 burp *aufstoßen*
choke *ersticken*
49 quell *bezwingen, beherrschen*
infidel *Ungläubige/r*
50 be routed *besiegen*
51 sink *hier: Sumpf*
hypocrite *Heuchler/in*
adulterer *Ehebrecher*
55 persecution *Hetzjagd*
62 urge *drängen*
mend one's ways *sich bessern*
65 usher out *hinausführen*

1 LOOKING AT THE TEXT

A Read the text and do the following activities.

1 Describe the setting of the incident and say from whose point of view it is told.
2 Copy and complete the table below. Outline Parvez's and Ali's conflicting opinions.

Parvez	*Ali*
drinks alcohol (whisky)	*rejects alcohol because it's against the Koran*

B Say what you think.

1 Explain the conflict between Parvez and Ali.
2 Describe Ali's idea of Muslim cultural identity in Britain and compare it to his father's.
3 Why do you think Ali has become a fanatic?

2 WORKING WITH WORDS

A Collect verbs and verb phrases that Hanif Kureishi uses to describe Ali's reaction to his father's behaviour.

Think about body language (facial expressions or gestures) that shows Ali's attitude, e.g. *(to) make a face*, as well as expressions such as *(to) speak harshly to sb, (to) be forbidden,* etc.

B How does Parvez defend himself against Ali's criticisms?

Find expressions Parvez uses to persuade his son that he is a hard-working and decent man who has integrated into English society, e.g. *(to) have few enjoyments/hobbies*, etc.

3 IMAGE ANALYSIS

> EXAM PREPARATION
> Bildbeschreibung mit Analyse (S. 172)

Wearing a Hijab (headscarf) in public is now banned in France. Describe what you can see in the photograph. Explain the women's message and relate it back to the text on page 126/7. Use the phrases below.

in the centre | (to) hold | (to) protest (against) | (to) wear | (to) claim | headscarf | poster

B The bigger picture

BEFORE YOU READ

A **How would you describe the racial make-up of America?**

B **What do you think the 'new face of America' (see the title of the text) could be like?**

The New Face of America

Leo Jimenez

Vin Diesel

Jessica Alba

Leo Jimenez, 25, is a New York model. His high cheekbones and jet-colored black hair and eyes suggest Asian or American-Indian ancestry. In fact, Jimenez is Colombian by birth, a product of the mixed racial heritage of that Latin-American country. He says his melting-pot looks have definitely opened doors for him.

People like Jimenez are both defining and benefiting from a big shift in American attitudes to race, a shift that has led Louis Vuitton, YSL Beauty and H&M to employ racially-mixed models. The popularity of movie stars like Vin Diesel and Jessica Alba with young audiences is due in part to their diverse ethnic backgrounds - and the same applies to sports stars like Derek Jeter and Tiger Woods.

"Today what's ethnically neutral, diverse or simply unclear has tremendous appeal," says Ron Berger, the chief executive of a New York advertising and trend-research company.

The new attitudes are evident not only in fashion, the media and entertainment. Nearly 7 million Americans said they were members of more than one race in the 2000 census. In addition, more than 14 million Hispanics - about 42 percent of Hispanic respondents - ticked "some other race".

The increasingly multiracial American population, demographers say, is due to intermarriage - which has become much more common and socially acceptable since the ending of segregation in the 1960s - and to waves of mixed-race immigrants, particularly from Latin America.

The multiracial bonus

For decades, art directors, magazine editors and casting agents wanted tall, blond, blue-eyed models and actors. But now the demand for the "Nordic look" is on its way out. Vin Diesel, 36, the star of action movies like *The Fast and the Furious* (2001) once hid his racial heritage by saying that his mother is Irish and his father's race unknown. But now he admits that his racial mix has been a big career asset that has enabled him to play all types of roles and many ethnicities.

Even megastars like Jennifer Lopez and Christina Aguilera borrow from diverse cultures and ethnic backgrounds. Lopez, who is Puerto Rican, features as a mixed-race Latina-Asian princess in the latest Louis Vuitton ad, while Aguilera, half Ecuadorean, poses as an Indian film star on a recent cover of *Allure* magazine.

According to Linda Wells, the magazine's editor-in-chief, this reflects a current fascination with the racial hybrid. "Uniformity just isn't appealing anymore," she says.

A recent study by the Lewis Mumford Center at the State University of New York at Albany noted that while nearly half of Hispanics chose the "some other race" category in the 2000 census, a big majority of Hispanics had chosen the "white" category 20 years earlier. "There used to be a sense that to be white was to have arrived," says John R. Logan, the Mumford Center's director. "Today there's a trend towards rejecting whiteness as a badge of success."

(479 words)

1 LOOKING AT THE TEXT

> EXAM PREPARATION
> Mediation (S. 171)

A **Sie arbeiten für eine erfolgreiche deutsche Modelagentur. Sie haben den englischen Bericht über kulturelle Integration gelesen und möchten Ihren Chef überzeugen, mehr Models mit unterschiedlichem kulturellem Hintergrund einzustellen. Schreiben Sie ihm eine E-Mail mit den passenden Informationen aus dem Text. Übersetzen Sie den Text nicht Wort für Wort.**

B **Find information in the article to support the following quotations.**

1 Ron Berger: "Today what's ethnically neutral, diverse or simply unclear has tremendous appeal."
2 Linda Wells: "Uniformity just isn't appealing anymore."
3 John R. Logan: "Today there's a trend towards rejecting whiteness as a badge of success."

C **Say what you think.**

1 Do you agree with Ron Berger and Linda Wells? Say why (not).
2 Can you name any German racially-mixed celebrities? Think particularly of sport and pop music.

2 WORKING WITH WORDS

A **The words in the table are all from the text. Give the missing verb or noun forms.**

B **Use some of the words from the table to write six sentences.**

Leave gaps where the words should go. Then swap your sentences with a partner. Can you complete each other's sentences?

	Verb	*Noun*
1	*(to) suggest*	...
2	...	*product*
3	*(to) employ*	...
4	...	*entertainment*
5	...	*respondent*
6	...	*marriage*
7	...	*segregation*
8	...	*action*
9	...	*fascination*
10	*(to) choose*	...
11	*(to) arrive*	...
12	...	*director*

3 SUMMARY

Read the dialogue and summarize the main points in English using your own words.

KATE I think a lot of Europeans have a completely out-dated idea of what America's really like.
MIKE Oh? What makes you say that?
KATE Well, just to start with, a lot of people think that black Americans make up the biggest minority. But that's no longer true. I read that people of Spanish origin – you know, "Hispanics" – now outnumber African-Americans.
MIKE Really? I didn't know that.
KATE Today, about 15% of the total population say that they are Hispanic. The comparable figure for Blacks is just over 13%.
MIKE OK. And the hispanic population is growing much faster, isn't it?
KATE Right. The black – and by the way also the white – share of the population is actually shrinking. But what I really wanted to say is that people of mixed race are becoming just as important as the traditional minorities.

MIKE Oh, yes. Now you mention it, I remember reading something about that. That was one finding of the last US census, wasn't it?

KATE Yes, it was. For the first time, people were allowed to name more than one race in the 2000 census. And a lot of people did so.

MIKE What, before 2000 you could only give Black or White?

KATE Of course not, Mike. But you could only give one race. You know, African-American, Caucasian, Hispanic, Asian, Native American and so on. Take sports stars like Derek Jeter and Tiger Woods, for example. They're both a fairly complicated racial mix, but until 2000 they were just Black.

Derek Jeter

Tiger Woods

4 LISTENING

3 11 **A Beantworten Sie auf Deutsch die unten stehenden Fragen zum Hörtext in ganzen Sätzen.**

> ZENTRALE KLASSENARBEIT
Hörverstehen (S. 175)

1 Worum geht es hauptsächlich in der Diskussion?
2 Wer nimmt an der Diskussion teil?
3 Welcher Teilnehmer befürwortet harte Strafen für illegale Einwanderer?
4 Sie sind Besitzer einer großen Farm in Südkalifornien. Welcher der beiden Teilnehmer versteht Ihre Sorgen besser?

B Hören Sie sich die Diskussion noch einmal an und ergänzen Sie das Raster mit Informationen aus dem Hörtext.

	Frank	*Julia*
Wieviele illegale mexikanische Einwanderer gibt es?	…	…
Warum wurde die illegale Einwanderung toleriert?		…
In welchen Bereichen arbeiten die illegalen Einwanderer?	… … … …	… … …
Was sollte man mit illegalen Einwanderern tun?	…	… …
Warum braucht die Wirtschaft illegale Einwanderer?		…
Warum braucht die Wirtschaft illegale Einwanderer nicht?	…	

5 COMPOSITION

> EXAM PREPARATION
> Materialgestützter Aufsatz (S. 173)

Refer to at least three of the materials below and write about the following: ***What is the role of Mexican immigrants in the United States?*** **Use the phrases below.**

Introduction:
Now that the number of Mexican immigrants in American has grown, we should ask ourselves the question: what role do they play in the USA?
Arguments:
The graph shows ... The cartoon contrasts the dual role of Mexican immigrants ...
The American attitude toward Mexicans is often contradictory: on the one hand, they need Mexicans for work ... However, on the other hand, ...
Moreover, ... What is more, ... Not only ..., but ... also ...
Conclusion:
To conclude, ... On the whole, ... It is clear that ...

1

Mexican population of the USA 1930–2008

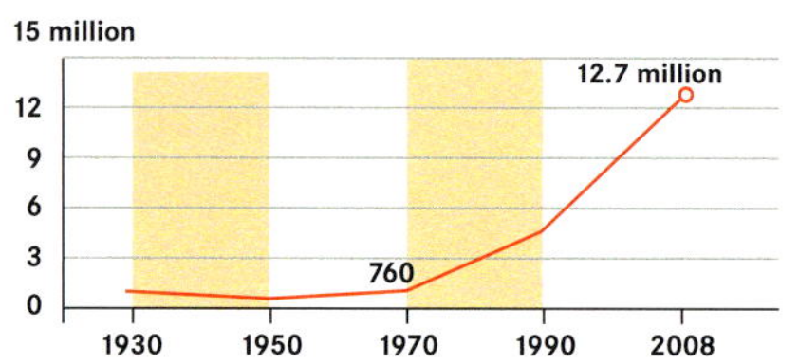

Source: Pew Hispanic Center

2

Illegal Mexican families with children in the USA, 2008

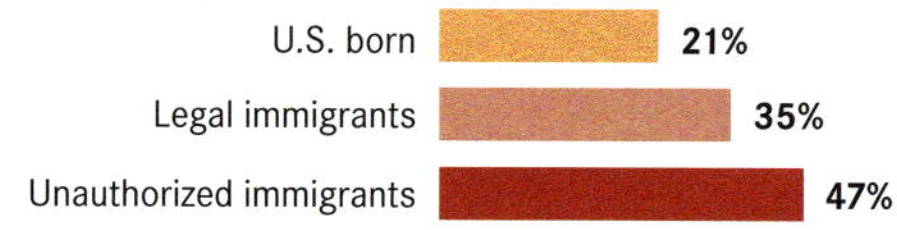

NOTE: Figures do not add to 100 due to rounding.

Source: Pew Hispanic Center

3

Wirtschaft hängt von illegalen Arbeitskräften ab

Die illegale Einwanderung mexikanischer Migranten in die Vereinigten Staaten ist ein hoch profitables Geschäft für amerikanische Arbeitgeber.

Die US-Regierung lässt es zu, dass arme Mexikaner einreisen und illegal für gewinnhungrige US-Arbeitgeber arbeiten, hauptsächlich in der Landwirtschaft und der Lebensmittelindustrie, aber Privathaushalte und Pflegeeinrichtungen profitieren auch davon. Ökonomen behaupten, dass die Wirtschaft in dem Südwesten der USA von diesen Billigarbeitskräften mittlerweile in hohem Maße abhängig ist.

From an Internet forum

4

5

H-2B Program helps small businesses

On Thursday, nine men will arrive from Mexico and start working in gardens across Augusta County the next day. They are part of the H-2B Visa Program that allows small, seasonal businesses to hire temporary workers from outside of the United States.

Chapman Williams, owner of the gardening business in Augusta County, claims, "If I didn't have full-time workers from Mexico, my business would have gone bankrupt years ago. It's not about cheap labour, because I have to pay the government fees to be part of the program. It's about the reliability that I can count on them coming to work and doing their job well. Sometimes people ask me why I hire workers from Mexico when we are having problems with unemployment in our own country ... Well, the rules of the program mean that I have to look for American workers first, before I look abroad. It is hard to find people here as the hours are long and it is hard work."

Source: whsv.com

C Further options

1 LOOKING AT THE SITUATION

You are on a student exchange programme in the USA. As a part of a project on immigration, you have been asked to answer questions on the situation in Germany.

With a partner, brainstorm what you know about immigration in Germany.

2 RESEARCHING THE TOPIC

Now with your partner use your ideas and the information in the portfolio below to ask and answer at least five questions (see examples) on immigration in Germany.

- *What percentage of the total population are foreigners or people of foreign descent?*
- *Which is/are the biggest group(s) of immigrants?*
- ...

THE PORTFOLIO

The German labour market

Population (2005): 82.4 million, expected to fall to 69–74 million by 2050*
Foreigners / People of foreign parentage as percentage of total (2006): 8.2% or 6.8 million*
People with migration background, including naturalized German citizens (*Spätaussiedler*) and their children: 18.6% or 15.3 million*

Avergage age of total population (2008): 42, expected to rise to 50 by 2050*
Average age of immigrant population: 31.7

Foreign employees as percentage of total labour force (2006): 9.1%**

Foreign population as of 31st December 2006, 10 most common citizenships

Citizenship	Total
Turkish	1,738,831
Italian	534,657
Polish	361,696
Serbian-Montenegrin	316,823
Greek	303,761
Croatian	227,510
Russian	187,514
Austrian	175,653
Bosnian-Herzegovinian	157,094
Ukrainian	128,950

*Federal Statistics Office
**OECD

Development of immigration

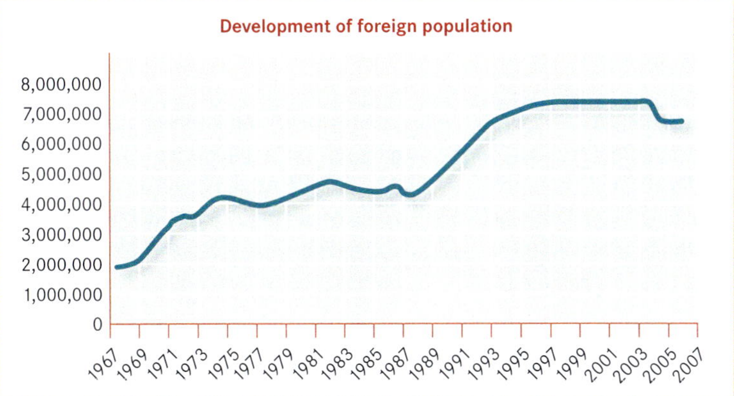

Quelle: Federal Statistics Office, Wiesbaden

3 COMPILING YOUR INFORMATION

Finally, compare your results with others and compile a catalogue of questions and answers for the class as a whole.

D Grammar checkpoint

1 REPORTED SPEECH – STATEMENTS

> Grammar summary S. 181

Read the statements and report the information.

1. There will soon be over ten million illegal immigrants in California alone.
   Governor Schwarzenegger complained that ...
2. Fewer immigrants crossed the Rio Grande last year.
   However, he added that ... the year before.
3. The US government has decided to build a fence along the border.
   The Mayor of San Diego said that ...
4. Surveillance cameras have been installed at every crossing point.
   An immigration official told reporters that ...
5. Maria Sanchez: "To be effective, the fence must be at least eight feet high."
   Ms Sanchez pointed out that ...
6. Maria Sanchez: "They are also going to introduce much stricter border controls."
   She went on to say that they ...

2 REPORTED SPEECH – QUESTIONS

> Grammar summary S. 183

A border guard has stopped a Mexican driver at a crossing point near San Diego. Report his questions.

1. "Can you understand English?"
   The guard asked the truck driver ...
2. "Do you have a valid entry visa?"
   He inquired ...
3. "May I see your vehicle papers, please?"
   The guard asked politely ...
4. "What is the purpose of your visit to the USA?"
   Then he wanted to know ...
5. "Where are you staying in California?"
   After that, he asked ...
6. "How long do you plan to stay in California?"
   He was interested to know ...

3 REPORTED SPEECH – INTRODUCTORY VERBS

> Grammar summary S. 181

Report the comments using as many different introductory verbs as you can.
These comments were made at a citizens' meeting in San Diego to discuss the problem of illegal immigration in southern California.

JEB DALE: In my opinion, the only answer is to build a high fence along the whole border. I'm a border guard and it's impossible to seal off a virtually open frontier.

SALLY-ANN MORRIS: Yes, but is that feasible? The fence would have to be at least eight feet high and the border's 1,400 miles long, for goodness' sake.

TOM BARNS: And it's not just the fence, either. There's the infrastructure, too – surveillance cameras and so on. And I know what I'm talking about, folks. I read something once about the iron curtain in Europe. You wouldn't believe it!

MADDY BARNS: It's good you mentioned the iron curtain. Is that what we really want? I mean do we want to build an iron curtain right across America?

ANNA GARCIA: I agree with that. No way! I think we need to do two things. First, a general amnesty for all illegal immigrants who already live and work here and, second, a fair quota system for poor Mexicans like for anybody else.

CARL HARMS: Well, I sure am glad that somebody has at last mentioned work, because that's what this is all about. I'm a fruit farmer and I'd go bust without the Mexicans, legal or illegal. The fact is, we need these people as much as they need us.

11

Main Course

Crime

FOCUS

1 Link the captions a–c to the cartoons 1–3.

a "... and our patience is exhausted. If you don't pay the ransom this year, we will ..."
b "You must admit, a strict diet, no alcohol and early to bed certainly keep you fit."
c "Open up, Benny. We know you're there. Fraud Squad."

2 Use the words and expressions below and the captions to describe the cartoons.

(to) be like a film set | (to) become an adult | breakout | (to) break out of/escape from prison | (to) deceive/trick sb into thinking sth | in captivity | kidnapper | (to) look over one's shoulder | victim (of a crime)

3 Which of these crimes do the cartoons focus on?

- graffiti-spraying
- kidnapping
- burglary
- escaping from prison
- drink driving
- shoplifting
- fraud
- armed robbery

4 Which of the eight crimes above do you think is the most/least serious? Why?

(to) be irresponsible | (to) be (relatively) trivial | minor/serious/trivial crime | (to) cause death/serious injury | (to) often involve children | (to) only involve property

1

2

3

A Personal perspectives

BEFORE YOU READ

A **Look at the headline and photos. What do you think the press report could be about?**

B **The US Constitution forbids 'cruel and unusual punishment' but the Supreme Court ruled that the death penalty is constitutional. What, then, do you think is meant by 'cruel and unusual punishment'?**

Karla Faye Tucker has an important place in American legal history. Her execution for murder broke the convention that women were not given the death penalty. Read on to find out more.

Execution by lethal injection
Death by lethal injection is painless. The victim is given a massive dose of a combination of fast-acting anaesthetics. Victims usually go into a coma almost immediately and die within about ten minutes.

3 12

A step too far?

1 ...

On the morning of Karla Faye Tucker's execution by lethal injection on 3 February 1998, the Governor's Office in Austin, Texas, received over 3,000 phone calls, faxes and emails, 80% of them asking the then governor, George W. Bush, to spare her life.

But nothing helped. Even if he had wanted to, Governor Bush felt he couldn't spare a convicted murderer's life 'just because she's a woman'. So the execution went ahead as planned, although even Texans – who routinely execute their killers without a thought – were troubled by it.

2 ...

By far the most important result of Ms Tucker's execution was to put an end to the legal convention that women may not be subjected to the death penalty. The last 'act of state' that discriminated between men and women simply because of their sex died with her. Since then, all attempts to save women from execution have similarly failed.

For feminists, Karla Faye's death was an awkward victory in the ongoing battle for equality with men. Whatever logic may say, many feel that equal wages and opportunity are one thing, capital and corporal punishment quite another. As civil rights activist Anna-Marie Barfield said, "Come on. We don't want to be that equal."

3 ...

The campaign for Karla Faye's life saw some surprising alliances. Civil rights campaigners, fundamentalist religious groups and male conservatives joined forces, although for widely differing reasons.

A large majority of civil righters are opposed to the death penalty on principle, seeing it as a 'cruel and unusual punishment' and hence unconstitutional. They also find the apparent racial bias repugnant. They would like to see the lives of all 369 offenders currently* on death row in Texas, of whom 40.9% are black and 27.9% Hispanic, spared.

Most fundamentalists are not opposed to capital punishment on principle – indeed, many are among its biggest fans – but nonetheless they thought that Ms Tucker's life should be spared. This was because during her 14 years on death row she had shown true remorse, had married a priest and had become a devout Christian. (The then Pope, John Paul II, agreed and sent a note to Governor Bush, himself a devout Christian, asking for clemency.)

Meanwhile, confused male conservatives just felt that women are, well, women and ought not to be executed. The more thoughtful among them pointed out that "as women don't kill by nature, those few that do must be insane".

4 ...

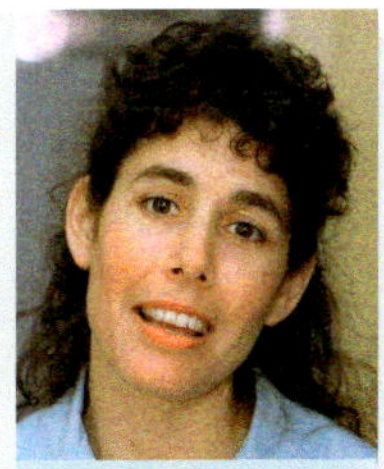

Karla Faye Tucker

Although many liberals also felt, at least in private, that executing women "somehow stinks", they were deeply worried by the passions aroused by the Tucker campaign. Would a reformed and repentant male have received such international attention? Would a black man who had killed an eldery white couple but then become a devout Muslim in prison have received such high-profile support? Almost certainly not. It was her sex and her prettiness and her uncanny natural ability to tear hearts on TV that made Karla Faye Tucker the campaigners' pin-up. (489 words)

* 15 February 2008

1 LOOKING AT THE TEXT

A Put four of these sub-headings into the text at the points shown.

Strange bedfellows | Public opinion | Women's lib? | What about victims' rights? | The liberal dilemma | Pleas for clemency

B Link the speech bubbles 1–8 to the people in the box. Say how you know.

an assistant in the Governor's Office, Austin, Texas | an aunt of Karla Faye's victim | a civil rights activist | a Christian fundamentalist | a feminist | Karla Faye's husband | a liberal | a male conservative

1. *Yes, gender equality can be really tough, but I believe inequality is even worse.*
2. *Being strapped to a bed and given a lethal injection is a cruel punishment. I believe humans deserve much better.*
3. *I'm not against capital punishment, but this is different. God has spoken to her. She's seen the Light.*
4. *I just feel that women – all women – should have our special protection and respect.*
5. *Look, Karla Faye Tucker's Christian, pretty and white, but what about the other 52 women on death row, not to mention the men?*
6. *This note has just arrived for the Governor. Guess who it's from?*
7. *What about victims' rights, I'd like to know? This woman killed our Jerry with an axe because she wanted to steal his motorcycle, for Pete's sake!*
8. *We didn't touch each other. We were only allowed to talk through a glass wall using microphones.*

2 WORKING WITH WORDS

Choose the most suitable connector, a) or b).

The US Supreme Court abolished the death penalty **a)** also | **b)** as[1] unconstitutional in 1972. **a)** However | **b)** Moreover[2], it was reintroduced in 1976 **a)** because of | **b)** because[3] a rise in violent crime **a)** what | **b)** which[4] many people saw **a)** as | **b)** like[5] being one result of abolition.

a) Furthermore | **b)** However[6], here we should be careful. The Supreme Court itself did not reintroduce capital punishment, **a)** and | **b)** but[7] only said that it was not unconstitutional – **a)** if | **b)** whether[8] to use it was for the states to decide.

Today, 36 states have reintroduced the death penalty, **a)** as a rule | **b)** in fact[9] by lethal injection **a)** because | **b)** while[10] this method is said to be more humane. **a)** But | **b)** Thus[11] this number can be a little misleading **a)** also | **b)** as[12] six of these states have not used the death penalty at all since reintroducing it, **a)** and | **b)** whereas[13] four more have only used it once. **a)** Moreover | **b)** Though[14] two-thirds of all executions since 1977 have been carried out in just five states, by far the most, 408, in Texas.

3 COMPOSITION

> **EXAM PREPARATION**
> Materialgestützter Aufsatz (S. 173)

Using the comments on page 137 and the materials below answer the following: Should the death penalty be abolished completely?

1

JUSTICE PARTY

BRING BACK THE DEATH PENALTY

Our world is full of murderers and terrorists, but we want a country that is safe for everyone again. We believe the only way to get it is to punish such crimes with death. Consider these points:

- The murderer will never murder again.
- Society delivers the justice of retribution.
- That retribution has a deterrent effect on others.
- Execution allows the victim's loved ones to 'draw a line' under their terrible experience.
- Every prisoner costs society £100,000 a year: execution is cheaper than life imprisonment.

2

Kommentar: Gerechtigkeit – aber zu welchem Preis?

Weltweit haben bereits etwa zwei Drittel aller Länder die Todesstrafe aus dem Gesetz gestrichen oder wenden sie nicht mehr an. Zu den Ländern, die sie noch praktizieren, gehören die USA, China und Russland, und in Großbritannien gewinnt die JUSTICE Party stark an Bedeutung und spricht sich für die Wiedereinführung der Todesstrafe in Mordfällen aus.

In jedem Rechtssystem geschehen Fehler, und infolgedessen werden zuweilen unschuldige Menschen hingerichtet. Wo liegt da die Gerechtigkeit? Bedenken wir auch, dass die überwältigende Mehrheit von Mordfällen im Affekt verübt werden. Häufig liegt auch eine psychische Störung des Täters vor. Sind wir dazu berechtigt, solchen Tätern die Chance auf Rehabilitierung zu verweigern? Genau dies erweist sich als ethisches Problem für die Gesellschaft. Indem wir die Todesstrafe zulassen, werden wir am Ende alle zu Mördern. Erinnern wir uns: Die Europäische Menschenrechtskonvention untersagt die Todesstrafe, und laut der UN-Menschenrechtscharta hat jeder Mensch das Recht auf Leben.

3

Two wrongs do not make a right.
An eye for an eye, a tooth for a tooth.

Common English sayings

4

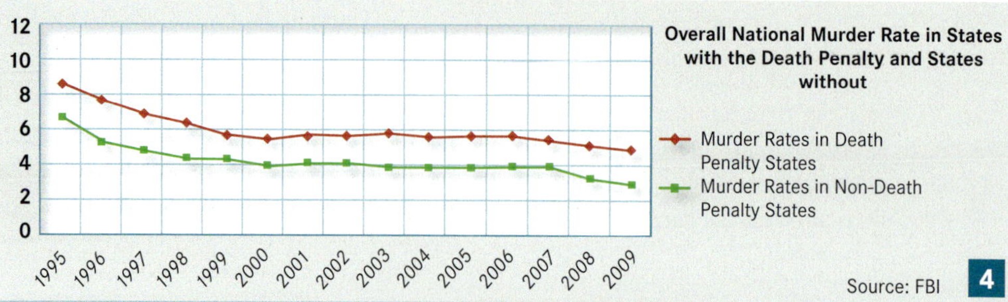

Source: FBI

B The bigger picture

BEFORE YOU READ

What do you think the title of the text means?

3 13

A stitch in time saves nine

In the late 1980s, New York City was sliding into lawlessness and chaos. South Bronx was just one of several 'no-go areas'; even the police only went there in heavily-armed groups. In 1991, the worst year for crime, the New York Police Department (NYPD) registered 2,245 murders, 2,818 rapes and 100,280 robberies. Few New Yorkers dared to use the subway or go into Central Park after dark. The city was fast becoming ungovernable.

Ten years later, New York had gone from being among America's most dangerous big cities to being one of its safest. In 2001, there were 633 murders, a drop of over 70%, 1,530 rapes and 27,229 robberies. And the subway? It had become one of the cleanest, safest and most efficient transport systems in the country. And that change has continued. In 2009, for example, the number of murders fell to 471, down a further 26% on the 2001 figure.

What made this turnaround possible? First, there was a sea change in public opinion. Ordinary, decent, tolerant New Yorkers wanted their big apple back - and were willing to support a tough new mayor, Rudolph Giuliani, and a tough new police chief, William J. Bratton, to do it.

Bratton's first step was to clean up the NYPD itself. The force was rotten with drug abuse, bribery, racism and nepotism. That is one reason why Giuliani hired Bratton from Boston. He was a stranger to New York; he owed no favours. And Bratton was merciless. Corrupt officers were weeded out with 'zero tolerance'. That is where the term really comes from. They were not only sacked with the loss of all pension rights, but they were also prosecuted and given tough sentences. The 'bad apples' were replaced by 2,000 better-educated officers taken from all of New York's communities. Great efforts were also made to build bridges and show a human face to all the city's ethnic groups.

After cleaning up the police, Bratton then introduced a policy called 'Crimes and Quality of Life' (CQL). "In the past, we just cut down trees," said Bratton. "But that's not enough. You must kill the seeds, so that the trees never grow. That's what CQL is all about."

To stop the seeds from growing into trees, the new and reformed NYPD focused on seven main areas: drug dealing, domestic violence, bad and threatening behaviour in public places, car theft, guns on the street, school violence and graffiti spraying. A special part of all this was the 'broken windows' approach. The basic idea is that low-level crime such as bad behaviour and graffiti spraying - and breaking windows - have to be stopped immediately. Otherwise, those who do these things will move on to more serious law breaking.

"I told my officers never ever to look the other way," said Bratton. "It's like in school. The biggest deterrent isn't getting punished, but getting caught."

Of course, these methods require a large number of police officers out on the streets. And with a force of roughly 40,000 - the largest in the country - the NYPD has the strength it needs to give New York today the lowest crime rate out of the 25 largest cities in the USA.

And it worked. As the seeds of crime were weeded out, the incidence of more serious crimes fell as well. "There's no such thing as a trivial crime," Bratton told his officers. "Never forget that most armed robbers started out as shoplifters."

(473 words)

1 LOOKING AT THE TEXT

> EXAM PREPARATION
> Beurteilen von Textaussagen (S. 172)

Decide whether the following statements are true or false and explain your choices in German.

1 In the late 1980s, South Bronx was the area which had by far the worst lawlessness of any part of New York.
2 It took over ten years for New York to change from one of the most dangerous large cities in the USA to being one of the safest.
3 The New York Subway is still one of the dirtiest in the United States.
4 Mayor Giuliani knew that Bratton, being a stranger to New York and its police, would be able to clean up the NYPD better than someone chosen from within the force.
5 Bratton increased the size of the NYPD by adding 2,000 better-educated officers who were chosen from all the city's different ethnic groups.
6 The new police chief's CQL policy aimed not just to catch people committing crimes, but also to catch corrupt officers in the city's police department.
7 Bratton was not so worried about stopping low-level crime: he wanted his officers to concentrate on bringing down the rates of serious crime.
8 New York has the largest police force in the country with nearly 40,000 officers.

2 WORKING WITH WORDS

Link the words or expressions on the left with their meanings on the right.

1	no-go area (*line 3*)	a	completely different way of looking at a situation
2	turnaround (*line 19*)	b	catch criminals
3	sea change (*line 20*)	c	corrupt people
4	big apple (*line 21*)	d	diametrically opposed direction
5	zero tolerance (*line 30*)	e	nickname of New York City
6	bad apples (*line 34*)	f	part of city too dangerous to enter
7	cut down trees (*line 41*)	g	stop people becoming criminals
8	kill the seeds (*line 42*)	h	absolute refusal to show understanding in any circumstances

3 SPEAKING

A Look at the photos and read the offenders' details. Which crimes do you think are most serious? Which are less serious or more understandable?

1

Chloe Martin, 35: caught stealing petrol from neighbour's car; single parent with two young children; first offence; says she can't afford to buy all the petrol she needs to drive to work

2

Jake Wilson, 32: broke into warehouse to steal electronic equipment; injured security guard with flick knife; history of burglary/violence; resisted arrest

3

Wim De Graf, 45: caused bad road accident (two people injured, one seriously) by dangerous driving; in UK on business and returning to Holland soon; first offence; claims he was late for an appointment

4

Holly Chang, 19: stole £400 from employer to finance gambling habit; second offence in six months; refuses to accept help from Gamblers Anonymous

B Study the possible punishments in the box and find one to fit each crime. Report your verdict to the class and give reasons for it.

Let the person off with a warning not to do it again ı
Put him/her on probation with a suspended sentence (say how long) ı
Make the offender do community service (say number of hours per week and for how long) ı
Impose a fine of up to £3,000 ı Sentence person to prison for at last three years ı
Make him/her repair or pay for any damage

4 GIVING A TALK

> Die Arbeitsergebnisse präsentieren S. 168

In small groups of three or four prepare a talk on crime trends in the USA.

Use the information in File 6, page 156, as well as any information you want from this Unit. You can also add other information you may have. As you prepare to present your talk to the class, divide it so that each of you takes a turn at presenting one part.

> TIP

- Spend time reading File 6, page 156. Think about other information that you would like to include.
- Discuss traditional European impressions of the USA as a violent country with particularly bad crime rates. Discuss reasons, e.g. films, TV crime drama series, the actual situation not long ago.
- Discuss information that you want to use to paint a truer picture of crime in America. Focus first on general crime trends, choosing statistical information to support your statements.
- Focus then on trends in particular crime areas and / or police activities, again using statistics.
- Conclude by highlighting the differences between European impressions and American reality.

5 IMAGE ANALYSIS

> EXAM PREPARATION
Bildbeschreibung mit Analyse (S. 172)

Describe what you can see in the photo and relate it back to the text on page 139.

6 LISTENING

3 14 **A** **Listen to a story about an old lady who was stopped for speeding. Then put the drawings into the correct order.**

B **Vervollständigen Sie auf Deutsch die unten stehenden Aussagen mit Informationen aus dem Hörtext.**

> ZENTRALE KLASSENARBEIT
Hörverstehen (S. 175)

1 Ein Motorrad-Polizist hält eine alte Dame an, weil ...
2 Er bittet sie, ...
3 Laut der alten Dame ist das unmöglich, weil ...
4 Danach möchte der Polizist ...
5 Sie erzählt ihm, dass ...
6 Sie fügt hinzu, dass ...
7 Laut der alten Dame befinden sich die Leichenteile ...
8 Der herbeigeeilte Sheriff bittet die alten Dame ...
9 Als sie den Kofferraum öffnet, finden sie ...
10 Die alte Dame möchte, dass der Sheriff glaubt, dass ...

C Further options

1 ANALYZING CASE STUDIES

Work with a partner. Read the three case studies below and identify patterns common to each.

Think about: sex/age; choice of victim; weapon; academic performance; school/social life; prior warning; how incident ended; motive.

1 **Columbine High School, Littleton, Colorado**
20 April 1999: Eric Harris and Dylan Klebold kill 12 students and a teacher, and injure a further 24 people, before killing themselves. Likely motive: both perpetrators suffered from depression and tended to blame their school for their personal failures.

2 **Albertville-Realschule, Winnenden, Germany**
11 March 2009: Former pupil Tim Kretschmer shoots dead 15 people and injures many others before taking his own life. Likely motive: he was treated for mental illness, but claimed he killed because "it was fun".

3 **Jokela High School, Tuusula, Finland**
7 November 2007: 18-year-old former student Pekka-Eric Auvinen shoots dead 7 students and a teacher, and injures 10 others, before shooting himself. Said to be 'a normal student from a normal home'. Posted his plans on YouTube. Motive: killing people he thinks are 'failures of natural selection' and hence unfit to live.

2 COMPARING YOUR RESULTS

Compare your analysis of the three school shootings with the research findings below. Identify the differences and similarities and present your results to the class.

Fact and fiction about school shootings

1 There is no 'standard shooter'. Though mostly teenage males, they come from all races and family backgrounds, with academic performance from very poor to excellent. Many shooters are mainstream and take part in sports/school activities.

2 Shooters seldom 'just snap'. There is a logical progression; 1) forming an idea, 2) planning an attack, 3) obtaining weapon(s), 4) selecting victims and 5) carrying out the attack.

3 Before most shootings, somebody else knows about the shooter's plan, but doesn't take it seriously. And this information is rarely reported.

4 Only about one in five shooters suffers from a mental disorder or takes drugs. However, most have problems handling personal failure, which they tend to blame on others.

3 DEVELOPING AN ACTION PLAN

Work with the class as a whole. Develop an action plan a) to prevent a shooting incident at your school and b) to protect the school community in the event of a shooting.

D Grammar checkpoint

1 ADVERB ORDER

> Grammar summary S. 187

Copy the table with eight writing lines into your exercise book and complete it with adverbs from the box. Sometimes more than one position is possible.

~~always~~ | ~~beautifully~~ | as a rule | at 6 o'clock | in the lesson | each spring | every day | fast | fortunately | in New York | in prison | last summer | loudly | naturally | nowadays | of course | often | once a month | on the whole | seldom | silently | since 2008

Front	*Mid*	*End-Position*		
		manner	*place*	*frequency/time*
	always	*beautifully*		

2 FORMING SENTENCES

> Grammar summary S. 187

Put the words or expressions in the correct order to make sensible sentences.

1 two hours' exercise | research | need | that | at least | a day | healthy prisoners | suggests
2 occupy | sometimes | a cell | two prisoners | unfortunately | designed for one
3 often | complain | critics | that | 'academies of crime' | are | prisons | in fact just
4 in street crime | has caused | mobile phones | it is said | that | a big increase | the theft of
5 clearly | a 'must have' status symbol | mobile phones | amongst | this is because | the young | have become
6 occur | or social group | most murders | within the family
7 no longer there | I returned | my car | to the car park | when | was
8 after dark | it's scandalous | many women | that | nervous | of walking | are | through our parks
9 in reality | crime | is falling | is increasing | it | many people | think | unfortunately, | when
10 FBI statistics | in states | less murders | perhaps surprisingly | show that | the death penalty | there are | without

3 TRANSLATING

Translate the sentences into English. Be careful about word order.

1 Vor dreißig Jahren war es noch möglich, ungefährdet auf der Straße zu spielen.
2 Viele New Yorker hatten Angst, nachts ihre Wohnungen zu verlassen.
3 Einige Wissenschaftler behaupten, dass Armut der Hauptgrund für Kriminalität ist.
4 Die Erfahrung zeigt, dass harte Bestrafung selten wirksam ist.
5 Leider ist eine große Mehrheit dafür, die Todesstrafe wieder einzuführen.
6 In der Tat wurde die Null-Toleranz hauptsächlich gegen korrupte Polizisten angewendet.
7 Selbstverständlich wollte der Polizist wissen, wo wir uns zur Tatzeit aufgehalten haben.
8 Man sagt, dass der Dieb sich während der Flucht schwer verletzt hat.
9 Im Interesse der Gleichbehandlung werden heutzutage Frauen in den USA genauso hart bestraft wie Männer.
10 Laut einer Meinungsumfrage aus dem Jahre 2007 sind 74 % der Wahlberechtigten (*electorate*) in Texas für die Todesstrafe.

12

Main Course

Future life, future living

FOCUS

1 Link the photos 1–8 to the captions a–h.

1

2

3
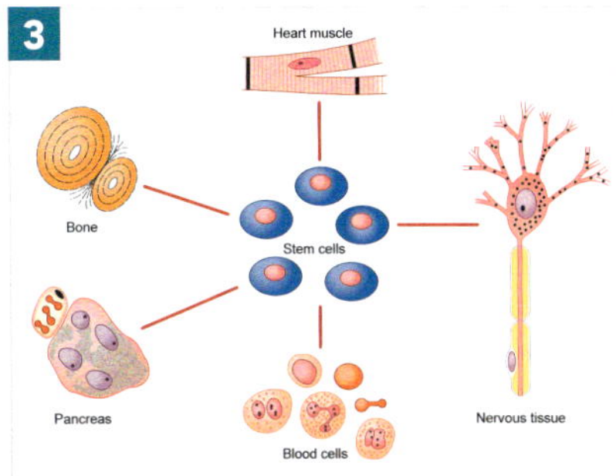

4

5
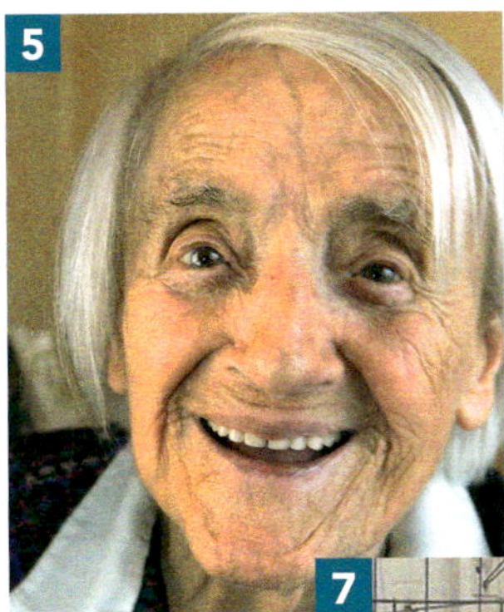

6

7

8
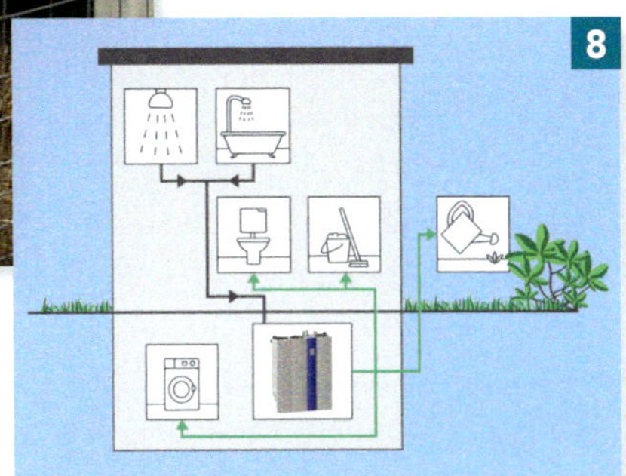

a your friend and helper
b more and better food
c 100+ and still going strong
d preventing hereditary diseases
e cloning
f conservation of resources
g the end of the service society
h cloned supercow's daughters give more milk

2 What is the overall theme of all the photos: a), b) or c)?
a) Future fears – b) Future developments – c) Future hopes

3 Which two developments do you find most interesting or useful? Say why. Then do a class survey.

4 How do you think life in Germany will have changed by, say, 2050?

A Personal perspectives

BEFORE YOU READ

A **What boycotts have you heard of, for example the boycott of BP after the Gulf oil spill in 2010?**

B **Do you think boycotts work or do they hurt the wrong people?**

C **Have you ever taken part in a boycott? If not, can you imagine doing so? Why (not)?**

According to this report from the Daily Mail, *the media and the big supermarkets are doing more to protect British consumers from the unknown risks of genetically-modified (GM) food than their government is.*

British supermarkets call for a boycott of 'cloned' meat and milk

Britain's biggest supermarkets last night announced a boycott of meat and milk from cloned farm animals and their offspring. The move follows Daily Mail revelations that a calf, the daugher of a US cloned cow, has been born on a British farm.

Separately, the government's Food Standards Agency (FSA) plans to hold emergency talks with EU officials tomorrow over the policing of food from cloned animals and their offspring.

Current food and health laws require the investigation and approval of any meat or milk from cloned farm animals. However, a loophole in the law means that there are no such controls on food which is produced by their offspring. As a result, meat and milk from animals who have a clone for a mother could be in the shops within a few years.

Last night, supermarkets, including Tesco, Sainsbury's, Asda, Morrisons and Marks & Spencer, reacted to this threat by announcing their own boycott. Tesco said: "We would not stock any products derived from cloned animals or their offspring." Marks & Spencer said: "We have long had a ban on all genetically modified ingredients in our food. That ban will now apply to any food from cloned animals and their offspring."

A Holstein calf called Dundee Paradise, the daughter of a US cloned cow, was born on a farm in Shropshire last month. This made clear that clone farming and the genetic modification of animals has now moved from science fiction to the reality of the supermarket.

In an astonishing failure, the government knew nothing at all about Dundee Paradise and the future birth of other calves from the same cloned cow.

Supporters of cloning claim that calves like Dundee Paradise will form the nucleus of the country's future dairy herds. And cloned and GM animals could, they say, provide cheap food for future generations. The idea is that 'supercows' will be capable of producing vast quantities of milk, as much as 70 pints (about 40 litres) a day.

However, the history of cloning and genetic modification is full of examples of animal suffering. The first cloned mammal, Dolly the sheep, died prematurely at the age of six in 2003 from a lung infection. She had also been diagnosed with the early onset of severe arthritis, and there are many more examples of miscarriages, ill health and abnormal organs.

Dundee Paradise and her sisters will start producing milk in around two years' time. As the law now stands, there is nothing to stop this going into stores without any form of labelling. (424 words)

from the *Daily Mail*, London, 10.01.07, abridged

1 LOOKING AT THE TEXT

> EXAM PREPARATION
> Mediation (S. 171)

A Sie haben erfahren, dass ab demnächst Milch von geklonten Kühen in Ihrer Schulmensa verwendet und verkauft wird. Sie sind dagegen und machen es sich zur Aufgabe, Ihre Mitschüler über die Vor- und Nachteile zu informieren. Entnehmen Sie dem englischen Artikel die relevanten Informationen und schreiben Sie einen Artikel für Ihre Schülerzeitung. Übersetzen Sie nicht Wort für Wort.

B Do the assignments.

1. Explain why the *Daily Mail* can claim that British supermarkets and the media are doing more to protect consumers than the government is.
2. Point out the difference between Tesco's and Marks & Spencer's policy on GM food.
3. Say why the *Daily Mail* speaks of 'an astonishing failure' on the part of the British government.
4. Describe what role Dolly the sheep plays in the text.

2 WORKING WITH WORDS

A Replace the highlighted words or phrases with a synonym from the text. They are not necessarily in the same order.

1. Supermarkets announced a refusal to sell[1] meat and milk from cloned animals or their young[2].
2. A serious omission in the regulations has allowed such meat to get into supermarkets.
3. This showed beyond a doubt[1] that the genetic alteration[2] of animals has now shifted[3] from science fiction to supermarket reality.
4. Dolly suffered an early death at the age of only six.
5. Exceptionally productive cows[1] will be able to deliver huge amounts[2] of milk.
6. As the law now stands, there is nothing to prevent[1] this milk finding its way[2] into stores without any type[3] of labelling.
7. The UK intends[1] to hold emergency discussions[2] with EU officials over the supervision[3] of food from cloned animals.
8. This calf and ones like her will make up the heart of Britain's future dairy herds.

B Work with a partner and complete the table.

The words in the table are all from the press report. If necessary, use a dictionary to find the missing forms. Please note: for some words, more than one noun is possible.

	Verb	*Noun(s)*	*Adjective*
1	*announce*	...; ...	
2	...	*revelation*	...
3		*law*; ...	...
4	*require*	...	
5	...	*investigation*	...
6	...	*approval*	...
7	*produce*	...; ...	...
8	...	*threat*	...
9	*apply*	...; ...	...
10	...	*modification*	...
11	...	...	*astonishing*
12	...	*infection*	...

C Replace the German words with words that you have found in exercise B. Be careful with tenses, etc.

1 The ... (*Ankündigung*) shocked supporters of GM farming.
2 Cloned cows are said to be more ... (*leistungsfähig*) than their natural sisters.
3 It is a ... ... (*gesetzliche Auflage*) to get approval for food from cloned animals.
4 The *Daily Mail* ... (*untersuchen*) food from cloned animals in Britain and ... (*aufdecken*) a loophole in the law.
5 The EU ... (*drohen*) to introduce stricter labelling.
6 The findings ... (*erstaunen*) the journalists.
7 Farmers ... (*verändern*) plants by natural selection for thousands of years.
8 Is it true that cloned animals suffer from more ... (*ansteckende*) diseases than natural ones do?

3 ANALYSING AN ADVERTISEMENT

Describe what you can see in the image. Explain its message and relate it back to the text on page 146.

The DNA of genetically modified plants may contain the genes of insects, animals or even viruses. These products may potentially cause harm to your health. Look for a "GMO Free" sign on the package.

> EXAM PREPARATION
Bildbeschreibung mit Analyse (S. 172)

B The bigger picture

BEFORE YOU READ

A Have you ever made use of FAQs yourself? If so, what did you want to find out?

B Work with a partner. Read this list of FAQs about gene technology. Then, skim the text and match as many questions as possible to the answers. Finally, read the text and match the remaining FAQs.

a Can we trust the food we eat?
b How do genetic engineers answer these arguments?
c How does gene technology differ from selective breeding?
d What are the ecological arguments against GM crops?
e What are the medical applications of GM?
f What is GM food?
g Why do some people think GM food may be harmful?

3 16

1 ...

GM food is produced from plants or animals whose genes have been changed by scientists. All living organisms have genes written in their DNA. They are the chemical instructions for creating and maintaining life. By changing the genes, scientists can alter the characteristics of an organism. Maybe, for example, we want a plant to produce bigger yields or an animal to produce more meat. Gene technology can do this.

2 ...

A tendency to suffer from many illnesses is 'genetically programmed' by the genes in a person's DNA. By changing the right genes, it becomes possible to get rid of this tendency. At present, such techniques are very promising in the treatment of dementia and diabetes in old age. A further, more distant, medical application of gene technology could be the production of transplant organs.

3 ...

Farmers have used selective breeding to improve crops and animals for thousands of years. They have also created new plants and animals by cross-breeding closely-related species. This is how they produced wheat and mules, for example. However, this was a very time-consuming business. Gene technology delivers much faster and more predictable results because it enables scientists to select a single gene for a single characteristic.

4 ...

Critics argue that we do not know enough about how genes interact with each other and with the environment. This means that we can't say with certainty what the long-term result of any modification will be. They worry that manipulations could accidentally lead to substances being produced that are poisonous, or could trigger allergies. Critics also argue that antibiotic-resistant genes in plants and farm animals could be passed to the micro-organisms that make us ill. If this happens, we might not have effective antibiotic drugs to fight back.

5 ...

They point out that there is no evidence that GM food has any bad effects. They argue that a lot of non-GM food is processed to remove unwanted or toxic substances – and that the regulations that govern GM foods are far stricter than those for non-GM products. Genetic modification might cause new allergies but so, too, can traditional selective breeding. In fact, gene technology may make it possible to rid our food of such problems altogether. Furthermore, GM enables us to improve not only the flavour, texture and shelf life of food, but also its nutritional value.

▶

6 …

All food is subject to regulation to ensure that it is safe for human consumption. Everybody involved in the production, processing and marketing of food, from farmers through to shopkeepers, must obey these strict rules. Food poisoning is usually caused by poor practice somewhere between the farm gate and the supermarket shelf. But consumers also have a responsibility. One of the main reasons why food poisoning has increased so dramatically in recent years is that we, the consumers, have not stored and prepared food properly in our own kitchens.

7 …

The green lobby fears that certain genes from GM crops could be passed on to other species, with harmful results. For two reasons, they are particularly worried about genes that make GM plants resistant to herbicides. Firstly, these genes could produce 'superweeds' that are resistant to all but the most powerful herbicides and, secondly, they could destroy insects and birds as their food becomes contaminated. But is this really new? The fact is that 'factory farming' is already playing havoc with nature. On the contrary, bioengineers argue, GM technology offers a real chance of improving the situation in the countryside - GM crops require less of the fertilizers and pesticides that are later washed into the rivers. And because GM crops produce higher yields, they need less land. This could save the few surviving uncultivated habitats.

(607 words)

1 LOOKING AT THE TEXT

> EXAM PREPARATION
> Beurteilen von Textaussagen (S. 172)

Decide whether the statements are true or false and explain your choices in German.

1 Scientists change the genes of plants to create GM crops.
2 In nature, a plant or animal's DNA has nothing to do with GM food.
3 Most human illnesses are genetically programmed.
4 In medicine, gene technology could be used to make transplant organs.
5 The use of selective breeding to improve crops is a relatively recent development.
6 Farmers use cross-breeding to produce new plants and animals.
7 Critics of GM technology say that we don't know enough about its long-term effects.
8 We already know that GM does not give rise to new allergies.
9 Supporters of GM technology say that GM food doesn't need to be as closely regulated as non-GM food.
10 GM technology can make food taste better and stay fresh longer.
11 Food poisoning has increased dramatically in recent years because of GM food.
12 Bioengineers think that GM food is less damaging to the environment than "factory farming".

2 WORKING WITH WORDS

A Explain the following in your own words.

1 get rid of sth (*paragraph 2*)
2 more distant (*paragraph 2*)
3 time-consuming business (*paragraph 3*)
4 long-term result (*paragraph 4*)
5 trigger sth (*paragraph 4*)
6 toxic substance (*paragraph 5*)
7 shelf life (*paragraph 5*)
8 be subject to sth (*paragraph 6*)
9 poor practice (*paragraph 6*)
10 play havoc with sth (*paragraph 7*)

B Complete the sentences with the missing prepositions.

1 GM tomatoes, …[1] example, are produced …[2] plants that have been genetically modified …[3] scientists.
2 DNA is often referred …[1] as 'the blueprint …[2] life', implying that it contains all the information needed to create life.
3 It is possible to get rid …[1] a tendency to suffer …[2] a particular illness by modifying the right genes …[3] a person's DNA.
4 Critics are worried …[1] the fact that not enough is known …[2] how genes interact …[3] each other …[4] the long term.
5 The spread …[1] seeds from GM crops could lead …[2] the unintentional production …[3] toxic substances …[4] the natural environment.
6 Supporters …[1] GM techniques point …[2] that selective breeding can also result …[3] the creation …[4] new allergies.
7 The genetic modification …[1] DNA is very promising …[2] the treatment …[3] conditions like dementia that occur …[4] old age.
8 The control …[1] so-called 'superweeds' depends …[2] the use …[3] very powerful herbicides because they are resistant …[4] conventional methods …[5] weed control.

3 LISTENING

> ZENTRALE KLASSENARBEIT
Hörverstehen (S. 175)

3 17

Vervollständigen Sie auf Deutsch die unten stehenden Aussagen mit Informationen aus dem Hörtext.

1 Ruth arbeitet in der Medizinforschung und ihrer Meinung nach … .
2 Sie glaubt, dass die Gentechnologie sowohl in der Medizin … .
3 Die Gentechnologie verspricht Heilung für … .
4 Längerfristig könnte sie auch verwendet werden, … .
5 Luke ist anderer Meinung und glaubt, dass … .
6 Um die wachsende Weltbevölkerung zu ernähren, glaubt Ruth, dass … .
7 Laut Luke wäre das Problem der Unterernährung auf der Welt leicht zu bewältigen, wenn … .
8 Luke behauptet, dass Gentechnologie die … .
9 Als Beispiele dafür nennt er … .

4 SPEAKING

Hold a debate on the motion 'Gene technology is of great benefit to humankind'.

1 Choose four speakers and a chairperson. A 'proposer' should speak in favour of the motion; the 'opposer' against it. Each should also have a 'second', who supports them with further arguments or information.
2 The speakers should prepare their speeches for and against the motion by collecting arguments and ideas from the texts in this unit. They can add any other information they may have.
3 Hold the debate. The chairperson should introduce the motion and the speakers and act as a referee.
4 At the end of the debate, the chairperson calls for a class vote for or against the motion.

5 COMPOSITION

> EXAM PREPARATION
> Materialgestützter Aufsatz (S. 173)

Refer to at least three of the following: the text on p. 149/50, and the materials below. Write a composition on the following:
Could GM food be a solution to world hunger?

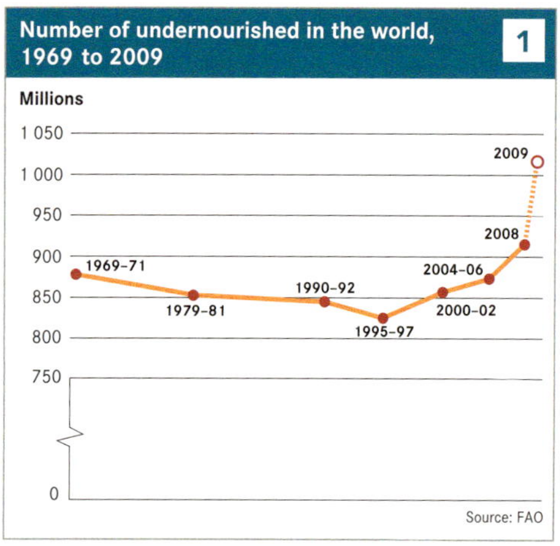

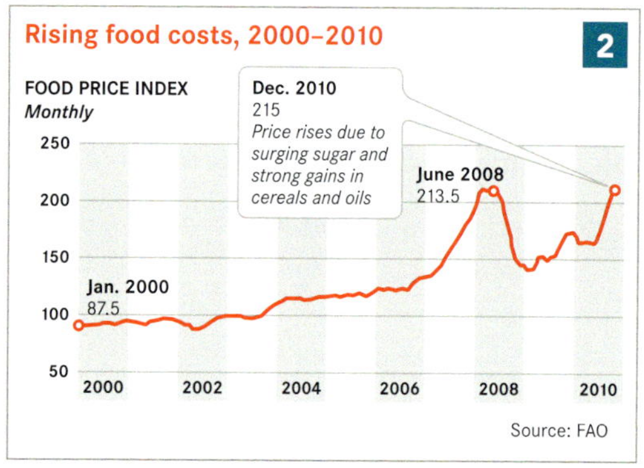

By permission of Michael Ramirez and Creators Syndicate, Inc.

4

Biokraftstoff führt zu höheren Lebensmittelpreisen und Hungersnot

Aufgrund steigender Preise können sich viele der ärmsten Menschen der Welt nicht ausreichend ernähren. Einen Anstieg der Preise schreiben zahlreiche Experten der Nutzung von Nahrungsmitteln in der Biokraftstofferzeugung zu. Ebenso wirken sich Ölpreise auf die Lebensmittelpreise aus, indem sie die Transportkosten erhöhen. Auch wenn der Prozess eine saubere und günstigere Alternative zu den üblichen fossilen Brennstoffen ist, sollte die Regierung ihn nicht aktiv fördern, denn die Nahrungsmittelvorräte sinken dadurch, und das Verhältnis von Angebot und Nachfrage verschiedener Grundnahrungsmittel gerät aus dem Gleichgewicht.

C Further options

1 ORGANIZING A PROJECT: Visions of the future

What is your vision of the future? Do you think things will stay much as they are with a few technical developments? Or do you think the future will be different from today in many ways? This project may give you the answer.

Divide into groups of four, then choose a topic from the list below to research. Check with other groups to make sure that there is a good spread of topics.

The topics

> The world of work	new jobs/workplaces, job security/fluctuation
> Transport/Communication	means of transport/communication
> Urban life	city of the future, design/layout, shopping
> Houses	design, housework, machines
> Leisure/Entertainment	new forms of leisure activity/entertainment
> Energy/Environment	new sources of energy, climate change, biodiversity
> Health/Welfare	medical advances, healthy living, life expectancy
> Education/Training	school, e-learning, personalized learning

2 THINKING, DISCUSSING, SHAPING THE FUTURE

Have a look at this project strategy and try to use it in your discussions.

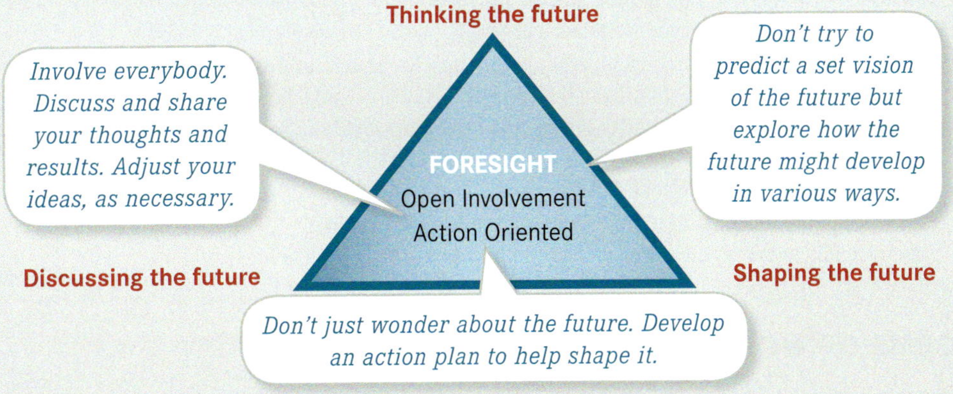

3 PRESENTING YOUR RESULTS

Present your ideas and results to the rest of the class.
The suggestions below may help:

> Write and give a talk.
> Produce part of an online newspaper for, say, 21 June 2050. Devote the main story to your topic. You could add shorter reports, for example on a major disaster, a scientific breakthrough, a sporting event, a celebrity marriage/love affair, ...
> Do a class/school/family/... survey on future developments in your topic area. List six questions and note down respondents' answers. Look for common patterns. Present your results to the class.

D Grammar checkpoint

Here is a grammar quiz on what you have learned in this course. In each case, choose the correct alternative – a) or b).

1 MIXED TENSES

1 The firm **a)** makes | **b)** has been making bikes for over a hundred years.
2 Work on genes **a)** became | **b)** has become possible when they discovered DNA.
3 They **a)** publish | **b)** are publishing a new magazine next year.
4 **a)** Did you make | **b)** Have you made back-up copies of these files yesterday?
5 Luke **a)** talked | **b)** was talking to Maria when I arrived.
6 They met after they **a)** have both left | **b)** had both left university.
7 Sarah **a)** is often travelling | **b)** often travels to the US on business.
8 We **a)** aren't going to have | **b)** won't have a holiday this year.
9 I **a)** didn't see | **b)** haven't seen that movie yet.
10 According to the timetable, our train **a)** leaves | **b)** will leave at 10:32.
11 The minister expects the EU **a)** is going to allow | **b)** will allow GM crops soon.
12 We read the documents while we **a)** waited | **b)** were waiting for the meeting to begin.

2 MIXED STRUCTURES

1 Frank has avoided **a)** going | **b)** to go to a doctor for years.
2 Do you remember **a)** seeing | **b)** to see your girlfriend for the first time?
3 Humans can only survive a short time without **a)** drinking | **b)** they drink.
4 Jack **a)** told | **b)** told me that he'd be late for the meeting.
5 If you hadn't called the police, the thieves **a)** had got away | **b)** would have got away.
6 I'm sorry, but stamps **a)** can only bought | **b)** can only be bought at post offices.
7 We **a)** don't have to | **b)** mustn't finish the project this week – next week is fine.
8 The car's OK, but it would be better if it **a)** didn't use | **b)** wouldn't use so much fuel.
9 Somebody at the bus stop told **a)** me the way | **b)** the way to me.
10 I'm sure we **a)** have already seen | **b)** have seen already this film.
11 Frank stopped **a)** buying | **b)** to buy some petrol on his way home.
12 The mechanic **a)** explained | **b)** explained me how to switch on the lights.

3 FORMS OF WORDS

1 You can earn **a)** a lot of | **b)** much money designing websites.
2 The Greens don't seem to like **a)** each other | **b)** themselves very much.
3 Can you lend me **a)** any | **b)** some money, please? – Sure. How much?
4 This project has been **a)** good organized | **b)** well organized.
5 The customs officer spoke to us **a)** friendly | **b)** in a friendly way.
6 We enjoyed **a)** ourselves | **b)** us a lot at the party.
7 Do you think **a)** there is water | **b)** water is on Mars?
8 Do you have to wear **a)** a | **b)** an uniform at school?
9 Please try **a)** not to be | **b)** to not be late.
10 The news **a)** are | **b)** is not very good, I'm afraid.
11 You will find some more **a)** information | **b)** informations on the next page.
12 Joshua's dad doesn't want **a)** him to get married | **b)** that he gets married so young.

Files

FILE 1 Unit 8, Further options, p. 113

Scoring

	a	b	c	d	e	f	g
1	2	4	6	–	–	–	–
2	6	4	7	2	1	–	–
3	4	2	5	7	6	–	–
4	4	6	2	1	–	–	–
5	6	4	3	2	–	–	–
6	6	4	2	–	–	–	–
7	6	2	4	–	–	–	–
8	6	7	5	4	3	2	1
9	7	6	4	2	1	–	–
10	4	2	3	5	6	1	–

What your personal score says about you

Over 60 People see you as extremely self-confident, even rather dominant.

51–60 Other people see you as an exciting and impulsive person, a risk-taker. People may find life more colourful when you're around, but they also think that you could be a bit chaotic.

41–50 Others see you as lively, charming, amusing, practical and never boring. You are popular, but you do not let it go to your head. People also find you kind and understanding.

31–40 Others see you as sensible, careful and practical. If you are clever, you are modest about it. You do not make friends easily but you are extremely loyal to your small circle of close friends, and you expect the same loyalty from them.

21–30 Other people see you as very careful and perhaps even a little too cautious. They expect you to think long and hard about a suggestion and then usually to decide against it. This is because your careful nature always makes you play safe.

Below 21 People think you are shy and indecisive. You're glad to let others make the decisions. Some people think you're a worrier, but those close to you know that you have hidden depths that you seldom show.

FILE 2 Unit 4, exercise 3, p. 71

Businessperson

You fear a large loss of trade, especially as car parking is already expensive in the city centre and the costs of running the business are high. You want the city councillor to understand clearly that if you have to close down, the city will lose your business rates (= local taxes). There may be thousands more like you.

role card

FILE 3 Unit 3, exercise 4, p. 58

Debbie

Personally, you would prefer the romantic comedy, and you particularly dislike science fiction, but you will watch it if that's what Dave wants. And anyway, you will accept the majority decision. You agree with Dave that a late movie would be a bad idea.
You would like to eat something before the film as you haven't had anything since breakfast.

role card

FILE 4 Unit 7, Further options, p. 103

A national union official

Gold Star has never allowed a union, but the workers are ready to join one now. You know how bad conditions are at the factory, and you know that your union has successfully supported other workers in similar situations. You therefore aim to do the same for Gold Star's employees. It helps that the Gold Star employees are very skilled, and you believe that this will stop Gold Star from moving production to another country. You want Now Look to make Gold Star accept your union. You want to persuade Now Look that this is the only way to make sure that employees will be treated fairly in future.

role card

FILE 5 Unit 3, exercise 4, p. 58

Claire

You would much prefer *One Night in New York*, and you think *Pirates of the Caribbean* is very silly – definitely something for 13-year-old boys. You are hungry and would quite like to eat before the film.

role card

FILE 6 Unit 11, exercise 4, p. 141

1 Nationwide general trends

U.S. crime statistics

According to the FBI's Preliminary Uniform Crime Report, the nation experienced a 5.5 percent drop in violent crime and a 4.9 percent drop in property crime in 2009 compared to 2008.

■ Crime by region

Percent change by geographic region

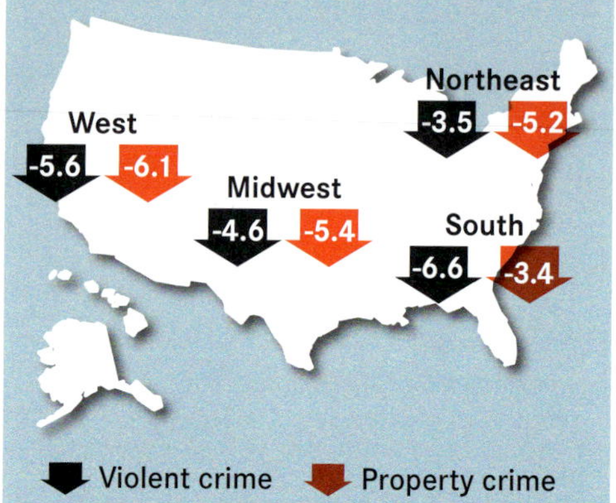

■ Violent Crime

Each of the violent crime offense categories decreased nationwide from January 2009 when compared to 2008.

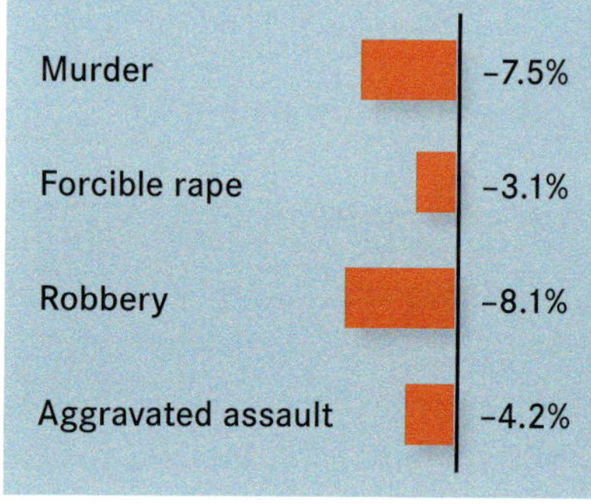

Source: U.S. Department of Justice, Bureau of Justice Statistics, *http//www.bjs.ojp.usdoj.gov*

2 Violent crime

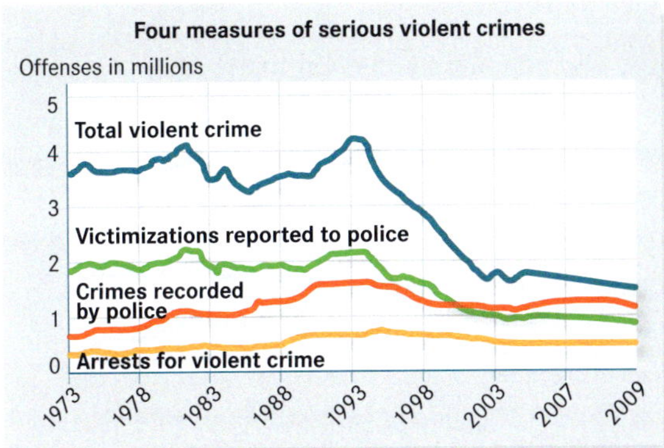

Serious violent crimes are 1) rape, 2) robbery, 3) armed assault and 4) homicide

Source: National Crime Victimization Survey

3 Homicide

4 Crime reported to the police

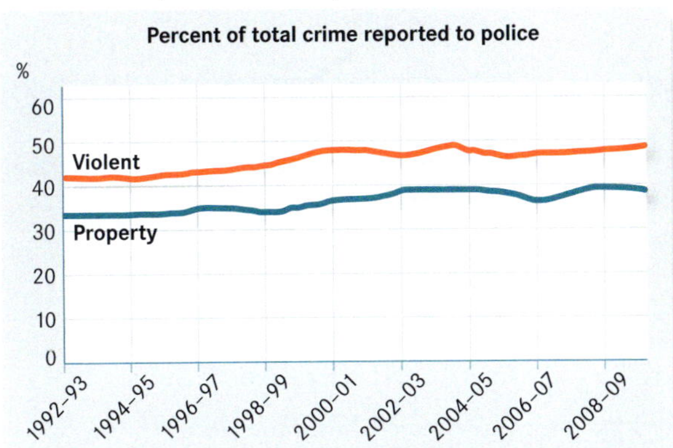

Source: *http//www.fbi.gov/headlines/uscrimestatistics*

FILE 7 Unit 4, exercise 3, p. 71

City councillor

As the chairperson of the meeting, you must make sure everyone speaks and help the meeting come to an agreement. You think that congestion charging is necessary, but you worry that it will cause terrible problems. You need the government money to help develop public transport, but you can only provide the city's 50% of the money from congestion charges. The city has no other spare money.

role card

FILE 8 Unit 7, Further options, p. 103

The Director of International Public Relations, Now Look

Up until now, you have been happy to use Gold Star: they have always produced good-quality goods at very competitive prices. However, you are very worried about the scandal and its bad effect on the Now Look brand. You are ready to end the Gold Star contract immediately to prevent further damage. You are sorry that this would close the factory and therefore destroy many jobs and hurt San Bernardo very badly, but for you the most important thing is to stop the bad publicity.

role card

FILE 9 Unit 7, Further options, p. 103

The owner of Gold Star

You believe that you cannot improve pay and conditions much at the factory because your products would become too expensive and you might lose the contract to a cheaper competitor. However, you may also lose the contract because of the scandal, and you will promise anything in order to prevent this. You then intend to forget about any 'expensive' promises. Later, you may move production to somewhere cheaper than the Philippines – to Cambodia perhaps. You are not sure, but you think you can find skilled workers there. You would offer slightly better conditions but pay lower wages and therefore keep prices down and keep the Now Look contract. (If you lose this, you will go out of business.) One thing you never want in any Gold Star factory anywhere is a union.

role card

FILE 10 Unit 8, Focus, p. 105

1B | 2A | 3B | 4B | 5B | 6B (2008) | 7B | 8C

FILE 11 Unit 6, Further options, p. 93

Answers

Numerical Test 1	1D | 2B
Numerical Test 2	3B | 4E
Coded Instructions	5E | 6B
Diagrammatic Test	7C | 8B

FILE 12 Unit 4, exercise 3, p. 71

Road commuter

You want much better public transport *before* congestion charging starts. You know that as things are, public transport can only carry up to 13% of commuters like you. You cannot afford to pay the daily congestion charge – (you know the figure for London is about £15 per day) – and you do not want to fight to find a place on public transport buses or trains every day.

role card

FILE 13 Unit 3, exercise 4, p. 58

Dave

You are more interested in driving than anything else today, and you don't really mind which film you go to – although you would quite like to see *Journey to the Stars*. However, you don't want to go to a late showing because you know your dad will be worried about the car. (You want to make sure he will lend you it many, many more times!)

role card

FILE 14 Unit 4, exercise 3, p. 71

Government transport official

You accept that congestion charging will cause problems for some people but believe that it must be part of the answer to the congestion problem. You can provide government money to help develop public transport if the city council provides the other 50%.

role card

FILE 15 Unit 7, Further options, p. 103

The Mayor of San Bernardo

You are very worried about pay and conditions at the Gold Star factory, (and you have been asking quietly for improvements). But the thing that worries you most is losing the jobs completely. You know that in today's world, producers like Gold Star often move production to cheaper parts of the world. And if the factory closed, this would destroy the town economically.

role card

FILE 16 Unit 7, Focus, p. 95

Australia

China

the EU

Germany

India

Japan

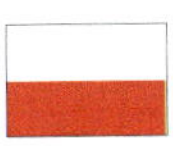
Poland

the UK

the USA

FILE 17 Unit 7, Culture Check, p. 98

a) EA | b) LA | c) NA | d) NA | e) EA

FILE 18 Unit 3, exercise 4, p. 58

Steve

You helped yourself to several things from the fridge before Claire arrived, so you're not hungry at all at the moment. Of all three films, you would much prefer to see *Pirates of the Caribbean*. (You have seen all the other 'Pirates' films at least twice each.) However, you know that Claire doesn't like *Pirates of the Caribbean*, and you don't want to have an argument with her. On the other hand, if you can quietly persuade Steve, then Debbie will probably agree with him – and then Claire will have to agree too.

role card

Skills

REZEPTION

Lesen schwieriger Texte

Texte werden zu unterschiedlichen Zwecken gelesen. Manchmal braucht man nur zu wissen, worum es geht, dann reicht in der Regel ein aufmerksames Überfliegen des Textes. Oft müssen gezielt Informationen herausgesucht werden, dann kommt es darauf an, die richtigen Schlüsselwörter zu finden. Will man sich gründlich mit einem Text auseinandersetzen, um z. B. Fragen zu beantworten oder einen Aufsatz dazu zu schreiben, ist gründliches, möglicherweise zweimaliges Lesen erforderlich.

Grobverständnis: Sich einen schnellen Überblick über einen Text verschaffen

Manchmal werden Sie aufgefordert, einen Text schnell zu lesen, um das Thema grob zu erfassen.

1. Schritt: Suchen Sie nach Anhaltspunkten, die Ihnen Aufschluss über den Textinhalt geben: Titel und Zwischenüberschriften, fett gedruckte Wörter, Bilder und Bildunterschriften.

2. Schritt: Sind Sie noch unsicher, lesen Sie die ersten und letzten Sätze jedes Absatzes. Bleiben Sie nicht an Einzelwörtern, schwierigen Zitaten usw. hängen.

Suche nach Einzelinformationen im Text

Bei vielen Textverständnisfragen oder Aufgaben vom Typ *True or false* geht es darum, schnell bestimmte Informationen im Text zu finden und nicht jedesmal den ganzen Text neu zu lesen.

1. Schritt: Suchen Sie den Text nach Schlüsselbegriffen für die gesuchten Informationen ab. Geht es etwa um die Meinung des Autors zu einem bestimmten Thema, halten Sie nach Wörtern wie *think, believe, opinion* usw. Ausschau. Geht es um Informationen zu einem Thema, rufen Sie sich ein paar Schlüsselbegriffe in Erinnerung, nach denen Sie Ausschau halten. Manchmal hilft es, sich den gesuchten Begriff als gedrucktes Wort vor dem geistigen Auge vorzustellen.

2. Schritt: Gehen Sie falls nötig mit dem Finger die Zeilen entlang, während Sie suchen. Wenn Sie sich wie oben beschrieben vorbereitet haben, springen Ihnen die gesuchten Begriffe sofort ins Auge.

> Beurteilen von Textaussagen S. 172

Detailverständnis: Gründliches Lesen

Lesen Sie nicht einfach drauflos. Ein paar einfache Schritte helfen Ihnen, den Text besser zu verstehen, ohne sich in Details zu verlieren.

1. Schritt: Der erste Schritt sollte darin bestehen, sich ein grobes Verständnis vom Textinhalt zu verschaffen (siehe oben). So werden Sie unklare Stellen besser in den Gesamtzusammenhang einordnen können. Es ist hilfreich, sich die wichtigsten Stichwörter kurz zu notieren. Zu dem Text *A step too far* auf S. 136 etwa könnten Sie nach kurzem Überfliegen aufschreiben: *The text is about the death penalty in the United States, in particular about the first woman who was executed.*

2. Schritt: Machen Sie sich die Struktur des Textes bewusst. Wo ist die Einleitung? Welcher Teil enthält die Hauptinformationen, und wie sind sie aufgebaut (Zwischenüberschriften, Absätze usw.)? Achten Sie auf Strukturwörter wie *only, but while, that's why, while, however* usw., mit denen der Verfasser seine Argumentation gliedert.

3. Schritt: Lesen Sie den Text nun aufmerksam. Notieren Sie sich Schlüsselstellen, z.B: *Karla Faye Tucker - first woman to be executed in the US; executed in Texas on 3 February 1998; case attracted a lot of interest - some felt only because she was white, attractive and showed remorse (married a priest and became a Christian); many pleas for clemency to Governor Bush from different groups and even from the Pope.* Schlagen Sie Wörter beim ersten Lesen nur nach, wenn die Bedeutung des ganzen Satzes an ihnen hängt. Oft lässt sich die wesentliche Bedeutung durch den Kontext erschließen.

4. Schritt: Notieren Sie sich den Textinhalt in strukturierter Form, etwa einer Mind Map oder einer Liste (Themen, pro/kontra). Fügen Sie auch Formulierungen hinzu, die Ihnen später helfen, sich in eigenen Worten über den Textinhalt zu äußern. Schlagen Sie jetzt das notwendige Vokabular nach. > Note Making S. 164

Umgang mit unbekannten Vokabeln

Fragen Sie sich bei neuen Vokabeln immer, ob sie für das Verständnis des Zusammenhangs unbedingt notwendig sind. Nachschlagen kostet Zeit und hilft oft nicht beim Verständnis des wirklich Wichtigen.

Erschließen der Bedeutung aus dem Kontext

> Ein Wort, das unbekannt scheint, kann z. B. mit einem anderen, Ihnen bekannten Wort verwandt sein (Ableitungen wie *aggressor* von *aggressive*). Oder das Wort hat einen bekannten Wortstamm und einen angehängten Wortteil, mit dessen Hilfe Sie die Bedeutung erkennen können (*formal - **in**formal, clockwise - **anti**clockwise, change - change**able**, stupid - stupid**ity***). Manche Wörter haben Ähnlichkeiten mit einem deutschen Wort (vgl. etwa *initial* und „Initialen", *potential* und „potenziell").

> Falls Sie den Sinn eines Wortes noch nicht verstehen, gehen Sie nach folgenden Schritten vor:
- Ist das Wort für den Sinn des Satzes wichtig? Falls nicht, ignorieren Sie es!
- Können Sie den Sinn des Wortes aus dem Zusammenhang erschließen?
- Ist das Wort vielleicht Teil eines Ausdrucks, der nur als Ganzes verständlich ist?
- Greifen Sie erst jetzt zum Wörterbuch. > Umgang mit dem einsprachigen Wörterbuch S. 161
- Prüfen Sie, ob die Wörterbuchdefinition wirklich zum Textzusammenhang passt.

> Manchmal verstehen Sie alle Wörter, aber zusammen wollen sie keinen Sinn ergeben. Gehen Sie diese Schritte durch, um den Satzbau zu verstehen:
- Finden Sie das finite Verb und umkreisen Sie es.
- Finden Sie das Subjekt des Verbs und unterstreichen Sie es.
- Klammern Sie eventuelle Nebensätze und Infinitivkonstruktionen aus.

> Ergibt der Satz immer noch keinen Sinn, fragen Sie sich: „Habe ich die Funktion eines Wortes missverstanden?" Es gibt im Englischen nämlich viele Wörter, die z. B. als Verb und als Nomen fungieren können, z. B. *demand* = „verlangen" und „Nachfrage"; *move* = „(sich) bewegen" und „Bewegung, Maßnahme". Dieser Umstand kann einen leicht auf den Holzweg bringen, so dass man dic ganze Satzstruktur falsch interpretiert.

Umgang mit dem einsprachigen Wörterbuch

Machen Sie sich mit Ihrem Wörterbuch vertraut, so dass Sie die Symbole, Abkürzungen und die Lautschrift verstehen und die Hilfen, die vorne und hinten im Wörterbuch oder auf Zusatzseiten angeboten werden, nutzen können. Auf der folgenden Seite sehen Sie ein Beispiel eines typischen Wörterbucheintrags.

- Achten Sie auf Ausdrücke, die den logischen Gedankengang verdeutlichen, z. B. *however, in my view, in conclusion* usw. Sie helfen Ihnen, den roten Faden nicht zu verlieren.
- Notieren Sie Informationen nur **stichpunktartig**, nie in ganzen Sätzen. Dabei kann ein Raster sehr hilfreich sein.
- Verwenden Sie Zeichen, Abkürzungen und Wortverkürzungen, um beim Notieren Zeit zu sparen:

Zeichen		Abkürzungen		Wortverkürzungen	
=	*the same as*	e.g.	*for example*	govt	*government*
≠	*not the same as*	km	*kilometres*	impt	*important*
+	*and*	w., w/o	*with, without*	kids	*children*

Nach dem Hören

- Formulieren Sie Ihre Stichpunkte so schnell wie möglich aus – vielleicht können Sie später Ihre Aufzeichnungen nicht mehr lesen oder Ihre Wortverkürzungen nicht mehr verstehen.
- Versuchen Sie, alle Fragen zu beantworten. Wenn Sie einige Informationen nicht verstanden haben, stellen Sie eine begründete Vermutung an.

> Hörverstehen S. 175

PRODUKTION

Note Making

Es ist sinnvoll, sich beim Lesen und Hören eines Textes Notizen zu machen. So können Sie später leichter auf die Informationen zurückgreifen.

Beim Lesen

Auf den ersten Blick scheint es ziemlich leicht, sich beim Lesen eines Textes Notizen zu machen. Trotzdem fällt es vielen schwer, wirklich kurze, sinnvolle Stichpunkte zu notieren. Oft führt die Sorge, etwas Wichtiges auszulassen, dazu, dass ganze Sätze des Originaltextes abgeschrieben werden. Damit verliert man nicht nur Zeit, sondern es wird später auch schwierig, seinen Text in eigenen Worten zu formulieren.

Hier einige Tipps, damit Sie diese Falle umgehen:

- Geben Sie Ihren Notizen eine Überschrift, die Ihr Thema klar umreißt, z. B. *Effects of genetic engineering on the environment.*
- Gehen Sie den Text durch und filtern Sie die wesentlichen Unterthemen heraus, die Sie als Überschriften verwenden können. Denken Sie daran, unter den Überschriften genug Platz für Ihre Stichpunkte zu lassen.

> Detailverständnis S. 160

- Halten Sie Ausschau nach Signalen wie Hervorhebungen, Wiederholungen und bedeutungstragenden Adjektiven wie *huge, incredible, devastating* usw. Diese zeigen, was der Verfasser für wichtig hält.
- Notieren Sie nur Stichwörter, nicht ganze Sätze.
- Verdeutlichen Sie den logischen Aufbau der Informationen, z. B. indem Sie bestimmte Punkte in einer Liste untereinanderschreiben, Themen durch Leerzeilen voneinander abheben oder die wichtigsten Begriffe unterstreichen.
- Kontrollieren Sie, ob Sie alle notwendigen Informationen zusammengetragen haben. Vergessen Sie nicht, dass sie oft über den gesamten Text verstreut sind.

Beim Hören

In diesem Fall ist es schwieriger Notizen zu machen, da man oft sehr schnell schreiben muss. Man muss sich auf das Wesentliche konzentrieren und sollte Abkürzungen verwenden, damit man den Faden nicht verliert.

> Das Hörverständnis üben S. 163, Hörverstehen, S. 175

Fragen zum Text beantworten

> Lesen schwieriger Texte S. 160

Bevor Sie mit dem Schreiben beginnen, vergewissern Sie sich, dass Sie den gesamten Text verstanden haben. (Nicht jedes Wort ist wichtig - überlegen Sie sich, ob Sie die Bedeutung des Satzes auch verstehen, ohne jedes Wort zu kennen.) Lesen Sie die Aufgabenstellung immer genau, um zu verstehen, worauf es bei der Beantwortung genau ankommt - ein häufiger Fehler ist das „Vorbeischreiben" an der Frage. Achten Sie auch darauf, keine Informationen zu „verpulvern", die Sie möglicherweise für die Beantwortung einer anderen Frage benötigen.

- Wenn Sie im Buch nichts anstreichen dürfen, machen Sie sich Notizen in Form von Stichpunkten und Listen, anstatt ganze Sätze aus dem Text herauszuschreiben. In der Klassenarbeit bzw. Prüfung sollten Sie die wichtigsten Passagen im Text markieren. Am besten markieren Sie alles, was für eine Textverständnisfrage wichtig ist, mit einer bestimmten Farbe, und nehmen dann eine andere Frage für die nächste Textverständnisfrage.
- Verwenden Sie in der Antwort die Zeitform der Fragestellung.
- Verwenden Sie so viele Synonyme und Umschreibungen der Begriffe und Formulierungen aus dem Text wie möglich, z. B. *recently - in recent years; violent crime - crime involving violence; think - believe; to a great extent - greatly; when she was a child - in her childhood* usw.
- Suchen Sie Signale im Text wie Hervorhebungen, Wiederholungen und bedeutungstragende Adjektive und Adverbien wie *absolutely, unbelievably, amazing*. Dies sind Signale dafür, was der Verfasser für wichtig hält.
- Versuchen Sie nicht, Ihre eigene Meinung einzubringen, wenn dies nicht in der Fragestellung gefordert ist.

Aus dem Text zitieren

Wenn Sie wirklich einmal eine wichtige Aussage aus dem Text zitieren möchten, um einen Punkt zu unterstreichen, so tun Sie dies nicht, indem Sie einfach die Formulierung des Textes übernehmen, sondern zeigen Sie, dass Sie bewusst zitieren und dies auch sprachlich deutlich machen können. Zitieren Sie in Ihrer Antwort höchstens einmal aus dem Text.

Zitate in die Antwort einbauen

- *To quote the author, ...*
- *According to the article, many stars are 'both defining and benefiting from a big shift in American attitudes to race'.*
- *Ron Berger highlights the positive aspects of this shift by saying 'what's ethnically neutral, diverse or simply unclear has tremendous appeal'.*

Eine Stellungnahme (*comment*) schreiben

> Materialgestützter Aufsatz, S. 173

Bei einer Stellungnahme geht es darum, Ihre Meinung zu einem bestimmten Thema darzulegen. Wichtig ist, dass Ihre Meinung begründet und mit Beispielen belegt ist.

1. Schritt: Machen Sie sich genau bewusst, worüber Sie schreiben sollen. Lesen Sie die Aufgabenstellung mehrmals durch.

2. Schritt: Machen Sie sich Notizen. Ordnen Sie Ihre Stichwörter übersichtlich an, z. B. in einer Mind Map, einer Liste oder einer Übersicht.

> Note Making S. 164

3. Schritt: Schreiben Sie einen Einleitungssatz, der sich auf die Aufgabenstellung beziehen sollte.

4. Schritt: Behandeln Sie jedes Argument in einem Absatz. Handelt es sich um ein Pro-/Kontra-Thema, können Sie erst die Pro- und dann die Kontra-Argumente anführen. Verdeutlichen Sie Ihre Argumentation durch die Verwendung von Strukturwörtern; hierzu siehe die Liste auf der hinteren Umschlagklappe dieses Buches (*Language for writing*).

> Einen Text sinnvoll gliedern S. 167

5. Schritt: Bringen Sie Ihre Argumentation in einem prägnanten Schlusssatz auf den Punkt.

Eine Stellungnahme einleiten
> *In the following I shall deal with the problem/subject/issue of ...*
> *I would like to discuss ...*
> *I intend to present arguments in favour of ... and against ...*

Eine Stellungnahme abschließen
> *All in all, I think it can be said that ...*
> *In conclusion, I would like to say that ...*
> *I would like to conclude by saying that ...*

Einen Text zusammenfassen

Die Fähigkeit, einen gelesenen Text zusammenzufassen, ist nicht nur wichtig, um den Text richtig zu verstehen, sondern sie hilft auch bei anderen Situationen, in denen Sie Informationen aus einem Text auf das Wesentliche reduzieren müssen. Zu solchen Situationen gehören z. B. die Beantwortung von Textverständnisfragen oder eine Mediation. > Mediation S. 171

1. Schritt: Lesen Sie den Text so oft wie möglich, bis Sie sicher sind, alles verstanden zu haben.

> Detailverständnis S. 160, Umgang mit unbekannten Vokabeln S. 161

2. Schritt: Fassen Sie in ein oder zwei einleitenden Sätzen zusammen, worum es in dem Text geht, z. B.: *The text is an extract from a radio phone-in show which is looking at people's attitudes to the EU.*

3. Schritt: Machen Sie sich bewusst, welche Informationen für den Leser wichtig sind, indem Sie *Wh*-Fragen beantworten: *Who? What? When? Where? Why?*, z. B.:
> *Who: Dr Peter Brown from Manchester University*
> *What: has been doing research into corruption in the EU*

4. Schritt: Machen Sie sich Notizen in Form von Stichwörtern. > Note Making S. 164

5. Schritt: Schreiben Sie Ihren Text. Beachten Sie dabei folgende Punkte:
> Lassen Sie Unwesentliches weg. Dazu gehören etwa Beispiele, Aufzählungen, Namen, Zitate usw.
> Verwenden Sie so weit wie möglich Ihre eigenen Worte.
> Vermeiden Sie es, zu dem Text Stellung zu nehmen. Dies gehört in der Regel nicht zur Aufgabenstellung.
> Denken Sie daran, Zitate in indirekte Rede umzuwandeln. > Reported speech S. 173

6. Schritt: Kontrollieren Sie Ihren Text auf Fehler und vergewissern Sie sich, dass Sie alle wichtigen Aspekte des Textes berücksichtigt haben.

Einen Aufsatz schreiben

> Materialgestützter Aufsatz, S. 173

Im Laufe der Oberstufe, in der Abschlussprüfung und auch später, z. B. im Studium, werden Sie immer wieder Aufsätze zu unterschiedlichsten Themen schreiben müssen. Es ist sinnvoll, sich von Anfang an einige Regeln zu eigen zu machen, um das Vorgehen möglichst zu automatisieren und sich gleich auf den Inhalt konzentrieren zu können. Dies ist besonders wichtig, wenn es – wie in der Abschlussprüfung – auf die Zeit ankommt.

1. Schritt: Verschaffen Sie sich Klarheit über Ihr Thema. Welche Aspekte gehören dazu, welche nicht?

2. Schritt: Machen Sie ein Brainstorming, indem Sie alle Ideen aufschreiben, die Ihnen zum Thema in den Kopf kommen. Wichtig: Die Ideen sollten Sie gleich in eine Struktur bringen, um nicht in einem Wust von ungeordnetem Gekritzel zu enden. Zur Strukturierung eignen sich z. B. Listen oder Mind Maps. > Note Making S. 164

3. Schritt: Überlegen Sie sich einen Aufbau für Ihren Text. Dies kann z. B. in Form einer Mind Map geschehen. Eine andere Möglichkeit ist eine Übersicht (*outline*) wie die folgende:

Should old towns be closed to private vehicles?

Einleitung: Umreißen des Themas
Hauptteil: Ausführung zum Thema, z. B.:
1. *Disadvantages for business*
  1.1 *Job losses*
    1.1.1 *retail trade*
    1.1.2 *fewer tourists*
  1.2 *What about town centre residents, delivery vehicles, etc.?*
2. *Advantages, positive effects on town and people*
...
Schluss: Zusammenfassung, Fazit

4. Schritt: Schreiben Sie Ihren Text. Lassen Sie Platz für Korrekturen, Änderungen oder Ergänzungen. Wichtig: Verdeutlichen Sie Ihre Argumentation durch die Verwendung von Strukturwörtern; hierzu siehe die Liste auf der hinteren Umschlagklappe dieses Buches (*Language for writing*) und den Abschnitt unten „Einen Text sinnvoll gliedern".

5. Schritt: Überprüfen Sie Ihren Entwurf auf:
- > **Rechtschreibfehler** (z. B. gleichlautende Wörter wie *there/their*, *meet/meat* usw.)
- > **Grammatikfehler** (z. B. Gebrauch der Zeitformen; *-ly*-Endung für Adverbien)
- > **Wortwahl** (z. B. Wiederholungen; *False friends* wie „aktuell" ≠ *actual*, „eventuell" ≠ *eventual*, „spenden" ≠ *spend*)
- > **Satzbau** (z. B. unvollständige Antworten, die mit *Because* beginnen)
- > **Gedankenführung** (z. B. Klarheit des Ausdrucks; Verwendung von Strukturwörtern wie *However, On the other hand, In addition, As a result* usw.)

Einen Text sinnvoll gliedern

> Materialgestützter Aufsatz, S. 173

Wann immer es darum geht, einen zusammenhängenden Text zu schreiben, sei es eine Antwort auf eine Frage zum Text, einen Aufsatz, eine Zusammenfassung o. Ä., ist es ganz wichtig, die Gedanken in einen logischen Zusammenhang zu bringen, damit der Leser den Faden nicht verliert. Dies alles gilt ebenso für mündliche Präsentationen, nur werden Sie dabei Ihre Materialien nicht Wort für Wort ablesen, sondern frei sprechen. Daher ist es wichtig, Formulierungen für die Gliederung auch mündlich parat zu haben.

Die wichtigsten Strukturwörter finden Sie auf der hinteren Umschlagklappe dieses Buches (*Language for writing*).

Diese Strukturwörter (*connectors*) sollten Sie sich so zu eigen machen, dass Sie sie möglichst in jedem Text verwenden. Dadurch gewöhnen Sie sich eine genaue und logische Ausdrucksweise an. Achten Sie auch beim Lesen von Texten auf Strukturwörter; so können Sie der Gedankenführung leichter folgen.

Die Arbeitsergebnisse präsentieren

Die Fähigkeit, wirkungsvoll vor einem Publikum zu referieren, ist wichtig im Berufsleben und zunehmend auch in der Schule. Dabei kommt es nicht nur auf den Inhalt an, sondern auch darauf, wie anschaulich Sie den Inhalt „verpacken", d.h. dass Sie Ihren Vortrag leicht nachvollziehbar gliedern, abwechslungsreich gestalten und lebendig illustrieren.

Vor der Präsentation

1. Schritt: Bereiten Sie Ihr Thema gründlich vor und machen Sie sich Notizen auf Englisch.

2. Schritt: Prüfen Sie Ihre Stichpunkte sprachlich und vergewissern Sie sich, dass Sie alles richtig aussprechen (anhand der Lautschrift in einem Wörterbuch oder der Aussprachebeispiele in gängigen Online-Wörterbüchern oder auf Wörterbuch-CD-ROMs).

3. Schritt: Überlegen Sie sich, wie Sie Ihren Vortrag interessanter und lebendiger machen können (Anschauungsmaterial, Audiobeispiele, Anekdoten, Handouts usw.).

4. Schritt: Organisieren Sie alle Hilfsmittel, die Sie benötigen (OHP, Flipchart usw.).

5. Schritt: Üben Sie die Präsentation, am besten vor Zuhörern.

Während der Präsentation

1. Schritt: Steigen Sie nicht gleich mitten ins Thema ein, sondern geben Sie einen Überblick über Ihre Präsentation.

2. Schritt: Machen Sie es den Zuhörern leicht, indem Sie sich klar ausdrücken, kurze Sätze benutzen und langsam sprechen.

3. Schritt: Achten Sie auf Ihre Körpersprache: Wenden Sie sich dem Publikum zu, halten Sie Blickkontakt mit den Zuhörern, sprechen Sie langsam und deutlich und benutzen Sie Gesten, um den Inhalt zu verdeutlichen.

4. Schritt: Fassen Sie zum Schluss das Wichtigste zusammen. Bedanken Sie sich bei den Zuhörern für ihre Aufmerksamkeit und ermuntern Sie sie, Fragen zu stellen.

Interpretation von Bildern und Karikaturen

> Bildbeschreibung mit Analyse, S. 172

Am besten eignen Sie sich einen Grundstock an Formulierungen zur Beschreibung und Interpretation von Bildern und Karikaturen an. Achten Sie darauf, sich auf die wesentlichen Bildaussagen zu konzentrieren, anstatt sich in Details zu verlieren.

1. Schritt: **Beschreibung des Bildes.** Betrachten Sie alle Einzelheiten der Bildvorlage, aber beschränken Sie sich bei der Beschreibung auf die Elemente, die für die Aussage wichtig sind.
Verwenden Sie bei der Beschreibung der Bildinhalte das *Present progressive* (außer bei Verben, die gewöhnlich nicht in dieser Zeitform vorkommen). Aber Vorsicht: Das *Present progressive* gilt nur für die Handlungen und Situationen, die im Bild dargestellt sind, nicht für die Verben, mit denen Sie den Cartoon beschreiben und interpretieren (*The cartoon* ***shows/describes*** *...*).

> Present progressive S. 176

2. Schritt: **Interpretation des Bildes.** Wenn Ihnen das Bild nicht viel sagt, können Sie dies in Ihre Interpretation miteinbeziehen, indem Sie es als *ambiguous* oder *unclear* bezeichnen.

3. Schritt: **Stellungnahme zur Bildaussage.** Bringen Sie die Hauptaussage der Bildvorlage auf den Punkt und/oder beziehen Sie Stellung, indem Sie z. B. die Wirkung des Bildes auf den Betrachter beurteilen.

1. **Beschreibung des Bildes**
   - > *In the foreground/background/centre there is ...*
   - > *The speech bubble* (Sprechblase) / *thought bubble* (Denkblase) / *caption* (Bildunterschrift) / *label* (Aufschrift) *says that ...*
   - > *The cartoon shows / appears to show ...*
   - > *The scene depicts/shows ...*
   - > *On the left/right you can see ...*
   - > *The ... looks as if ...*
   - > *The person on the left appears to ... / It seems as if the person ...*
   - > *He/She is wearing/holding ...*
2. **Interpretation der Bildaussage**
   - > *The picture/cartoon deals with the recent discussion of ...*
   - > *I think the cartoonist's/artist's/photographer's use of irony/exaggeration is intended to create ... / is aimed at making ... / conveys ...*
   - > *The person in the centre represents/symbolizes/shows ...*
   - > *This indicates/shows/reveals that ...*
   - > *The cartoonist/artist/photographer criticizes / wants to say / express the idea that ...*
   - > *The point of the cartoon seems to be that ...*
3. **Stellungnahme, Beschreibung der Wirkung auf den Betrachter**
   - > *I think the cartoon is quite right / makes a fair point.*
   - > *I agree with the cartoonist / artist, but ...*
   - > *In my opinion, the cartoonist is partly right / exaggerates a little / a lot / is quite wrong.*
   - > *Because of ..., the picture touches me / leaves me cold.*

Interpretation von Grafiken, Diagrammen und Tabellen

> Bildbeschreibung mit Analyse, S. 172

Wie im Falle von Cartoons ist es auch bei Grafiken, Diagrammen und Tabellen sinnvoll, einen Grundstock an Formulierungen zur Beschreibung und Interpretation parat zu haben. Halten Sie die folgenden Schritte ein, um Ihre Antwort sinnvoll zu gliedern:

1. Schritt: **Beschreibung der Vorlage.** Hier geht es nicht darum, alle Details aufzuzählen, sondern zu beschreiben, worum es in der Vorlage geht und welche Daten dargestellt werden.

2. Schritt: **Zusammenfassung der dargestellten Tendenzen, Entwicklungen bzw. Größen.** Welche Schlussfolgerungen ergeben sich aus den Daten? Kann man zusammenfassend ein Ergebnis oder Fazit formulieren?

Sprechen über Zahlen und Mengenangaben (*values, amounts*)
- > *more / less than ...*
- > *no less than ...*
- > *eighty-five per cent (said that ...)*
- > *On the other hand, almost ...*

Sprechen über Proportionen (*proportions, shares, percentages*)
- > *(over) half of ...*
- > *more / less than one third / quarter of ...*
- > *the (vast) majority of ...*
- > *a mere third of ...*

Sprechen über Entwicklungen (*developments*) und Tendenzen (*tendencies*)
- > *a huge / sharp increase / decrease*
- > *a small / slight raise / dip*
- > *levels out, remains constant*
- > *drastically, gradually, sharply, steadily*
- > *rises / increases / hits a maximum*
- > *drops / decreases / falls / plunges*
- > *over a period of ...*
- > *between 2000 and 2008*

Typen von Diagrammen

Tabelle (*table*)

	USA	UK
1995	495	105
2005	718	85

Kurvendiagramm (*graph, line graph*)

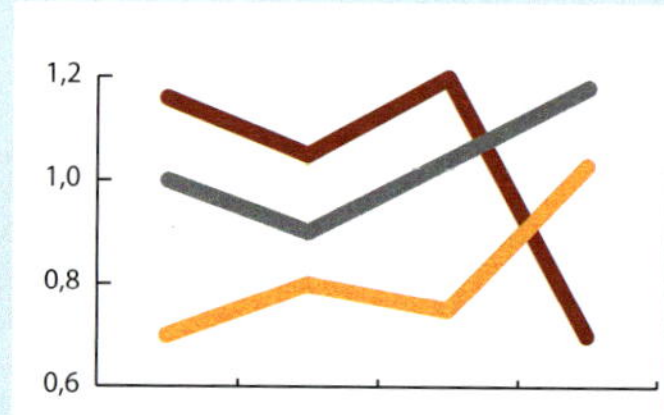

Balkendiagramm (*bar chart*)

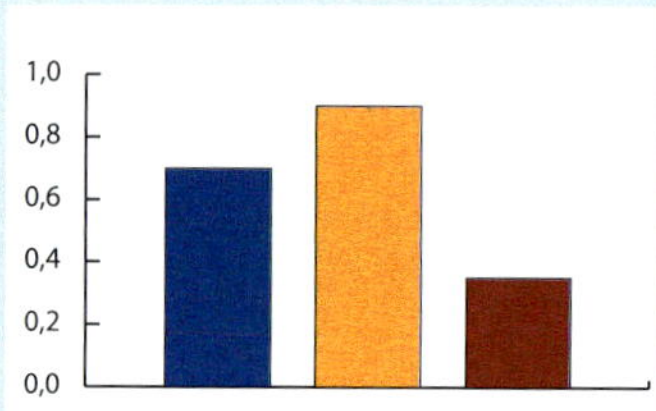

Kreis-/Tortendiagramm (*pie chart*)

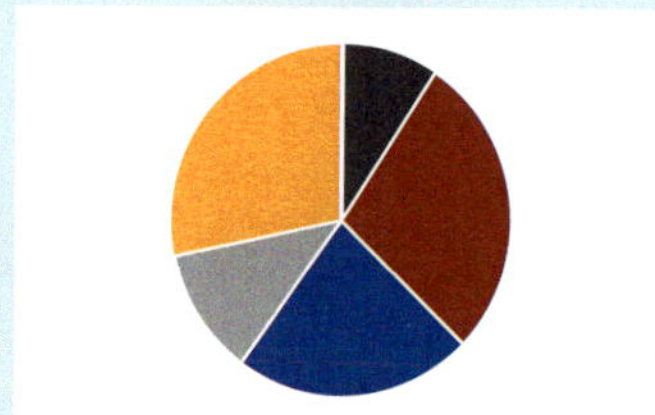

INTERAKTION

Gruppengespräche und Diskussionen führen

Ob es um Gruppengespräche, Diskussionen oder Rollenspiele geht: Machen Sie das meiste daraus, indem Sie die folgenden Punkte beherzigen.

> Lernen Sie die Formulierungen auf der hinteren Umschlagklappe dieses Buches (*Language for discussion*). Klappen Sie diese während des Unterrichts aus. Die Formulierungen helfen Ihnen, sich klar und logisch auszudrücken.
> Bereiten Sie sich inhaltlich vor, indem Sie sich einzelne Aspekte des Themas nochmal in Stichworten ins Gedächtnis rufen und Schlüsselbegriffe auf Englisch notieren.
> Legen Sie sich, wenn genügend Zeit ist, ein paar Fragen/Antworten zum Thema zurecht.
> Bleiben Sie immer ruhig und denken Sie nach, bevor Sie sprechen.
> Bleiben Sie beim Thema und schweifen Sie nicht ab.
> Gehen Sie auf Ihre Gesprächspartner ein und halten Sie Blickkontakt.
> Beteiligen Sie sich und hören Sie nicht bloß still zu: Gruppenarbeit ist eine hervorragende Gelegenheit zum freien Sprechen.

Sich zu Wort melden

> *Can I just say that ...* > *Well, if you ask me ...*

Jemand anderen ins Gespräch einbringen

> *What do you think, Sven / Svenja?*

Verständnis, Erstaunen usw. ausdrücken	
Ach so. / Ah ja.	*I see. / Right. / Oh, right.*
Oh je!	*Oh dear!*
Echt?	*Really?*
Gut. / Okay.	*Fine.*
Alles klar.	*OK then.*
Das ist doch wohl nicht dein Ernst!	*You're kidding!*

Exam preparation

MEDIATION

In dieser Aufgabe müssen Sie relevante Informationen aus einem englischen Text (ca. 450 Wörter) im Deutschen wiedergeben. Form und Inhalt Ihrer Zusammenfassung hängen von folgenden Faktoren ab, die in der Aufgabenstellung vorgegeben werden:
- Adressat (Mitschüler/innen, Kunden einer Firma usw.)
- Form (Info-Broschüre, Artikel usw.)
- Ort (Schule, Arbeitsplatz, Jugendgruppe usw.)
- Zweck (Infos/Ratschläge/Argumente zu einem spezifischen Thema aufbereiten)

Was ist Mediation?

Mediation bedeutet „Vermittlung". In einer Mediationsaufgabe übermittelt man die Informationen aus fremdsprachlichen Unterlagen an jemanden, der die Fremdsprache nicht beherrscht. Sprachmittlung ist in der alltäglichen und beruflichen Kommunikation von großer Bedeutung.
In der Abschlussprüfung werden Sie aufgefordert, eine schriftliche Mediation aus dem Englischen ins Deutsche vorzunehmen. Bei einer Übersetzung muss man sich möglichst getreu nach dem Original richten; bei einer Mediation dagegen geht es lediglich darum, die wesentlichen Informationen im Originaltext zu verstehen und in die andere Sprache zu übertragen. Als Faustregel sollte eine Mediation ungefähr der Hälfte der Länge des Originaltextes entsprechen.

Welche sind die „wesentlichen" Informationen?

Hier sind der Adressat und dessen Interesse am Text entscheidend. Die Aufgabenstellung gibt darüber Auskunft. Sie müssen die Aufgabe also genau lesen, um zu entscheiden, welche Informationen übertragen werden müssen. Behalten Sie also die Situation, für die der Text übertragen werden soll, im Auge, während Sie die wesentlichen Textstellen unterstreichen.

Wie erkenne ich „unwesentliche" Textstellen?

Folgende Textstellen können bei einer Mediationsaufgabe als unwesentlich betrachtet werden:
- Wiederholungen (oft eingeleitet durch *in other words, to put it another way*)
- Anekdoten und Exkurse (oft eingeleitet durch *by the way, incidentally*).

Solche Textstellen können Sie rasch überfliegen und dann meist ausklammern und nicht weiter beachten.
Stilmittel wie Vergleiche sollen vereinfacht werden: *The authorities received a flood of complaints* überträgt man etwa so: „Die Behörden erhielten viele Beschwerden."
Mit Zitaten müssen Sie etwas vorsichtiger umgehen: Manchmal werden sie nur aufgeführt, um eine Ausführung zu veranschaulichen. In diesem Fall sind sie unwesentlich. Bei journalistischen Texten jedoch sind manchmal Kernaussagen des Textes in Zitaten enthalten (um den Text abwechslungsreicher und interessanter zu machen). Sie müssen also jedes Zitat einzeln bewerten.
Auf jeden Fall sollten Sie ein Zitat auf seine Kernaussage reduzieren: Die Identität des Sprechers und die Umstände des Zitats sind fast immer unwesentlich.
Dasselbe gilt für Beispiele (oft eingeleitet durch *for instance, for example, e.g.*). Sind sie nur da, um einen Punkt zu veranschaulichen, oder enthalten sie wichtige zusätzliche Informationen? Sie müssen entscheiden.

> Einen Text zusammenfassen, S. 166

Schritte zum Erfolg

1. Schritt: Lesen Sie den Text schnell durch, um sich einen Überblick zu verschaffen. Lesen Sie bei kleineren Verständnisproblemen einfach weiter - wahrscheinlich ergibt sich der Sinn schwieriger Stellen aus dem Kontext.

2. Schritt: Lesen Sie die Aufgabe genau durch. Finden Sie heraus, welche Informationen aus dem Text Sie benötigen.

3. Schritt: Gehen Sie den Text jetzt Absatz für Absatz durch. Unterstreichen Sie die wesentlichen Sätze und Satzteile.

4. Schritt: Fassen Sie die unterstrichenen Teile auf Deutsch zusammen.

5. Schritt: Gehen Sie alle Textteile nochmals durch, die Sie unterstrichen haben. Vergewissern Sie sich, dass Sie sie alle in Ihrem Text berücksichtigt haben.

6. Schritt: Falls Sie Zeit haben: Gehen Sie sicherheitshalber die nicht unterstrichenen Stellen noch einmal durch, um sich zu vergewissern, dass Sie nichts Wesentliches übersehen haben.

7. Schritt: Prüfen Sie: Ist der Aufbau klar? Sind die Sätze vollständig? Ist die Rechtschreibung korrekt?

Häufige Fehler

- Man übersetzt den gesamten Text, anstatt sich auf das Wesentliche zu beschränken, und verschenkt so wertvolle Zeit.
- Man übersieht wichtige Aspekte des Textes, weil man nicht systematisch genug arbeitet.

BEURTEILEN VON TEXTAUSSAGEN

> Lesen schwieriger Texte, S. 160

Für diese Aufgabe müssen Sie einen längeren englischen Text (ca. 600 Wörter) lesen. Ihr Textverständnis wird geprüft, indem Sie entscheiden, ob Aussagen zum Text richtig oder falsch sind und Ihre Entscheidung auf Deutsch begründen. Es wird zehn Aussagen zum Text geben, von denen sich zumindest zwei oder drei übergreifend auf den gesamten Text beziehen sollen.

Schritte zum Erfolg

1. Schritt: Lesen Sie den Text schnell durch, um sich einen Überblick zu verschaffen. Lassen Sie sich von schwierigen Stellen nicht aufhalten.

2. Schritt: Lesen Sie die zehn Aussagen genau durch. Greifen Sie nur notfalls zum Wörterbuch.

3. Schritt: Suchen Sie nach Anhaltspunkten im Text.

4. Schritt: Lesen Sie die relevanten Absätze sorgfältig durch. Setzen Sie das Wörterbuch nur dann ein, wenn es für das Verständnis unentbehrlich ist.

5. Schritt: Entscheiden Sie, ob die Aussagen richtig oder falsch sind.

6. Schritt: Begründen Sie Ihre Entscheidung.

Häufige Fehler

- Man greift zu oft zum Wörterbuch und gerät dadurch in Zeitnot.
- Man übersieht relevante Stellen im Text und beurteilt die Aussage als falsch, weil man die Informationen im Text nicht gefunden hat.
- Man begründet seine Entscheidung durch die eigene Meinung/durch eigene Kenntnisse, statt sich auf den Text zu beziehen.

BILDBESCHREIBUNG MIT ANALYSE

> Interpretation von Bildern und Karikaturen, S.168, Interpretation von Grafiken, Diagrammen und Tabellen, S.169

Sie werden aufgefordert, ein Bild (z. B. ein Foto, eine Karikatur oder eine Anzeige) zu beschreiben und seine Beziehung zum Text in Aufgabe 2 (Beurteilen von Textaussagen) zu interpretieren.

Schritte zum Erfolg

1. Schritt: Halten Sie Ihre erste Reaktion gleich fest, während sie noch frisch ist, indem Sie einige Stichwörter notieren.

2. Schritt: Betrachten Sie das Bild eingehend und erwähnen Sie möglichst viele Einzelheiten in Ihrem Aufsatz.

3. Schritt: Es gibt keine „richtige" Lösung - es geht hier um Ihre persönliche Interpretation. Scheuen Sie sich also nicht, Vermutungen anzustellen und auch Ihre Fantasie zu benutzen.

4. Schritt: Überlegen Sie, wie sich das Bild auf den Text in Aufgabe 2 bezieht: Bestätigt es eine Meinung, die dort zum Ausdruck gebracht wurde? Vertritt es eine andere Position als die des Textes?

5. Schritt: Wenn Ihnen das Bild nicht viel sagt, können Sie das auch in Ihre Bewertung einbeziehen, indem Sie es als *ambiguous* oder *unclear* bezeichnen.

MATERIALGESTÜTZTER AUFSATZ

> Einen Aufsatz schreiben, S.166

Sie werden aufgefordert, einen Aufsatz über ein bestimmtes Thema zu schreiben. Das Thema kann sowohl aus dem gesellschaftlich-politischen als auch aus dem naturwissenschaftlich-technischen Bereich stammen. Erwartet werden ungefähr 300 Wörter.
Für diese Aufgabe werden vier bis fünf unterschiedliche Materialien (Bildvorlage, Statistik, Schaubild, Zitat, Textausschnitt usw.) als Schreibanlass und inhaltliche Hilfestellung vorgelegt, von denen Sie mindestens drei in Ihren materialgestützten Aufsatz einbeziehen sollen. Sie können den Aufsatz durch eigene Kenntnisse ergänzen. Was nicht fehlen sollte: Ihre eigene Meinung zu der Thematik.
Die Materialien werden das Thema aus verschiedenen Perspektiven beleuchten, Sie können sie also kombinieren, um das Für und Wider zu erörtern oder mehrere Aspekte des Themas zu besprechen.
Ganz wichtig: Sie sollen Ihre eigenen Worte verwenden, die Textquellen nicht wörtlich wiedergeben.

Wie teile ich meine Zeit ein?

Phase	Beschreibung	Dauer
Recherche	Alle Materialien durchlesen; erste Notizen auf Konzeptpapier machen	10 Minuten
Planen	Ideen in ca. fünf Hauptideen ordnen (Gedankengerüst); Notizen ergänzen	20 Minuten
Schreiben	ca. 300 Wörter in vollständigen Sätzen, in ca. sieben Absätze geordnet (einschließlich Einleitung und Zusammenfassung)	50 Minuten
Kontrolle	Überprüfung der Struktur, Fehlerkontrolle	10 Minuten

Phase 1: Recherche

Lesen Sie das Aufsatzthema und die Materialien sorgfältig durch. Benutzen Sie falls nötig Ihr Wörterbuch, um Schlüsselbegriffe nachzuschlagen. Kreisen Sie wichtige Themen ein und/oder notieren Sie Stichwörter auf Konzeptpapier.
Überblick über die Materialien

> **Statistik:** Dies könnte z. B. in Form eines Diagramms, eines Schaubilds oder einer Tabelle sein. Sie können sie verwenden, um eine These zu unterstützen oder zu widerlegen, oder den Hintergrund darzustellen: *Statistics tell us that a large part of our carbon emissions come from burning fossil fuels. Does this mean that ... ?*

Denken Sie immer daran, mittels der Statistik Vergleiche zu ziehen (*Compared to Europeans, Chinese people use less ...*) oder Trends zu kommentieren (*Over the last ten years, water consumption has risen by ...*) .

- **Bildvorlage:** Das könnte z.B. eine Karikatur über das Thema sein. Sie sollen keine unwichtigen Bilddetails beschreiben, sondern die Aussage des Bildes erkennen und diese in Ihren Aufsatz eingliedern, etwa: *It is easy to joke about the effects of climate change in chilly northern countries, and it is probably true that there will be some positive changes ...* (Karikatur mit einem Eisbären, der sich am Nordpol am Strand sonnt.)
- **Kurztext:** Dies könnte entweder ein neutraler Sachtext oder eine Stellungnahme zum Thema sein. Sie können daraus Tatsachen und Argumente für Ihren Aufsatz erschließen. Einzelne Vokabeln und Redewendungen aus dem Text können Sie in Ihrem Aufsatz wiederverwenden, aber Sie sollten es vermeiden, ganze Sätze oder Textteile wiederzugeben - dafür gibt es keine Punkte!
- **Zitat:** Dies könnte eine provokative These einer berühmten Person zum Thema sein. Sie können sich in Ihrem Aufsatz direkt darauf beziehen, etwa: *Former US vice president Al Gore considers that ...*
  Achtung: das Zitat nicht wörtlich wiederholen, sondern den Standpunkt des Sprechers in Ihren eigenen Worten schildern.
- **Deutscher Text:** Ähnlich wie der Kurztext, aber auf Deutsch. Der Vorteil davon ist natürlich, dass der Inhalt ohne Weiteres verständlich ist; der Nachteil, dass Sie dadurch keine nützlichen Vokabeln vorgelegt bekommen.

Phase 2: Planen

> Einen Text sinnvoll gliedern, S.167

Sammeln Sie nun Ideen aus den Materialien. Am Ende der Planungsphase sollten Sie ca. fünf Hauptargumente bzw. -themen vor sich haben, die den Kern Ihres Aufsatzes bilden, mitsamt mehreren Stichwörtern, Ausdrücken und Redewendungen, die Sie benutzen können, um die Argumente auszugestalten.
Haben Sie mehr als fünf Hauptthemen, können Sie überzählige vorläufig ausklammern - wobei Sie natürlich diejenigen behalten, zu denen Ihnen am meisten einfällt, oder die am besten in Ihr Schema passen. Sie halten die ausgeklammerten Themen in Reserve, für den Fall, dass Sie mehr Stoff brauchen.
Ganz wichtig: Machen Sie Ihre Planung ausschließlich auf Englisch.

Phase 3: Schreiben

> Eine Stellungnahme schreiben, S.165

Jeder Absatz sollte eine Hauptidee beinhalten. Der erste Absatz leitet immer das Thema des Aufsatzes ein, der letzte Absatz fasst die Argumente zusammen und zieht eine Schlussfolgerung oder ein Fazit.
Benutzen Sie Ausdrücke wie *firstly, secondly, on the one hand, on the other hand, however, furthermore*, um die logische Abfolge Ihrer Argumente zu verdeutlichen.

Phase 4: Kontrolle

Wenn Sie Ihren Aufsatz fertig haben, lesen Sie ihn aufmerksam durch und überprüfen Sie ihn auf Rechtschreibung, Wortstellung und Satzbau, Grammatik, Wortwahl und Aufbau.

Vor der Prüfung

- Seien Sie vielseitig interessiert und informiert, damit Ihnen zum Thema etwas einfällt!
- Lesen Sie in englischsprachigen Zeitschriften und im Internet so viel wie möglich über Themen, die in der Prüfung vorkommen könnten.
- Nur durch eine gründliche Vorbereitung werden Sie über einen ausreichenden Aktivwortschatz verfügen, um Ihre Ideen auf Englisch auszudrücken.

Während der Prüfung

- Halten Sie sich streng an Ihre Zeiteinteilung.
- Schreiben Sie nicht einfach drauflos, sondern beginnen Sie immer mit der Planungsphase.
- Lassen Sie beim Schreiben genügend Platz für spätere Korrekturen und Ergänzungen.
- Vergessen Sie nicht, Ihren Aufsatz zum Schluss nochmal durchzulesen.

Häufige Fehler

- Man schweift vom vorgegebenen Aufsatzthema ab.
- Man gerät unter Zeitdruck und überspringt die Vorbereitungsphase. Das Ergebnis: ein schlecht gegliederter Aufsatz.
- Man übersieht Rechtschreib- und Grammatikfehler.

HÖRVERSTEHEN

Bei der zentralen Klassenarbeit, wird das Hörverstehen auch geprüft. Dabei können verschiedene Aufgabentypen vorkommen.

Aufgabentyp: Sätze vervollständigen

Bei dieser Aufgabe geht es darum, Deutsche Sätze mit Informationen aus dem Hörtext zu vervollständigen.

> Detailverständnis, S.160

Aufgabentyp: Fragen zum Text

Bei dieser Aufgabe müssen sie Fragen zum Text in vollständigen Sätzen auf Deutsch beantworten.

> Fragen zum Text beantworten, S.165

Aufgabentyp: Raster ausfüllen

Bei dieser Aufgabe müssen sie einen Raster mit Details aus dem Hörtext auf Deutsch ausfüllen.

> Suche nach Einzelinformationen im Text, S.160

Aufgabentyp: Mediation

In dieser Aufgabe müssen Sie die wesentlichen Informationen aus dem Hörtext auf Deutsch zusammenfassen. Die Form und Inhalt der Zusammenfassung hängen von der Situation ab, die in der Aufgabenstellung vorgegeben wird.

> Mediation, S.171

Aufgabentyp: Wahre und falsche Aussagen

Bei dieser Aufgabe müssen sie entscheiden, ob (englische) Aussagen zum Hörtext richtig oder falsch sind. Dabei müssen Sie Ihre Antworten auf Deutsch begründen. Wichtig ist, dass Sie nach Ihrer eigenen Meinung nicht gefragt werden, sondern nur nach dem, was im Text steht.

> Detailverständnis, S.160

Schritte zum Erfolg

1. Schritt: Lesen Sie die Aufgabenstellung sorgfältig durch, damit Sie genau wissen, was von Ihnen verlangt wird.

2. Schritt: Hören Sie sich den gesamten Text zunächst in Ruhe an, um zu verstehen, worum es geht. Machen Sie sich in dieser Phase keine Notizen.

3. Schritt: Lesen Sie die Aufgabenstellung noch einmal durch und notieren Sie relevante Details (auf Englisch!) aus dem Hörtext.

4. Schritt: Vervollständigen Sie Ihre Notizen beim 2. Zuhören.

5. Schritt: Nach dem 2. Zuhören können Sie Ihre Antworten aufschreiben und korrigieren, wenn nötig.

Grammar summary

THE SIMPLE PRESENT

1 I **go** to the disco once a week.
2 We **live** in Bavaria.
3 Mr Brown **teaches** us English every day.
4 **I don't like** chocolate.
5 **Does** he **like** chocolate?

> Man gebraucht das **simple present** für regelmäßige, sich wiederholende Ereignisse oder Handlungen (1, 3) und für Dauerzustände (2, 4, 5).
> Mit Ausnahme der 3. Person Singular (*he, she, it*) hat das **simple present** dieselbe Form wie der Infinitiv (1, 2).
⚠ Die **3. Person Singular** endet auf *-(e)s* (3).
> Ist **kein Hilfsverb** im Satz vorhanden, werden **Verneinung** und **Fragen** mit der entsprechenden Form von *to do* gebildet (4, 5).

Das **simple present** wird häufig mit den folgenden **Zeitangaben** benutzt:

> *always, never, often, rarely, seldom, sometimes*
> *generally, mostly, normally, regularly, usually*
> *every day/week/month/..., every morning/afternoon/...*
> *on Mondays/Tuesdays/..., on weekdays*
> *in (the) summer/winter/...*
> *at Christmas/Easter, at weekends*

THE PRESENT PROGRESSIVE

1 **I'm calling** to say that Ben's ill.
2 He**'s staying** in bed today.
3 The computer **isn't working**.
4 **Are** you **sleeping**?

> Man benutzt das **present progressive** (auch **present continuous** genannt) für Vorgänge oder Handlungen, die im Moment des Sprechens oder Schreibens passieren und noch nicht abgeschlossen sind (1, 3, 4).
> Es wird auch für vorübergehende Situationen gebraucht (2).
> Das **present progressive** wird mit dem Präsens von *to be* und der *-ing*-Form des Vollverbs gebildet.
> Da beim **present progressive** immer ein Hilfsverb vorhanden ist, wird die **Verneinung** mit *not/n't* gebildet (3).
> Fragen werden durch Umstellung gebildet (4).

Das **present progressive** wird oft mit den folgenden **Zeitangaben** benutzt:

at the moment, at present, now, this week/month

⚠ Diese Verben bilden normalerweise **keine progressive-Form**:

be, believe, doubt, feel (meinen), *hate, hear, imagine, know, like/dislike, love, mean, notice, prefer, realize, recognize, remember, see* (begreifen), *seem, suppose, think* (meinen), *understand, want, wish*

THE SIMPLE PAST

1 We **wanted** to go to the USA last year.
2 She **went** on a school trip to London.
3 Jasmin **did not enjoy** her holiday in Rimini last summer.
4 Where **did** you **go** last year?

> Man benutzt das **simple past**, um über Vergangenes zu berichten.
> Das **simple past** wird auch gebraucht, wenn man sagen will, **wann** etwas geschehen ist (1, 3, 4).
> Bei **regelmäßigen** Verben wird das **simple past** durch das Anhängen von *-ed* an den Infinitiv gebildet (1).
⚠ Die unregelmäßigen Verben haben eine Sonderform (2), die man sich merken - auswendig lernen! - muss. > Irregular Verbs (S. 252)
> Ist **kein Hilfsverb** im Satz vorhanden, bildet man die **Verneinung** und **Fragen** mit *did/didn't* (3, 4).

Das **simple past** wird häufig mit den folgenden **Zeitangaben** benutzt:

> *yesterday, the day before yesterday, the week/month/... before last*
> *last night/week/month/summer/December/Easter/...*
> *two/three/... hours/days/years/... ago*
> *in 2005 / in the 20th century ...*
> *at that time, in those days*

THE PAST PROGRESSIVE

1 The teacher **was talking** to Heather **during the break**.
2 The tourists **were taking** photos when a lion (suddenly) **sprang** towards them.
3 I **wasn't doing** anything particular when he **arrived**.
4 **Were** you **having** breakfast when I **phoned**?

> Wenn man ausdrücken möchte, dass eine Handlung zu einem bestimmten Zeitpunkt oder während eines bestimmten Zeitraumes in der Vergangenheit **im Gange** war, benutzt man das **past progressive** (auch **past continuous** genannt) (1).
> Das **past progressive** wird auch benutzt, um zu verdeutlichen, dass eine Handlung im Gange war, als ein neues Ereignis (plötzlich) eintrat (2–4).
> Man bildet das **past progressive** mit *was/were* und der *-ing*-Form des Vollverbs (1).
> Die **Verneinung** wird mit *was not / wasn't* bzw. *were not / weren't* gebildet (3).
> **Fragen** bildet man durch Umstellung (4).
⚠ Einige Verben haben normalerweise **keine progressive-Form** (siehe die Liste unter **present progressive**).

THE PRESENT PERFECT

1 I've **bought** a new car.
2 I **haven't seen** the new film yet.
3 How long **have** you **had** a laptop?
4 We**'ve had** snow **for** two weeks.
5 She**'s had** a cold **since** December.

> Wenn man ausdrücken will, dass etwas geschehen ist, ohne dass der genaue Zeitpunkt des Ereignisses wichtig ist, wird das **present perfect** benutzt (1, 2).
> Man gebraucht das **present perfect** auch, um zu sagen, seit wann oder wie lange ein Zustand oder eine Handlung schon andauert (3–5). Dafür wird sehr oft *for* bzw. *since* verwendet. (Im Deutschen steht dafür „seit" plus Gegenwart.)
> Das **present perfect** wird mit *have/has* und der 3. Form des Vollverbs gebildet (1, 4, 5).
⚠ Die unregelmäßigen Verben haben eine Sonderform (1, 2), die man auswendig lernen muss.

> Irregular verbs (S. 252)

> Die **Verneinung** wird durch das Einfügen von *not/n't* nach *have/has* gebildet (2).
> **Fragen** bildet man durch Umstellung (3).

Das **present perfect** wird oft mit den folgenden Zeitangaben benutzt:

> *already, still (not), (not) yet*
> *(not) ever, just, lately, never, recently*
> *so far this week/month/..., till/until now*

THE PRESENT PERFECT PROGRESSIVE

1 I**'ve been learning** English since I was 10.
2 They**'ve not been speaking** to each other lately.
3 **Has** he **been singing** in the choir for long?

> Das **present perfect progressive** (auch **present perfect continuous** genannt) benutzt man für Handlungen und Vorgänge, die in der Vergangenheit begonnen haben und zum Zeitpunkt des Sprechens bzw. Schreibens noch nicht beendet sind.
> Das **present perfect progressive** wird mit *have/has been* und der *-ing*-Form des Vollverbs gebildet (1).
> Die **Verneinung** bildet man durch das Einfügen von *not/n't* unmittelbar nach *have/has* (2).
> **Fragen** werden durch Umstellung gebildet (3).
⚠ Einige Verben haben normalerweise **keine progressive-Form** (siehe die Liste unter **present progressive**, S. 177).

THE PAST PERFECT

1 Laura couldn't pay. She **had forgotten** her purse.
2 Nina **had** already **left** the coffee bar by the time I arrived.
3 When I visited John in hospital, he **had been** there for ten days.

> Mit Hilfe des **past perfect** drückt man aus, dass zwei Handlungen oder Vorgänge in der Vergangenheit aufeinander folgten (1, 2). Die Handlung, die zeitlich voranging, steht im **past perfect**.
> Das **past perfect** wird auch verwendet, um auszudrücken, dass ein Zustand vor einem Zeitpunkt der Vergangenheit begann und zu diesem Zeitpunkt noch andauerte (3).

⚠ Wenn zwei oder mehrere kurze Handlungen in der Vergangenheit direkt aufeinander folgen, wird für alle Handlungen das **simple past** verwendet:
*The cat **ran** out when Joanne **opened** the door.*

THE PAST PERFECT PROGRESSIVE

1 Rod **had been travelling** for three months when he ran out of money.
2 When I found Mary, I could see that she **had been crying**.

> Das **past perfect progressive** (auch **past perfect continuous** genannt) wird verwendet, wenn man ausdrücken will, dass eine Handlung oder ein Vorgang vor einem Zeitpunkt in der Vergangenheit begonnen hatte und bis (oder fast bis) zu diesem Zeitpunkt andauerte.

THE FUTURE

A will

1 In the future people **will use** public transport more often.
2 We can only hope that everyone **will accept** this shift in attitudes.
3 You've forgotten your purse? Don't worry. I**'ll lend** you some money.
4 Ms Smith **will not be** at the meeting this afternoon.
5 I **won't come** either.
6 **Will** he **get** the job?

> Das **will future** benutzt man, um Vorhersagen zu machen (1) oder Vermutungen über die Zukunft zu äußern (2).
> Man benutzt es auch, wenn man sich spontan zu etwas entschließt, Angebote oder Versprechen macht (3).
> Das **will future** wird mit *will* + Infinitiv des Vollverbs gebildet. Es hat für alle Personen die gleiche Form (1-3).
> Die **Verneinung** bildet man durch das Einfügen von *not* unmittelbar nach *will* (4). Im gesprochenen Englisch sagt man häufig *won't* (5).
> **Fragen** werden durch Umstellung gebildet (6).

Das **will future** kommt häufig mit den folgenden einleitenden Verben und Ausdrücken vor:

> *believe, expect, forecast, hope, imagine, suppose, think*
> *It's clear/obvious that ..., There's no doubt that ...*

B going to

1 Look at these clouds. It**'s going to rain** soon.
2 This time I**'m going to get** good marks in the class test.
3 Tom **isn't going to work** at the club any more.
4 When **are** you **going to take** your driving test?

> Das **going to future** benutzt man für Ereignisse und Situationen, die nach Meinung des Sprechers bald eintreten werden (weil es bereits Anzeichen dafür gibt) (1).
> Es wird auch für Pläne und Absichten gebraucht (2).
> Das **going to future** wird mit *am/is/are* + *going to* + Infinitiv gebildet (1, 2).
> Die **Verneinung** bildet man durch das Einfügen von *not/n't* unmittelbar nach *am/is/are* (3).
> **Fragen** werden durch Umstellung gebildet (4).

⚠ Der **Gebrauch des Futurs** hängt in gewissem Maße von der Absicht oder Sichtweise des Sprechers ab. Dies gilt insbesondere für das **going to future** und für zukünftige Ereignisse. Daher ist es im Zweifelsfall ratsam, das neutralere **will future** zu benutzen.

C The present progressive / The simple present

1 We**'re leaving** the house at 10.30.
2 The bus **goes** at 11 o'clock.

> Man kann das **present progressive** auch **mit einer Zeitbestimmung der Zukunft** (*at 10.30, this afternoon, on Sunday*) für bereits feststehende Pläne und Verabredungen verwenden (1).
> Genau wie im Deutschen wird auch im Englischen das **simple present mit einer Zeitangabe** benutzt, um fest terminierte Vorgänge (Fahrpläne, Stundenpläne, Programme usw.) anzugeben (2).

MODAL AUXILIARY VERBS

1 He **can speak** several languages.
2 You **must accept** your new situation.
3 We **needn't go** to work today.
4 **May** I **interrupt** you?

> Um zu sagen, was geschehen kann, muss, darf, soll usw., benutzt man ein modales Hilfsverb in Verbindung mit einem Vollverb (1-4).

⚠ Im Englischen steht ein Hilfsverb - anders als im Deutschen - nie ohne Vollverb:
- Lena kann Spanisch. ⟶ *Lena can speak Spanish.* NICHT: ~~Lena can Spanish.~~

> Modale Hilfsverben - nicht jedoch die Ersatzverben (siehe unten) - haben bei allen Personen immer die gleiche Form, einschließlich der 3. Person Singular (keine *-s*-Endung) (1, 2).
> Die **Verneinung** wird durch das Einfügen von *not/n't* unmittelbar nach dem Hilfsverb gebildet (3).
> **Fragen** bildet man durch Umstellung (4).
> Abgesehen von *could* (wenn es für eine Fähigkeit gebraucht wird) kann man modale Hilfsverben nur im Präsens und - mit einer geeigneten Zeitangabe - mit zukünftiger Bedeutung benutzen, zum Beispiel:
- *You **can go** home now.* (Präsens)
  *You **can go** home an hour early tomorrow.* (Futur)
- *I **must write** these letters now.* (Präsens)
  *I **must write** a long report next week.* (Futur)

⚠ Um andere Zeitformen bei modalen Hilfsverben zu bilden, z. B. die Vergangenheit, muss ein geeignetes Ersatzverb gebraucht werden:

must *The provider **had to block** access to the internet last December.*
can *I **couldn't start** the car yesterday.* (Fähigkeit)
*We **weren't allowed to go** home early last Friday.* (Erlaubnis)

Übersicht der modalen Hilfsverben nach Funktion

Funktion	Modale(s) Hilfsverb(en)	
Fähigkeit	*He **can** speak several languages.*	
	*The first satellites **could** only transmit sound.*	
Möglichkeit	*With your qualifications you **could** work abroad.*	
	*The boss **may** come in at any moment.*	
	*He **might** ask you what you are doing.*	
Bitte	***Can** I have a word with Ms Sims, please?*	(neutral)
	***Could** I speak to Ms Sims, please?*	(höflich)
	***May** I interrupt you?*	(betont höflich)
	***Might** I ask you a personal question?*	(äußerst höflich)
Erlaubnis	*You **can** go in now.*	(neutral)
	*The boss is free. You **may** go in now.*	(gefällig)
Verbot	*We **mustn't** be late for work tomorrow.*	
Pflicht	*You **must** wear a hard hat in the factory.*	
Wahl	*Most shop workers **needn't** work on Sundays.*	
Empfehlung	*You **should** get better qualifications.*	(neutral)
	*You **ought to** get better qualifications.*	(betont)
	*You **must** get better qualifications.*	(streng)

REPORTED SPEECH

A Aussagesätze

1 Some people **claim** that 'servant' robots **are putting** people out of work.
2 The speaker **reminded** his audience that there **were** some jobs robots **couldn't do**.

> Wenn man einem Dritten berichten möchte, was während eines Gespräches gesagt wurde, benutzt man die **indirekte Rede**.

> Bei Verwendung der indirekten Rede benutzt man ein einleitendes Verb wie *claim, say, remind, answer, think, mention* usw., um zu verdeutlichen, dass eine Äußerung wiedergegeben wird.
Steht das einleitende Verb in der Vergangenheit – also *said, answered, mentioned* usw. –, dann verschieben sich die Zeiten wie folgt:

direkte Rede		indirekte Rede
simple present *she works hard*	→	**simple past** *she worked hard*
present progressive *she is working hard*	→	**past progressive** *she was working hard*
simple past *she worked hard*	→	**past perfect** *she had worked hard*
past progressive *she was working hard*	→	**past perfect progressive** *she had been working hard*
present perfect *she has worked hard*	→	**past perfect** *she had worked hard*

> Beim Gebrauch von modalen Hilfsverben wird nach folgendem Muster verfahren:

bei Aussagen	Hilfsverb + *to be* + 3. Form	*must be displayed*
bei Fragen	Hilfsverb + Subjekt + *to be* + 3. Form	*Can ... be persuaded?*

⚠ Das Verb *to be* bleibt im Infinitiv immer unverändert.

THE IMPERSONAL PASSIVE

1 **It is said that** petrol will soon cost more.
2 He **is thought** to have gone to hospital.

> Das **impersonal passive** wird vor allem dann benutzt, wenn man sich objektiv bzw. unbeteiligt ausdrücken möchte. Daher kommt diese Struktur oft in Polizeiberichten, seriösen Zeitungsartikeln usw. vor.

> Bei Verben des Berichtens, Denkens usw. benutzt man häufig das Satzmuster:
It is/was/... + 3. Form des einleitenden Verbs + *that*-Satz (1).
Hier sind weitere Beispiele dieses Musters:

Aktiv	*Some **say** that companies which cause pollution should be heavily fined.*
Passiv	***It is said that** companies which cause pollution should be heavily fined.*
Aktiv	*Experts **recommended** that more be spent on public transport.*
Passiv	***It was recommended** that more be spent on public transport.*

> Um das Subjekt des *that*-Satzes zu betonen, kann man folgendes Muster benutzen:
Subjekt + *is/was/...* + 3. Form + *to be* + andere Satzteile (2):

Aktiv	*Many **believe** that the minister is thinking of raising fuel taxes.*
Passiv	*The minister **is believed to be** thinking of raising fuel taxes.*

⚠ Der *by agent* wird in solchen Passivsätzen folgendermaßen verwendet:

Aktiv	*The speaker felt that the idea was too radical.*
Passiv	*The idea was felt to be too radical **by** the speaker.*

CONDITIONALS

1 If we **invest** in new technology, a lot of people **will lose** their jobs.
2 A lot of people **will lose** their jobs if we **invest** in new technology.
3 If more people **took part** in re-training schemes, they **wouldn't have to worry** about finding new employment.
4 We **won't have** political censorship if we **don't start** to censor the internet.
5 **Will** we soon **have** political censorship if we **start** to censor the internet?

> Ein **Konditionalsatz** besteht aus zwei Teilen: dem ***if*-Teil** und dem **Hauptteil**.
Der ***if*-Teil** drückt eine **Bedingung** aus, der Hauptteil eine **Folge**.

> Bei **Konditionalsätzen** kommen folgende **Zeitmuster** am häufigsten vor:

Typ I	*If + simple present*	+	*will*-Futur
Typ II	*If + simple past*	+	*would* + Infinitiv
Typ III	*If + past perfect*	+	*would have* + 3. Form des Verbs

> Der *if*-Teil kann hinter dem Hauptteil stehen. In diesem Fall steht kein Komma dazwischen (2, 4, 5).

> Je nach Sinn kann der *if*-Teil, der Hauptteil oder beide Teile des Satzes **verneint** werden (3, 4).

> Bei **Fragen** kann nur der **Hauptteil** zu einer Frage geformt werden. Dann steht dieser Teil **an erster Stelle** (5).

- *if*-Sätze werden gemäß der **Wahrscheinlichkeit** der zu erwartenden Folge eingesetzt:
  Typ I: Folge (fast) sicher.
  *If we **invest in** new technology, a lot of people **will lose** their jobs.*
  D.h. viele Leute werden (vermutlich) ihre Stellen verlieren, da wir (sehr wahrscheinlich) in die neue Technologie investieren werden.
  Typ II: Folge theoretisch möglich, aber kaum wahrscheinlich.
  *If we **invested in** new technology, a lot of people **would lose** their jobs.*
  D.h. es ist kaum zu erwarten, dass viele Leute ihre Stellen verlieren werden, da wir (wahrscheinlich) nicht in die neue Technologie investieren werden.
  Typ III: Folge unmöglich, da die Bedingung nicht erfüllt wurde und bereits in der Vergangenheit liegt.
  *If we **had invested in** new technology, a lot of people **would have lost** their jobs.*
  D.h. der Sprecher weiß schon, dass keiner den Job verloren hat, da wir in die neue Technologie nicht investiert haben.

GERUND/INFINITIVE

1 Max **enjoys playing** football.
2 Can you **afford to buy** that DVD collection?
3 Cem and Julie **continued to meet** even though they had spilt up.
4 Cem and Julie **continued meeting** even though they had split up.
5 Alison **normally likes going** to parties, but **today** she would **prefer to stay** at home.

- Nach einigen Verben folgt immer die *-ing*-Form **(gerund)** (1).
  Am wichtigsten sind:

  admit, avoid, consider, deny, enjoy, finish, give up, imagine, mention, (not) mind (etwas/nichts dagegen haben), *miss, practise, recommend, risk, stop, suggest*

- **Nach einigen Verben** folgt immer der Infinitiv **(infinitive)** (2).
  Die **wichtigsten** Verben dieser Gruppe sind:

  afford, choose, decide, expect, hope, manage, mean, plan, promise, refuse, want

⚠ Nach den Verben *begin, continue, intend* und *start* kann der **Infinitiv** oder die ***-ing*-Form beliebig benutzt werden** (3, 4).

- Einige Verben werden **je nach Bedeutung** entweder mit dem **Infinitiv** oder mit der ***-ing*-Form** benutzt. Die **wichtigsten** Verben dieser Gruppe sind:

  like, dislike, love, hate, prefer

- Wenn von einer **allgemeingültigen Situation** die Rede ist, folgt auf diese Verben die ***-ing*-Form**. Handelt es sich aber um eine **Ausnahmesituation**, dann verwendet man den **Infinitiv** (5).

advise, allow, encourage, forbid, permit, recommend
Handelt es sich um einen **konkreten Einzelfall**, wird mit diesen Verben ein **Objekt + Infinitiv** verwendet.
*I strongly **advise you to** be more polite to people.*
Wenn es sich aber um eine **allgemeine Situation** handelt, dann steht das nachfolgende Verb in der ***-ing*-Form**.
*Most firms don't **allow smoking** in their offices.*

forget/remember

Die Struktur ***forget/remember*** **+ *-ing*-Form** bezieht sich auf die Vergangenheit. Sie drückt etwa die Idee „Ich werde nie vergessen ..." aus.

⚠ „Vergangenheit" bezieht sich hier nicht auf *forget/remember*, sondern auf das nachfolgende Verb.

*I still **remember getting** my first bicycle.*

*I'll never **forget going** to the Rock against Hunger concert last year.*

Die Struktur ***forget/remember*** **+ Infinitiv** dagegen bezieht sich auf die Zukunft. Sie drückt etwa die Idee aus „Ich darf nicht vergessen, etwas zu tun" bzw. „ich habe noch etwas zu tun, weil ich es bis jetzt vergessen habe".

*Dad, please **remember / don't forget to pick me up** from the station.*

*Oh dear. I **forgot / didn't remember to pick Sally up** from the station.*

regret

Die Struktur ***regret*** **+ *-ing*-Form** drückt Bedauern über eine vergangene Situation bzw. einen vergangenen Vorfall aus. Häufig geht es dabei um verpasste Chancen.

*I really **regret leaving** school without any qualifications.*

*I know they will **regret buying** such a big, expensive car.*

Die Struktur ***regret*** **+ Infinitiv** – fast immer mit einem Verb des Mitteilens wie *inform, say, tell* kombiniert – drückt eine schlechte Nachricht aus.

*I **regret to say** that I can't attend the meeting tomorrow.*

*We **regret to inform** you that the vacancy has now been filled.*

stop

Bedeutet ***stop*** „aufhören, etwas zu tun", steht das nachfolgende Verb in der ***-ing*-Form**.
Bedeutet aber ***stop*** „kurz anhalten, um etwas anderes zu tun", folgt ein Verb im **Infinitiv**.

*For heaven's sake **stop shouting** at me.*

*I'm a little late because I **stopped to give** somebody a lift.*

try

Bedeutet ***try*** „etwas ausprobieren", steht das nachfolgende Verb in der ***-ing*-Form**. Bedeutet aber ***try*** „sich anstrengen, etwas zu tun", folgt ein Verb im **Infinitiv**.

*I **tried phoning** Ellie, but she wasn't at home.*

*We'll **try to repair** your computer by the weekend.*

ADJECTIVES AND ADVERBS

1 John has a **new** DVD player.
2 He always buys **expensive** equipment.
3 My computer has become **very slow**.
4 That CD sounds **terrible**.
5 We can make printouts **quickly** and **cheaply**.

> Um **Personen** oder **Sachen** näher zu beschreiben, benutzt man **Adjektive** (1–4).
> Adjektive stehen **unmittelbar** vor Substantiven oder **unmittelbar nach** einer Form von *be* (bzw. *become* oder *seem*, die *be* ersetzen können) (3).
> **Adjektive** können mit Verben wie *feel, look* (aussehen), *sound, smell* und *taste* eine **sinnliche Wahrnehmung** ausdrücken (4).
> Um einen **Tätigkeitsverb** näher zu beschreiben, setzt man ein Adverb **unmittelbar hinter das Verb** bzw. Verb + Objekt (5).

⚠ Im Englischen können ein Verb und sein Objekt - anders als im Deutschen - nicht durch ein Adverb getrennt werden. Also NICHT: ~~We can make quickly printouts~~. (siehe **Word order** unten)

> Adverbien werden auch benutzt, um **Adjektive, andere Adverbien** und **ganze Sätze** näher zu bestimmen:
*MP3 players have become **surprisingly cheap**.* (Adverb + Adjektiv)
*My fax machine prints out **terribly slowly**.* (Adverb + Adverb)
***Luckily** Gerd left a message on my mailbox.* (Satzadverb)

> Die meisten Adverbien werden durch Anhängen von *-ly* an das Adjektiv gebildet (5). Eine kleine Anzahl von Adverbien hat dieselbe Form wie Adjektive; die häufigsten sind *fast, hard, early late, long, daily*.

COMPARISON OF ADJECTIVES AND ADVERBS

1 A hundred years ago life was **slower** and people may have been **happier**.
2 Which technological innovation is the **most/least important**?
3 Today you can copy data **more easily than** ever before.

> **Einsilbige** und **zweisilbige Adjektive**, die auf *-y* enden - zum Beispiel *easy, happy* und *lucky* -, werden mit *-(i)er/-(i)est* gesteigert (1).

> **Mehrsilbige Adjektive** und **Adverbien**, die auf *-ly* enden, werden mit *more/most* gesteigert (2, 3).
⚠ Die Adverbien, die dieselbe Form wie das entsprechende Adjektiv haben (*fast, hard, early* usw.), werden mit *-er/-est* gesteigert.

> Um Personen oder Sachen im Satz miteinander zu vergleichen, gibt es folgende Möglichkeiten:

Kein Unterschied	*as good as*	genau so gut wie
Unterschied	*not as good as*	nicht so gut wie
Unterschied	*better than*	besser als

WORD ORDER

positions of adverbs of time, place and frequency

1 She goes shopping **every week**.
2 They play in a club **in Doherty Street**.
3 **Last year** we went to India for our holidays.
4 Paul and Emily went to **the USA last year**.
5 She **always finishes** school early on Fridays.
6 He **is never** at home when I call.
7 I like to stay at home **now and then**.
8 Gina acted **strangely at the party last night**.

> Zeitangaben (Wann?) und Ortsangaben (Wo?, Wohin?) stehen in der Regel am Satzende (1, 2).

> Um die Zeit eines bestimmten Ereignisses hervorheben, kann man die Zeitangabe an die erste Stelle setzen (3).

> Stehen eine Zeitangabe und eine Ortsangabe zusammen am Satzende, dann gilt die Reihenfolge Ort vor Zeit (alphabetisch merken: O vor Z!) (4).

> Besteht eine Häufigkeitsangabe aus einem Wort, z.B. *always, often, sometimes*, steht sie unmittelbar vor dem Vollverb (5).

> Lautet das Vollverb *to be*, steht das Adverb direkt dahinter (6).

- Besteht die Häufigkeitsangabe aus mehreren Wörtern, z.B. *every day, now and then*, steht sie wie eine Zeitangabe am Satzende (7).
- Adverbien der Art und Weise stehen in der Regel am Satzende. Kommen noch Zeit- oder Ortsadverbien hinzu, lautet die Reihenfolge: Art und Weise - Ort - Zeit (AOZ) (8).

RELATIVE CLAUSES AND CONTACT CLAUSES

1 Car manufacturers are designing cars **which/that** can use hydrogen fuel cells.
2 Wildernesses are being spoiled by tourists **who/that** want to go to 'unspoiled' places.
3 Tony filled in a Dateline questionnaire **(which/that)** he found on the internet.
4 Fred Foley is a paparazzo **whose** photos sell for huge sums of money.
5 Call centre employees, most **of whom** come from India, work long hours.
6 Some non-GM crops are attacked by pests **against which** they have no resistance.

- Relativsätze werden benutzt, um den Hauptsatz durch zusätzliche Informationen genauer zu bestimmen.
- Für **Sachen** benutzt man das Relativpronomen *which* bzw. *that* (1) und für Personen *who* bzw. *that* (2).
- Steht das Relativpronomen für das **Objekt des Hauptsatzes**, dann kann man es weglassen (3). Solche Relativsätze heißen **contact clauses**.
- Um **Besitz** bzw. **Zugehörigkeit** anzuzeigen, gebraucht man *whose* unmittelbar vor dem **Substantiv** bei Personen und Sachen (4).
- Steht eine **Präposition** vor dem **Relativpronomen**, wird *whom* für Personen und *which* für Sachen benutzt (5, 6). In solchen Fällen ist der Gebrauch von *that* nicht möglich.

DEFINING AND NON-DEFINING RELATIVE CLAUSES

1 The first Europeans **who** settled in Australia came from Britain.
2 Sydney, **which** is famous for its unusually designed opera house, is situated on the south-eastern coast of Australia.

- Im **ersten Beispielsatz** ist der Sinn des Hauptsatzes *The first Europeans came from Britain* ohne den Relativsatz *who settled in Australia* offensichtlich falsch bzw. unvollständig. Relativsätze dieser Art - die wesentlich für das Verständnis des gesamten Satzes sind - nennt man **defining relative clauses** (notwendige oder bestimmende Relativsätze).
- Im **zweiten Beispielsatz** ist die Aussage des Hauptsatzes *Sydney is situated on the south-eastern coast of Australia* ohne den Relativsatz völlig verständlich, weil der Relativsatz *which is famous for its unusually designed opera house* eine zusätzliche, also nebensächliche, Information enhält. Daher werden solche Relativsätze ***non-defining relative clauses*** (nicht notwendige oder nicht bestimmende Relativsätze) genannt.
  ⚠ Notwendige Relativsätze werden immer **ohne** trennende **Kommas** benutzt. Dies signalisiert, dass sie fester Bestandteil der Hauptaussage sind.

PARTICIPLE CONSTRUCTIONS

1 Malaria, preventable with a treated bed net **costing** less than one pound, is endemic.
2 Many men believe that any work **involved** with cooking is a woman's chore.
3 **Losing** more and more people to AIDS, Africa now needs effective help more urgently than ever before.

4 **Burdened** with declining life-expectancy, large parts of Africa are caught in a poverty trap.
5 **Having fetched** water from a river for many years, some women in developing countries are now happy to be able to use the Hippo Roller.
6 **Despite facing** extreme destitution, many rural residents haven't given up hope.
7 Donors should invest in projects that help local inhabitants become self-supporting, **thereby making** sure that the money isn't wasted.
8 Poor infrastructure is a key barrier to economic growth in Nepal, **thus causing** huge additional costs to the transport of commercial goods.
9 Life is becoming hard in the developing countries, **with** many small farmers **going** out of business.
10 AIDS represents a major challenge to sub-Saharan Africa, currently **killing** more than two million people every year.

Die englische Sprache ist geprägt durch häufige Verwendung von Partizipialkonstruktionen. Diese ermöglichen einen eleganteren Sprachfluss.

> Partizipialkonstruktionen verkürzen Relativsätze; dabei kann entweder das **present participle** (1) oder das **past participle** (2) verwendet werden.
> Sie werden auch verwendet, um adverbiale Nebensätze zu vekürzen. In diesen Fällen unterscheidet man zwischen Partizipialkonstruktionen ohne Konjunktion (3–5) und solchen mit Konjunktion (6–9). In Sätzen ohne Konjunktion ist der Inhalt des Satzes auch ohne eine solche klar. Dagegen sind Konjunktionen nötig, um zu verhindern, dass der logische Zusammenhang des Satzes verloren geht. Zum Beispiel wird der Inhalt von Satz 6 unklar, wenn die Konjunktion *despite* ausgelassen wird.
> Wie bei der Verkürzung von Relativsätzen kommen auch bei der Verkürzung von adverbialen Nebensätzen das **present participle** (3, 6–9) und das **past participle** (4) zur Anwendung. Darüber hinaus wird hier auch noch das **perfect participle** verwendet (5), und zwar um die Vorzeitigkeit der Handlung im Nebensatz auszudrücken. *(Nachdem sie jahrelang Wasser aus dem Fluss geholt hatten, ...)*
> Schließlich verknüpft man mit einer Partizipialkonstruktion zwei Hauptsätze zu einem einzigen Satz, und zwar ausnahmslos mittels **present participle** (10).

COUNTABLE AND UNCOUNTABLE NOUNS

1	Visit our website for more **information** on our firm.	NICHT ~~informations~~
2	Have you read the paper today? The political **news** is interesting.	NICHT ~~news are~~
3	Where can I get some **advice**?	NICHT ~~an advice~~

> Einige wichtige **Substantive** sind **zählbar im Deutschen, nicht jedoch im Englischen**. Diese Substantive können also nicht ohne weiteres mit dem unbestimmten Artikel *a/an* oder mit einem Zahlwort benutzt werden.
Hier ist eine Liste solcher Wörter, die Sie auswendig lernen sollten:

advice, baggage, damage, data, equipment, evidence, furniture, information, knowledge, luck, luggage, machinery, news, progress, research, rubbish, work (housework, homework)

> Um diese Substantive im Plural zu verwenden, muss *some, a bit of* bzw. *a piece of* hinzugefügt werden (3).

THE DEFINITE ARTICLE

1 **Sociologists** say that **violence** is increasing among young people.
2 Is **the current trend** partly caused by **the violent films** they watch?
3 **Most sentences** are not tough enough.
4 Nearly **half the prisoners** in **British prisons** are under 25.
5 **Spring** is my favourite season but **the spring** we're having this year is more like **winter**.
6 We had **breakfast** late this morning so we came to school **by car** instead of **by bus**.
7 They are thinking of legalizing soft drugs in **the Netherlands**.

> Hat ein Substantiv eine allgemeine, uneingeschränkte Bedeutung - also „alle ohne Ausnahme“ - dann steht es ohne Artikel (1, 5).

> Ist die Bedeutung eines Substantives auf bestimmte Fälle eingeschränkt, benutzt man den Artikel (2, 5).

> Ferner wird der Artikel in den folgenden Fällen und Wendungen im Englischen - z. T. anders als im Deutschen - nicht gebraucht:
- bei *most* in der Bedeutung „die meisten" (3),
- bei öffentlichen Gebäuden im allgemeinen Sinn (4),
- bei Mahlzeiten (6),
- bei Verkehrsmitteln (6),
- bei Straßennamen,
- bei Tageszeiten, Wochentagen, Monaten und Jahreszeiten im allgemeinen Sinn (5).

> Der Artikel wird verwendet nach *all* und *half* (4) und mit den Pluralnamen von Staaten (7).
⚠ Der bestimmte Artikel steht im Englischen (viel) seltener als im Deutschen. Daher: *When in doubt, leave it out!*

Basic word list

Diese Liste enthält ca. 1000 Wörter und Ausdrücke, die in **Focus on Success – Ausgabe Baden-Württemberg** als bekannt vorausgesetzt werden. Nicht aufgeführt, jedoch vorausgesetzt, sind einige elementare Wörter wie einfache Strukturwörter, Präpositionen, Zahlen, Wochentage usw. sowie internationale Wörter wie *email*, *hotel*, *cowboy* usw.

> TIP

Die folgende Grundwortschatzliste ist nach Themenbereichen angelegt. Auch innerhalb der Themenbereiche sind die Vokabeln nach sinnvollen Wortfeldern angeordnet. Dadurch eignet sich die Liste nicht nur zum Nachschlagen, sondern auch zum Lernen. Hierzu gibt es eine einfache, aber effektive Übung. Nehmen Sie sich einen Themenbereich vor und verdecken Sie ein paar Wörter in der linken Spalte. Schauen Sie nun auf die Übersetzungen in der rechten Spalte und bilden Sie englische Sätze, die so viele Übersetzungen der verdeckten deutschen Wörter wie möglich enthalten. Anschließend kontrollieren Sie Ihre Übersetzungen, indem Sie die linke Spalte aufdecken.

PEOPLE
(Menschen)

people *Personen*
population *Bevölkerung, Einwohner*
nationality *Staatsangehörigkeit*
race *Rasse*
racist *rassistisch; Rassist/in*
society *Gesellschaft*
social *sozial*
human *menschlich*
adult *Erwachsene/r*
child *Kind*
teenager *Teenager/in*
sex *Geschlecht*
lady *Dame*
man *Mann, Mensch*
men *Männer, Menschen*
woman *Frau*
women *Frauen*
male *männlich*
female *weiblich, Frauen-*
boy *Junge*
girl *Mädchen*
couple *Paar*
married *verheiratet*
to get married *heiraten*
Mr *Herr*
Mrs, Ms *Frau*
name *Name*
age *Alter*
born *geboren*
life *Leben*
death *Tod*
anybody *jemand, jede/r/s*
anyone *jemand, jede/r/s*
nobody *niemand*
some *einige, etwas*
somebody *jemand*
someone *jemand*
everybody *jede/r/s*
everyone *jede/r/s, alle*
friend *Freund/in*
guest *Gast*
host *Gastgeber/in*
leader *Leiter/in*
loser *Verlierer/in*
member *Mitglied*
group *Gruppe*
crowd *(Menschen-)Menge*
together *zusammen*

FAMILY
(Familie)

family *Familie*
parents *Eltern*
father *Vater*
mother *Mutter*
dad *Papa*
mum, mom ***(AE)*** *Mama*
stepfather *Stiefvater*
stepmother *Stiefmutter*
husband *(Ehe-)Mann*
wife *(Ehe-)Frau*
children *Kinder*
son *Sohn*
daughter *Tochter*
brother *Bruder*
sister *Schwester*
brothers and sisters *Geschwister*
cousin *Cousin/e*
grandparents *Großeltern*
grandfather *Großvater*
grandmother *Großmutter*
grandchildren *Enkel(kinder)*

EMOTIONS
(Gefühle)

to feel *(sich) fühlen*
feeling, emotion *Gefühl*
happy *glücklich, froh, zufrieden*
joy *Freude*
pleased *zufrieden*
(to) surprise *Überraschung; überraschen*
mad *verrückt, toll*
unhappy *unglücklich*
sad *traurig*
to cry *schreien, weinen*
angry *wütend, zornig*
crazy *verrückt*
afraid of *ängstlich*
to be frightened of *sich fürchten vor*
tired *müde*
care *Sorge*

BODY AND CLOTHING
(Körper und Kleidung)

body *Körper*
physical *physisch, körperlich*
leg *Bein*
arm *Arm*
hand *Hand*
shoulder *Schulter*
hair *Haar(e)*
to touch *anfassen, berühren*
head *Kopf*
face *Gesicht*
eye *Auge*
to look *(aus)sehen, blicken*
nose *Nase*

to smell *riechen*
mouth *Mund*
voice *Stimme*
to smile *lächeln*
to speak *sprechen, reden*
ear *Ohr*
to listen *zuhören*
to hear *hören*
to sound *klingen*
tooth *Zahn*
heart *Herz*
skin *Haut*
health *Gesundheit*
healthy *gesund*
well *gesund, gut*
able *fähig, in der Lage*
flexible *flexibel*
illness *Krankheit*
ill/sick *krank*
painful *schmerzhaft*
fat *dick*
thin *dünn*
short *kurz, klein*
small *klein*
tall/big *groß*
weak *schwach*
strong *stark, kräftig*
old *alt*
young *jung*
clothing *Bekleidung*
clothes *Kleidung, Kleider*
fashion *Mode*
design *Design*
(to) dress *Kleid; (be)kleiden*
to wear *tragen, anhaben*
to cover *(be)decken*
to wash *waschen*
to spray *(be)sprühen*
comfortable *bequem*
uncomfortable *unbequem*
elegant *elegant*
coat *Mantel*
shirt *Hemd*
shoes *Schuhe*
trainers *Turnschuhe*
boot *Stiefel*
bag *Tasche*
uniform *Uniform*

JOBS AND WORK
(Jobs und Arbeit)

to work *arbeiten, funktionieren*
worker *Arbeiter/in*
job *Arbeit, Stelle*
factory *Fabrik*
business *Geschäft, Firma*
company *Firma, Unternehmen*
firm *Firma*
office *Büro, Amt*
assistant *Assistent/in, Verkäufer/in*
director *Direktor/in, Geschäftsführer/in*
boss *Chef/in*
customer *Kunde, Kundin*
meeting *Konferenz, Besprechung*
model *Modell, Model*
project *Projekt*
programme *Programm*
expert *Fachmann/frau*
doctor *Arzt, Ärztin*
police *Polizei*
politician *Politiker/in*
farmer *Bauer, Bäuerin*

SCHOOL
(Schule)

education *Erziehung, (Ausbildung)*
school *Schule*
to learn *lernen, erfahren*
college *Fachhochschule*
to train *trainieren, ausbilden*
university *Universität*
to study *lernen, studieren*
course *Kurs, Lehrgang,*
class *Klasse*
desk *(Schreib-)Tisch*
seat *Sitz(platz)*
teacher *Lehrer/in*
to teach *unterrichten, lehren*
pupil *Schüler/in*
student *Student/in, Lernende/r*
subject *(Schul-)Fach, Thema*
English *englisch*
German *deutsch*
history *Geschichte*
topic *Thema*
question *Frage*
exercise *Übung*
homework *Hausaufgaben*
rule *Vorschrift, Regel*
to match *zuordnen, (zusammen) passen*
correct *richtig*
true *richtig, wahr*
false *falsch*

HOUSES AND HOMES
(Haus und Einrichtung)

house *Haus*
home *Zuhause, Heim; nach Hause*
flat *Wohnung*
to live *wohnen, leben*
address *Adresse*
door *Tür*
key *Schlüssel*
roof *Dach*
window *Fenster*
stairs *Treppe*
room *Zimmer, Raum*
(to) clean *sauber; reinigen, säubern*
furniture *Möbel*
bed *Bett*
table *Tisch*
bath *Bad*
shower *Dusche*
kitchen *Küche*
floor *Etage, (Fuß-)Boden*
alarm *Alarm(anlage)*

HOBBIES AND SPORT
(Hobbys und Sport)

to like *mögen, gern tun*
to interest *interessieren*
to enjoy *genießen, gefallen*
to love *lieben, sehr gern mögen*
favourite *Lieblings-*
fun *Spaß*
sport *Sport*
active *aktiv, tätig, aktiviert*
to play *spielen*
match *Spiel, Wettkampf*
game *Spiel*
ball *Ball, Kugel*
to kick *treten*
score *Ergebnis, Punkt(estand)*
to win *gewinnen, siegen*
winner *Gewinner/in, Sieger/in*
to swim *schwimmen*
to fish *angeln*
cycling *Radfahren*
bike *Rad*
to ride *reiten, (Rad) fahren*
(to) dance *Tanz; tanzen*
dancer *Tänzer/in*
television *Fernsehen, Fernseher*
viewer *Zuschauer/in*
TV programme *Fernsehprogramm*
to smoke *rauchen*

SOCIETY AND SOCIAL PROBLEMS
(Gesellschaft und soziale Probleme)

religion *Religion*
politics *Politik*
political *politisch*
rights *Rechte*
vote *Stimme, Abstimmung*
to allow *erlauben, (zu)lassen*
to control *kontrollieren, regeln*
control *Kontrolle*
poor *arm, schlecht, mangelhaft*
rich *reich, wohlhabend*
protest *Protest*
crime *Verbrechen*
conflict *Konflikt*
problem *Problem*
crisis *Krise*

danger *Gefahr*
dangerous *gefährlich*
serious *schwer, ernst*
wrong *falsch*
to hurt *verletzen*
to hit *schlagen, treffen*
to break *brechen*
to burn *(ver)brennen*
to fight *(be)kämpfen*
to die *sterben*
dead *tot*
to kill *töten*
gun *Schusswaffe, Pistole*
to protect *(be)schützen*
to hide *verstecken, verbergen*
drug *Droge*
risk *Risiko*
mistake *Fehler, Irrtum*
to forbid *verbieten*
to forget *vergessen*
to ignore *ignorieren*
to steal *stehlen*
personal *persönlich*
chance *Chance, Gelegenheit*
responsible *verantwortlich*
law *Gesetz, Recht*
case *Fall*

INTERACTING WITH PEOPLE
(Umgehen mit Menschen)

to communicate *sich mit jdm verständigen*
to talk *sprechen, reden*
to say *sagen*
to tell *sagen, erzählen*
truth *Wahrheit*
to ask *fragen, bitten*
to answer *(be)antworten*
to reply *antworten*
to realize *bemerken, realisieren*
to understand *verstehen, begreifen*
to translate *übersetzen, -tragen*
to explain *erklären*
to repeat *wiederholen*
to agree *zustimmen, vereinbaren*
to express *ausdrücken*
to be sorry *leidtun*
to discuss *diskutieren (über), besprechen*
to argue *argumentieren, streiten*
argument *Argument; Streit*
to shout *schreien*
to order *befehlen, bestellen, ordnen*
to direct *leiten*
to shock *erschüttern, schockieren*
reaction *Reaktion*
to warn *warnen*
to disappoint *enttäuschen*
to promise *versprechen*
to help *helfen*
to share *(sich) teilen, gemeinsam (be)nutzen*
to show *zeigen*
to connect *verbinden*
to call *(an)rufen*
to phone *anrufen*
to ring *läuten, anrufen*
to chat *sich unterhalten, chatten (mit)*
dialogue *Dialog*
conversation *Unterhaltung*
to introduce *(sich) vorstellen*
to meet *(zusammen)treffen, begegnen*
to greet *(be)grüßen*
(to) kiss *Kuss; küssen*
to laugh *lachen*
(to) joke *Witz; scherzen*
(to) offer *Angebot; (an)bieten*
to invite *einladen*
party *Party, Partei*
to arrange *arrangieren, vereinbaren*
to inform *informieren*
to report *berichten*
to notice *bemerken*
to guess *raten, schätzen*

READING AND WRITING
(Lesen und Schreiben)

to read *lesen*
reader *Leser/in*
story *Erzählung, Geschichte*
mail *Post*
letter *Brief, Buchstabe*
to send *senden, schicken*
document *Dokument, Papier*
briefcase *Aktentasche*
key *Taste*
table *Tabelle*
diagram *Diagramm, Grafik*
content *Inhalt*
to write *schreiben*
paper *Papier, Zeitung*
pencil *Bleistift*
point *Punkt; Sinn*
word *Wort*
sentence *Satz*
message *Mitteilung, Nachricht*
slogan *Werbespruch*
form *Form, Formular*
summary *Zusammenfassung*
page *Seite*
title *Titel*
information *Auskunft, Information(en)*
dictionary *Wörterbuch*
to mean *bedeuten, meinen, heißen*
meaning *Bedeutung*
emphasis *Hervorhebung*
to copy *kopieren*
to list *auflisten, notieren*
to note *beachten, notieren*
to complete *vervollständigen*
to comment *kommentieren*
to describe *beschreiben*
description *Beschreibung, Schilderung*
detail *Detail*
stereotype *Klischee*
example *Beispiel*
language *Sprache*
grammar *Grammatik*
vocabulary *Wortschatz*
style *Stil*
clear *klar, deutlich*
formal *formell, förmlich*
dear *liebe/r*

BELIEFS AND ATTITUDES
(Glaube und Einstellungen)

to believe *glauben*
to consider *nachdenken über, halten für*
to think *denken, meinen, finden, glauben*
view *Ansicht, Aussicht*
opinion *Meinung, Einschätzung*
positive *positiv, bejahend*
opposite *Gegenteil; gegensätzlich*
to dislike *nicht mögen*
to hate *hassen, nicht mögen*
option *Option, Wahl, Alternative*
idea *Idee, Gedanke*
to hope *hoffen*
(to) dream *Traum; träumen*
to want *wollen*
to wish *wünschen*
to remember *sich erinnern, daran denken*
to suppose *vermuten*
to imagine *sich vorstellen*
to seem *(er)scheinen*
to prove *beweisen*
real *echt, wirklich*
to worry *sich Sorgen machen*
to know *kennen, wissen*
reason *Vernunft, Grund*
to need *brauchen, benötigen*
necessary *nötig, erforderlich*

MOVEMENT
(Bewegung)

to move *(sich) bewegen, umziehen*
fast *schnell*
slow *langsam*
to go *gehen, fahren*
to walk *(zu Fuß) gehen*
step *Schritt*
to run *laufen*
to jump *springen*

to climb *klettern, steigen*
to fall *fallen*
to sit *sitzen, sich hinsetzen*
to stand *stehen, aushalten*
to rise *steigen*
to turn *(sich) drehen*
to arrive *ankommen*
to come *kommen*
to enter *eintreten, eingeben*
to leave *(ver)lassen*
to bring *bringen, holen*
to carry *tragen*
to put *setzen, stellen, legen*
to press *drücken*
to push *drücken, schieben*
to pull *ziehen*
to lead *führen*
to follow *(be)folgen*
to pass *vorbeigehen, vergehen; bestehen*
to hurry *sich beeilen*
to rush *sich beeilen*
to reach *greifen, erreichen*
to catch *fangen*
to disappear *verschwinden*

TOWNS AND BUILDINGS
(Städte und Gebäude)

city *(Groß-)Stadt*
town *Stadt*
village *Dorf*
neighbourhood *Nachbarschaft*
street *Straße*
path *(Fuß-)Weg, Pfad*
road *(Land-)Straße*
sign *Zeichen, Schild*
corner *Ecke*
map *Karte*
local *örtlich, lokal*
building *Gebäude*
bank *Bank*
church *Kirche*
tower *Turm*
hospital *Krankenhaus*
supermarket *Supermarkt*
market *Markt*
entrance *Eingang, Einfahrt*
bridge *Brücke*
farm *Bauernhof*

TRAFFIC, TRAVEL AND HOLIDAYS
(Verkehr, Reisen und Urlaub)

holiday *Ferien, Urlaub, Feiertag*
abroad *im/ins Ausland*
foreign *fremd*
international *international*
national *national, staatlich*
country *Land, Staat*
European *europäisch*
American *amerikanisch*
tour *Tour, Rundgang*
trip *Ausflug, Reise, Besuch*
tourist *Tourist/in*
visitor *Besucher/in, Gast*
to travel *reisen, fahren*
to visit *besuchen, besichtigen*
to plan *planen*
boat *Boot, Schiff*
ship *Schiff*
bus *(Linien-)Bus*
truck *Laster, Lkw*
car *Auto*
vehicle *Fahrzeug, Wagen*
to drive *(Auto) fahren*
driver *Fahrer/in*
plane *Flugzeug*
helicopter *Hubschrauber*
flight *Flug*
to fly *fliegen*
airport *Flughafen*
train *Zug*
underground *unterirdisch; U-Bahn*
station *Bahnhof*
ticket *Fahrkarte, Eintrittskarte*
to miss *verpassen, vermissen*
to return *zurückkehren, -gehen*
hotel *Hotel*
beach *Strand*
to relax *sich erholen*
photo *Foto*

MONEY AND SHOPPING
(Geld und Einkaufen)

money *Geld*
to earn *verdienen*
to afford *es sich leisten können*
to spend *ausgeben, verbringen*
to buy *kaufen*
to pay *(be)zahlen*
to sell *(sich) verkaufen*
to charge *berechnen, verlangen, (auf)laden*
to cost *kosten*
price *(Kauf-)Preis*
worth *wert*
bill *Rechnung*
present *Geschenk*
prize *Preis*
free *kostenlos, frei*
cheap *billig, günstig*
expensive *teuer*
luxury *Luxus*
card *Karte*
cash *Bargeld*
to change *(aus)wechseln, (sich) ändern*
to borrow *borgen, leihen*
to belong *gehören zu*
to own *besitzen*
to prefer *vorziehen, bevorzugen*
to choose *(aus)wählen*
available *verfügbar*
product *Produkt, Erzeugnis*
to produce *produzieren, herstellen*
shop *Laden, Geschäft*
shopping *Einkaufen*
sale *Verkauf*
success *Erfolg*
to open *öffnen*
to close *schließen*
open *offen*
closed *geschlossen*

EATING AND DRINKING
(Essen und Trinken)

to eat *essen*
food *Essen, Nahrung*
to cook *kochen*
to prepare *(sich) vorbereiten*
meal *Essen, Mahlzeit*
breakfast *Frühstück*
lunch *Mittagessen*
dinner *(Abend-)Essen*
to taste *schmecken*
hunger *Hunger*
hungry *hungrig*
thirst *Durst*
thirsty *durstig*
meat *Fleisch*
potato *Kartoffel*
vegetable *Gemüse*
fruit *Obst, Frucht*
fresh *frisch*
salt *Salz*
burger *Hamburger*
chicken *Huhn, Hähnchen*
egg *Ei*
cheese *Käse*
chocolate *Schokolade, Praline*
cake *Kuchen, Torte*
sweet *süß; Süßigkeit*
to drink *trinken*
mineral water *Mineralwasser*
tea *Tee*
juice *Saft*
alcohol *Alkohol*
wine *Wein*
beer *Bier*
bar *Bar*
cup *Tasse*
glass *Glas*
bottle *Flasche*
knife *Messer*
fork *Gabel*
spoon *Löffel*
plate *Platte, Teller*
bowl *Schüssel*
box *Kiste, Kästchen, Schachtel*
packet *Schachtel, Packung*

NATURE AND WEATHER
(Natur und Wetter)

nature *Natur*
natural *natürlich*
planet *Planet*
world *Welt*
continent *Erdteil, Kontinent*
environment *Umwelt, Umfeld*
earth *Erde*
air *Luft*
water *Wasser*
ice *Eis*
fire *Feuer*
sky *Himmel*
mountain *(größerer) Berg*
river *Fluss*
wind *Wind*
rain *Regen*
sun *Sonne*
storm *Sturm*
heat *Hitze*
hot *heiß, warm*
warm *warm*
cold *kalt*
to dry *trocknen*
wet *nass*
light *Licht, hell, leicht*
to shine *scheinen*
dark *dunkel*
animal *Tier*
dog *Hund*
cat *Katze*
bird *Vogel*
fish *Fisch*
flower *Blume*
plant *Pflanze*
tree *Baum*
to recycle *wieder verwerten*
to waste *verschwenden*

SCIENCE AND TECHNOLOGY
(Wissenschaft und Technik)

science *Wissenschaft*
scientist *Wissenschaftler/in*
chemical *chemisch; Chemikalie*
technical *technisch*
to build *(auf)bauen*
tool *Werkzeug*
device *Gerät, Apparat*
machine *Maschine*
computer *Computer*
data *Daten*
image *Bild*
to switch on *an-, einschalten*
to click *klicken*
to print *drucken*
electric *elektrisch, Strom-*
electricity *Elektrizität, Strom*
power *Kraft, Strom*
instruction *Anleitung*
method *Methode, Verfahren*
system *System*
to repair *reparieren*
modern *modern*
new *neu*
safe *sicher*
automatic *automatisch*

ART AND CULTURE
(Kunst und Kultur)

art *Kunst*
picture *Bild*
symbol *Symbol, Zeichen*
to draw *zeichnen*
scene *Szene*
to represent *darstellen*
culture *Kultur*
to act *handeln*
movie *Film*
book *Buch*
author *Autor/in*
article *Artikel*
newspaper *Zeitung*
magazine *Zeitschrift*
news *Neuigkeit(en), Nachricht(en)*
media *Medien*
song *Lied*
singer *Sänger/in*
music *Musik*
band *Kapelle*

QUALITIES AND CHARACTERISTICS
(Eigenschaften und Besonderheiten)

character *Charakter*
kind *Art, Sorte*
similar *ähnlich*
different *anders, verschieden*
difference *Unterschied*
advantage *Vorteil*
disadvantage *Nachteil*
to be *sein*
to become *werden*

DESCRIBING PEOPLE AND SITUATIONS
(Menschen und Situationen beschreiben)

friendly *freund(schaft)lich*
kind *nett*
interesting *interessant*
individual *individuell*
boring *langweilig*
funny *komisch, merkwürdig*
busy *beschäftigt, besetzt*
lazy *faul*
helpful *hilfreich, nützlich*
careful *vorsichtig, sorgfältig*
creative *gestalterisch, kreativ*
romantic *romantisch*
smart *schick, clever*
stupid *dumm*
silly *albern*
nice *schön, nett*
tough *zäh*
strict *streng, strikt*
polite *höflich*
rude *unhöflich, rüde*
pretty *hübsch*
beautiful *schön*
ugly *hässlich*
positive *positiv*
negative *negativ, verneinend*
strange *fremd, seltsam*
normal *normal*
perfect *vollkommen, perfekt*
special *besondere*
well-known *sehr bekannt, berühmt*
famous *berühmt*
popular *beliebt, populär*
unknown *unbekannt*
good *gut*
better *besser*
best *beste/r/s, am besten*
great *groß(artig)*
amazing *erstaunlich*
excellent *ausgezeichnet*
wonderful *wunderbar, -voll*
fantastic *fantastisch, wunderbar*
bad *schlecht, schlimm*
worse *schlechter, schlimmer*
worst *schlechteste/r/s, schlimmste/r/s*
horrible, awful, terrible *furchtbar, schrecklich*
easy *leicht, einfach*
basic *elementar*
simple *einfach*
hard *schwer, schwierig, hart*
difficult *schwer, schwierig*
important *wichtig*
successful *erfolgreich*
exciting *aufregend, spannend*
useful *nützlich*
unfair *unfair*
poor *arm*
wealthy *reich*
loud *laut*
quiet, silent *ruhig, still*
wet *nass*
dry *trocken*
slow *langsam*
quick *schnell, rasch*

Unit word list

Dieses Wörterverzeichnis enthält alle Wörter in **Focus on Success – Ausgabe Baden-Württemberg** in der Reihenfolge ihres Erscheinens. Nicht aufgeführt sind die Wörter aus der *Basic word list* sowie internationale Wörter wie *hotel, email* usw.
Die Wörter der *Further Options*-Seiten werden in den darauf folgenden Units nicht vorausgesetzt. Wörter, die in den Hörverständnistexten vorkommen, sind mit einem CD-Symbol gekennzeichnet.

AE = American English
BE = British English
abbrev = abbreviation (*Abkürzung*)
n = noun (*Substantiv*)
v = verb
adj = adjective
adv = adverb

inf = informal (*informell, Umgangssprache*)
phr = phrase (*feststehende Wendung*)
<> = opposite (*Gegensatz*)
fem = feminine
pl = plural
esp = especially

REFRESHER COURSE

UNIT A

page 6

to chill out	[ˌtʃɪl 'aʊt]	*(inf)* to relax	*sich entspannen*
to hang around	[ˌhæŋ ə'raʊnd]	*(inf)* to spend a lot of time in a place	*rumhängen*
speech bubble	['spiːtʃ bʌbl]	circle with words to show what someone says	*Sprechblase*
text message	['tekst mesɪdʒ]	written message sent by phone	*SMS*
chatroom	['tʃætruːm]	internet site where you can communicate with other people online	*Chatroom, Diskussionsforum*
to discover	[dɪ'skʌvə]	*n* discovery	*entdecken*
movies	['muːviz]	*(AE) BE:* cinema	*Kino*
to go clubbing	[gəʊ 'klʌbɪŋ]	to go out to clubs	*in Discos gehen*
net	[net]	*(abbrev)* internet	*Internet*
to carry out	[ˌkæri 'aʊt]	to do (a task)	*ausführen*
survey	['sɜːveɪ]	set of questions used to find out people's opinions	*Umfrage*

page 7

according to	[ə'kɔːdɪŋ tə]	as reported by	*nach, gemäß*
Red Cross	[ˌred 'krɒs]	a community service that helps people in need	*Rotes Kreuz*
worthwhile	[ˌwɜːθ'waɪl]	important, worth doing	*der Mühe wert*
the box	[ðə 'bɒks]	*(inf)* television	*die Kiste*
the homeless	[ðə 'həʊmləs]	people who have no home	*die Obdachlosen*
to get a lot out of sth	[ˌget ə lɒt 'aʊt əv]	to benefit from sth	*viel davon haben*
Are you joking?	[ɑː ju 'dʒəʊkɪŋ]	used to show surprise	*Ist das dein Ernst?*
schoolwork	['skuːlwɜːk]	homework	*Hausaufgaben*
to suffer	['sʌfə]	to become worse	*leiden*
to look round	[ˌlʊk 'raʊnd]	to visit a place and see what is there	*sich umsehen*
I'm afraid	[aɪm ə'freɪd]	unfortunately, sorry	*leider*
coach	[kəʊtʃ]	trainer	*Trainer/in*
to expect	[ɪk'spekt]	*phr* to expect sb to do sth	*erwarten*
violent	['vaɪələnt]	*n* violence	*gewalttätig*
stuff	[stʌf]	things	*Zeug*
to test	[test]	to examine	*prüfen*
skill	[skɪl]	thing you are good at	*Fähigkeit, Geschick*
to network	['netwɜːk]	to link up with	*vernetzen*
all over the place	[ɔːl ˌəʊvə ðə 'pleɪs]	everywhere	*überall*
voluntary	['vɒləntri]	*v* to volunteer	*freiwillig*

competitive	[kəm'petətɪv]	*phr* competitive sports	*Wettkampf-*
part-time job	[ˌpɑːt 'taɪm dʒɒb]	*v* to work part-time	*Teilzeitjob*
expression	[ɪk'spreʃn]	word or phrase	*Ausdruck*
definition	[ˌdefɪ'nɪʃn]	explanation of a word	*Definition*
valuable	['væljuəbl]	useful, important	*wertvoll*
permanent	['pɜːmənənt]	<> temporary	*ständig, dauerhaft*
certain	['sɜːtn]	definite	*gewiss, sicher*
ability	[ə'bɪləti]	skill	*Fähigkeit*

page 8

not necessarily	[nɒt ˌnesə'serəli]	*adj* necessary	*nicht unbedingt*
order	['ɔːdə]	sequence	*Reihenfolge*
employer	[ɪm'plɔɪə]	*v* to employ	*Unternehmer, Arbeitgeber*
qualification	[ˌkwɒlɪfɪ'keɪʃn]	*phr* job qualifications	*Qualifikation, Ausbildung*
cinema	['sɪnəmə]	*(BE) AE:* movie theater	*Kino*
instead of	[ɪn'sted əv]	rather than	*statt, anstatt (von)*
petrol	['petrəl]	*(BE) AE:* gas	*Benzin*
to refer to	[rɪ'fɜː tə]	to talk about sth specific	*sich beziehen auf*
to replace	[rɪ'pleɪs]	to put sth in the place of sth else	*ersetzen*
underlined	[ˌʌndə'laɪnd]	with a line underneath the word	*unterstrichen*
suitable	['suːtəbl]	appropriate	*passend, geeignet*
to score a goal	[skɔːr ə 'gəʊl]	e.g. Ronaldo scored three goals.	*ein Tor erzielen*
to be lucky	[bi 'lʌki]	not: ~~to have luck~~	*Glück haben*
times	[taɪmz]	*phr* many times	*mal*

page 9

rare	['reə]	not very often, unusual	*selten*
seldom	['seldəm]	not very often, rarely	*selten*
general	['dʒenrəl]	most of the time, basic	*allgemein*
weekday	['wiːkdeɪ]	*phr* on weekdays	*Wochentag*
drum	[drʌm]	*phr* to play the drums	*Trommel*
to surf	[sɜːf]	*phr* to surf the net	*surfen*
mark	[mɑːk]	result at school	*Note*
better	['betə]	<> worse	*besser*

page 10

below	[bɪ'ləʊ]	<> above	*unten*
pub	[pʌb]	*(BE) AE:* bar	*Kneipe*
mate	[meɪt]	*(inf)* friend	*Kumpel*
at present	[ət 'preznt]	at the moment	*gegenwärtig*
currently	['kʌrəntli]	at the moment	*zurzeit*

page 11

to serve	[sɜːv]	to give (a meal) to sb	*servieren*
ordinary	['ɔːdnri]	normal	*gewöhnlich, normal*
exercise bike	['eksəsaɪz baɪk]	bike which is used for keeping fit	*Heimtrainer*
to practise	['præktɪs]	*n* practice	*üben*
penalty	['penlti]	*phr* to take a penalty	*Strafstoß*
cash machine	['kæʃ məʃiːn]	machine which lets people take money from their bank accounts	*Geldautomat*
to manage	['mænɪdʒ]	to control sth, to deal with sth	*zurechtkommen, fertig werden (mit), (es) schaffen*
to try on	[ˌtraɪ 'ɒn]	to put on a piece of clothing to see whether you like it	*anprobieren*

UNIT B

page 12

to ban	[bæn]	to say that sth is not allowed	*verbieten*
discrimination	[dɪˌskrɪmɪ'neɪʃn]	*v* to discriminate against	*Diskriminierung*
public school	[ˌpʌblɪk 'skuːl]	*(AE) BE:* state school	*staatliche Schule*
requirement	[rɪ'kwaɪəmənt]	thing that is necessary	*Erfordernis*
to make up	[ˌmeɪk 'ʌp]	to form	*bilden*
awesome	['ɔːsəm]	very difficult or impressive	*überwältigend*
challenge	[tʃælɪndʒ]	a difficult task	*Herausforderung*
to wrestle	['resl]	to fight sb as a sport	*ringen*
mat	[mæt]	piece of material that people wrestle on	*Matte*

rival	['raɪvl]	person or team who plays against sb	*Gegner/in, Rivale, -lin*
unblinking	[ʌn'blɪŋkɪŋ]	to blink = blinzeln	*unbewegt*
shiver	['ʃɪvə]	*phr* a shiver of fear	*Zittern*
fear	[fɪə]	*v* to fear	*Furcht*
hulk	[hʌlk]	big strong man	*Kerl wie ein Baum*
stretcher	['stretʃə]	piece of equipment used to carry sb who has been hurt	*Trage*
hold	[həʊld]	*v* to hold	*Griff*
to twist	[twɪst]	to turn	*(ver)drehen*
muscle	['mʌsl]	⚠ Aussprache	*Muskel*
to injure	['ɪndʒə]	to hurt	*verletzen*
stereotype	['steriətaɪp]	e.g. racial stereotype	*Klischee*
to compete	[kəm'pi:t]	to play against other people or teams	*konkurrieren*
teammate	['ti:mmeɪt]	person who is on the same team as you	*Mannschaftskamerad/in*
session	['seʃn]	time spent doing a particular activity	*Treffen, Termin*
nasty	['nɑ:sti]	not nice	*gemein*
sweetie	['swi:ti]	*(inf)* darling	*Liebling, Schatz*
next door	[ˌnekst 'dɔ:]	in the next room or building	*nebenan*
to set to work	[set tə 'wɜ:k]	to begin a task or project	*ans Werk gehen*
to impress	[ɪm'pres]	*adj* impressive	*imponieren*
to beat	[bi:t]	to win against sb	*schlagen*
to back off	[ˌbæk 'ɒf]	to stop making things difficult for sb	*zurücktreten*
warrior	['wɒriə]	someone who fights in a war	*Krieger*
princess	[ˌprɪn'ses]	daughter of king or queen	*Prinzessin*
guy	[gaɪ]	*(inf)* boy, man	*Kerl, Typ*
equal	['i:kwəl]	person who is treated the same as others	*Gleichberechtigte/r, Ebenbürtige/r*

page 13

statement	['steɪtmənt]	*v* to state	*Aussage*
proud	[praʊd]	pleased with oneself	*stolz*
ice-hockey	['aɪs hɒki]	hockey played on ice	*Eishockey*
first aider	[ˌfɜ:st 'eɪdə]	*phr* first aid	*Sanitäter*
opponent	[ə'pəʊnənt]	person or team who plays against sb	*Gegner/in*
feminine	['femənɪn]	connected with women	*weiblich*
to teach sb a lesson	[ti:tʃ ə 'lesn]	to show sb they were wrong by making sth bad happen to them	*jdm eine Lektion erteilen*
glad	[glæd]	pleased	*froh*
to accept	[ək'sept]	*adj* acceptable	*akzeptieren*
private	['praɪvət]	<> public	*privat, persönlich*
precise	[prɪ'saɪs]	exactly	*genau*
frightening	['fraɪtnɪŋ]	scary	*beängstigend, erschreckend*
increasing	[ɪn'kri:sɪŋ]	getting bigger	*zunehmend*
pleasant	['pleznt]	nice	*angenehm*
to discriminate	[dɪ'skrɪmɪneɪt]	to contrast, but: to discriminate against sb	*unterscheiden, diskriminieren*
to require	[rɪ'kwaɪə]	*n* requirement	*erfordern*
injury	['ɪndʒəri]	*v* to injure	*Verletzung*
competition	[ˌkɒmpə'tɪʃn]	*v* to compete	*Wettkampf*
impression	[ɪm'preʃn]	a feeling or an idea about sth	*Eindruck*
to challenge	['tʃælɪndʒ]	to test sb's skills with a difficult task	*herausfordern*
to rival	['raɪvl]	to compete with	*konkurrieren*
wrestler	['reslə]	*v* to wrestle	*Ringer/in*
missing	['mɪsɪŋ]	absent	*fehlend*

page 14

EU	[ˌi: 'ju:]	*(abbrev)* European Union	*EU*
football	['fʊtbɔ:l]	*AE:* American football	*American Football (BE: Fußball)*
phenomenal	[fə'nɒmɪnl]	*n* phenomenon	*phänomenal*
talent	['tælənt]	special natural ability	*Talent*
although	[ɔ:l'ðəʊ]	even though	*obwohl*
grade	[greɪd]	result in school	*Note*

page 15

planner	['plænə]	book in which people write their plans	*(Termin-)Kalender*
further	['fɜ:ðə]	additional	*weiter*

lunchtime	['lʌntʃtaɪm]	time when people eat their mid-day meal	*Mittagspause*
ironing	['aɪənɪŋ]	*v* to iron	*Bügeln*
hairdresser	['heədresə]	person who cuts and styles hair	*Friseur/in*
to record	[rɪ'kɔ:d]	to store a film or TV programme on video/DVD	*aufzeichnen*
BBC	[ˌbi: bi: 'si:]	*(abbrev)* British Broadcasting Corporation	*BBC*
to swap	[swɒp]	to switch	*tauschen*
role	[rəʊl]	role-play	*Rolle*
at least	[ət 'li:st]	at the minimum	*mindestens*
to go camping	[gəʊ 'kæmpɪŋ]	to go on holiday in a tent or caravan	*campen*
leisure centre	['leʒə sentə]	place where people go to keep fit	*Freizeitzentrum*
to go on a date	[gəʊ ɒn ə 'deɪt]	to meet a (possible) boyfriend or girlfriend	*eine Verabredung haben*

UNIT C

page 16

case study	['keɪs stʌdi]	detailed description of a particular person/situation	*Fallstudie*
double life	['dʌbl laɪf]	*phr* to lead a double life	*Doppelleben*
genuine	['dʒenjuɪn]	real	*echt*
eating disorder	[ˌi:tɪŋ dɪs'ɔ:də]	e.g. anorexia, bulimia	*Essstörung*
anorexia	[ˌænə'reksiə]	illness where people don't eat because they want to be very thin	*Magersucht*
bulimia	[bju:'lɪmiə]	illness where people eat and make themselves sick to stay thin	*Bulimie, Ess-Brech-Sucht*
charming	['tʃɑ:mɪŋ]	*n* charm	*charmant*
attractive	[ə'træktɪv]	*v* to attract	*attraktiv*
community	[kə'mju:nəti]	people who live together in an area/ a society	*Gemeinde*
secret	['si:krɪt]	*phr* to keep sth secret	*geheim*
double-decker	[ˌdʌbl 'dekə]	*phr* double-decker bus	*Doppeldecker*
packet	['pækɪt]	small paper or plastic container	*Schachtel, Packung, Tüte*
tub	[tʌb]	small round plastic container	*Becher*
to scream	[skri:m]	here: to attract attention with big writing and bright colours	*schreien*
familiar	[fə'mɪliə]	*n* familiarity	*bekannt*
tingling	['tɪŋglɪŋ]	*v* to tingle	*kribbelnd, prickelnd*
to lose control over	[lu:z kən'trəʊl əʊvə]	to no longer be able to control sth	*die Beherrschung verlieren*
to stuff	[stʌf]	to push sth into a space	*stopfen*
greedy	['gri:di]	*n* greed	*gierig*
in no time	[ɪn 'nəʊ taɪm]	very quickly	*im Handumdrehen*
counter	['kaʊntə]	*phr* over the counter	*Tresen, Ladentisch*
dessert	[dɪ'zɜ:t]	sweet food eaten at the end of a meal	*Nachspeise, -tisch*
caramel	['kærəmel]	sweet sauce made by melting sugar	*Karamel*
donut	['dəʊnʌt]	*(AE) BE:* doughnut	*Pfannkuchen, Krapfen*
cheeky	['tʃi:ki]	a bit rude but in a funny way	*frech, kess*
to grin	[grɪn]	smile	*lächeln, grinsen*
to sink	[sɪŋk]	to go down	*sinken*
dirty	['dɜ:ti]	<> clean	*schmutzig*
guilty	['gɪlti]	<> innocent	*schuldig*
cubicle	['kju:bɪkl]	e.g. shower/toilet cubicle	*Kabine*
to bend	[bend]	*phr* to bend over	*(sich) beugen*
toilet pan	['tɔɪlət pæn]	*(AE) BE:* toilet bowl	*Kloschüssel*
to throw up	[ˌθrəʊ 'ʌp]	to be sick	*(sich) erbrechen*
to not be able to help	[nɒt bi ˌeɪbl tə 'help]	to not be able to avoid sth	*nicht umhin können*
association	[əˌsəʊsi'eɪʃn]	group of people with a common goal or interest	*Verband, Verein*
to go down a road	[gəʊ ˌdaʊn ə 'rəʊd]	to experience sth	*etwas erleben*
to refuse	[rɪ'fju:z]	to reject, turn down	*ablehnen, sich weigern, widerstehen*
to put on weight	[ˌpʊt ɒn 'weɪt]	<> to lose weight	*zunehmen*
addiction	[ə'dɪkʃn]	*v* to be addicted	*Sucht, Abhängigkeit*
to vomit	['vɒmɪt]	to throw up	*erbrechen*

page 17

task	[tɑ:sk]	work, assignment	*Aufgabe*
to compare	[kəm'peə]	*n* comparison	*vergleichen*
evidence	['evɪdəns]	proof	*Beweis, Beleg*
embarrassed	[ɪm'bærəst]	*n* embarrassment	*verlegen*
ashamed	[ə'ʃeɪmd]	*n* shame	*beschämt*
attitude	['ætɪtju:d]	*phr* attitude towards sth	*Haltung, Einstellung*
to disagree (with)	[ˌdɪsə'gri: wɪð]	<> agree	*widersprechen, nicht zustimmen*
choice	[tʃɔɪs]	*v* to choose	*Wahl*
to starve yourself	[stɑ:v]	to not allow yourself to eat	*hungern*
otherwise	['ʌðəwaɪz]	if not	*sonst, ansonsten*
to get real	[get 'ri:əl]	to accept the truth	*die Realität anerkennen*
to pull oneself together	[ˌpʊl wʌnself tə'geðə]	to take control of your feelings	*sich zusammenreißen*
mental	['mentl]	*n* mentality	*mental*
treatment	['tri:tmənt]	*v* to treat	*Behandlung*
sufferer	['sʌfərə]	sb who suffers from an illness	*Leidende/r*
sympathetic	[ˌsɪmpə'θetɪk]	*n* sympathy	*mitfühlend, verständnisvoll*
medical	['medɪkl]	connected with illnesses and treatments	*medizinisch*
criticism	['krɪtɪsɪzəm]	negative feedback	*Kritik*
phrase	[freiʒ]	expression	*Wendung, Ausdruck*
waiter	['weɪtə]	*fem* waitress	*Kellner, Ober*

page 18

to attract	[ə'trækt]	to draw attention to	*anziehen, anlocken*
special offer	[ˌspeʃl 'ɒfə]	*phr* on special offer	*Sonderangebot*
to get drunk	[get 'drʌŋk]	to drink so much alcohol that you can no longer think clearly	*sich betrinken*
good-looking	[ˌgʊd 'lʊkɪŋ]	attractive	*gut aussehend*
ad	[æd]	*(inf)* advertisement	*Anzeige*
disgusting	[dɪs'gʌstɪŋ]	*n* disgust	*ekelhaft*
to overcome	[ˌəʊvə'kʌm]	to beat or deal with (a problem or illness)	*überwinden*
capital	['kæpɪtl]	main city in a country	*Hauptstadt*
equivalent (of)	[ɪ'kwɪvələnt əv]	sth that is equal in size/importance, etc. to sth else	*Entsprechung*
curable	['kjʊərəbl]	*v* to cure	*heilbar*
fatty	['fæti]	containing a large amount of fat	*fetthaltig, fettig*
What's the matter with ...?	[ˌwɒts ðə 'mætə wɪð]	What's wrong with ...?	*Was ist los mit ...?*

page 19

countable	['kaʊntəbl]	which can be counted	*zählbar*
uncountable	[ˌʌn'kaʊntəbl]	which cannot be counted	*nicht zählbar*
ham	[hæm]	type of meat from a pig	*Schinken*
research	[rɪ'sɜ:tʃ]	study to find out more about a subject	*Forschung*
advice	[əd'vaɪs]	suggestion	*Rat(schlag)*
luggage	['lʌgɪdʒ]	suitcases	*Gepäck*
hardware	['hɑ:dweə]	parts of a computer	*Hardware, Geräte*
software	['sɒftweə]	computer programs	*Software, Programme*
knowledge	['nɒlɪdʒ]	what sb knows	*Wissen*
police officer	[pə'li:s ɒfɪsə]	policeman/-woman	*Polizeibeamter/-beamtin*
column	['kɒləm]	vertical sections which separate a page	*Spalte*
mustard	['mʌstəd]	yellow-brown sauce usually served with meat	*Senf*
paint	[peɪnt]	*v* to paint	*Farbe*
can	[kæn]	e.g. a can of beans	*Dose*
queue	[kju:]	*v* to queue up for sth	*(Warte-)Schlange*
loaf	[ləʊf]	e.g. a loaf of bread	*(Laib) Brot*
tube	[tju:b]	e.g. a tube of toothpaste	*Tube*
jar	[dʒɑ:]	e.g. a jam jar	*(Einmach)Glas*

page 20

unspecified	[ˌʌn'spesɪfaɪd]	unclear	*unbestimmt*
quantity	['kwɒntəti]	amount	*Menge, Quantität*

cookbook	['kʊkbʊk]	book that shows how to cook different meals	*Kochbuch*
to have room	[həv 'ru:m]	to have enough space for	*Platz haben*
barbecue	['bɑ:bɪkju:]	outdoor party where food is cooked on a metal frame over a fire	*Grillparty*
plenty of	['plenti əv]	many of	*viel(e)*
freezer	['fri:zə]	cupboard where food can be stored at a very low temperature	*Gefrierschrank*

page 21

to panic	['pænɪk]	<> to stay calm	*in Panik geraten*
Why on earth?	[ˌwaɪ ɒn 'ɜ:θ]	phrase used to emphasize the question 'why?'	*Warum um Himmels willen?*
not ... either	[nɒt 'aɪðə]	e.g. Pete can't go and I can't either.	*auch nicht*
carrot	['kærət]	long orange vegetable	*Karotte*
fridge	[frɪdʒ]	cupboard where food can be stored at a low temperature	*Kühlschrank*
understandable	[ˌʌndə'stændəbl]	which can be understood	*verständlich*
time off	[ˌtaɪm 'ɒf]	*phr* to take time off	*Freizeit*

UNIT D

page 22

time out	[ˌtaɪm 'aʊt]	*phr* to take time out	*Freizeit*
financial	[faɪ'nænʃə]	connected with money	*finanziell*
exotic	[ɪg'zɒtɪk]	exciting because it is strange or unusual	*exotisch*
destination	[ˌdestɪ'neɪʃn]	place to which people travel, the end of a journey	*(Fahrt-)Ziel*
proper	['prɒpə]	real, full, correct	*richtig, geeignet, korrekt, ordentlich*
bright	[braɪt]	clever	*hell; glänzend, schlau*
to pick fruit	[pik 'fru:t]	to take fruit from trees or plants	*Obst pflücken*
absolutely	['æbsəlu:tli]	definitely	*absolut*
especially	[ɪ'speʃəli]	particularly	*besonders, insbesondere*
uncool	[ˌʌn'ku:l]	⚠ Betonung	*uncool*
come on	[ˌkʌm 'ɒn]	used to show that you think sb is wrong	*komm (schon)*
living expenses	[ˌlɪvɪŋ ɪk'spensɪz]	money spent on everyday things	*Lebenshaltungskosten*

page 23

to break into	['breɪk ɪntə]	to enter by force	*einbrechen*

page 24

to give a lift	[gɪv ə 'lɪft]	to give sb a ride	*mit dem Auto mitnehmen*
weatherman	['weðəmæn]	man on TV who predicts the weather	*Meteorologe*
to watch out	[ˌwɒtʃ 'aʊt]	to be careful	*aufpassen*
visa	['vi:zə]	mark in a passport which allows you to enter a country	*Visum*
to take off	[ˌteɪk 'ɒf]	(of an aeroplane) to leave the ground	*starten*

page 25

several	['sevrəl]	a few more than one	*mehrere, einige*
school-leaver	[ˌsku:l 'li:və]	person who has just left school	*Schulabgänger/in*
farewell	[ˌfeə'wel]	saying goodbye to sb	*Abschied*
definitely	['defɪnətli]	certainly	*bestimmt, definitiv*

UNIT E

page 26

pushy	['pʊʃi]	trying to persuade sb to do sth	*aufdringlich*
sales	[seɪlz]	selling goods	*Verkaufs-*
staff	[stɑ:f]	a group of workers or employees	*Personal, Angestellte, Mitarbeiter/innen*
virtual	['vɜ:tʃuəl]	existing only on a computer screen	*virtuell*
mail-order catalogue	[meɪl 'ɔ:də kætəlɒg]	book with a list of goods that will be sent to customers by post	*Versandhauskatalog*
bargain	['bɑ:gɪn]	special offer	*Sonderangebot*
department store	[dɪ'pɑ:tmənt stɔ:]	large shop selling clothes, food, etc.	*Kauf-, Warenhaus*
purchase	['pɜ:tʃəs]	*v* to purchase	*(Ein-) Kauf*

fabulous	['fæbjələs]	great, wonderful	*fabelhaft*
blouse	[blauz]	piece of clothing like a shirt for women	*Bluse*
quality	['kwɒləti]	<> quantity	*Qualität*
fashion-conscious	['fæʃn kɒnʃəs]	very interested in fashionable clothes	*modebewusst*
exclusive	[ɪk'sklu:sɪv]	good quality and expensive and only bought by a small number of people	*exklusiv*
label	['leɪbl]	*phr* brand label	*Label, Marke*
wardrobe	['wɔ:drəʊb]	large cupboard for clothes	*Kleiderschrank, Garderobe*
thrill	[θrɪl]	*adj* thrilling	*Spannung*
lovely	['lʌvli]	nice, pleasant	*hübsch*
pure	[pjʊə]	*n* purity	*rein*
silk	[sɪlk]	a soft shiny material	*Seide*
site	[saɪt]	*(inf)* website	*Website*
shopping trolley	['ʃɒpɪn trɒli]	*AE:* shopping cart	*Einkaufswagen*
in the meantime	[ɪn ðə 'mi:ntaɪm]	in the time between two events	*inzwischen*
to run up debts	[ˌrʌn 'ʌp dets]	to spend more money than you have	*sich verschulden, Schulden anhäufen*

page 27

second-hand	[ˌsekənd 'hænd]	which used to belong to somebody else	*gebraucht*
auction	['ɔ:kʃn]	*phr* to put sth up for auction	*Auktion*
to link	[lɪŋk]	to connect, to join	*verbinden*

page 28

sceptical	['skeptɪkl]	having doubts	*skeptisch*
to keep in touch with	[ˌki:p ɪn 'tʌtʃ wɪð]	to stay in contact with	*in Verbindung bleiben*
creditor	['kredɪtə]	person who gives money to people who must pay it back later	*Gläubiger/in*
to repay	[rɪ'peɪ]	*n* repayment	*zurückzahlen*
convenient	[kən'vi:niənt]	*n* convenience	*bequem*
honest	['ɒnɪst]	*n* honesty	*ehrlich*
display	[dɪ'spleɪ]	⚠ Betonung	*Ausstellung*
row	[rəʊ]	line	*Reihe*
occasional	[ə'keɪʒənl]	now and then, sometimes	*gelegentlich*
fixed	[fɪkst]	set in place	*befestigt*
anti-theft pad	['æntɪ θeft pæd]	piece of material designed to stop people stealing goods	*Diebstahlsicherung*
to glow	[gləʊ]	to produce light	*leuchten*
reliable	[rɪ'laɪəbl]	which can be trusted	*zuverlässig*
value	['vælju:]	how much sth is worth	*Wert*
feature	['fi:tʃə]	aspect of a product	*Eigenschaft*
to switch off	[ˌswɪtʃ 'ɒf]	to turn off	*abschalten*

page 29

position	[pə'zɪʃn]	arrangement	*Stellung*
fortunately	['fɔ:tʃənətli]	luckily	*glücklicherweise*
actually	['æktʃuəli]	in fact	*tatsächlich, eigentlich*
unluckily	[ʌn'lʌkɪli]	unfortunately	*unglücklicherweise*
obviously	['ɒbviəsli]	clearly	*offensichtlich*
irresponsible	[ˌɪrɪ'spɒnsəbl]	<> responsible	*unverantwortlich*
from time to time	[frəm ˌtaɪm tə 'taɪm]	sometimes	*von Zeit zu Zeit*
now and then	[naʊ ənd 'ðen]	sometimes	*ab und zu*
frequency	['fri:kwənsi]	*adj* frequent	*Häufigkeit*
retailer	['ri:teɪlə]	person or company that sells products	*Einzelhändler/in*
shoplifting	['ʃɒplɪftɪŋ]	stealing from a shop	*Ladendiebstahl*
punishment	['pʌnɪʃmənt]	*v* to punish	*Strafe, Bestrafung*
shoplifter	['ʃɒplɪftə]	person who steals things from a shop	*Ladendieb/in*
sale	[seɪl]	event where goods are sold at a cheaper price	*Schlussverkauf*
to buy sth on credit	[baɪ ɒn 'kredɪt]	to buy sth using borrowed money	*etw auf Kredit kaufen*
congratulations	[kənˌgrætʃu'leɪʃnz]	*v* to congratulate	*Glückwunsch*

UNIT F

page 30

questionnaire	[ˌkwestʃə'neə]	list of questions	*Fragebogen*
to fit	[fɪt]	to be suitable	*passen*
to stay up	[ˌsteɪ 'ʌp]	to not go to bed	*aufbleiben*
to text	[tekst]	to write a text message	*SMS schicken, simsen*
loads	[ləʊdz]	*(inf)* a lot	*eine Menge*
to depend	[dɪ'pend]	to be dependent upon	*abhängen von*
social life	[ˌsəʊʃl 'laɪf]	time spent meeting friends	*Sozialkontakte*
to hand in	[ˌhænd 'ɪn]	to give in (e.g. your homework)	*abgeben*
to sit back	[ˌsɪt 'bæk]	to relax and not play an active role in sth	*sich zurückhalten, sich zurücklehnen*

page 31

sensible	['sensəbl]	<> silly	*vernünftig*
careers adviser	[kə'rɪəz ədvaɪzə]	person whose job is to give people advice about different jobs	*Berufsberater/in*
to interview	['ɪntəvju:]	to have a conversation with questions and answers	*interviewen*
theme	[θi:m]	a topic or subject	*Thema*
don't mention it	['menʃn]	you're welcome	*gern geschehen*
to concentrate	['kɒnsntreɪt]	to focus on sth	*sich konzentrieren*
to get by	[ˌget 'baɪ]	to have just enough money to live	*durchkommen*
to increase	[ɪn'kri:s]	to grow	*ansteigen, zunehmen*
since	[sɪns]	before the present time	*seit*
generation	[ˌdʒenə'reɪʃn]	people born around the same time	*Generation*
at a disadvantage	[ət ə ˌdɪsəd'vɑ:ntɪdʒ]	having more problems than other people	*benachteiligt*
job-related	['dʒɒb rɪleɪtɪd]	having to do with the job	*beruflich*
shelf	[ʃelf]	flat surface on a wall or in a cupboard where things can be placed	*Regal*

page 32

objection to	[əb'dʒekʃn tə]	*v* to object to	*Ablehnung gegenüber*
misunderstanding	[ˌmɪsʌndə'stændɪŋ]	*v* to misunderstand	*Missverständnis*
cartoon	[kɑ:'tu:n]	a humorous drawing	*Karikatur*
brochure	['brəʊʃə]	e.g. advertising brochure	*Broschüre, Prospekt*
careless	['keələs]	<> careful	*sorglos, nachlässig*
travel agency	['trævl eɪdʒənsi]	company that helps to organize holidays	*Reisebüro*
rack	[ræk]	object used to hold things or hang things from	*Ständer*
to sort	[sɔ:t]	to organize	*sortieren*
to deal with	['di:l wɪð]	to work with	*sich beschäftigen mit, mit jdm zu tun haben*
to complain	[kəm'pleɪn]	*n* complaint	*reklamieren, sich beklagen, beschweren*

page 33

to take it in turns	[ˌteɪk ɪt ɪn 'tɜ:nz]	to alternate	*sich abwechseln*
bartender	['bɑ:tendə]	*(AE) BE:* barman, barmaid	*Barmann, -frau*
cashier	[kæ'ʃɪə]	person who takes money from and gives money to customers in a shop or bank	*Kassierer/in*
shelf-stacker	['ʃelf stækə]	person who works in a supermarket putting products on shelves	*Regalauffüller/in*
tuition	[tju'ɪʃn]	*v* to tutor	*Unterricht*
old people's home	[ˌəʊld 'pi:plz həʊm]	place where old people live together and are cared for	*Seniorenheim*
filling station	['fɪlɪŋ steɪʃn]	petrol station	*Tankstelle*
recently	['ri:sntli]	lately, not long ago	*kürzlich, neulich*

page 34

day off	[ˌdeɪ 'ɒf]	*phr* to take a day off	*freier Tag*
part-timer	[ˌpɑ:t 'taɪmə]	person who works part-time	*Teilzeitarbeiter/in*
arrival	[ə'raɪvl]	*v* to arrive	*Ankunft*

MAIN COURSE

UNIT 1

page 35

focus	['fəʊkəs]	theme	*Blickpunkt*
quotation	[kwəʊ'teɪʃn]	*v* to quote	*Zitat*
to set foot in	[set 'fʊt ɪn]	to enter	*betreten*
to feature	['fi:tʃə]	to appear	*eine Rolle spielen*
to appear	[ə'pɪə]	*n* appearance	*auftauchen, vorkommen*
sequence	['si:kwəns]	part of a film	*Episode, Sequenz*

page 36

perspective	[pə'spektɪv]	view point	*Perspektive, Ansicht*
to contrast	[kən'trɑ:st]	to compare differences	*gegenüberstellen*
to scan	[skæn]	read sth quickly to find a piece of information	*überfliegen, absuchen*
state	[steɪt]	e.g. California, Kentucky	*(Bundes-)Staat*
roughly	['rʌfli]	<> exactly	*ungefähr*
exciting	[ɪk'saɪtɪŋ]	*n* excitement	*spannend, aufregend*
to happen	['hæpən]	to take place, occur	*geschehen, passieren*
particular	[pə'tɪkjələ]	specific, especially	*bestimmt, speziell*
urban	['ɜ:bən]	<> rural	*städtisch*
rural	['rʊərəl]	<> urban	*ländlich*
calm	[kɑ:m]	quiet	*ruhig*
enjoyable	[ɪn'dʒɔɪəbl]	*v* to enjoy	*angenehm*
gentle	['dʒentl]	kind	*freundlich*
intense	[ɪn'tens]	*n* intensity	*intensiv*

page 37

to check out	[ˌtʃek 'aʊt]	to find out about	*herausfinden*
pretty soon	[ˌprɪti 'su:n]	very soon	*sehr bald*
to get used to	[get 'ju:st tə]	to become familiar with sth	*sich gewöhnen an*
to yell	[jel]	to shout	*schreien*
really something	['ri:əli sʌmθɪŋ]	something impressive	*toll, beeindruckend*
downtown	['daʊntaʊn]	*(esp AE)* in the city centre	*im Stadtzentrum*
skyline	['skaɪlaɪn]	buildings, etc. that can be seen against the background of the sky	*Silhouette*
to blow sb away	[ˌbləʊ ə'weɪ]	to really impress sb	*jdn überwältigen*
scary	['skeəri]	frightening	*unheimlich, beängstigend*
elevator	['elɪveɪtə]	*(AE) BE:* lift	*Lift*
senior	['si:niə]	student in the last year of high school in the US	*Schüler/in im letzten Schuljahr*
skyscraper	['skaɪskreɪpə]	very tall building	*Wolkenkratzer*
huge	[hju:dʒ]	very big	*gewaltig*
forest	['fɒrɪst]	woods	*Wald*
waterfall	['wɔ:təfɔ:l]		*Wasserfall*
to be stuck	[bi 'stʌk]	to be unable to get away	*feststecken*
nightmare	['naɪtmeə]	*adj* nightmarish	*Albtraum*

page 38

context	['kɒntekst]	circumstances	*Kontext, Zusammenhang*
shopping mall	['ʃɒpɪŋ mɔ:l]	a large building with many shops inside	*Einkaufszentrum*
exhibition	[ˌeksɪ'bɪʃn]	*v* to exhibit	*Ausstellung*
ferry	['feri]	a large boat used to transport people	*Fähre*
geography	[dʒi'ɒgrəfi]	layout	*Lage, Geographie*
gateway	['geɪtweɪ]	entrance	*Tor, Pforte*
to rent	[rent]	to hire	*mieten*
lake	[leɪk]	area of water surrounded by land	*(Binnen-)See*
ride	[raɪd]	*phr* to go for a ride	*Tour, Fahrt, Flug*
tight	[taɪt]	*phr* a tight fit	*knapp, eng*
budget	['bʌdʒɪt]	amount of money you plan to spend	*Budget, Etat*
security check	[sɪ'kjʊərəti tʃek]	a measure to stop dangerous items/people entering a building/country, etc.	*Sicherheitskontrolle*

greeting	['gri:tɪŋ]	*v* to greet	*Begrüßung*
to receive	[rɪ'si:v]	to get	*empfangen*
relationship	[rɪ'leɪʃnʃɪp]	a connection between two or more people	*Verhältnis*

page 39

immigrant	['ɪmɪgrənt]	*v* to immigrate	*Einwanderer/Einwanderin*
bite	[baɪt]	*phr* to take a bite of sth	*Bissen, Happen*
sub-heading	[ˌsʌb 'hedɪŋ]	title that comes under the main title	*Untertitel*
encyclopedia	[ɪnˌsaɪklə'pi:diə]	book that gives information about many different subjects	*Lexikon, Enzyklopädie*
entry	['entri]	piece of written information in a book	*Eintrag*
novel	['nɒvl]	book containing a story	*Roman*
guidebook	['gaɪdbʊk]	book which gives information on a particular place	*Reiseführer*

page 40

distant	['dɪstənt]	*n* distance	*fern*
to shine	[ʃaɪn]	*adj* shiny	*glänzen*
magical	['mædʒɪkl]	wonderful	*magisch*
to take sb's breath away	[teɪk 'breθ əweɪ]	to surprise sb by being very impressive	*jdm den Atem rauben*
to explore	[ɪk'splɔ:]	to travel around and see different areas	*erkunden*
borough	['bʌrə]	area, quarter in a city	*(Stadt-)Bezirk*
shore	[ʃɔ:]	place where land meets water	*Ufer*
island	['aɪlənd]	land which is surrounded by water	*Insel*
within	[wɪ'ðɪn]	inside	*innerhalb*
characteristic	[ˌkærəktə'rɪstɪk]	quality	*Eigenschaft, Merkmal*
sense	[sens]	a feeling	*Sinn, Gefühl*
melting pot	['meltɪŋ pɒt]	place where people from different cultures live together	*Schmelztiegel*
variety	[və'raɪəti]	*adj* various	*Vielfalt*
cultural	['kʌltʃərəl]	connected with culture	*kulturell*
ethnic	['eθnɪk]	connected with origin or race	*ethnisch*
tradition	[trə'dɪʃn]	*adj* traditional	*Tradition*
wave	[weɪv]	large number of people moving somewhere	*Welle*
effect	[ɪ'fekt]	result	*Auswirkung*
dish	[dɪʃ]	plate or shallow bowl	*Gericht*
crowded	['kraʊdɪd]	filled with people	*überfüllt*
energy	['enədʒi]	force	*Energie*
newly	['nju:li]	recently	*kürzlich*
to invent	[ɪn'vent]	*n* invention	*erfinden*
steel-frame	['sti:l freɪm]	with a frame of steel (strong metal)	*Stahlträger*
construction	[kən'strʌkʃn]	building	*Bau, Bauweise*
area	['eəriə]	a space	*Gebiet, Bereich*
including	[ɪn'klu:dɪŋ]	*abbrev:* incl.	*einschließlich, inbegriffen, darunter*
finance	['faɪnæns]	*adj* financial	*Finanzen*
advertising	['ædvətaɪzɪŋ]	industry connected with producing adverts	*Werbung*
to take over	[ˌteɪk 'əʊvə]	to start to have control over people or things	*übernehmen*
taxpayer	['tækspeɪə]	person who pays taxes	*Steuerzahler/in*
bankrupt	['bæŋkrʌpt]	*n* bankruptcy	*bankrott, pleite*
terrorist	['terərɪst]	person who takes part in political attacks	*Terrorist/in*
attack	[ə'tæk]	assault	*Angriff*
failure	['feɪljə]	<> success	*Versagen*
unemployment	[ˌʌnɪm'plɔɪmənt]	*adj* unemployed	*Arbeitslosigkeit*
former	['fɔ:mə]	from an earlier time	*früher*
recovery	[rɪ'kʌvəri]	*v* to recover	*Erholung*

page 41

structure	['strʌktʃə]	something that has been built, a foundation and organized system	*Gebäude, Struktur, Aufbau*
man-made	['mæn meɪd]	<> natural	*von Menschenhand*
industry	['ɪndəstri]		*Industrie*

birth	[bɜːθ]	*v* to be born	*Geburt*
aspect	['æspekt]	area, part	*Aspekt, Seite*
to collect	[kə'lekt]	to bring together	*sammeln*
to differ	['dɪfə]	to be different	*sich unterscheiden*
to immigrate	['ɪmɪgreɪt]	to come to live in a new country	*einwandern*
attraction	[ə'trækʃn]	feeling of being attracted to sth/sb	*Anziehung*
sleepy	['sliːpi]	tired	*müde*
informative	[ɪn'fɔːmətɪv]	*v* to inform	*informativ*
to strengthen	['streŋθn]	to make stronger	*stärken*
page 42			
large-scale	['lɑːdʒ skeɪl]	in large numbers	*in großer Zahl*
basic	['beɪsɪk]	simple	*elementar*
chart	[tʃɑːt]	*diagram*	*Diagramm, Tabelle*
figure	['fɪgə]	number	*Zahl*
to prove	[pruːv]	*n* proof	*beweisen*
income	['ɪnkʌm]	money earned	*Einkommen*
increase	['ɪŋkriːs]	*adj* increasing	*Anstieg, Steigerung*
to express	[ɪk'spres]	*n* expression	*ausdrücken*
page 43			
heavyweight	['heviweɪt]	very important person	*Schwergewicht*
screen	['skriːn]	television	*Bildschirm*
period drama	['pɪəriəd drɑmə]	TV programme which tells a story set in a period of history	*Historiendrama*
to concern	[kən'sɜːn]	to be about	*betreffen*
invention	[ɪn'venʃn]	act of inventing sth	*Erfindung*
genius	['dʒiːniəs]	an extremely intelligent person	*Genie*
intermission	[ˌɪntə'mɪʃn]	short pause between parts of a play/film	*(Werbe-)Pause*
dozen	['dʌzn]	twelve	*Dutzend*
sensation	[sen'seɪʃn]	*adj* sensational	*Sensation*
to form the spine of	[fɔːm ðə 'spaɪn əv]	to be the main part of	*das Rückgrat bilden*
worldwide	['wɜːldwaɪd]	all over the world	*weltweit*
smash	[smæʃ]	film/play, etc. that is very successful	*Kassenschlager*
for a song	[fər ə 'sɒŋ]	*(inf)* at a very low price	*spottbillig*
apiece	[ə'piːs]	each	*je, das Stück*
box office	['bɒks ɒfɪs]	place where tickets for films/plays, etc. can be bought	*(Theater-)Kasse*
performance	[pə'fɔːməns]	*v* to perform	*Vorstellung*
noon	[nuːn]	midday	*mittags*
to wait in line	[weɪt ɪn 'laɪn]	to stand in a queue and wait for sth	*anstehen*
curtain	['kɜːtn]	beginning of a play	*Vorhang*
discounted	[dɪs'kaʊntɪd]	*n* discount	*reduziert*
to apologize for	[ə'pɒlədʒaɪz fə]	*n* apology	*sich entschuldigen für*
to include	[ɪn'kluːd]	to contain	*einschließen, einbeziehen*
sight	[saɪt]	*phr* to see the sights	*Sehenswürdigkeit*
event	[ɪ'vent]	sth that is happening	*Veranstaltung, Ereignis*
page 44			
comparison	[kəm'pærɪsn]	comparing things	*Vergleich, Steigerung*
approx.	[ə'prɒksɪmətli]	*(abbrev)* approximately	*ungefähr, etwa, zirka*
clue	[kluː]	something which helps solve a puzzle	*Schlüssel*
farther	['fɑːðə]	= further	*weiter*
to guess	[ges]	to try to answer	*raten*
junior	['dʒuːniə]	low-ranking	*untergeordnet*
comment	['kɒment]	*v* to comment	*Kommentar*
length	[leŋθ]	measurement of time, distance, etc.	*Länge, Dauer*
departure	[dɪ'pɑːtʃə]	*v* to depart	*Abfahrt*
frequent	['friːkwənt]	*n* frequency	*häufig*
service	['sɜːvɪs]	assistance	*(Bus-/Zug-)Verbindung*

UNIT 2

page 45

advertisement	[əd'vɜ:tɪsmənt]	*abbrev:* ad, advert	*Anzeige, Werbespot*
classified	['klæsɪfaɪd]	arranged by subject	*nach Rubriken geordnet*
panel	['pænl]	section of a page	*hier: Spalte, Fläche*
leaflet	['li:flət]	flyer	*Broschüre, Flugblatt*
pop-up ad	['pɒp ʌp æd]	advert that appears on the screen when you are online	*Internet-Anzeige*
banner ad	['bænər æd]	advert that covers the top/bottom/ side of an internet page	*Bannerwerbung*
product placement	['prɒdʌkt pleɪsmənt]	advertising products by showing them in films or on TV shows	*Schleichwerbung*
commercial	[kə'mɜ:ʃl]	advertisement	*Anzeige, Werbespot*
sponsorship	['spɒnsəʃɪp]	giving financial support to a group/ event, etc.	*finanzielle Unterstützung*
annoying	[ə'nɔɪɪŋ]	irritating	*lästig, ärgerlich*
glamorous	['glæmərəs]	*n* glamour	*glamourös*
aim	[eɪm]	goal	*Ziel*
to vary	['veəri]	*n* variety	*variieren*
to promote	[prə'məʊt]	to advertise	*fördern*
brand	[brænd]	*phr* brand name	*Marke*

page 46

agency	['eɪdʒənsi]	e.g. advertising agency	*Agentur*
to design	[dɪ'zaɪn]	to create	*entwerfen*
sponsor	['spɒnsə]	*v* to sponsor	*Sponsor/in*
freelance	['fri:lɑ:ns]	e.g. freelance journalist	*freiberuflich*
developer	[dɪ'veləpə]	person whose job is to create new products	*Entwickler/in*
to expand	[ɪk'spænd]	to get bigger	*expandieren, (sich) ausdehnen*
potential	[pə'tenʃl]	possible	*potentiell*
client	['klaɪənt]	customer	*Kunde/Kundin*
campaign	[kæm'peɪn]	*phr* advertising campaign	*(Werbe-)Feldzug, Kampagne*
to pitch	[pɪtʃ]	to present an idea or a product to persuade people to use or buy it	*anbieten, anpreisen*
contract	['kɒntrækt]	a formal document or agreement	*(Arbeits-)Vertrag*
account manager	[ə'kaʊnt mænɪdʒə]	person who looks after regular customers	*Kundenbetreuer/in*
to get the green light	[get ðə ˌgri:n 'laɪt]	to be allowed to begin	*grünes Licht erhalten*
to launch	[lɔ:ntʃ]	to start	*einführen, starten*
journey	['dʒɜ:ni]	trip	*Reise, Fahrt*

page 47

successful	[sək'sesfl]	*n* success	*erfolgreich*
flow chart	['fləʊ tʃɑ:t]	diagram showing the order in which a process happens	*Flussdiagramm*
to set up	[ˌset 'ʌp]	to found	*begründen*
booker	['bʊkə]	person whose job is to book appointments	*Besteller/in*
slot	[slɒt]	appointment	*Termin*
PA	[ˌpi: 'eɪ]	*(abbrev)* personal assistant	*persönliche/r Assistent/in*
to be due to	[bi 'dju: tə]	due to = because of	*darauf zurückzuführen sein*
stressful	['stresfl]	*n* stress	*stressig, anstrengend*
process	['prəʊses]	systematic action	*Prozess, Vorgang*

page 48

to sponsor	['spɒnsə]	*n* sponsor, sponsorship	*finanziell unterstützen*
to supply	[sə'plaɪ]	to provide	*liefern*
supply	[sə'plaɪ]	giving people what they want or need	*Lieferung; Stoff, Material*
urgent	['ɜ:dʒənt]	*n* urgency	*dringend, eilig*
innovative	['ɪnəʊveɪtɪv]	*n* innovation	*innovativ*
application	[ˌæplɪ'keɪʃn] (fɔ:m)]	*v* to apply to/for	*Bewerbung*
Human Resources	[ˌhju:mən rɪ'sɔ:sɪz]	*abbrev:* HR	*Personal(abteilung)*

candidate	['kændɪdət]	person who has applied for a job	*Kandidat/in, Bewerber/in*
shortlisted	['ʃɔːtlɪstɪd]	chosen to go on a list of possible candidates	*in der engeren Wahl*
to confirm	[kən'fɜːm]	*n* confirmation	*bestätigen*
to attend	[ə'tend]	to be present at	*teilnehmen (an)*
correspondence	[ˌkɒrɪ'spɒndəns]	letters sent and received by people	*Korrespondenz*
to suggest	[sə'dʒest]	*n* suggestion	*vorschlagen, andeuten*
closeness	['kləʊsnəs]	*adj* close	*Vertrautheit*

page 49

heading	['hedɪŋ]	title	*Überschrift*
forum	['fɔːrəm]	discussion	*Forum*
discussion	[dɪ'skʌʃn]	*v* to discuss sth	*Diskussion*
to drown in	['draʊn ɪn]	to be surrounded by	*ertränken in*
terrible	['terəbl]	awful	*schrecklich, furchtbar*
commercial break	[kəˌmɜːʃl 'breɪk]	pause between TV programmes when adverts are shown	*Werbepause*
to cut	[kʌt]	to get rid of sth	*ausblenden*
lively	['laɪvli]	fun	*lebhaft*
to lighten up	[ˌlaɪtn 'ʌp]	to feel less worried	*aufheitern*
to escape	[ɪ'skeɪp]	to get away from	*flüchten*
advertiser	['ædvətaɪzə]	person or company that advertises	*Werbefirma*
branded	['brændɪd]	showing the name of a company	*Marken-*
entertainment	[ˌentə'teɪnmənt]	amusement	*Unterhaltung*
placement	['pleɪsmənt]	*v* to place	*(Produkt-)Werbung*
extended	[ɪk'stendɪd]	*n* extension	*verlängert*
viral	['vaɪrəl]	like a virus	*viral, Virus-*
to pass	[pɑːs]	to move, go by	*weitergegeben werden*
to spread	[spred]	*n* spread	*(sich) verbreiten*
word of mouth	[ˌwɜːd əv 'maʊθ]	*phr* to spread by word of mouth	*Mundpropaganda*
to recognize	['rekəgnaɪz]	to see sth or sb familiar	*erkennen*
channel	['tʃænl]	*phr* to change channels	*Kanal*
to admit	[əd'mɪt]	to confess	*zugeben, gestehen*
wasteful	['weɪstfə]	*v* to waste	*verschwenderisch*
to drop	[drɒp]	to fall	*fallen*
to collapse	[kə'læps]	to fail suddenly	*zusammenbrechen*
to fail	[feɪl]	to not succeed	*versagen, scheitern*
Middle Ages	[ˌmɪdl 'eɪdʒɪz]	period from about 600 AD to 1450 AD	*Mittelalter*

page 50

hard sell	[ˌhɑːd 'sel]	selling technique that puts a lot of pressure on the customer	*aggressive Verkaufstechnik*
soft sell	[ˌsɒft 'sel]	selling technique that persuades customers without putting pressure on them	*zurückhaltende Verkaufstechnik*
to influence	['ɪnfluəns]	*n* influence	*beinflussen*
raw material	[ˌrɔː mə'tɪəriəl]	material that is used to make a product	*Rohstoff*
disagreement	[ˌdɪsə'griːmənt]	*v* to disagree	*Widerspruch, Uneinigkeit*
to exaggerate	[ɪg'zædʒəreɪt]	*n* exaggeration	*übertreiben*
one-sided	[ˌwʌn 'saɪdɪd]	showing only one aspect of a situation	*einseitig*

page 51

leading	['liːdɪŋ]	*v* to lead	*führend*
technique	[tek'niːk]	method	*Methode, (Arbeits-)Technik*
college of further education	[ˌkɒlɪdʒ əv ˌfɜːðər ˌedʒu'keɪʃn]	vocational school	*Fachoberschule, Weiterbildungskolleg*
to stand for sth	['stænd fə]	to mean	*für etw stehen*
formula	['fɔːmjələ]	method	*Formel*
immediate	[ɪ'miːdiət]	happening without delay, straight away	*umgehend, sofort*
acronym	['ækrənɪm]	an abbreviation pronounced as a word	*Akronym, Initialwort*
attention	[ə'tenʃn]	*phr* to pay attention to	*Aufmerksamkeit*
to raise	[reɪz]	to build up	*wecken*
to create	[kri'eɪt]	*adj* creative	*hervorrufen, erzeugen, wecken*
desire	[dɪ'zaɪə]	*adj* desirable	*Begehren, Verlangen*
to encourage	[ɪn'kʌrɪdʒ]	to promote	*anregen*

to analyze	['ænəlaɪz]	to study in detail	*analysieren*
aimed at	['eɪmd ət]	*v* to aim sth at	*abgezielt auf, gerichtet an*
play on words	[pleɪ ɒn 'wɜ:dz]	pun	*Wortspiel*
to work out	[ˌwɜ:k 'aʊt]	to train	*trainieren*
membership	['membəʃɪp]	*phr* gym membership	*Mitgliedschaft*
to join	[dʒɔɪn]	to sign up	*beitreten, sich anmelden*
message	['mesɪdʒ]	written or spoken information	*Aussage, Botschaft*
foreground	['fɔ:graʊnd]	front	*Vordergrund*
thought bubble	['θɔ:t bʌbl]	expressing someone's thoughts in a cartoon	*Denkblase*
to satirize	['sætəraɪz]	*n* satire	*satirisch darstellen*
to illustrate	['ɪləstreɪt]	to represent	*darstellen*
to mention	['menʃn]	to name, list	*erwähnen, aufzählen*
required	[rɪ'kwaɪəd]	necessary	*erforderlich*
imagination	[ɪˌmædʒɪ'neɪʃn]	*v* to imagine	*Fantasie*

page 52

explanation	[ˌeksplə'neɪʃn]	*v* to explain	*Erklärung, Erläuterung*
to decline	[dɪ'klaɪn]	to decrease	*abnehmen, sinken, zurückgehen*
slight	[slaɪt]	a little, small	*leicht*
statistical	[stə'tɪstɪkl]	*n* statistic	*statistisch*
presentation	[ˌprezn'teɪʃn]	a talk	*Vorstellung, Präsentation*
decrease	['di:kri:s]	to decrease	*Abnahme, Rückgang*
rapid	['ræpɪd]	happening in a short period	*rapide, schnell*
sharp	[ʃɑ:p]	sudden(ly) and by a large amount	*rasch, schnell, stark*
steady	['stedi]	even(ly), stable	*stetig, fest, regelmäßig*
gradual	['grædʒuəl]	happening slowly over a period of time	*allmählich, nach und nach*
decline	[dɪ'klaɪn]	decrease	*Rückgang*
to remain	[rɪ'meɪn]	to stay the same	*bleiben*
trend	[trend]	general way in which things are changing, fashion	*Trend*

page 53

extremely	[ɪk'stri:mli]	*adj* extreme	*äußerst*
analysis	[ə'næləsɪs]	*v* to analyze	*Analyse*
arrangement	[ə'reɪndʒmənt]	the way that things are placed	*Anordnung*
to construct	[kən'strʌkt]	to create	*entwickeln, ausarbeiten*
accessory	[ək'sesəri]	e.g. handbag, jewellery	*Zubehör, Accessoire*
to persuade	[pə'sweɪd]	to convince	*überzeugen*

page 54

sales figures	['seɪlz fɪgəz]	the amount of things that have been sold	*Verkaufszahlen*
account executive	[əˌkaʊnt ɪg'zekjətɪv]	manager for regular customers or clients	*Kundenberater/in, -betreuer/in*
microwave	['maɪkrəweɪv]	oven which heats food quickly using electromagnetic waves	*Mikrowelle*
to not break the bank	[nɒt ˌbreɪk ðə 'bæŋk]	to not cost too much	*nicht die Welt kosten*

UNIT 3

page 55

madness	['mædnəs]	*adj* mad	*Wahnsinn*
contact	['kɒntækt]	*phr* to stay in contact	*Kontakt, Verbindung*
celebrity	[sə'lebrəti]	sb famous	*Promi(nente/r)*
interactive	[ˌɪntər'æktɪv]	*v* to interact with sb	*interaktiv*
newsletter	['nju:zletə]	printed report of news	*Rundschreiben, (Info-)Blatt*
blog	[blɒg]	an online journal	*Blog*
to react	[ri'ækt]	*n* reaction	*reagieren*
hurricane	['hʌrɪkən]	severe storm	*Orkan, Wirbelsturm*
latest	['leɪtɪst]	newest	*neueste, letzte*
public	['pʌblɪk]	in front of other people	*öffentlich*
to raise	[reɪz]	*phr* to raise money for sth	*sammeln*
charity	['tʃærəti]	*phr* an act of charity	*wohltätiger Verein*

in need	[ɪn 'ni:d]	needing help	*bedürftig*
communication	[kəˌmju:nɪ'keɪʃn]	*v* to communicate	*Kommunikation, Mitteilung, Benachrichtigung*
refugee	[ˌrefju'dʒi:]	sb fleeing their country	*Flüchtling*
background	['bækgraʊnd]	origin	*Hintergrund, Herkunft*
library	['laɪbrəri]	place where books can be borrowed	*Bücherei, Bibliothek*

page 56

reality TV	[riˌæləti ti: 'vi:]	shows using real people, not actors	*Reality TV*
bother	['bɒðə]	difficulty, trouble	*Ärger*
long-running	['lɒŋrʌnɪŋ]	having been on TV for a long time	*mit langer Laufzeit*
to screen	['skri:nɪŋ]	to show a programme on TV	*ausstrahlen*
series	['sɪəri:z]	programme in episodes	*Serie*
producer	[prə'dju:sə]	film-maker, manufacturer	*Produzent/in, Erzeuger*
action	['ækʃn]	*phr* to take action	*Aktion, Handlung*
entertaining	[ˌentə'teɪnɪŋ]	*n* entertainment	*unterhaltsam*
audience	['ɔ:diəns]	viewers	*Zuschauer*
to vote	[vəʊt]	*phr* to vote in favour of/against	*abstimmen, wählen*
to throw out	[ˌθrəʊ 'aʊt]	to force sb to leave	*hinauswerfen*
trouble	['trʌbl]	problem	*Schwierigkeiten, Ärger*
actress	['æktrəs]	female actor	*Schauspielerin*
popular press	[ˌpɒpjələ 'pres]	media that aims to reach a wide audience	*Boulevardpresse*
to exploit	[ɪk'splɔɪt]	*n* exploitation	*be-, ausnutzen*
abuse	[ə'bju:s]	*v* to abuse sb	*Anpöbelung, Beschimpfung(en)*
to blame sb	[bleɪm]	to think that sb is responsible for sth	*die Schuld geben, verantwortlich machen*
psychological	[ˌsaɪkə'lɒdʒɪkl]	mental	*psychologisch*
profile	['prəʊfaɪl]	description	*Profil, Ansicht, Herkunft, Berufsbild, Porträt*
personality	[ˌpɜ:sə'næləti]	a person's character	*Persönlichkeit*
clash	[klæʃ]	conflict	*Konflikt, Zusammenstoß*
profit	['prɒfɪt]	*adj* profitable	*Profit, Gewinn*
to survive	[sə'vaɪv]	*n* survival	*überleben*
addicted	[ə'dɪktɪd tə]	*n* addiction	*süchtig nach*
embarrassing	[ɪm'bærəsɪŋ]	*v* to embarrass	*peinlich*
fame	[feɪm]	*adj* famous	*Ruhm*
to wonder	['wʌndə]	to think about	*sich fragen, sich wundern*
psychology	[saɪ'kɒlədʒi]	*adj* psychological	*Psychologie*
to behave	[bɪ'heɪv]	to act in a certain way	*sich benehmen, sich verhalten*
contestant	[kən'testənt]	sb taking part in a contest	*Kandidat/in*
grotesque	[grəʊ'tesk]	terrible	*grotesk*
Roman	['rəʊmən]	inhabitant of the ancient Roman empire	*Römer/in*

page 57

to force	[fɔ:s]	to make sb do sth that they don't want to do	*zwingen*
housemate	['haʊsmeɪt]	person that you share a house with	*Mitbewohner/in*
remark	[rɪ'mɑ:k]	*phr* to make a remark about sth	*Bemerkung*
abusive	[ə'bju:sɪv]	*n* abuse	*beleidigend, ausfallend*
accurate	['ækjərət]	correct, precise	*genau*
legal	['li:gl]	*v* to legalize	*legal*
legible	['ledʒəbl]	clear enough to read	*leserlich*
logical	['lɒdʒɪkl]	sensible or reasonable	*logisch*
moral	['mɒrəl]	*n* morality	*moralisch*
perfect	['pɜ:fɪkt]	*n* perfection	*vollkommen*
relevant	['reləvənt]	*phr* to be relevant to sth/sb	*relevant, wichtig*
behaviour	[bɪ'heɪvjə]	*phr* good/bad behaviour	*Verhalten, Benehmen*

page 58

brave	[breɪv]	*n* bravery	*tapfer*
to be up for	[bi 'ʌp fə]	to be keen to do	*bereit sein für, Lust haben auf*
to pick up	[ˌpɪk 'ʌp]	to collect	*abholen*
either	['aɪðə]	*phr* either one or the other	*hier: beides*

genre	['ʒɑːnrə]	type or style	*Genre*
comedy	['kɒmədi]	funny film	*Komödie, Comedy*
documentary	[ˌdɒkju'mentri]	programme about sth real	*Dokumentarbericht, -film*
satire	['sætaɪə]	*adj* satirical	*Satire*
sci-fi	['saɪ faɪ]	*(abbrev)* science fiction	*Science-Fiction, wissenschaftlich-utopisch*
spy	[spaɪ]	person who tries to find out secret information	*Spion/in, Spionage-*
pirate	['paɪrət]	*phr* pirate DVDs	*Pirat*
all-star	['ɔːl stɑː]	full of celebrities	*Star-, mit vielen Stars*
to put forward	[ˌpʊt 'fɔːwəd]	to suggest or present	*vorbringen, zur Diskussion stellen*
point of view	[ˌpɔɪnt əv 'vjuː]	opinion	*Standpunkt, Ansicht*
ought to	['ɔːt tə]	should	*sollte/n*
it's a pity	[ɪts ə 'pɪti]	it's a shame	*es ist schade*
whatever	[wɒt'evə]	no matter what	*was (auch) immer*

page 59

medium	['miːdiəm]	way of communicating	*Medium*
butterfly	['bʌtəflaɪ]	type of winged insect	*Schmetterling*
altogether	[ˌɔːltə'geðə]	in total	*alles in allem*
stranger	['streɪndʒə]	person you don't know	*Fremde/r*
unusual	[ʌn'juːʒuəl]	strange	*ungewöhnlich*
applicant	['æplɪkənt]	person who applies for a job, etc.	*Bewerber/in*
offline	['ɒflaɪn]	<> online	*offline, nicht im Internet*
to make no sense	[meɪk nəʊ 'sens]	to be hard to understand	*nicht sinnvoll sein*
freely	['friːli]	willingly and honestly	*freimütig*
provider	[prə'vaɪdə]	*v* to provide	*Anbieter*
user	['juːzə]	person who uses sth	*Anwender/in, Benutzer/in*
at risk	[ət 'rɪsk]	in danger of	*gefährdet*
to be worried	[bi 'wʌrid]	to be afraid	*befürchten*
identity	[aɪ'dentəti]	who sb is	*Identität*
thief	[θiːf]	*pl:* thieves	*Dieb/in*
bank details	['bæŋk diːteɪlz]	bank account numbers, etc.	*Bankverbindung, Kontoangaben*
researcher	[rɪ'sɜːtʃə]	*v* to research sth	*Forscher/in*
reunion	[riː'juːniən]	*v* to reunite	*Treffen, Wiedersehen*
to abridge	[ə'brɪdʒ]	to make (a text) shorter	*(ab)kürzen*
to adapt	[ə'dæpt]	to change	*adaptieren*

page 60

to lie	[laɪ]	<> to tell the truth	*lügen*
circle	['sɜːkl]	*phr* circle of friends	*Kreis*
experience	[ɪk'spɪəriəns]	*v* to experience	*Erfahrung(en)*

page 61

to bet	[bet]	to be sure that	*wetten*

page 62

netiquette	['netɪket]	*(inf)* rules for behaving correctly online	*Netiquette, Umgangsformen (im Internet)*
range	[reɪndʒ]	*phr* a wide range of	*Reihe, Spektrum*
polite	[pə'laɪt]	*n* politeness	*höflich*
capital (letter)	['kæpɪtl]	e.g. A, B, C	*Groß(buchstabe)*
to be considered	[bɪ kən'sɪdəd]	to be thought of as	*berücksichtigt werden*
to emphasize	['emfəsaɪz]	*n* emphasis	*betonen, hervorheben*
bold	[bəʊld]	in a thick dark print	*fett*
to underline	[ˌʌndə'laɪn]	to draw a line under a word	*unterstreichen*
spelling	['spelɪŋ]	*phr* a spelling mistake	*Rechtschreibung*
to avoid	[ə'vɔɪd]	to try not to do sth	*(ver)meiden*
over the top	[ˌəʊvə ðə 'tɒp]	too much	*übertrieben*
to bet	[bet]	to be sure that	*wetten*
punctuation	[ˌpʌŋktʃu'eɪʃn]	marks used to separate phrases/sentences	*Zeichensetzung, Interpunktion*
abbreviation	[əˌbriːvi'eɪʃn]	short form of a word or phrase	*Abkürzung*
unnecessary	[ʌn'nesəsəri]	<> necessary	*unnötig*

to shut up	[ˌʃʌt 'ʌp]	*(inf)* to be quiet	*den Mund halten*
kid	[kɪd]	*(inf)* child	*Kind*

page 63

to publish	['pʌblɪʃ]	*n* publication	*veröffentlichen*
fictional	['fɪkʃənl]	*n* fiction	*erfunden*
surveillance	[sɜː'veɪləns]	careful observation	*Überwachung*
society	[sə'saɪəti]	*adj* social	*(die) Gesellschaft*
term	[tɜːm]	phrase	*Ausdruck*
extract	['ekstrækt]	short piece taken from a longer text	*Auszug, Extrakt*
similarity	[ˌsɪmə'lærəti]	*adj* similar	*Ähnlichkeit*

page 64

fundraising	['fʌndreɪzɪŋ]	raising money for a charity/organization	*Wohltätigkeitsveranstaltung, Spendensammeln*
suggestion	[sə'dʒestʃən]	recommendation	*Vorschlag*
to hire sth	['haɪə]	*(esp AE)* to borrow sth for money	*mieten*
bouncy castle	['baʊnsi kɑːsl]	plastic castle filled with air for children to play on	*Hüpfburg*
soft drink	[ˌsɒft 'drɪŋk]	cold drink containing no alcohol	*alkoholfreies Getränk*
exchange	[ɪks'tʃeɪndʒ]	conversation	*(Kurz-)Dialog*
exam results	[ɪgˌzæm rɪ'zʌlts]	grades or marks	*Examensnoten*
secure	[sɪ'kjuə]	*n* security, safe	*sicher*
goods	[gʊdz]	merchandise	*Ware(n), Güter*

UNIT 4

page 65

on the move	[ɒn ðə 'muːv]	travelling	*unterwegs*
various	['veəriəs]	a range of	*verschieden*
transport	['trænspɔːt]	*phr* means of transport	*Verkehr(smittel)*
salesman	['seɪlzmən]	man whose job is to sell goods	*Verkäufer*
ideal	[aɪ'diːəl]	perfect	*ideal*
budget	['bʌdʒɪt]	cheap	*hier: Billig-*
extent	[ɪk'stent]	*phr* to a certain extent	*(Aus-)Maß, Umfang, Grad*
reality	[ri'æləti]	*adj* real	*Wirklichkeit*
amazed	[ə'meɪzd]	*n* amazement	*erstaunt*
annoyed	[ə'nɔɪd]	*v* to annoy sb	*verärgert*
anxious	['æŋkʃəs]	*n* anxiety	*besorgt, beunruhigt*
delighted	[dɪ'laɪtɪd]	happy	*(sehr) erfreut, entzückt*
depressed	[dɪ'prest]	*n* depression	*deprimiert, niedergeschlagen*
disappointed	[ˌdɪsə'pɔɪntɪd]	*n* disappointment	*enttäuscht*
excited	[ɪk'saɪtɪd]	*n* excitement	*aufgeregt, erregt*
exhausted	[ɪg'zɔːstɪd]	*n* exhaustion	*erschöpft*
frustrated	[frʌ'streɪtɪd]	*n* frustration	*frustriert*
nervous	['nɜːvəs]	*n* nervousness	*nervös*
relaxed	[rɪ'lækst]	*n* relaxation	*entspannt, locker*
shocked	[ʃɒkt]	*n* shock	*schockiert*
surprised	[sə'praɪzd]	*n* surprise	*überrascht, erstaunt*
terrified	['terɪfaɪd]	very scared	*erschrocken*
upset	[ˌʌp'set]	unhappy	*bestürzt, entsetzt*

page 66

traffic jam	['træfɪk dʒæm]	*phr* to be stuck in a traffic jam	*(Verkehrs-)Stau*
to reduce	[rɪ'djuːs]	*n* reduction	*reduzieren, verringern*
nursery	['nɜːsəri]	*phr* day nursery, nursery school	*Kindertagesstätte, Kita,*
dry cleaner's	[ˌdraɪ 'kliːnəz]	shop where clothes are cleaned using chemicals	*chemische Reinigung*
fortune	['fɔːtʃuːn]	*phr* to cost a fortune	*Vermögen*
surely	['ʃʊəli]	almost certainly	*sicherlich*
government	['gʌvənmənt]	*v* to govern	*Regierung*
fuel	['fjuːəl]	e.g. petrol, coal, gas	*Kraftstoff*
tax	[tæks]	*phr* tax increases/cuts	*Steuer*
tailback	['teɪlbæk]	long line of still or slow-moving traffic	*Autoschlange*
freedom	['friːdəm]	*adj* free	*Freiheit*

flexibility	[ˌfleksəˈbɪləti]	*adj* flexible	*Flexibilität*
privacy	[ˈprɪvəsi]	*adj* private	*Privatsphäre*
campaigner	[kæmˈpeɪnə]	a person who campaigns for/ against sth	*Aktivist/in, Kämpfer/in*
pollution	[pəˈluːʃn]	*v* to pollute	*(Umwelt)Verschmutzung*
environmental	[ɪnˌvaɪrənˈmentl]	*n* environment	*Umwelt-*
damage	[ˈdæmɪdʒ]	physical harm	*Schaden, Schäden*
exhaust	[ɪɡˈzɔːst]	pipe in a car through which waste gases pass	*Auspuff(rohr)*
fumes	[fjuːmz]	smoke or gas	*Abgase*
to choke	[tʃəʊk]	to be unable to breathe	*ersticken*
gridlock	[ˈɡrɪdlɒk]	situation where there are so many cars that none can move	*Verkehrskollaps*
to contain	[kənˈteɪn]	to hold, include	*enthalten*
passenger	[ˈpæsɪndʒə]	person in a car who is not the driver	*Fahrgast*
minister	[ˈmɪnɪstə]	government official	*Minister/in*
congestion	[kənˈdʒestʃən]	*adj* congested	*Verkehrsstau, Verstopfung*
congested	[kənˈdʒestɪd]	full of traffic	*verstopft*
chaos	[ˈkeɪɒs]	*adj* chaotic	*Chaos*
to improve	[ɪmˈpruːv]	to get better, <> to worsen	*verbessern, besser werden*
balance	[ˈbæləns]	of equal weight	*Gleichgewicht*
efficient	[ɪˈfɪʃnt]	*n* efficiency	*effizient, leistungsfähig*
emission	[ɪˈmɪʃn]	*v* to emit	*Emission, Ausstoß*
suburb	[ˈsʌbɜːb]	*adj* suburban	*Vorort, Außenbezirk*
saving	[ˈseɪvɪŋ]	*v* to save (money)	*Einsparung, Ersparnis*
impact	[ˈɪmpækt]	*phr* to have an impact on sth	*(Aus-)Wirkung, Einfluss*
colleague	[ˈkɒliːɡ]	person you work with	*Kollege/Kollegin*
car sharing	[ˈkɑː ʃeərɪŋ]	sharing a ride to reduce costs/ pollution, etc.	*gemeinsame Pkw-Nutzung*

page 67

idiomatic	[ˌɪdiəˈmætɪk]	*n* idiom	*idiomatisch*
illegal	[ɪˈliːɡl]	<> legal	*verboten, illegal*
idiom	[ˈɪdiəm]	*adj* idiomatic	*Idiom, Redewendung*
accident	[ˈæksɪdənt]	*phr* car accident	*Unfall*
mile	[maɪl]	= 1609 metres	*Meile*
motorway	[ˈməʊtəweɪ]	wide road where cars travel long distances	*Autobahn*
to brainstorm	[ˈbreɪnstɔːm]	to write down or think of different ideas quickly	*(Ideen) sammeln*
route	[ruːt]	(in US road names) main road	*Route, Strecke, Weg*
commuter	[kəˈmjuːtə]	person who travels a long way to get to work every day	*Pendler/in*

page 68

distinction	[dɪˈstɪŋkʃn]	*v* to distinguish	*Unterscheidung*
in contrast to sb/sth	[ɪn ˈkɒntrɑːst tə]	*v* to contrast	*im Gegensatz zu, im Unterschied zu*
conflicting	[kənˈflɪktɪŋ]	different	*gegensätzlich*
advanced	[ədˈvɑːnst]	sophisticated	*fortgeschritten, hochentwickelt*
to disappear	[ˌdɪsəˈpɪə]	to vanish	*verschwinden*
showroom	[ˈʃəʊruːm]	where cars are put on display	*Austellungsraum, Verkaufsraum*
to mark	[mɑːk]	*to signify*	*bedeuten, bezeichnen*
SUV	[ˌes juː ˈviː]	*(abbrev)* sport utility vehicle	*Geländewagen (mit Vierradantrieb)*
to claim	[kleɪm]	to state sth as true	*behaupten, erklären*
awareness	[əˈweənəs]	*adj* aware	*Bewusstsein*
downmarket	[ˌdaʊnˈmɑːkɪt]	cheap	*auf den Massenmarkt ausgerichtet*
upmarket	[ˌʌpˈmɑːkɪt]	expensive	*anspruchsvoll, exklusiv*
to jump start	[ˈdʒʌmp stɑːt]	to start or get a process or activity to move faster	*etwas auf die Sprünge helfen*
to report	[rɪˈpɔːt]	*n* report	*melden, berichten*
gas	[ɡæs]	*(AE) BE:* petrol	*Benzin, Treibstoff*
to support	[səˈpɔːt]	to help, back up	*unterstützen*
to oppose	[əˈpəʊz]	to contradict	*widersprechen*
to relate to sb/sth	[rɪˈleɪt tə]	to connect	*sich beziehen auf*

page 69

satellite	['sætəlaɪt]	*phr* satellite television	*Satellit*
zone	[zəʊn]	area	*Zone, Bereich*
rush hour	['rʌʃaʊə]	time when roads are busy	*Hauptverkehrszeit, Berufsverkehr*
unless	[ən'les]	if not	*wenn nicht*
satnav	['sætnæv]	*(abbrev)* satellite navigation	*Satellitennavigation, Navi*
location	[ləʊ'keɪʃn]	*v* to locate	*(Stand-)Ort, Position*
monthly	['mʌnθli]	every month	*monatlich*
haulier	['hɔːliə]	person who transports goods by road	*Spediteur, Fuhrunternehmen*
to destroy	[dɪ'strɔɪ]	*n* destruction	*zerstören, vernichten*
to estimate	['estɪmeɪt]	*n* estimation	*schätzen*
zero	['zɪərəʊ]	the number 0	*Null*
owner	['əʊnə]	person who owns sth	*Besitzer/in*
environmentalist	[ɪn,vaɪrən'mentəlɪst]	person who wants to protect the environment	*Umweltschützer/in*
engineer	[,endʒɪ'nɪə]	person who designs/builds roads/machines, etc.	*Ingenieur/in, Techniker/in*
to race	[reɪs]	to compete to be the first to do sth	*sich ein Wettrennen liefern*
dweller	['dwelə]	inhabitant	*Bewohner/in*
electricity	[ɪ,lek'trɪsəti]	*adj* electric, electrical	*Elektrizität, Strom*
traditional	[trə'dɪʃənl]	*n* tradition	*traditionell*
power station	['paʊə steɪʃn]	building where electricity is produced	*Kraftwerk*
hybrid	['haɪbrɪd]	using a mixture of fuels	*hybrid*
cleverly	['klevəli]	in a clever way	*klug, intelligent*
movement	['muːvmənt]	*v* to move	*Bewegung*
motor	['məʊtə]	device that uses fuel to produce movement	*Motor*
engine	['endʒɪn]	part of vehicle that produces power to move	*Motor*
hill	[hɪl]	*adj* hilly	*Hügel, Berg*
complicated	['kɒmplɪkeɪtɪd]	complex, intricate	*kompliziert*
development	[dɪ'veləpmənt]	progress	*Entwicklung*
production	[prə'dʌkʃn]	creation, manufacture	*Produktion, Herstellung*
to combine	[kəm'baɪn]	*n* combination	*(sich) verbinden*
hydrogen	['haɪdrədʒən]	chemical element H	*Wasserstoff*
oxygen	['ɒksɪdʒən]	chemical element O	*Sauerstoff*
waste	[weɪst]	*phr* waste product	*Abfall*
to manufacture	[,mænju'fæktʃə]	to produce	*herstellen, produzieren*
renewable	[rɪ'njuːəbl]	*phr* renewable energy	*erneuerbar*
source	[sɔːs]	*phr* energy source	*Quelle*
environmentally friendly	[ɪn,vaɪrən,mentəli 'frendli]	not harmful to the environment	*umweltfreundlich*

page 70

issue	['ɪʃuː]	problem	*Frage, Thema, Anliegen*
conventional	[kən'venʃənl]	traditional	*konventionell, herkömmlich*
doubtful	['daʊtfl]	*v* to doubt	*fraglich, zweifelhaft*

page 71

congestion charging	[kən'dʒestʃən tʃɑːdʒɪŋ]	money you have to pay for driving your car in the city centre	*Staugebühr*
charge	[tʃɑːdʒ]	*phr* free of charge	*Gebühr*
to enter	['entə]	to go into	*hineingehen, -fahren*
result	[rɪ'zʌlt]	*phr* as a result of	*Resultat, Ergebnis*
reduction	[rɪ'dʌkʃn]	*v* to reduce	*Verringerung, Senkung*
central	['sentrəl]	in the centre	*zentral*
anger	['æŋgə]	*v* to anger sb	*Zorn, Ärger*
to affect	[ə'fekt]	to have an effect on	*betreffen*
to benefit from	['benɪfɪt frəm]	to be in a better position because of sth	*Nutzen ziehen aus, profitieren von*
businessperson	['bɪznəspɜːsn]	businessman, businesswoman	*Geschäftsmann/-frau*
official	[ə'fɪʃl]	person in a position of authority	*Beamter/Beamtin*
councillor	['kaʊnsələ]	member of a council	*Ratsmitglied*
to persuade	[pə'sweɪd]	*n* persuasion	*überzeugen, überreden*

page 72

solution	[sə'luːʃn]	*v* to solve	*Lösung*
to maintain	[meɪn'teɪn]	to support	*unterhalten, warten*
road network	[ˌrəʊd 'netwɜːk]	country roads, motorways, etc.	*Straßennetz*
to subsidize	['sʌbsɪdaɪz]	to provide financial support for sth	*subventionieren*
to limit	['lɪmɪt]	to reduce	*limitieren, begrenzen, auf etwas beschränken*
essential	[ɪ'senʃl]	vital, necessary, important	*notwendig, wesentlich*
major	['meɪdʒə]	large or important	*groß, größer*
complete	[kəm'pliːt]	total	*völlig*
unavailable	[ˌʌnə'veɪləbl]	<> available	*nicht verfügbar*
extremely	[ɪk'striːmli]	very	*äußerst, außerordentlich*
personally	['pɜːsənəli]	individually	*persönlich*

page 73

to rank	[ræŋk]	to put in order of importance	*einstufen, -ordnen*
lane	[leɪn]	section of a road	*(Fahr-)Spur*
sensor	['sensə]	device that reacts to light/sound/heat, etc.	*Sensor, Messgerät*
to detect	[dɪ'tekt]	*n* detection	*entdecken*
safety	['seɪfti]	*phr* a safety measure	*Sicherheit*
monitor	['mɒnɪtə]	*v* to monitor	*Monitor*
to fall asleep	[fɔːl ə'sliːp]	to go to sleep	*einschlafen*
to sound	[saʊnd]	to make a noise	*ausgelöst werden, ertönen*
disabler	[dɪs'eɪblə]	to disable	*Sperre*
braking	['breɪkɪŋ]	to slow a vehicle	*Bremssystem*
roadside	['rəʊdsaɪd]	side of a road	*(am) Straßenrand*
signal	['sɪgnəl]	sign	*Signal*
to override	[ˌəʊvə'raɪd]	to stop a process and take control	*ausschalten*
to prevent	[prɪ'vent]	to stop sth happening	*verhindern*
blind spot	['blaɪnd spɒt]	area that you cannot see	*blinder Fleck*
radar	['reɪdɑː]	system that uses radio waves to find objects	*Radar*
ahead	[ə'hed]	in front	*voraus, kommend*
in addition to	[ɪn ə'dɪʃn tə]	as well as	*zusätzlich zu, neben*
communications technologies	[kəˌmjuːnɪˌkeɪʃnz tek'nɒlədʒiz]	e.g. email, text messages, mobile phone	*Kommunikationstechnologien*
to direct	[də'rekt]	*n* direction	*leiten*
parking space	['pɑːkɪŋ speɪs]	place where cars can be parked	*Parkplatz, Parklücke*
insurance	[ɪn'ʃʊərəns]	*phr* to take out insurance	*Versicherung*
premium	['priːmiəm]	money paid for insurance	*Prämie*
air conditioning	['eə kəndɪʃnɪŋ]	*adj* air-conditioned	*Klimaanlage*
heating	['hiːtɪŋ]	system which supplies heat to a car/building, etc.	*Heizung*

page 74

return	[rɪ'tɜːn]	ticket to go to a place and back again	*(hin und) zurück*
election	[ɪ'lekʃn]	a political vote	*(politische) Wahl*

UNIT 5

page 75

disaster	[dɪ'zɑːstə]	a very bad situation or event	*Katastrophe, Unglück*
mixture	['mɪkstʃə]	combination	*Mischung*
brief	['briːf]	quick, for a short time	*kurz*
asteroid	['æstərɔɪd]	a small planet which revolves around the sun	*Asteroid*
catastrophe	[kə'tæstrəfi]	disaster	*Katastrophe*
destruction	[dɪ'strʌkʃn]	*v* to destroy	*Zerstörung, Vernichtung*
epidemic	[ˌepɪ'demɪk]	outbreak of a disease or illness	*Epidemie*
flood	[flʌd]	a place that is filled or covered with water	*Flut, Überschwemmung*
to be set in	[bi 'set ɪn]	the film is set in …, NOT: ~~the film plays in …~~	*spielen in*

page 76

report	[rɪ'pɔːt]	*v* to report	*Bericht, Reportage*
fitted	['fɪtɪd]	*v* to fit in place	*eingebaut*
low-energy	[ˌləʊ 'enədʒi]	small or little amount of power	*Niedrigenergie-, Spar-*
bulb	[bʌlb]	*phr* light bulb	*Glühbirne, -lampe*
matter	['mætə]	situation, problem	*Sache, Ding, Angelegenheit*
journalist	['dʒɜːnəlɪst]	a person who collects and writes news stories	*Journalist/in*
progress	['prəʊgres]	⚠ Betonung	*Fortschritt/e*
to turn down	[ˌtɜːn 'daʊn]	*phr* to turn down the temperature	*herunterregeln*
sweater	['swetə]	a piece of clothing for the upper body	*Pullover*
alternative	[ɔːl'tɜːnətɪv]	different option	*alternativ*
turbine	['tɜːbaɪn]	⚠ Aussprache	*Turbine, Rad*
strength	[streŋθ]	*adj* strong	*Kraft, Stärke*
unreliable	[ˌʌnrɪ'laɪəbl]	<> reliable	*unzuverlässig*
solar	['səʊlə]	using the sun's energy to create power	*Sonnen-, Solar-*
to meet needs	[miːt 'niːdz]	to get sth done	*Bedürfnisse decken*
insulation	[ˌɪnsju'leɪʃn]	*phr* wall insulation	*Isolierung*
to face	[feɪs]	*phr* to face a decision	*sich gegenübersehen, vor sich haben*
cycle	['saɪkl]	*n* bicycle	*radfahren*
double-glazing	[ˌdʌbl 'gleɪzɪŋ]	*phr* double-glazed windows	*mit Isolierverglasung versehen*
previous	['priːviəs]	before	*vorher(gehend)*
to run out of	[ˌrʌn 'aʊt əv]	*phr* to run out of money	*ausgehen*
tonne	[tʌn]	1000 kilograms	*Tonne*
amount	[ə'maʊnt]	quantity	*Menge*
average	['ævərɪdʒ]	typical, normal	*durchschnittlich*
lifestyle	['laɪfstaɪl]	how a person lives and works	*Lebensstil*
somehow	['sʌmhaʊ]	in a way which is not clear	*irgendwie*

page 77

timeline	['taɪmlaɪn]	diagram showing the order in which events happened	*Zeitachse, -leiste*
benefit	['benɪfɪt]	advantage	*Nutzen, Vorteil*

page 78

to rewrite	[ˌriː'raɪt]	to write again	*umschreiben, neu schreiben*
original	[ə'rɪdʒənl]	*phr* the original words from the text	*original, ursprünglich*
to advise	[əd'vaɪz]	to suggest, offer an opinion	*raten, beraten*
to request	[rɪ'kwest]	to ask for	*anfordern, bitten (um)*
junction	['dʒʌŋkʃn]	a place or point where two things come together	*Kreuzung*
bored	[bɔːd]	uninterested	*gelangweilt*
switch	[swɪtʃ]	a device for turning off and on an electrical current	*Schalter*
machinery	[mə'ʃiːnəri]	*n* machine	*Maschine(n), Gerät*
appliance	[ə'plaɪəns]	electronic device	*Gerät*
worried	['wʌrɪd]	*v* to worry	*besorgt*
cloudy	['klaʊdi]	*n* cloud	*bewölkt*
valley	['væli]	the lowest point between two mountains	*Tal*
path	[pɑːθ]	a walkway	*Pfad, Weg*
direction	[də'rekʃn]	*phr* to change direction	*Richtung*

page 79

global	['gləʊbl]	worldwide	*global, weltweit*
desperate	['despərət]	urgent	*verzweifelt*
airwaves	['eəweɪvz]	radio waves used to broadcast radio and TV	*Äther*
atmosphere	['ætməsfɪə]	the mixture of gases that surround the earth	*Atmosphäre*
twice	[twaɪs]	once, twice, three times	*zweimal, doppelt*
level	['levl]	amount	*Niveau, Stand*
industrial	[ɪn'dʌstriəl]	*n* industry	*industriell*
revolution	[ˌrevə'luːʃn]	radical change	*Revolution*
climate	['klaɪmət]	weather	*Klima*

eastern	['iːstən]	<> western, northern, southern	*östlich*
cyclone	['saɪkləʊn]	bad storm with wind and rain	*Zyklon*
desert	['dezət]	dry empty land	*Wüste*
moreover	[mɔːr'əʊvə]	also	*außerdem, zudem*
sheet	[ʃiːt]	*phr* sheet of ice	*Platte, Decke*
to melt	[melt]	<> freeze	*schmelzen*
centimetre	['sentɪmiːtə]	unit for measuring length	*Zentimeter*
low-lying	[ˌləʊ 'laɪɪŋ]	located at a low level	*tief gelegen*
coastal	['kəʊstl]	on the coast	*Küsten-*
to prevent	[prɪ'vent]	to stop sth from happening	*verhindern, verhüten*
champagne	[ʃæm'peɪn]	French sparkling white wine	*Champagner*
to celebrate	['selɪbreɪt]	*phr* to celebrate a birthday	*feiern*
atmospheric	[ˌætməs'ferɪk]	in the atmosphere	*atmosphärisch*
ppm	[ˌpiː piː 'em]	*(abbrev)* parts per million	*Teile pro Million*
economy	[ɪ'kɒnəmi]	*phr* the world economy	*Wirtschaft*
stabilization	[ˌsteɪbəlaɪ'zeɪʃn]	*adj* stable	*Stabilisierung*
coal	[kəʊl]	type of fuel	*Kohle*
fossil fuel	['fɒsl fjuːəl]	type of fuel	*fossiler Brennstoff*
tidal	['taɪdl]	*n* tides	*Gezeiten-*
hydroelectric	[ˌhaɪdrəʊɪ'lektrɪk]	using the power of water to make electricity	*hydroelektrisch*
nuclear	['njuːkliə]	*phr* nuclear weapons	*Atom-*
fusion	['fjuːʒn]	joining things together to make one	*Fusion, Verschmelzung*
thanks to	['θæŋks tə]	because of	*dank*
vision	['vɪʒn]	goal	*Vision, Vorausschau*
to delay	[dɪ'leɪ]	*n* delay	*aufschieben, hinauszögern*
warming	['wɔːmɪŋ]	*adj* warm	*Erwärmung*
severe	[sɪ'vɪə]	very bad	*ernst, schwer, stark*
wise	[waɪz]	smart	*weise, klug*
leader	['liːdə]	*phr* leader of the group	*Führer/in*
to owe	[əʊ]	*phr* to owe money	*verdanken, schulden*
to emerge	[ɪ'mɜːdʒ]	to come out of some place	*heraustreten, hervorkommen*
carbon	['kɑːbən]	a chemical element	*Kohlenstoff*

page 80

century	['sentʃəri]	100 years	*Jahrhundert*
to power	['paʊə]	*adj* powerful	*antreiben*
fraction	['frækʃn]	a part of a whole	*Bruch(teil)*
percentage	[pə'sentɪdʒ]	%	*Prozentsatz*
climate change	['klaɪmət tʃeɪndʒ]	alteration of the world's weather patterns	*Klimawandel*
rise	[raɪz]	increase	*Anstieg*
carbon dioxide	[ˌkɑːbən daɪ'ɒksaɪd]	the gas CO_2	*Kohlendioxid*
though	[ðəʊ]	however	*doch, jedoch*
poverty	['pɒvəti]	*adj* poor	*Armut*
standard of living	[ˌstændəd əv 'lɪvɪŋ]	quality of life	*Lebensstandard*
to make up for	[ˌmeɪk 'ʌp fə]	to compensate for	*ausgleichen*
to hold down	[ˌhəʊld 'daʊn]	to prevent from increasing	*niedrig halten*
cut	[kʌt]	reduction	*Kürzung, Senkung*
target	['tɑːgɪt]	goal	*Ziel(vorgaben), Soll(zahlen)*

page 81

to describe	[dɪ'skraɪb]	*n* description	*beschreiben*
view	[vjuː]	picture, image	*Ansicht*

page 82

to present	[prɪ'zent]	to put forward	*vorstellen, behandeln*
demand	[dɪ'mɑːnd]	*v* to demand	*Nachfrage*
carefully	['keəfəli]	*n* care	*sorgfältig*
to turn one's back on sb/sth	[ˌtɜːn wʌnz 'bæk ɒn]		*jdm/etwas den Rücken kehren*
surprising	[sə'praɪzɪŋ]	*n* surprise	*überraschend*
to put sth in perspective	[ˌpʊt ɪn pə'spektɪv]	to compare with something similar to get a clearer, more accurate idea	*etwas ins rechte Licht rücken, etw relativieren*

page 83

purpose	['pɜ:pəs]	reason	*Zweck, Ziel*
overall	[ˌəʊvər'ɔ:l]	including all things	*allgemein*
mains	[meɪnz]	*(inf, BE)* circuit outlets	*(Strom-)Netz*
afterwards	['ɑ:ftəwədz]	at a later time	*danach, hinterher*
wrinkly	['rɪŋkli]	*n* wrinkles	*runzlig*
tap	[tæp]	*phr* tap water	*(Wasser-)Hahn*
standby	['stændbaɪ]	sth ready to use when it is needed	*Bereitschaft, Ruhezustand*
secondary	['sekəndri]	second	*Zweit-*
household	['haʊshəʊld]	all the people who live in one house	*Haushalt*
whopping	['wɒpɪŋ]	*(inf, AE)* very big	*gewaltig*
kWh	[ˌkeɪ dʌblju: 'eɪtʃ]	*(abbrev)* kilowatt-hour	*Kilowattstunde*
overnight	[ˌəʊvə'naɪt]	throughout the night	*über Nacht*
worth of	['wɜ:θ əv]	value	*im Wert von*
floodlight	['flʌdlaɪt]	powerful light	*Flutlicht*
premiership	['premiəʃɪp]	*phr* the premiership football leagues in the United Kingdom	*Bundesliga*
professional	[prə'feʃənl]	*phr* to have professional skills	*Profi-*
league	[li:g]	*phr* football league	*Liga*
stadium	['steɪdiəm]	*phr* football or sports stadium	*Stadion*
to brush	[brʌʃ]	*phr* to brush your teeth	*bürsten, putzen*
tooth	[tu:θ]	*pl:* teeth	*Zahn*
to fancy	['fænsi]	to be interested in	*sich vorstellen*
stupid	['stju:pɪd]	dumb	*dumm*
toilet	['tɔɪlət]	*BE* also: loo	*Toilette*
to flush	[flʌʃ]	*phr* to flush the toilet	*spülen*
to add up to	[ˌæd 'ʌp tə]	to accumulate	*sich addieren zu*
to exist	[ɪg'zɪst]	to be present	*existieren*
greenhouse gas	[ˌgri:nhaʊs 'gæs]	type of pollution	*Treibhausgas*
to commit	[kə'mɪt]	to be loyal	*(sich) verpflichten*
commitment	[kə'mɪtmənt]	*v* to commit	*(Selbst-)Verpflichtung*

page 84

dramatic	[drə'mætɪ]	*adv.* dramatically	*dramatisch, drastisch*

UNIT 6

page 85

to operate	['ɒpəreɪt]	to run	*betreiben*
seaside	['si:saɪd]	along the ocean	*Bade-, Strand-, See-*
resort	[rɪ'zɔ:t]	a place where people go to on holiday to relax	*Erholungsort*
accountant	[ə'kaʊntənt]	person who looks after and checks financial accounts	*Buchhalter/in*
booking	['bʊkɪŋ]	*v* to book	*Buchung*
clerk	[klɑ:k]	a worker in charge of accounts and records, etc.	*(Bank-)Angestellte/r*
customer relations officer	[ˌkʌstəmə rɪ'leɪʃnz ɒfɪsə]	person who deals with customers	*Kundendienstmitarbeiter/in, Kundenbetreuer/in*
IT technician	[ˌaɪ 'ti: tek'nɪʃn]	person who is skilled with information technology	*Informationstechniker/in*
receptionist	[rɪ'sepʃənɪst]	works in a reception	*Empfangsdame, -chef*
publicity	[pʌb'lɪsəti]	*n* public	*Öffentlichkeitsarbeit*
activities officer	[æk'tɪvətiz ɒfɪsə]	person who is in charge of organizing events	*Verantwortliche/r für Aktivitäten und Veranstaltungen*
salesperson	['seɪlzpɜ:sn]	salesman, saleswoman	*Verkaufsmitarbeiter/in, Verkäufer/in*
instructor	[ɪn'strʌktə]	person who gives instructions	*Lehrer/in, Ausbilder/in*
temporary	['temprəri]	<> permanent	*zeitlich befristet*
seasonal	['si:zənl]	*n* season	*Saison-*
paid	[peɪd]	*phr* to get paid money	*bezahlt*
irregular	[ɪ'regjələ]	<> regular	*unregelmäßig*
outdoors	[ˌaʊt'dɔ:z]	outside	*draußen, im Freien*
independent	[ˌɪndɪ'pendənt]	self-reliant	*unabhängig*

office-based	['ɒfɪs beɪst]	to be working within an office	*im Büro, bürogebunden*
routine	[ruː'tiːn]	a regular fixed way of doing things	*Routine, Ablauf*
challenging	['tʃælɪndʒɪŋ]	difficult	*herausfordernd, anstrengend*
reasonable	['riːznəbl]	okay	*vernünftig*
salary	['sæləri]	amount of money earned	*Gehalt, Lohn*
fringe benefits	['frɪndʒ benəfɪts]	extra things that an employer gives you as well as your salary	*zusätzliche Leistungen, freiwillige Sozialleistungen*
page 86			
workplace	['wɜːkpleɪs]	area where one works	*Arbeitsplatz*
complex	['kɒmpleks]	complicated	*komplex, kompliziert*
diploma	[dɪ'pləʊmə]	graduation certificate	*Diplom*
secretarial course	[ˌsekrə'teəriəl kɔːs]	course on how to become a secretary	*Sekretariatskurs*
CV	[ˌsiː 'viː]	*(abbrev)* Curriculum Vitae	*Lebenslauf*
to drift	[drɪft]	to move slowly and casually	*treiben, zufällig kommen*
stock control	['stɒk kəntrəʊl]	control of supplies	*Lagersteuerung, Lagerkontrolle*
dead-end	[ˌded 'end]	*phr* a dead-end job	*ohne Perspektiven*
redundant	[rɪ'dʌndənt]	made unemployed	*arbeitslos*
to upgrade	[ˌʌp'greɪd]	to make better or to improve	*erweitern, verbessern*
to apply for	[ə'plaɪ fə]	*n* application	*sich bewerben um*
page 87			
vocational	[vəʊ'keɪʃənl]	preparing sb for a specific occupation or trade	*in der beruflichen Ausbildung, beruflich, Berufs-*
to outline	['aʊtlaɪn]	to summarize	*umreißen, skizzieren*
to matter	['mætə]	to be of importance	*von Bedeutung sein*
backwards	['bækwədz]	<> forward(s)	*rückwärts*
page 88			
employment	[ɪm'plɔɪmənt]	job	*Arbeit, Beschäftigung, Beruf*
wages	['weɪdʒɪz]	amount of money earned by or paid to sb	*Lohn, Löhne*
pressure	['preʃə]	stress	*Druck*
responsibility	[rɪˌspɒnsə'bɪləti]	*adj* responsible	*Verantwortung, Verantwortlichkeit*
export sales	['ekspɔːt seɪlz]	things that are being sold to other countries	*Exportverkäufe, Auslandsverkäufe*
marketing	['mɑːkɪtɪŋ]		*Marketing, Vermarktung*
IT	[ˌaɪ 'tiː]	*(abbrev)* information technology	*Informationstechnologie*
to mess up	[ˌmes 'ʌp]	*(inf)* to do badly	*es verderben, es verpeilen*
skint	[skɪnt]	*(inf)* having no money	*pleite*
to put down	[ˌpʊt 'daʊn]	to pay up front	*anzahlen*
solar heating	[ˌsəʊlə 'hiːtɪŋ]	system which uses the sun's energy to heat a house	*Solarheizung*
to push up	[ˌpʊʃ 'ʌp]	to increase	*ausbauen, hochtreiben*
to hire	[haɪə]	to recruit, look for new employees	*anstellen*
IT officer	[ˌaɪ 'tiː 'ɒfɪsə]	= IT technician	*EDV-Techniker/in*
support	[sə'pɔːt]	help	*Hilfe, Unterstützung*
pen	[pen]	*phr* ballpoint pen	*Stift*
car seat	['kɑː siːt]	seat in a car	*Autositz*
page 89			
beyond	[bɪ'jɒnd]	apart/aside from	*abgesehen von*
aptitude	['æptɪtjuːd]	ability	*Fähigkeit, Eignung*
prospect	['prɒspekt]	a probable future	*Aussicht*
commitment	[kə'mɪtmənt]	*v* to commit	*Einsatz, Engagement*
retired	[rɪ'taɪəd]	having finished working, usually late in life	*pensioniert, im Ruhestand*
grandad	['grændæd]	grandfather	*Opa*
hardly	['hɑːdli]	barely	*kaum*
terms	[tɜːmz]	conditions	*Bedingungen, Konditionen*
generous	['dʒenərəs]	*n* generosity	*großzügig*
subsidized	['sʌbsɪdaɪzd]	supported financially	*subventioniert*
healthcare	['helθkeə]	service of providing medical care	*medizinische Versorgung*
travel insurance	[ˌtrævl ɪn'ʃʊərəns]	*phr* to take out travel insurance	*Reiseversicherung*
maternity leave	[mə'tɜːnəti liːv]	the amount of paid time soon-to-be mothers have off from work	*Mutterschaftsurlaub*

paternity leave	[pəˈtɜːnəti liːv]	the amount of paid time soon-to-be fathers have off from work	*Vaterschaftsurlaub*
creche facilities	[ˌkreʃ fəˈsɪlətiz]	a place where babies and small children are taken care of	*Krippeneinrichtungen*
employee	[ɪmˈplɔɪiː]	worker	*Arbeitnehmer/in, Beschäftigte/r*
union	[ˈjuːniən]	group of working people	*Gewerkschaft*
to invest	[ɪnˈvest]	to put money into a business	*investieren*
workforce	[ˈwɜːkfɔːs]	the workers	*Belegschaft*
resource	[rɪˈsɔːs]	reserves	*Reserve, Ressource*
white-collar	[ˌwaɪt ˈkɒlə]	working in an office	*Schreibtisch-, Büro-*
clerical	[ˈklerɪkl]	connected with office work	*Schreib-, Büro-*
low-cost	[ˌləʊˈkɒst]	inexpensive	*Niedriglohn-*
page 90			
to illustrate	[ˈɪləstreɪt]	to visually show	*illustrieren, veranschaulichen*
conclusion	[kənˈkluːʒn]	summary	*(Schluss-)Folgerung*
performance-related pay	[pəˌfɔːməns rɪleɪtɪd ˈpeɪ]	when rate of pay is based on how well sb does their job	*leistungsbezogene Bezahlung*
goal-oriented	[ˈgəʊl ɔːriəntɪd]	working towards a goal	*ergebnisorientiert, zielorientiert*
repetitive	[rɪˈpetətɪv]	*n* repetition	*monoton*
page 91			
ID	[ˌaɪ ˈdiː]	*(abbrev)* (proof of) identity	*Ausweis*
letter of appointment	[ˌletər əv əˈpɔɪntmənt]	letter sent to a new employee	*Bewerbungsschreiben*
as a matter of fact	[əz ə ˌmætər əv ˈfækt]	actually	*um genau zu sein*
to be off to	[bi ˈɒf tə]	to be about to go to	*losgehen*
page 92			
indirectness	[ˌɪndəˈrektnəs]	to be indirect	*Indirektheit*
absurd	[əbˈsɜːd]	ridiculous	*absurd*
reply	[rɪˈplaɪ]	*v* to reply	*Antwort, Erwiderung, Reaktion*
freezing	[ˈfriːzɪŋ]	very cold	*eiskalt, sehr kalt*
elderly	[ˈeldəli]	older	*älter*
parcel	[ˈpɑːsl]	package	*Paket*
to guide	[gaɪd]	to lead	*führen, leiten*
page 93			
aptitude test	[ˈæptɪtjuːd test]	test used to measure skills	*Eignungs-, Fähigkeitstest*
numerical	[njuːˈmerɪkl]	*n* number	*numerisch, Zahlen-*
to select	[sɪˈlekt]	to choose	*auswählen*
to complete	[kəmˈpliːt]	to finish	*vervollständigen, abschließen*
maximum	[ˈmæksɪməm]	highest	*maximal*
gross profit	[ˌgrəʊs ˈprɒfɪt]	the amount of money earned after costs are deducted	*Bruttogewinn*
labour	[ˈleɪbə]	physical work	*Arbeit*
production rate	[prəˈdʌkʃn reɪt]	speed at which sth is produced	*Produktionsrate*
clockwise	[ˈklɒkwaɪz]	the direction the clock moves in	*im Uhrzeigersinn*
degree	[dɪˈgriː]	angle	*Grad*
diagrammatic	[ˌdaɪəgrəˈmætɪk]		*grafisch, schematisch*
page 94			
for ages	[fər ˈeɪdʒɪz]	for a very long time	*eine Ewigkeit*
How have you been keeping?	[ˌhaʊ həv ju biːn ˈkiːpɪŋ]	How are you doing?	*Wie geht es dir?*
revision	[rɪˈvɪʒn]	review	*Wiederholung*
appropriate	[əˈprəʊpriət]	suitable	*angemessen, passend, entsprechend*

UNIT 7

page 95			
directed at	[dəˈrektɪd ət]	aimed at	*gerichtet auf, abzielend auf*
microchip	[ˈmaɪkrəʊtʃɪp]	a chip used in computers	*Mikrochip*
studio	[ˈstjuːdiəʊ]	the place where art, films or music is created	*Studio*

checklist	['tʃeklɪst]	a list of items	*Checkliste*
equipment	[ɪ'kwɪpmənt]	the things necessary for a particular kind of job	*Ausrüstung*

page 96

globalization	[ˌgləʊbəlaɪ'zeɪʃn]	the expansion of the economy, industry, market or culture	*Globalisierung*
transmission	[træns'mɪʃn]	transfer	*Übertragung*
opportunity	[ˌɒpə'tju:nəti]	a good chance to advance oneself	*Chance, Möglichkeit*
textile	['tekstaɪl]	e.g. weaving, knitting, etc.	*Textil-*
to be required to	[bi rɪ'kwaɪəd tə]	to have to	*müssen*
overtime	['əʊvətaɪm]	working more hours	*Überstunden*
to sack	[sæk]	to fire	*entlassen, feuern*
slave	[sleɪv]	person who is forced to work for no money	*Sklave / Sklavin*
offshore	[ˌɒf'ʃɔ:]	to be relocated in a new country	*ins / im Ausland*
paycheck	['peɪtʃek]	*(AE) BE:* wages, salary, income	*Gehalt(sscheck)*
to rescue	['reskju:]	to save	*retten*
to redevelop	[ˌri:dɪ'veləp]	to restore	*erneuern, neu entwickeln*
reborn	[ˌri:'bɔ:n]	new	*wiedergeboren*
competitive advantage	[kəm'petətɪv ədvɑ:ntɪdʒ]	e.g. lower price, better quality, etc.	*Wettbewerbsvorteil*
cutting-edge	[ˌkʌtɪŋ 'edʒ]	modern	*Spitzen-, Hightech-, modern*

page 97

branch	[brɑ:ntʃ]	an office of a company abroad	*Niederlassung*

page 98

body language	['bɒdi læŋgwɪdʒ]	the signs and gestures we make with our body	*Körpersprache*
personal space	['pɜ:sənl speɪs]	the space around us	*Distanzzone, Abstand zwischen Personen*
acceptable	[ək'septəbl]	approved	*annehmbar, akzeptabel*
sensitive	['sensətɪv]	being easily affected by sth	*empfindlich*
to dominate	['dɒmɪneɪt]	to have command or influence over	*dominieren*
listener	['lɪsnə]	*v* to listen	*Zuhörer / in*
dishonest	[dɪs'ɒnɪst]	<> honest	*unehrlich*
to trust	[trʌst]	to believe or have confidence in sth or sb	*vertrauen*
warmth	[wɔ:mθ]	*adj* warm	*Wärme*
to shake	[ʃeɪk]	*phr* to shake hands	*schütteln*
activist	['æktɪvɪst]	sb who actively stands up for a cause / belief	*Aktivist / in*

page 99

to rely on	[rɪ'laɪ ɒn]	to depend on	*angewiesen sein auf, sich verlassen auf*
supply chain	[sə'plaɪ tʃeɪn]	the chain through which products are distributed from producer to retailer	*Versorgungskette*
casual	['kæʒuəl]	occasional	*Gelegenheits-*
picker	['pɪkə]	*v* to pick	*Pflücker / in*
to despair	[dɪ'speə]	to lose hope	*verzweifeln*
to bury	['berɪ]	*phr* to bury your feelings / hopes / dreams	*begraben*
concern	[kən'sɜ:n]	worry	*Sorge, Interesse, Anliegen*
to hurt	[hɜ:t]	to harm	*wehtun, hier: negativ beinflussen*
coordinator	[kəʊ'ɔ:dɪneɪtə]	organizer	*Koordinator / in*
weakness	['wi:knəs]	*adj* weak	*Schwäche*
guaranteed	[ˌgærən'ti:d]	secured	*garantiert*
craft	[krɑ:ft]	handmade art pieces	*(Kunst-)Handwerk*
middlemen	['mɪdlmən]	people in the middle of the supply chain	*Zwischenhändler*
precarious	[prɪ'keəriəs]	risky	*unsicher, prekär*
shareholder	['ʃeəhəʊldə]	sb who owns stocks in a company	*Aktionär / in*
to offload	[ˌɒf'ləʊd]	unload	*weitergeben*
to seek	[si:k]	to look for	*suchen*
sub-contractor	[ˌsʌbkən'træktə]		*Subunternehmer*

page 100

to identify	[aɪ'dentɪfaɪ]	to find	*herausfinden*
to relate to	[rɪ'leɪt tə]	to connect	*sich beziehen auf*

page 101

hectare	['hekteə]	= 10,000 square metres	*Hektar*
co-operative	[kəʊ 'ɒpərətɪv]	workers' group	*Kooperative*
coffee mill	['kɒfi mɪl]	where coffee is produced	*Kaffeemühle*
to install	[ɪn'stɔːl]	to set up	*installieren*
earnings	['ɜːnɪŋz]	money made	*Einkünfte*

page 102

deficit	['defɪsɪt]	<> surplus	*Defizit*
to address sth	[ə'dres]	to tackle, do sth about sth	*sich mit etw befassen, etw angehen*
to solve	[sɒlv]	*n* solution	*lösen*
sustainable	[sə'steɪnəbl]	*v* to sustain	*nachhaltig*

page 103

consignment	[kən'saɪnmənt]	a shipment of goods to a dealer to sell or keep safe	*(Waren-)Sendung, Lieferung*
customs	['kʌstəmz]	taxes on imports and exports	*Zoll*
duty	['djuːti]		*Zoll, Abgabe*
commission	[kə'mɪʃn]	*phr* to earn commission	*Provision, Gebühr*
destination	[ˌdestɪ'neɪʃn]	end of a journey	*Ziel(hafen), Entladehafen*
port	[pɔːt]	a harbour	*Hafen*
to handle	['hændl]	to deal with	*umgehen mit, bearbeiten*
distribution	[ˌdɪstrɪ'bjuːʃn]	*v* to distribute	*Vertrieb, (Waren-)Verteilung*
packaging	['pækɪdʒɪŋ]	*v* to pack	*Verpacken*
manner	['mænə]	way	*Art (und Weise)*
visual	['vɪʒuəl]	*n* vision	*visuell, optisch*
scandal	['skændl]	event that causes feelings of shock	*Skandal*
offence	[ə'fens]	a crime	*Straftat, Vergehen*
compulsory	[kəm'pʌlsəri]	obligatory	*obligatorisch, zwangsweise*
sacking	['sækɪŋ]	firing	*Entlassung(en)*

page 104

dryer	['draɪə]	a machine that dries	*Trockner*
dried	[draɪd]	when sth lacks water	*Trocken-*
basket	['bɑːskɪt]	an object used to hold things	*Korb*
specialist	['speʃəlɪst]	expert	*speziell, Fach-*
payment	['peɪmənt]	*v* to pay (for)	*Bezahlung*
receipt	[rɪ'siːt]	written statement that money has been received	*Eingang, Erhalt*

UNIT 8

page 105

treaty	['triːti]	an agreement between countries	*Vertrag*
headquarters	[ˌhed'kwɔːtəz]	main office	*Hauptsitz, Zentrale*
commission	[kə'mɪʃn]	an official group of people who control sth	*Kommission*
voter	['vəʊtə]	*v* to vote	*Wähler/in*
to reject	[rɪ'dʒekt]	to refuse	*ablehnen*
constitution	[ˌkɒnstɪ'tjuːʃn]	an established arrangement	*Verfassung*
anthem	['ænθəm]	*phr* national anthem	*Hymne*
peace	[piːs]	a state of mutual harmony	*Frieden*
prosperity	[prɒ'sperəti]	success	*Wohlstand*

page 106

internship	['ɪntɜːnʃɪp]	work providing experience in firm	*Volontariat*
to involve	[ɪn'vɒlv]	to include	*einschließen, beinhalten*
tourism	['tʊərɪzəm]	*n* tourist	*Tourismus, Fremdenverkehr*
practical	['præktɪkl]	basic	*praktisch*
intern	['ɪntɜːn]	person doing an internship	*Praktikant/in, Volontär/in*
to contact	['kɒntækt]	to get in touch with sb	*Kontakt aufnehmen zu, sich wenden an*
to specialize in	['speʃəlaɪz ɪn]	to be good at sth specific	*sich spezialisieren auf*

sector	['sektə]	section	*Sektor, Bereich*
duty	['dju:ti]	task	*Pflicht, Aufgabe*
enquiry	[ɪn'kwaɪəri]	question	*Anfrage*
accommodation	[əˌkɒmə'deɪʃn]	food and lodging	*Unterkunft*
fluent	['flu:ənt]	*phr* to be fluent in a language	*fließend, gewandt, flüssig*
licence	['laɪsns]	*phr* driving licence	*Führerschein*
outgoing	['aʊtgəʊɪŋ]	confident and friendly	*kontaktfreudig*
contribution	[ˌkɒntrɪ'bju:ʃn]	*v* to contribute	*Beitrag, Beihilfe*
expenses	[ɪk'spensɪz]	costs	*Kosten, Ausgaben*
negotiation	[nɪˌgəʊʃi'eɪʃn]	discussion	*Verhandlung*
attachment	[ə'tætʃmənt]	*v* to attach	*Anlage*
reference	['refrəns]	written statement about character and skills	*Zeugnis*
to provide	[prə'vaɪd]	to supply	*(an)bieten, sorgen für, zur Verfügung stellen*
fee	[fi:]	*phr* admission fee	*Gebühr*
council	['kaʊnsl]	an assembly of people	*Rat, Gemeinderat*
to gain	[geɪn]	to receive	*sammeln, erlangen*
to attach	[ə'tætʃ]	to join onto sth	*beilegen, -fügen*
query	['kwɪəri]	question	*Frage, Rückfrage*
Yours faithfully	[jɔ:z 'feɪθfʊli]	phrase used to end formal letters	*Mit freundlichen Grüßen*

page 107

unpaid	[ˌʌn'peɪd]	<> paid	*unbezahlt*
enthusiasm	[ɪn'θju:ziæzəm]	excitement	*Begeisterung (-sfähigkeit)*
agreement	[ə'gri:mənt]	*v* to agree	*Vertrag, Abkommen, Zusage*
department	[dɪ'pɑ:tmənt]	a section of a business	*Abteilung*
theoretical	[ˌθɪə'retɪkl]	<> practical	*theoretisch*
request	[rɪ'kwest]	*v* to request	*Bitte, Aufforderung, Wunsch*

page 108

referee	[ˌrefə'ri:]	person who writes a job reference	*Referenzgeber/in*
regarding	[rɪ'gɑ:dɪŋ]	concerning	*bezüglich, betreffend*
marital status	[ˌmærɪtl 'steɪtəs]	whether or not you are married	*Familienstand*

page 109

landline	['lændlaɪn]	home phone	*Festnetz(leitung)*
Do you mind if ...?	[də ju 'maɪnd ɪf]	Is it all right if ...?	*Haben Sie etwas dagegen, wenn ...?*
cyclist	['saɪklɪst]	bike rider	*Fahrradfahrer/in*
outdoor clothing	['aʊtdɔ: kləʊðɪŋ]	clothes for hiking, camping, etc.	*Wanderbekleidung*
typical	['tɪpɪkl]	ordinary	*typisch*

page 110

corruption	[kə'rʌpʃn]	*v* to corrupt	*Korruption*
bureaucracy	[bjʊə'rɒkrəsi]		*Bürokratie*
interference	[ˌɪntə'fɪərəns]	*v* to interfere	*Einmischung*
affair	[ə'feə]	event or happening	*Angelegenheit*
undemocratic	[ˌʌndemə'krætɪk]	not practising social equality	*undemokratisch*
bunch	[bʌntʃ]	a lot of	*Gruppe, Haufen*
unelected	[ˌʌnɪ'lektɪd]	people who were not chosen	*nicht gewählt*
bang	[bæŋ]	expression used when sth starts dramatically	*Paukenschlag*
misleading	[ˌmɪs'li:dɪŋ]	leading in the wrong direction	*irreführend*
frank	['fræŋk]	honest	*offen, ehrlich*
to recommend	[ˌrekə'mend]	to suggest	*empfehlen*
to defend	[dɪ'fend]	to ward off attack from sb or sth	*verteidigen*
take on	['teɪk ɒn]	opinion on	*Einstellung zu*
relatively	['relətɪvli]	quite, somewhat	*verhältnismäßig*
frontier	['frʌntɪə]	boundary	*Grenze*
currency	['kʌrənsi]	system of money that a country uses	*Währung*

page 111

stability	[stə'bɪləti]	*adj* stable	*Stabilität*
sovereignty	['sɒvrənti]	independent power/authority	*Souveränität, Unabhängigkeit*
anyhow	['enihaʊ]	in any case	*sowieso*
selfish	['selfɪʃ]	only interested in oneself	*egoistisch*

threat	[θret]	sth that is a source of danger	*Bedrohung, Drohung*
scarcity	['skeəsəti]	*adj* scarce	*Knappheit*
migration	[maɪ'greɪʃn]	to move from one part of the world to another	*Wanderung(sbewegung)*
border	['bɔ:də]	boundary	*Grenze, Grenz-*
to pull on the same rope	[ˌpʊl ɒn ðə ˌseɪm 'rəʊp]	to work together, cooperate	*an einem Strang ziehen*
to integrate	['ɪntɪgreɪt]	to become part of sth	*sich integrieren*
tyre	['taɪə]	a rubber ring placed over the wheel of a vehicle	*Reifen*
widening	['waɪdnɪŋ]	increase in size	*Erweiterung*

page 112

recommendation	[ˌrekəmen'deɪʃn]	*v* to recommend	*Empfehlung*
lawyer	['lɔ:jə]	person who has studied law	*(Rechts-)Anwalt/Anwältin*
to evaluate	[ɪ'væljueɪt]	to assess	*einschätzen, bewerten*
federal	['fedərəl]	*phr* federal government of the USA	*föderal(istisch)*
to unite	[ju'naɪt]	to bring together	*vereinigen*
diverse	[daɪ'vɜ:s]	differing from one another	*verschieden, unterschiedlich*

page 113

worse	[wɜ:s]	<> better	*schlechter, schlimmer*
to fold	[fəʊld]	to bend	*verschränken, falten*
to clasp	[klɑ:sp]	to embrace	*verschränken*
hip	[hɪp]		*Hüfte*
chin	[tʃɪn]		*Kinn*
to smooth	[smu:ð]	to make straight	*glatt streichen, glätten*
knee	[ni:]		*Knie*
to stretch out	[stretʃ 'aʊt]	*phr* to stretch your body	*ausstrecken*
to curl	[kɜ:l]	to sit or lie down cosily	*(Beine) unterschlagen*
beneath	[bɪ'ni:θ]	below	*unter(halb)*
to chuckle	['tʃʌkl]	to give a small laugh or a giggle	*in sich hineinlachen, kichern*
to interrupt	[ˌɪntə'rʌpt]	to make a break in the middle of sth	*unterbrechen*
extreme	[ɪk'stri:m]	very different	*Extrem*
stomach	['stʌmək]		*Magen*
cover	['kʌvə]	*phr* bed covers	*(Bett-)Decke*
to float	[fləʊt]	to not touch the ground	*schweben*
dreamless	['dri:mləs]	to not have dreams	*traumlos*
self-confident	[ˌself 'kɒnfɪdənt]	to be full of assurance	*selbstsicher, -bewusst*
dominant	['dɒmɪnənt]	controlling	*beherrschend, dominant*
impulsive	[ɪm'pʌlsɪv]	doing things without thinking first	*impulsiv*
risk-taker	['rɪsk teɪkə]	person who takes risks	*Mensch mit Risikobereitschaft*
chaotic	[keɪ'ɒtɪk]	unorganized	*chaotisch*

page 114

pound	[paʊnd]	currency of the United Kingdom	*Pfund (Sterling)*
to adopt	[ə'dɒpt]	to vote to accept	*einführen*
to opt out	[ˌɒpt 'aʊt]	to choose not to participate in sth	*austreten, aussteigen*
isolated	['aɪsəleɪtɪd]	being separated from	*isoliert*
referendum	[ˌrefə'rendəm]	when everyone in a country votes on an important issue	*Volksentscheid*
gigantic	[dʒaɪ'gæntɪk]	huge	*gigantisch, riesig*
office block	['ɒfɪs blɒk]	tall building containing offices	*Bürogebäude, -hochhaus*
nonsense	['nɒnsns]	not making sense	*Unsinn*
luck	[lʌk]	*adj* lucky	*Glück*

UNIT 9

page 115

heritage	['herɪtɪdʒ]	sth that is passed on through generations	*Erbe, Herkunft*
musician	[mju:'zɪʃn]	a person who writes or performs music	*Musiker/in*
peer group	['pɪə gru:p]	people who have equal standing in age, class or rank	*Gleichaltrige, Clique*
role model	['rəʊl mɒdl]	sb whose actions other people follow	*Vorbild*

page 116

to bring up	[ˌbrɪŋ 'ʌp]	to raise	*großziehen*
washing powder	['wɒʃɪŋ paʊdə]	clothes detergent	*Waschpulver*
to polish	['pɒlɪʃ]	to make clean	*polieren, putzen*
emotional	[ɪ'məʊʃənl]	sad, happy, in love, angry, fearful, etc.	*emotional*
childcare	['tʃaɪldkeə]	taking care of children	*(Kinder-)Erziehung*
abandoned	[ə'bændənd]	deserted	*verlassen*
rejected	[rɪ'dʒektɪd]	*v* to reject	*abgelehnt*
to care for sb	['keə fə]	to raise or nurture sb	*jdn pflegen, sich um jdn kümmern*

page 117

childminder	['tʃaɪldmaɪndə]	babysitter	*Kinderbetreuer/in, Tagesmutter/-vater*
nervous breakdown	[ˌnɜːvəs 'breɪkdaʊn]	illness when you are mentally not be able to deal with life	*Nervenzusammenbruch*
social services	[ˌsəʊʃl 'sɜːvɪsɪz]	a service that ensures child safety within the household	*Sozialamt, Sozialdienste*
to retire	[rɪ'taɪə]	to go into retirement	*in Rente/Pension gehen*

page 118

custom	['kʌstəm]	practices, habits, norms, traditions	*Brauch*
psychiatric	[ˌsaɪki'ætrɪk]	*n* psychiatrist	*psychiatrisch*
to come to terms with	[kʌm tə 'tɜːmz]	to accept	*zurechtkommen mit*
board game	['bɔːd geɪm]	e.g. monopoly, backgammon, etc.	*Brettspiel*
to catch sb off guard	[kætʃ ˌɒf 'gɑːd]	to surprise	*jdn überraschen, ertappen*
braid	[breɪd]	small tight plait	*(geflochtener) Zopf*
input	['ɪnpʊt]	contribution	*hier: Aufwendung, Hingabe*
schoolyard	['skuːljɑːd]	*(AE) BE:* (school) playground	*Schulhof*
myth	[mɪθ]	rumour	*Legende*
literally	['lɪtərəli]	honestly	*buchstäblich*
to fail sb	[feɪl]	to not give sb what they need	*jdn enttäuschen, jdm etw nicht geben können*
ultimate	['ʌltɪmət]	definitive example of	*ultimativ*
baggage	['bægɪdʒ]	*phr* emotional baggage	*Gepäck, Last*
to miss out on	[ˌmɪs 'aʊt ɒn]	to not get to do	*verpassen*
nail polish	['neɪl pɒlɪʃ]	paint for fingernails	*Nagellack*
to lean on	['liːn ɒn]	to support oneself against	*sich lehnen an*
once in a while	[ˌwʌns ɪn ə 'waɪl]	now and then, from time to time	*dann und wann*
overly	['əʊvəli]	excessively	*übermäßig*
minor	['maɪnə]	very small	*geringfügig*
wound	[wuːnd]	injury	*Wunde*
to rub	[rʌb]	*phr* to rub salt into the wound	*reiben*
to carry on	[ˌkæri 'ɒn]	to keep going	*weitermachen*
motherly	['mʌðəli]	maternal	*mütterlich*
you bet	[ju 'bet]	of course	*ganz bestimmt, und ob*
effort	['efət]	attempt	*Bemühung, Anstrengung*
depressing	[dɪ'presɪŋ]	very sad	*bedrückend, deprimierend*
tiring	['taɪərɪŋ]	exhausting	*anstrengend, ermüdend*

page 119

nurse	[nɜːs]	sb who looks after sick people	*Krankenschwester, -pfleger/in*
priest	[priːst]	a minister of any religion	*Priester/in, Geistliche/r*
solicitor	[sə'lɪsɪtə]	legal advisor	*(Rechts-)Anwalt/Anwältin*
powerful	['paʊəfl]	*n* power	*mächtig, stark*
shade	[ʃeɪd]		*Schattierung*
march	[mɑːtʃ]	*phr* peace march	*(Protest-)Marsch*
disobedience	[ˌdɪsə'biːdiəns]	misbehaving, breaking rules	*Ungehorsam*
demonstration	[ˌdemən'streɪʃn]	a public display of discontent	*Demonstration*
arrest	[ə'rest]	*v* to arrest	*Verhaftung, Festnahme*
violence	['vaɪələns]	physical fighting	*Gewalt*
sympathy	['sɪmpəθi]	feeling sorry for	*Mitgefühl, Mitleid*
suffragette	[ˌsʌfrə'dʒet]	female supporter of votes for women	*Frauenrechtlerin*
battle	['bætl]	a conflict or struggle	*Kampf*

logging	['lɒgɪŋ]	cutting down and removing trees	*Abholzung*
rope	[rəʊp]	cord	*Seil, Tau*
mainstream	['meɪnstriːm]	dominant, popular	*vorherrschend(e Meinung)*

page 120

single-issue politics	[sɪŋgl ˌɪʃuː 'pɔlɪtɪks]		*Interessenpolitik*
to achieve	[ə'tʃiːv]	to accomplish sth	*erreichen*
demo	['deməʊ]	*(abbrev)* demonstration	*Demo(nstration)*
foot	[fʊt]	measurement: 30.48cm	*Fuß*
height	[haɪt]	distance from ground upwards	*Höhe, Größe*
to be concerned with	[bi kən'sɜːnd wɪð]	to be worried about	*sich befassen mit, sich kümmern um*

page 121

broad	[brɔːd]	wide	*breit*
proportion	[prə'pɔːʃn]	dimensions or size	*Teil, Verhältnis*
registered	['redʒɪstəd]	*v* to register	*registriert, eingetragen*
a fifth	[ə 'fɪfθ]	a third, a fourth, a fifth	*Fünftel*
runner-up	[ˌrʌnər 'ʌp]	person or team that finished second	*Zweite/r*
to extend	[ɪk'stend]	to make bigger	*ausweiten, ausbauen*
extension	[ɪk'stenʃn]	development	*Ausbau*
to recap	['riːkæp]	to repeat the main facts	*rekapitulieren, zusammenfassen*
runway	['rʌnweɪ]	landing strip	*Landebahn*
to knock down	[ˌnɒk 'daʊn]	to demolish	*abreißen*
to crash	[kræʃ]	to have an accident	*(ab)stürzen*
air pollution	[eə pə'luːʃn]	*v* to pollute	*Luftverschmutzung*
to go ahead	[ˌgəʊ ə'hed]	to continue as planned	*vorangehen, vonstatten gehen*
to summarize	['sʌməraɪz]	*n* summary	*zusammenfassen*
estuary	['estʃuəri]	where a river meets the sea	*Mündung*

page 122

non-governmental organization	[ˌnɒn gʌvənˌməntl ɔːgənaɪ'zeɪʃn]	an organization independent of governments	*Nichtregierungsorganisation*
to hunt	[hʌnt]	*n* hunter	*jagen*
follower	['fɒləʊə]	*v* to follow	*Anhänger*
involvement	[ɪn'vɒlvmənt]	being involved in sth	*Beteiligung, Engagement*

page 123

poem	['pəʊɪm]	writing in verses	*Gedicht*
verse	[vɜːs]	a poem with metrical composition	*Vers, Strophe*
ridiculous	[rɪ'dɪkjələs]	silly	*lächerlich*
to drag	[dræg]	to trail on the ground	*schleifen*
hedge	[hedʒ]	a row of bushes	*Hecke*
to reveal	[rɪ'viːl]	to expose	*enthüllen, zeigen*
neckline	['neklaɪn]	*phr* shirt neckline	*Ausschnitt*
navel-line	['neɪvl laɪn]	bellybutton-line	*tiefer Ausschnitt (bis zum Nabel)*
to plunge	[plʌndʒ]	to fall in a downward position	*(ab)stürzen, tief fallen*
outfit	['aʊtfɪt]	*phr* clothing outfit	*Kleidung, Outfit*

page 124

high	[haɪ]	effect experienced when taking drugs	*high, auf Drogen*
to snort	[snɔːt]	to inhale power through the nose	*sniffen, schnupfen*
needle	['niːdl]	medical instrument used to insert liquid into the body	*Nadel*
to break	[breɪk]	to give up addiction to sth	*abbrechen*
overdose	['əʊvədəʊs]	consuming too much of sth	*Überdosis*
to get clear of	[get 'klɪər əv]	*phr* to get clear of sth bad	*wegkommen von*
enemy	['enəmi]	sb you hate	*Feind*
experienced	[ɪk'spɪəriənst]	having a lot of experience	*erfahren*
social worker	['səʊʃl wɜːkə]	sb whose job is social work	*Sozialarbeiter/in*
broken	['brəʊkən]	used for a family where the parents are divorced or separated	*getrennt, kaputt*
foster family	[ˌfɒstə 'fæməli]	foster mother/father, foster parents	*Pflegefamilie*

UNIT 10

page 125

multiculturalism	[ˌmʌlti-ˈkʌltʃərəlɪzəm]	different cultures coexisting in a society	*Multikulturalismus*
Afro-Caribbean	[ˌæfrəʊ ˌkærəˈbiːən]	African and Caribbean	*afro-karibisch*
headscarf	[ˈhedskɑːf]	worn by Muslim women to cover their heads	*Kopftuch*
sari	[ˈsɑːri]	a garment worn by Hindu women	*Sari (Kleidungsstück)*

page 126

fanatic	[fəˈnætɪk]	*n* fanatic, fanaticism	*Fanatiker/in*
to tremble	[ˈtrembl]	to shake with fear, nerves or cold	*zittern*
to loosen	[ˈluːsn]	to make less tight	*lockern*
tie	[taɪ]	garment worn around the neck	*Krawatte, Schlips*
harsh	[hɑːʃ]	unpleasant	*scharf, harsch*
forbidden	[fəˈbɪdn]	not allowed	*verboten*
gambling	[ˈgæmblɪŋ]	betting money in a game	*Glücksspiel*
accompaniment	[əˈkʌmpənimənt]	*v* to accompany	*Begleitung*
disgust	[dɪsˈgʌst]	repulsion, horror	*Ekel*
censure	[ˈsenʃə]	disapproval	*Tadel, Missbilligung*
temper	[ˈtempə]	*phr* to lose one's temper	*Beherrschung*
to stare	[steə]	to look directly and fixedly at sth	*starren*
conscience	[ˈkɒnʃəns]	inner sense of what is right and wrong	*Gewissen*
monotonous	[məˈnɒtənəs]	to speak using one tone of voice	*monoton*
countless	[ˈkaʊntləs]	so many that they cannot be counted	*zahllos*
for instance	[fəˈrɪnstəns]	for example	*zum Beispiel*
to demand	[dɪˈmɑːnd]	to ask in a bold, authoritative way	*(nach)fragen*

page 127

to deny	[dɪˈnaɪ]	to state that sth is not true	*bestreiten*
mushroom	[ˈmʌʃrʊm]	*phr* fried mushrooms	*Pilz*
fried	[fraɪd]	cooked in oil	*gebraten, geröstet*
perplexed	[pəˈplekst]	confused	*perplex, verblüfft*
civilisation	[ˌsɪvəlaɪˈzeɪʃn]	an advanced state of human society	*Zivilisation*
materialist	[məˈtɪəriəlɪst]	person only concerned with material things	*Materialist/in*
miserable	[ˈmɪzrəbl]	unhappy	*kläglich*
rowdy	[ˈraʊdi]	disorderly	*laut, randalierend*
to convince	[kənˈvɪns]	to persuade	*überzeugen*
homosexual	[ˌhəʊməˈsekʃuəl]	person sexually attracted to people of the same sex	*Homosexuelle/r*
prostitute	[ˈprɒstɪtjuːt]	person who engages in sexual acts for money	*Prostituierte/r*
paradise	[ˈpærədaɪs]	a state of supreme happiness	*Paradies*
to swallow	[ˈswɒləʊ]	muscle movement used when eating and drinking	*(ver)schlucken*

page 128

setting	[ˈsetɪŋ]	scene	*Szenerie, Schauplatz*
incident	[ˈɪnsɪdənt]	event	*Vorfall, Ereignis*

page 129

cheekbones	[ˈtʃiːkbəʊnz]	bones at the top of the cheeks, below the eyes	*Wangenknochen*
jet-colored	[ˌdʒet ˈkʌləd]	*(AE) BE:* jet-coloured	*pechschwarz*
ancestry	[ˈænsestri]	lineage, parentage	*Abstammung, Herkunft*
to define	[dɪˈfaɪn]	to describe sth accurately	*(sich) definieren*
to apply to	[əˈplaɪ tə]	to count for	*gelten für, zutreffen auf*
neutral	[ˈnjuːtrəl]	indifferent	*neutral*
unclear	[ˌʌnˈklɪə]	<> clear	*unklar*
tremendous	[trɪˈmendəs]	huge	*gewaltig*
appeal	[əˈpiːl]	attraction	*Anziehungskraft, Anreiz*
census	[ˈsensəs]	periodic count of population	*(Volks-)Zählung*
respondent	[rɪˈspɒndənt]	person who responds	*Befragte/r*
to tick	[tɪk]	to mark an option with a tick	*ankreuzen*

multiracial	[ˌmʌlti'reɪʃl]	of many races, mixed-race	*ethnisch gemischt*
demographer	[dɪ'mɒgrəfi]	person who studies population data	*Demograph*
intermarriage	[ˌɪntə'mærɪdʒ]	the marriage of two people of different races	*Mischehe*
segregation	[ˌsegrɪ'geɪʃn]	the separation of different races	*Rassentrennung*
casting agent	['kɑːstɪŋ eɪdʒənt]	person who chooses models and actors for events/films	*Besetzungsagent/in*
Nordic	['nɔːdɪk]	connected with the countries of Scandinavia	*nordisch*
asset	['æset]	a valuable thing to own or have	*Wert, Vorteil*
to enable	[ɪ'neɪbl]	to help to make possible	*(es) ermöglichen, in die Lage versetzen*
ethnicity	[eθ'nɪsəti]	race	*ethnische Zugehörigkeit*
to pose	[pəʊz]	to take on the role of sb	*posieren, darstellen*
to reflect	[rɪ'flekt]	to show	*widerspiegeln*
fascination	[ˌfæsɪ'neɪʃn]	strong interest	*Faszination*
uniformity	[ˌjuːnɪ'fɔːməti]	quality or state of being alike	*Gleichmäßigkeit*
badge	[bædʒ]	trademark	*Abzeichen*
page 130			
out-dated	[ˌaʊt 'deɪtɪd]	old-fashioned	*überholt, veraltet*
minority	[maɪ'nɒrəti]	<> majority	*Minderheit*
to outnumber	[ˌaʊt'nʌmbə]	to exceed in amount	*übertreffen*
to shrink	[ʃrɪŋk]	to get smaller	*schrumpfen, zurückgehen*
page 131			
Caucasian	[kɔː'keɪziən]	person of European descent	*Weiße/r, Hellhäutige/r*
Native American	[ˌneɪtɪv ə'merɪkən]	person descended from the original inhabitants of America	*Indianer/in, indianisch*
fairly	['feəli]	quite	*ziemlich*
to tolerate	['tɒləreɪt]	*adj* tolerant	*tolerieren, ertragen*
entire	[ɪn'taɪə]	complete	*vollkommen, gänzlich*
limitless	['lɪmɪtləs]	boundless	*grenzenlos, uneingeschränkt*
cooperative	[kəʊ'ɒpərətɪv]	willing to help	*kooperativ*
to be to blame	[bi tə 'bleɪm]	he's to blame = it's his fault	*an etwas schuld sein*
law-abiding	['lɔː əbaɪdɪŋ]	non-criminal	*gesetzestreu*
domestic	[də'mestɪk]	in the household	*in der Familie, häuslich*
nanny	['næni]	child-minder	*Kindermädchen*
citizenship	['sɪtɪznʃɪp]	membership of a country	*Staatsbürgerschaft*
humane	[hjuː'meɪn]	kind to humans and animals	*human*
civil rights	[ˌsɪvl 'raɪts]	democratic rights	*bürgerliche Rechte*
to reward	[rɪ'wɔːd]	to give a prize to	*belohnen*
to break a law	[breɪk ə 'lɔː]	to commit a crime	*das Gesetz brechen/übertreten*
to deport	[dɪ'pɔːt]	to remove sb from a country	*ausweisen, abschieben*
to ship	[ʃɪp]	to send by boat	*verschiffen, transportieren*
for sb's sake	[fə 'seɪk]	for the good of sb (used as an exclamation of annoyance)	*um jds willen*
wage	[weɪdʒ]	salary	*Lohn*
to flood	[flʌd]	to fill to overflowing	*überschwemmen*
page 132			
full-time	[ˌfʊl 'taɪm]	<> part-time	*Vollzeit-*
to go bankrupt	[ˌgəʊ 'bæŋkrʌpt]	to no longer have enough money to pay off your debts	*in Konkurs gehen, Pleite gehen*
reliability	[rɪˌlaɪə'bɪləti]	*adj* reliable	*Zuverlässigkeit*
to count on sb/sth	['kaʊnt ɒn]	to rely on sb/sth	*sich auf jdn/etwas verlassen, auf jdn/etwas zählen*
contradictory	[ˌkɒntrə'dɪktəri]	opposite	*widersprüchlich*
page 133			
exchange	[ɪks'tʃeɪndʒ]	*phr* an exchange programme	*Austausch*
immigration	[ˌɪmɪ'greɪʃn]	moving to a new country and living there	*Einwanderung*
labour market	['leɪbə mɑːkɪt	the people who work	*Arbeitsmarkt*
population	[ˌpɒpju'leɪʃn]	the number of people living in a certain area	*Bevölkerung*
parentage	['peərəntɪdʒ	*n* parent	*elterliche Abstammung*
naturalized	['nætʃrəlaɪzd]	made a citizen of a country you were not born in	*eingebürgert*

page 134

governor	['gʌvənə]	the executive head of a state in the US	*Gouverneur/in*
crossing point	['krɒsɪŋ pɔɪnt]	place where people cross a border	*Übergang(sstelle)*
fence	[fens]	barrier to confine or prevent entrance	*Zaun*
guard	[gɑːd]	person who protects a place or people	*Wache*
valid	['vælɪd]	relevant	*gültig*
to inquire	[ɪn'kwaɪə]	to ask	*fragen, sich erkundigen*
vehicle papers	['viːəkl peɪpəz]	car registration documents	*Wagenpapiere*
to seal off	[ˌsiːl 'ɒf]	to close	*absperren, abriegeln*
virtually	['vɜːtʃuəli]	entirely	*praktisch, nahezu*
feasible	['fiːzəbl]	capable of being done	*(praktisch) durchführbar, machbar*
amnesty	['æmnəsti]	a general pardon for offences	*Amnestie*
quota system	['kwəʊtə sɪstəm]	a proportional share assigned to each person	*Quotensystem*
to go bust	[gəʊ 'bʌst]	to fall apart or lose money	*Pleite gehen*

UNIT 11

page 135

patience	['peɪʃns]	*adj* patient	*Geduld*
ransom	['rænsəm]	money paid to kidnappers	*Lösegeld*
diet	['daɪət]	*phr* to be on a strict diet	*Ernährung, Diät*
to deceive	[dɪ'siːv]	to lie to, trick	*betrügen*
to trick	[trɪk]	to deceive or create an illusion	*betrügen, hereinlegen*
victim	['vɪktɪm]	someone who suffers injury, loss or death	*Opfer*
burglary	['bɜːgləri]	breaking into a building with the intention of stealing something	*Einbruch*
prison	['prɪzn]	a place where criminals are locked up	*Gefängnis*
drink driving	['drɪŋk draɪvɪŋ]	driving after drinking too much alcohol	*Trunkenheit am Steuer*
fraud	[frɔːd]	using lies and deceit to get access to money	*Betrug, Unterschlagung*
armed robbery	[ˌɑːmd 'rɒbəri]	a robbery with weapons involved	*bewaffneter Raubüberfall*
trivial	['trɪviəl]	not important	*trivial, geringfügig*
property	['prɒpəti]	what sb owns	*Eigentum*

page 136

cruel	[kruːəl]	unfeeling and harsh	*grausam*
Supreme Court	[suˌpriːm 'kɔːt]	highest judicial body in the US	*Oberster Gerichtshof*
to rule	[ruːl]	to decide (legally)	*entscheiden*
death penalty	['deθ penlti]	execution of a person by the state as punishment for a crime	*Todesstrafe*
constitutional	[ˌkɒnstɪ-'tjuːʃənl]	acceptable to the US Constitution	*verfassungsgemäß*
execution	[ˌeksɪ'kjuːʃn]	the act of killing by law as a punishment	*Hinrichtung*
murder	['mɜːdə]	the crime of killing sb	*Mord*
convention	[kən'venʃn]	socially accepted way of doing sth	*Konvention*
lethal	['liːθl]	deadly	*tödlich*
injection	[ɪn'dʒekʃn]	fluid introduced into body using a needle	*Spritze, Injektion*
painless	['peɪnləs]	without pain	*schmerzlos*
massive	['mæsɪv]	very large	*massiv, enorm*
dose	[dəʊs]	amount	*Dosis*
fast-acting	[ˌfɑːst 'æktɪŋ]	taking effect quickly	*schnell wirkend*
anaesthetic	[ˌænəs'θetɪk]	a substance that causes no physical pain and in large amounts is deadly	*Narkosemittel*
routinely	[ruː'tiːnli]	*n* routine	*routinemäßig*
to be troubled	[bi 'trʌbld]	to be concerned	*beunruhigt sein*
to subject	[səb'dʒekt]	to force sb to suffer sth	*unterwerfen, aussetzen*
attempt	[ə'tempt]	try	*Versuch*
feminist	['femənɪst]	person who supports women's rights	*Feministin*
awkward	['ɔːkwəd]	uncomfortable	*unangenehm, lästig, peinlich*
victory	['vɪktəri]	win	*Sieg*
capital punishment	[ˌkæpɪtl 'pʌnɪʃmənt]	execution as punishment	*Todesstrafe*
corporal punishment	[ˌkɔːpərəl 'pʌnɪʃmənt]	physical injury as punishment	*körperliche Züchtigung*

alliance	[ə'laɪəns]	union, agreement	*Allianz, Bündnis*
fundamentalist	[ˌfʌndə-'mentəlɪst]	believing strongly in one idea	*fundamentalistisch*
conservative	[kən'sɜːvətɪv]	favouring traditional views and values	*Konservative/r*
to be opposed to sth	[bi ə'pəʊzd tə]	to be against sth	*gegen etw sein*
principle	['prɪnsəpl]	personal rule for correct conduct	*Prinzip*
hence	[hens]	therefore	*daher*
apparent	[ə'pærənt]	visible	*offensichtlich, deutlich*
bias	['baɪəs]	supporting sth more due to external factors	*Vorurteil*
repugnant	[rɪ'pʌgnənt]	offensive, unpleasant	*widerlich*

page 137

remorse	[rɪ'mɔːs]	regret	*Reue*
devout	[dɪ'vaʊt]	committed (religious)	*fromm*
clemency	['klemənsi]	mercy	*Milde, Nachsicht*
confused	[kən'fjuːzd]	*n* confusion	*verwirrt*
insane	[ɪn'seɪn]	mentally ill, crazy	*geisteskrank*
liberal	['lɪbərəl]	sb who supports progress and change	*Liberale/r*
passion	['pæʃn]	powerful emotion	*Leidenschaft, Emotion*
reformed	[rɪ'fɔːmd]	made better, altered	*gebessert*
repentant	[rɪ'pentənt]	feeling guilty for committing a sin	*reuig, reumütig*
uncanny	[ʌn'kæni]	extraordinary, strange	*ungeheuer, unheimlich*
bedfellow	['bedfeləʊ]	companion	*Bettgenosse, Schlafkamerad*
to strap	[stræp]	to tie down	*anschnallen, festbinden*
to deserve	[dɪ'zɜːv]	to be worthy of receiving sth	*verdienen*
axe	[æks]	tool used to chop wood	*Axt*
microphone	['maɪkrəfəʊn]	device used to record/emit sound	*Mikrophon*

page 138

to abolish	[ə'bɒlɪʃ]	to get rid off	*abschaffen*
to reintroduce	[ˌriːˌɪntrə'djuːs]	to introduce again	*wieder einführen*
abolition	[ˌæbə'lɪʃn]	*v* to abolish	*Abschaffung*
justice	['dʒʌstɪs]	fair outcome	*Gerechtigkeit*
to deliver	[dɪ'lɪvə]	to give or provide	*hier: schaffen, erzielen*
retribution	[ˌretrɪ'bjuːʃn]	punishment which was deserved	*Vergeltung*
deterrent	[dɪ'terənt]	making people not want to do sth	*abschreckend*
loved one	['lʌvd wʌn]	close relatives	*Angehörige/r, Nahestehende/r*
to draw a line	[ˌdrɔː ə 'laɪn]	to move on	*einen Schlussstrich ziehen*
prisoner	['prɪznə]	*n* prison	*Häftling, Gefangene/r*
imprisonment	[ɪm'prɪznmənt]	being kept in prison	*Haft, Gefängnis(strafe)*

page 139

to associate	[ə'səʊʃieɪt]	to connect with, be in the company of	*assoziieren, verbinden*
stitch	[stɪtʃ]	A stitch in time saves nine = *Vorsicht ist besser als Nachsicht*	*Stich*
to slide	[slaɪd]	to glide smoothly downwards	*(ab)rutschen, (ab)sacken*
heavily-armed	[ˌhevɪli 'ɑːmd]	protected using weapons	*schwer bewaffnet*
to register	['redʒɪstə]	to record	*registrieren*
rape	[reɪp]	unwanted sexual assault	*Vergewaltigung*
robbery	['rɒbəri]	*v* to rob	*Raub, Überfall*
to dare	[deə]	to try sth risky	*(es) wagen*
turnaround	['tɜːnəraʊnd]	big change/improvement	*Kehrtwendung, Umschwung*
decent	['diːsnt]	respectable	*anständig*
tolerant	['tɒlərənt]	able to endure/accept sth	*tolerant*
to be willing	[bi 'wɪlɪŋ]	to be inclined/open to	*bereit/gewillt sein*
rotten	['rɒtn]	corrupt	*korrupt*
drug abuse	[ˌdrʌg ə'bjuːs]	excessive use of drugs	*Drogenmissbrauch*
bribery	['braɪbəri]	*v* to bribe	*Bestechung*
nepotism	['nepətɪzəm]	when people hire relatives	*Vetternwirtschaft*
merciless	['mɜːsiləs]	*n* mercy	*unbarmherzig*
to weed out	[ˌwiːd 'aʊt]	weed = *Unkraut*	*aussondern, -merzen*
tolerance	['tɒlərəns]	*adj* tolerant	*Toleranz*
pension	['penʃn]	payment made by the government to those not in work due to age/illness	*Rente, Pension*

to prosecute	['prɒsɪkjuːt]	to accuse sb of a crime and question them	*anklagen, strafrechtlich verfolgen*
policy	['pɒləsi]	rule	*Politik, Linie*
seed	[siːd]	thing from which a plant grows, starting point	*Samen(korn)*
to focus on	['fəʊkəs ɒn]	to concentrate on sth	*sich konzentrieren auf*
dealing	['diːlɪŋ]	*phr* drug dealing	*Handel*
crime rate	['kraɪm reɪt]	the number of crimes each year	*Krimininalitätsrate*
incidence	['ɪnsɪdəns]	recorded number of sth	*Vorkommen, Häufigkeitsrate*

page 140

diametrically opposed	[ˌdaɪə'metrɪkli əpəʊzd]	completely different	*diametral entgegengesetzt*
nickname	['nɪkneɪm]	an informal name for a person	*Spitzname*
offence	[ə'fens]	sth done against the law	*Delikt, Straftat*
warehouse	['weəhaʊs]	a building that stores supplies	*Lager(halle)*
flick knife	['flɪk naɪf]	a folding pocket knife	*Springmesser*
to resist	[rɪˌzɪst]	to refuse	*Widerstand leisten gegen, sich etw widersetzen*
appointment	[ə'pɔɪntmənt]	an arranged meeting	*Termin, Verabredung*

page 141

verdict	['vɜːdɪkt]	a decision (legal)	*Urteil, Beurteilung*
warning	['wɔːnɪŋ]	*v* to warn	*Verwarnung, Warnung, Aufforderung*
probation	[prə'beɪʃn]	test period to monitor good behaviour	*Bewährung*
suspended sentence	[səˌspendɪd 'sentəns]	a possible punishment used as a threat	*(Freiheits-)Strafe auf Bewährung*
to impose	[ɪm'pəʊz]	to force	*auferlegen, erlassen*

page 142

speeding	['spiːdɪŋ]	driving above the speed limit	*Geschwindigkeitsüberschreitung*
deputy	['depjuti]	officer ranked just below the head of a police department	*Hilfs-, Vertretungs-*
drunk driving	['drʌŋk draɪvɪŋ]	*(AE) BE:* drink driving	*Trunkenheit am Steuer*
registration papers	[ˌredʒɪ'streɪʃn peɪpəz]	official documents (for a car)	*Papiere, Zulassung*
to hack up	[ˌhæk 'ʌp]	to roughly cut up into pieces	*zerstückeln*
trunk	[trʌŋk]	*(AE) BE:* boot (of car)	*Kofferraum*
to back away	['bæk ə'weɪ]	to retreat	*zurückgehen*
backup	['bækʌp]	help	*Hilfe, Unterstützung*
to approach	[ə'prəʊtʃ]	to go towards	*sich nähern, zugehen auf*
to dig into	['dɪg ɪntə]	to rummage in	*wühlen in*
puzzled	['pʌzld]	confused	*verdutzt*
liar	['laɪə]	*v* to lie	*Lügner/in*

page 143

pattern	['pætn]	recurring theme	*Muster*
weapon	['wepən]	e.g. gun, sword, knife, axe, saw, etc.	*Waffe*
academic performance	[ˌækəˌdemɪk pə'fɔːməns]	measurement of how well a person did or is doing at school	*(Ober-)Schulleistungen*
prior	['praɪə]	before	*vorherig*
motive	['məʊtɪv]	reason	*Motiv, Beweggrund*
perpetrator	['pɜːpətreɪtə]	person who commit sth	*Täter/in*
depression	[dɪ'preʃn]	*adj* depressed	*Depression*
to tend	[tend]	to be likely to do sth	*dazu neigen*
to post	[pəʊst]	to announce sth publicly in written form	*veröffentlichen, bekanntgeben*
unfit	[ʌn'fɪt]	unable	*ungeeignet*
standard	['stændəd]	basic	*Standard-, Normal-*
to snap	[snæp]	to suddenly lose control	*ausflippen, ausrasten*
progression	[prə'greʃn]	forward movement	*Werdegang, Entwicklung*
to obtain	[əb'teɪn]	to be in possession of sth	*erwerben*
disorder	[dɪs'ɔːdə]	problem	*Störung, Erkrankung*

page 144

cell	[sel]	room in a prison where inmates live	*(Gefängnis-)Zelle*
scandalous	['skændələs]	socially inappropriate, shocking	*skandalös*

UNIT 12

page 145

hereditary	[hə'redɪtri]	sth that passes from parent to offspring	*erblich*
cloning	['kləʊnɪŋ]	to make a genetic replica of sth	*Klonen*
conservation	[ˌkɒnsə'veɪʃn]	preservation, protection	*Schutz, Erhaltung*

page 146

boycott	['bɔɪkɒt]	refusing to buy or use a product	*Boykott*
genetically modified	[dʊəˌnetɪkli 'mɒdɪfaɪd]	when genes have been altered in food	*genmanipuliert*
to announce	[ə'naʊns]	to declare	*ankündigen*
offspring	['ɒfsprɪŋ]	children	*Nachkommen*
revelation	[ˌrevə'leɪʃn]	to reveal information	*Enthüllung*
separate	['seprət]	<> together	*getrennt*
loophole	['lu:phəʊl]	when a law can be disobeyed due to ambiguous word use	*Schlupfloch*
to stock	[stɒk]	to have sth in a shop, warehouse, etc.	*führen, anbieten*
to derive	[dɪ'raɪv]	to come from, originate	*abstammen*
ban	[bæn]	an official rule that says sth is not allowed	*Verbot*
ingredient	[ɪn'gri:diənt]	one of the foods that make up a dish	*Zutat, Bestandteil*
astonishing	[ə'stɒnɪʃɪŋ]	unexpected or amazing	*erstaunlich*

page 147

nucleus	['nju:kliəs]	the centre of a cell where DNA is located	*Kern*
dairy	['deəri]	e.g. the dairy industry	*hier: Milchvieh*
herd	[hɜ:d]	a group of grazing animals	*Herde*
to be capable of	[bi 'keɪpəbl əv]	to be able to	*können, fähig sein*
vast	[vɑ:st]	immense	*riesig, ungeheuer*
mammal	['mæml]	animal that gives birth to live young and feeds them on milk	*Säugetier*
premature	['premətʃə]	unexpectedly early	*vorzeitig, frühzeitig*
lung	[lʌŋ]	organ used to breathe	*Lunge*
infection	[ɪn'fekʃn]	*adj* infectious	*Entzündung*
to diagnose	['daɪəgnəʊz]	to identify a disease or an illness	*diagnostizieren*
arthritis	[ɑ:'θraɪtɪs]	painful inflammation of the joints	*Arthritis, Gelenkentzündung*
miscarriage	[ˌmɪs'kærɪdʒ]	failed pregnancy	*Fehlgeburt*
abnormal	[æb'nɔ:ml]	<> normal	*abnorm, anomal, ungewöhnlich*
organ	['ɔ:gən]	body part with specific function	*Organ*
labelling	['leɪblɪŋ]	system of labels on products	*Kennzeichnung*
omission	[ə'mɪʃn]	leaving sth out	*Lücke*
doubt	[daʊt]	uncertainty	*Zweifel*
alteration	[ˌɔ:ltə'reɪʃn]	change	*Veränderung*
exceptional	[ɪk'sepʃənl]	unusually (positive)	*außergewöhnlich*
supervision	[ˌsu:pə'vɪʒn]	watching/observing sb	*Überwachung*

page 148

supporter	[sə'pɔ:tə(r)]	*v* to support	*Anhänger/in*
to introduce	[ˌɪntrə'dju:s]	to make sth available for use	*einführen*

page 149

gene	[dʒi:n]	*adj* genetic	*Gen*
to alter	['ɔ:ltə]	to change	*(ver)ändern*
organism	['ɔ:gənɪzəm]	a living thing	*Organismus*
yield	[ji:ld]	e.g. crop yield, milk yield	*Ertrag*
tendency	['tendənsi]	inclination, trend	*Tendenz*
dementia	[dɪ'menʃə]	mental illness	*Demenz*
diabetes	[ˌdaɪə'bi:ti:z]	metabolic disorder	*Zuckerkrankheit, Diabetes*
transplant	['trænsplɑ:nt]	operation to replace damaged organ	*Transplantation*
breeding	['bri:dɪŋ]	producing offspring	*Zucht, Züchtung*
crop	[krɒp]	agricultural plant	*(Anbau)Pflanze*
to cross-breed	['krɒs bri:d]	to breed from two different species	*kreuzen*
species	['spi:ʃi:z]	animal type, e.g. monkeys, dogs, birds, etc.	*Art(en)*

mule	[mju:l]	male donkey used for farm labour	*Maultier, -esel*
time-consuming	['taɪm kənsju:mɪŋ]	taking up a lot of time	*zeitraubend*
predictable	[prɪ'dɪktəbl]	*n* prediction	*voraussagbar*
to interact	[ˌɪntər'ækt]	to work with one another	*sich gegenseitig beeinflussen*
manipulation	[məˌnɪpju'leɪʃn]	*v* to manipulate	*Manipulation, Veränderung*
accidental	[ˌæksɪ'dentəl]	unintentional	*zufällig, versehentlich*
substance	['sʌbstəns]	matter	*Substanz, Stoff*
poisonous	['pɔɪzənəs]	toxic	*giftig*
to trigger	['trɪgə]	to make sth active	*auslösen*
allergy	['ælədʒi]	*adj* allergic	*Allergie*
antibiotic-resistant	[ˌæntibaɪˌɒtɪk rɪ'zɪstənt]	not affected by antibiotic drugs	*resistent gegen Antibiotika*
micro-organism	[ˌmaɪkrəʊ 'ɔ:gənɪzəm]	very small organism	*Mikroorganismus*
flavour	['fleɪvə]	taste	*Geschmack*
shelf life	['ʃelf laɪf]	date when a product expires	*Haltbarkeit*
nutritional	[nju'trɪʃənl]	to do with food and health	*Nähr-*
page 150			
consumption	[kən'sʌmpʃn]	when sb uses/eats sth	*Verzehr*
to obey	[ə'beɪ]	to follow a rule	*befolgen*
to store	[stɔ:]	to keep sth somewhere	*lagern, aufbewahren*
lobby	['lɒbi]	e.g. gun lobby	*Lobby, Interessengruppe*
harmful	['hɑ:mfl]	bad, dangerous	*schädlich*
herbicide	['hɜ:bɪsaɪd]	chemical substance used to inhibit the growth of unwanted plants	*Unkrautvernichtungsmittel*
contaminated	[kən'tæmɪneɪtɪd]	polluted	*verunreinigt, verseucht*
to play havoc	[pleɪ 'hævək]	to ruin, to mess sth up	*verheerende Schäden anrichten*
contrary	['kɒntrəri]	*phr* on the contrary	*Gegenteil*
bioengineer	[ˌbaɪəʊ-ˌendʒɪ'nɪə]	a person who has studied genetic engineering	*Gentechniker/in*
fertilizer	['fɜ:təlaɪzə]	a substance added to soil which improves plant growth	*Dünger*
pesticide	['pestɪsaɪd]	chemical used to kill pests on plants	*Schädlingsbekämpfungsmittel*
uncultivated	[ʌn'kʌltɪveɪtɪd]	untidy, not looked after carefully	*brachliegend*
habitat	['hæbɪtæt]	the natural home and environment of an organism	*Lebensraum*
toxic	['tɒksɪk]	poisonous	*giftig, toxisch*
page 151			
blueprint	['blu:prɪnt]	prototype, plan	*Blaupause, Bauplan*
to imply	[ɪm'plaɪ]	to suggest	*andeuten, implizieren*
unintentional	[ˌʌnɪn'tenʃənl]	not on purpose	*unabsichtlich*
radiation	[ˌreɪdi'eɪʃn]	energy transmitted as electromagnetic waves	*Strahlung*
mast	[mɑ:st]	pole, tower	*Mast*
spare part	[ˌspeə 'pɑ:t]	replacement	*Ersatzteil*
potential	[pə'tenʃl]	possibilities	*Potenzial*
cure	[kjʊə]	remedy	*Heilung, Heilmittel*
downside	['daʊnsaɪd]	disadvantage	*Nachteil*
to abuse	[ə'bju:z]	to use for a bad purpose	*missbrauchen*
clone	[kləʊn]	exact genetic copy	*Klon*
media hype	['mi:diə haɪp]	over-the-top journalism	*Medienrummel*
to feed	[fi:d]	*n* food	*ernähren*
field trial	['fi:ld traɪəl]	test in natural conditions	*Freilandversuch*
superweed	['su:pəwi:d]	weed which is hard to kill	*hoch resistentes Unkraut*
bee	[bi:]		*Biene*
cross-breeding	['krɒsbri:dɪŋ]	*v* to cross-breed	*Kreuzung*
page 152			
undernourished	[ˌʌndə'nʌrɪʃt]	undernourishment	*Unterernährte/r*
surging	['sɜ:dʒɪŋ]	to surge	*(Preis:) anziehend, steigend*
page 153			
to divide	[dɪ'vaɪd]	to split into many pieces or sections	*(sich) teilen*
spread	[spred]	variety	*Verteilung*

leisure	['leʒə]	free time	*Freizeit*
welfare	['welfeə]	well-being	*Fürsorge, Soziales*
security	[sɪ'kjʊərəti]	stability	*Sicherheit*
fluctuation	[ˌflʌktʃʊ'eɪʃn]	irregular changes	*Fluktuation*
biodiversity	[ˌbaɪəʊ daɪ'vɜːsəti]	different plants and animals in an environment	*Artenvielfalt*
expectancy	[ɪk'spektənsi]	*v* to expect	*Erwartung*
e-learning	['iː lɜːnɪŋ]	online learning	*Lernen am Computer*
to adjust	[ə'dʒʌst]	to change for proper function or meaning	*anpassen, abstimmen*

page 154

to publish	['pʌblɪʃ]	to make e.g. a book public	*veröffentlichen, herausgeben*
timetable	['taɪmteɪbl]	e.g. train timetable	*Zeitplan, Fahrplan*
stamp	[stæmp]	mark of payment on an envelope	*Briefmarke*

A–Z word list

Dieses Wörterverzeichnis enthält alle Wörter aus **Focus on Success – Ausgabe Baden-Württemberg** in alphabetischer Reihenfolge. Nicht aufgeführt sind die Wörter aus der *Basic word list* sowie internationale Wörter wie *hotel, email* usw.
Wörter, die in den Hörverständnistexten vorkommen, sind mit einem ***t*** hinter der Seitenzahl gekennzeichnet.

A

abandoned *116* verlassen
abbreviation *62* Abkürzung
ability *7* Fähigkeit
able: to not be able to help *16* nicht umhin können
abnormal *147* abnorm, anomal, ungewöhnlich
to abolish *138* abschaffen
abolition *138* Abschaffung
to abridge *59* (ab)kürzen
absolutely *22* absolut
absurd *92* absurd
abuse *56* Anpöbelung, Beschimpfung(en)
to abuse *151t* missbrauchen
abusive *57* beleidigend, ausfallend
academic performance *143* (Ober-)Schulleistungen
to accept *13* akzeptieren
acceptable *98* annehmbar, akzeptabel
accessory *53* Zubehör, Accessoire
accident *67* Unfall
accidental *149* zufällig, versehentlich
accommodation *106* Unterkunft
accompaniment *126* Begleitung
according to *7* nach, gemäß
account executive *54* Kundenberater/in, -betreuer/in
account manager *46* Kundenbetreuer/in
accountant *85* Buchhalter/in
accurate *57* genau
to achieve *120* erreichen
acronym *51t* Akronym, Initialwort
action *56* Aktion, Handlung
activist *98* Aktivist/in
activities officer *85* Verantwortliche/r für Aktivitäten und Veranstaltungen
actress *56* Schauspielerin
actually *29* tatsächlich, eigentlich
ad *18* Anzeige
to adapt *59* adaptieren
to add up to *83* sich addieren zu
addicted *56* süchtig nach
addiction *16* Sucht, Abhängigkeit
addition: in addition to *73* zusätzlich zu, neben
to address sth *102* sich mit etw befassen, etw angehen
to adjust *153* anpassen, abstimmen
to admit *49* zugeben, gestehen
to adopt *114* einführen
advanced *68* fortgeschritten, hochentwickelt
advertisement *45* Anzeige, Werbespot
advertiser *49* Werbefirma
advertising *40* Werbung
advice *19* Rat(schlag)
to advise *78* raten, beraten
affair *110* Angelegenheit
to affect *71* betreffen
afraid: I'm afraid *7* leider
Afro-Caribbean *125* afro-karibisch
afterwards *83* danach, hinterher
agency *46* Agentur
ages: for ages *94* eine Ewigkeit
agreement *107* Vertrag, Abkommen, Zusage
ahead *73* voraus, kommend; **to go ahead** *121t* vorangehen, vonstatten gehen
aim *45* Ziel
aimed at *51t* abgezielt auf, gerichtet an
air conditioning *73* Klimaanlage
air pollution *121t* Luftverschmutzung
airwaves *79* Äther
all over the place *7* überall
allergy *149* Allergie
alliance *136* Allianz, Bündnis
all-star *58t* Star-, mit vielen Stars
to alter *149* (ver)ändern
alteration *147* Veränderung
alternative *76* alternativ
although *14* obwohl
altogether *59* alles in allem
amazed *65* erstaunt
amnesty *134* Amnestie
amount *76* Menge
anaesthetic *136* Narkosemittel
analysis *53* Analyse
to analyze *51t* analysieren
ancestry *129* Abstammung, Herkunft
anger *71* Zorn, Ärger
to announce *146* ankündigen
annoyed *65* verärgert
annoying *45* lästig, ärgerlich
anorexia *16* Magersucht
anthem *105* Hymne
antibiotic-resistant *149* resistent gegen Antibiotika
anti-theft pad *28* Diebstahlsicherung
anxious *65* besorgt, beunruhigt
anyhow *111* sowieso
apiece *43* je, das Stück
to apologize for *43* sich entschuldigen für
apparent *136* offensichtlich, deutlich
appeal *129* Anziehungskraft, Anreiz
to appear *35* auftauchen, vorkommen
appliance *78* Gerät
applicant *59* Bewerber/in
application *48* Bewerbung
to apply for *86* sich bewerben um
to apply to *129* gelten für, zutreffen auf
appointment *140* Termin, Verabredung
to approach *142t* sich nähern, zugehen auf
appropriate *94* angemessen, passend, entsprechend
approx. *44* ungefähr, etwa, zirka
aptitude *89* Fähigkeit, Eignung
aptitude test *93* Eignungs-, Fähigkeitstest
area *40* Gebiet, Bereich
armed robbery *135* bewaffneter Raubüberfall
arrangement *53* Anordnung
to arrest *142* festnehmen, verhaften
arrival *34* Ankunft
arthritis *147* Arthritis, Gelenkentzündung
ashamed *17* beschämt
asleep: to fall asleep *73* einschlafen

aspect *41* Aspekt, Seite
asset *129* Wert, Vorteil
to associate *139* assoziieren, verbinden
association *16* Verband, Verein
asteroid *75* Asteroid
astonishing *146* erstaunlich
atmosphere *79* Atmosphäre
atmospheric *79* atmosphärisch
to attach *106* beilegen, -fügen
attachment *106* Anlage
attack *40* Angriff
attempt *136* Versuch
to attend *48* teilnehmen (an)
attention *51t* Aufmerksamkeit
attitude *17* Haltung, Einstellung
to attract *18* anziehen, anlocken
attraction *41* Anziehung
attractive *16* attraktiv
auction *27* Auktion
audience *56* Zuschauer
average *76* durchschnittlich
to avoid *62* (ver)meiden
awareness *68* Bewusstsein
awesome *12* überwältigend
awkward *136* unangenehm, lästig, peinlich
axe *137* Axt

B

to back away *142t* zurückgehen
to back off *12* zurücktreten
background *55* Hintergrund, Herkunft
backup *142t* Hilfe, Unterstützung
backwards *87* rückwärts
badge *129* Abzeichen
baggage *118t* Gepäck, Last
balance *66* Gleichgewicht
ban *146* Verbot
to ban *12* verbieten
bang *110* Paukenschlag
bank details *59* Bankverbindung, Kontoangaben
bank: to not break the bank *54* nicht die Welt kosten
bankrupt *40* bankrott, pleite; **to go bankrupt** *132* in Konkurs gehen, Pleite gehen
banner ad *45* Bannerwerbung
barbecue *20* Grillparty
bargain *26* Sonderangebot
bartender *33* Barmann, -frau
basic *42* elementar
basket *104* Korb
battle *119* Kampf
to beat *12* schlagen
bedfellow *137* Bettgenosse, Schlafkamerad
bee *151t* Biene
to behave *56* sich benehmen, sich verhalten
behaviour *57* Verhalten, Benehmen
below *10* unten
to bend *16* (sich) beugen
beneath *113* unter(halb)
benefit *77* Nutzen, Vorteil
to benefit from *71* Nutzen ziehen aus, profitieren von
to bet *61,62* wetten; **you bet** *118t* ganz bestimmt, und ob
better *9* besser
beyond *89* abgesehen von
bias *136* Vorurteil
biodiversity *153* Artenvielfalt
bioengineer *150* Gentechniker/in
birth *41* Geburt
bite *39* Bissen, Happen
to blame sb *56* die Schuld geben, verantwortlich machen; **to be to blame** *131t* an etwas schuld sein
blind spot *73* blinder Fleck
blog *55* Blog
blouse *26* Bluse
to blow sb away *37* jdn überwältigen
blueprint *151* Blaupause, Bauplan
board game *118t* Brettspiel
body language *98* Körpersprache
bold *62* fett
booker *47* Besteller/in
booking *85* Buchung
border *111* Grenze, Grenz-
bored *78* gelangweilt
borough *40* (Stadt-)Bezirk
bother *56* Ärger
bouncy castle *64* Hüpfburg
box: the box *7* die Kiste
box office *43* (Theater-)Kasse
boycott *146* Boykott
braid *118t* (geflochtener) Zopf
to brainstorm *67* (Ideen) sammeln
braking *73* Bremssystem
branch *97* Niederlassung
brand *45* Marke
branded *49* Marken-
brave *58t* tapfer
to break *124* abbrechen
to break a law *131t* das Gesetz brechen/übertreten
to break into *23* einbrechen
breath: to take sb's breath away *40* jdm den Atem rauben
breeding *149* Zucht, Züchtung
bribery *139* Bestechung
brief *75* kurz
bright *22* hell; glänzend, schlau
to bring up *116* großziehen
broad *121* breit
brochure *32* Broschüre, Prospekt
broken *124* getrennt, kaputt
to brush *83* bürsten, putzen
budget *38t, 65* Budget, Etat; Billig-
bulb *76* Glühbirne, -lampe
bulimia *16* Bulimie, Ess-Brech-Sucht
bunch *110* Gruppe, Haufen
bureaucracy *110* Bürokratie
burglary *135* Einbruch
to bury *99* begraben
businessperson *71* Geschäftsmann/-frau
bust: to go bust *134* Pleite gehen
butterfly *59* Schmetterling
to buy sth on credit *29* etw auf Kredit kaufen

C

calm *36* ruhig
campaign *46* (Werbe-)Feldzug, Kampagne
campaigner *66* Aktivist/in, Kämpfer/in
camping: to go camping *15* campen
can *19* Dose
candidate *48* Kandidat/in, Bewerber/in
capable: to be capable of *147* können, fähig sein
capital *18* Hauptstadt
capital (letter) *62* Groß(buchstabe)
capital punishment *136* Todesstrafe
car seat *88t* Autositz
car sharing *66* gemeinsame Pkw-Nutzung
caramel *16* Karamel
carbon *79* Kohlenstoff
carbon dioxide *80t* Kohlendioxid
to care for sb *116* jdn pflegen, sich um jdn kümmern
careers adviser *31* Berufsberater/in
carefully *82* sorgfältig
careless *32* sorglos, nachlässig
carrot *21* Karotte
to carry on *118t* weitermachen
to carry out *6* ausführen
cartoon *32* Karikatur
case study *16* Fallstudie
cash machine *11* Geldautomat
cashier *33* Kassierer/in
casting agent *129* Besetzungsagent/in
casual *99* Gelegenheits-
catastrophe *75* Katastrophe
to catch sb off guard *118t* jemanden überraschen, ertappen
Caucasian *131* Weiße/r, Hellhäutige/r
to celebrate *79* feiern
celebrity *55* Promi(nente/r)
cell *144* (Gefängnis-)Zelle
censure *126* Tadel, Missbilligung
census *129* (Volks-)Zählung

centimetre *79* Zentimeter
central *71* zentral
century *80* Jahrhundert
certain *7* gewiss, sicher
challenge *12* Herausforderung
to challenge *13* herausfordern
challenging *85* herausfordernd, anstrengend
champagne *79* Champagner
channel *49* Kanal
chaos *66* Chaos
chaotic *113* chaotisch
characteristic *40* Eigenschaft, Merkmal
charge *71* Gebühr
charity *55* wohltätiger Verein
charming *16* charmant bezaubernd
chart *42* Diagramm, Tabelle
chatroom *6* Chatroom, Diskussionsforum
to check out *37* herausfinden
checklist *95* Checkliste
cheekbones *129* Wangenknochen
cheeky *16* frech, kess
childcare *116* (Kinder-)Erziehung
childminder *117* Kinderbetreuer/in, Tagesmutter/-vater
to chill out *6* sich entspannen
chin *113* Kinn
choice *17* Wahl
to choke *66* ersticken
to chuckle *113* in sich hineinlachen, kichern
cinema *8* Kino
circle *60* Kreis
citizenship *131t* Staatsbürgerschaft
civil rights *131t* bürgerliche Rechte
civilisation *127* Zivilisation
to claim *68* behaupten, erklären
clash *56* Konflikt, Zusammenstoß
to clasp *113* verschränken
classified *45* nach Rubriken geordnet
clemency *137* Milde, Nachsicht
clerical *89* Schreib-, Büro-
clerk *85* (Bank-)Angestellte/r
cleverly *69* klug, intelligent
client *46* Kunde/Kundin
climate *79* Klima
climate change *80t* Klimawandel
clockwise *93* im Uhrzeigersinn
clone *151t* Klon
cloning *145* Klonen
closeness *48* Vertrautheit
cloudy *78* bewölkt
clubbing: to go clubbing *6* in Discos gehen
clue *44* Schlüssel
coach *7* Trainer/in
coal *79* Kohle
coastal *79* Küsten-
coffee mill *101t* Kaffeemühle
to collapse *49* zusammenbrechen
colleague *66* Kollege/Kollegin
to collect *41* sammeln
college of further education *51t* Fachoberschule, Weiterbildungskolleg
column *19* Spalte
to combine *69* (sich) verbinden
come on *22* komm (schon)
comedy *58* Komödie, Comedy
comment *44* Kommentar
commercial *45* Anzeige, Werbespot
commercial break *49* Werbepause
commission *103, 105* Provision, Gebühr; Kommission
to commit *83* (sich) verpflichten
commitment *83, 89* (Selbst-)Verpflichtung, Einsatz, Engagement
communication *55* Kommunikation, Mitteilung, Benachrichtigung
communications technologies *73* Kommunikationstechnologien
community *16* Gemeinde
commuter *67* Pendler/in
to compare *17* vergleichen
comparison *44* Vergleich, Steigerung
to compete *12* konkurrieren
competition *13* Wettkampf
competitive *7* Wettkampf-
competitive advantage *96* Wettbewerbsvorteil
to complain *32* reklamieren, sich beklagen, beschweren
complete *72* völlig
to complete *93* vervollständigen, abschließen
complex *86* komplex, kompliziert
complicated *69* kompliziert
compulsory *103* obligatorisch, zwangsweise
to concentrate *31* sich konzentrieren
concern *99* Sorge, Interesse, Anliegen
to concern *43* betreffen; **to be concerned with** *120* sich befassen mit, sich kümmern um
conclusion *90* (Schluss-)Folgerung
to confirm *48* bestätigen
conflicting *68* gegensätzlich
confused *137* verwirrt
congested *66* verstopft
congestion *66* Verkehrsstau, Verstopfung
congestion charging *71* Staugebühr
congratulations *29* Glückwunsch
conscience *126* Gewissen
conservation *145* Schutz, Erhaltung
conservative *136* Konservative/r
considered: to be considered *62* berücksichtigt werden
consignment *103* (Waren-)-Sendung, Lieferung
constitution *105* Verfassung
constitutional *136* verfassungsgemäß
to construct *53* entwickeln, ausarbeiten
construction *40* Bau, Bauweise
consumption *150* Verzehr
contact *55* Kontakt, Verbindung
to contact *106* Kontakt aufnehmen zu, sich wenden an
to contain *66* enthalten
contaminated *150* verunreinigt, verseucht
contestant *56* Kandidat/in
context *38* Kontext, Zusammenhang
contract *46* (Arbeits-) Vertrag
contradictory *132* widersprüchlich
contrary *150* Gegenteil
contrast: in contrast to sb/sth *68* im Gegensatz zu, im Unterschied zu
to contrast *36* gegenüberstellen
contribution *106* Beitrag, Beihilfe
convenient *28* bequem
convention *136* Konvention
conventional *70* konventionell, herkömmlich
to convince *127* überzeugen
cookbook *20* Kochbuch
cooperative *131t* kooperativ
co-operative *101t* Kooperative
coordinator *99* Koordinator/in
corporal punishment *136* körperliche Züchtigung
correspondence *48* Korrespondenz
corruption *110* Korruption
council *106* Rat, Gemeinderat
councillor *71* Ratsmitglied
countable *19* zählbar
counter *16* Tresen, Ladentisch
to count on sb/sth *132* sich auf jdn/etwas verlassen, auf jdn/etwas zählen
countless *126* zahllos
cover *113* (Bett-)Decke
craft *99* (Kunst-)Handwerk
to crash *121t* (ab)stürzen
to create *51t* hervorrufen, erzeugen, wecken
crèche facilities *89* Krippeneinrichtungen
creditor *28* Gläubiger/in
crime rate *139* Krimininalitätsrate
criticism *17* Kritik
crop *149* (Anbau)Pflanze
to cross-breed *149* kreuzen
cross-breeding *151t* Kreuzung

crossing point *134* Übergang(sstelle)
crowded *40* überfüllt
cruel *136* grausam
cubicle *16* Kabine
cultural *40* kulturell
curable *18* heilbar
cure *151t* Heilung, Heilmittel
to curl *113* (Beine) unterschlagen
currency *110* Währung
currently *10* zurzeit
curtain *43* Vorhang
custom *118* Brauch
customer relations officer *85* Kundendienstmitarbeiter/in, Kundenbetreuer/in
customs *103* Zoll
cut *80t* Kürzung, Senkung
to cut *49* ausblenden
cutting-edge *96* Spitzen-, High-tech-, modern
CV *86* Lebenslauf
to cycle *76* radfahren
cyclist *109t* Fahrradfahrer/in
cyclone *79* Zyklon

D

dairy *147* hier: Milchvieh
damage *66* Schaden, Schäden
to dare *139* (es) wagen
date: to go on a date *15* eine Verabredung haben
day off *34* freier Tag
dead-end *86* ohne Perspektiven
to deal with *32* sich beschäftigen mit, mit jdm zu tun haben
dealing *139* Handel
death penalty *136* Todesstrafe
to deceive *135* betrügen
decent *139* anständig
decline *52* Rückgang
to decline *52* abnehmen, sinken, zurückgehen
decrease *52* Abnahme, Rückgang
to defend *110* verteidigen
deficit *102* Defizit
to define *129* (sich) definieren
definitely *25* bestimmt, definitiv
definition *7* Definition
degree *93* Grad
to delay *79* aufschieben, hinauszögern
delighted *65* (sehr) erfreut, entzückt
to deliver *138* hier: schaffen, erzielen
demand *82* Nachfrage
to demand *126* (nach)fragen
dementia *149* Demenz
demo *120* Demo(nstration)
demographer *129* Demograph
demonstration *119* Demonstration
to deny *127* bestreiten
department *107* Abteilung
department store *26* Kauf-, Warenhaus
departure *44* Abfahrt
to depend on *30* abhängen von
to deport *131t* ausweisen, abschieben
depressed *65* deprimiert, niedergeschlagen
depressing *118* bedrückend, deprimierend
depression *143* Depression
deputy *142t* Hilfs-, Vertretungs-
to derive *146* abstammen
to describe *81* beschreiben
desert *79* Wüste
to deserve *137* verdienen
to design *46* entwerfen
desire *51t* Begehren, Verlangen
to despair *99* verzweifeln
desperate *79* verzweifelt
dessert *16* Nachspeise, -tisch
destination *22* (Fahrt-)Ziel; *103* Ziel(hafen), Entladehafen
to destroy *69* zerstören, vernichten
destruction *75* Zerstörung, Vernichtung
to detect *73* entdecken
deterrent *138* abschreckend
developer *46* Entwickler/in
development *69* Entwicklung
devout *137* fromm
diabetes *149* Zuckerkrankheit, Diabetes
to diagnose *147* diagnostizieren
diagrammatic *93* grafisch, schematisch
diametrically opposed *140* diametral entgegengesetzt
diet *135* Ernährung, Diät
to differ *41* sich unterscheiden
to dig into *142t* wühlen in
diploma *86* Diplom
to direct *73* leiten
directed at *95* gerichtet auf, abzielend auf
direction *78* Richtung
dirty *16* schmutzig
disabler *73* Sperre
disadvantage: at a disadvantage *31* benachteiligt
to disagree (with) *17* widersprechen, nicht zustimmen
disagreement *50* Widerspruch, Uneinigkeit
to disappear *68* verschwinden
disappointed *65* enttäuscht
disaster *75* Katastrophe, Unglück
discounted *43* reduziert
to discover *6* entdecken
to discriminate *13* unterscheiden, diskriminieren
discrimination *12* Diskriminierung
discussion *49* Diskussion
disgust *126* Ekel
disgusting *18* ekelhaft
dish *40* Gericht
dishonest *98* unehrlich
disobedience *119* Ungehorsam
disorder *143* Störung, Erkrankung
display *28* Ausstellung
distant *40* fern
distinction *68* Unterscheidung
distribution *103* Vertrieb, (Waren-) Verteilung
diverse *112* verschieden, unterschiedlich
to divide *153* (sich) teilen
documentary *58* Dokumentarbericht, -film
domestic *131t* in der Familie, häuslich
dominant *113* beherrschend, dominant
to dominate *98* dominieren
donut *16* Pfannkuchen, Krapfen
dose *136* Dosis
double life *16* Doppelleben
double-decker *16* Doppeldecker
double-glazing *76* mit Isolierverglasung versehen
doubt *147* Zweifel
doubtful *70* fraglich, zweifelhaft
downmarket *68* auf den Massenmarkt ausgerichtet
downside *151t* Nachteil
downtown *37* im Stadtzentrum
dozen *43* Dutzend
to drag *123* schleifen
dramatic *84* dramatisch, drastisch
to draw a line *138* einen Schlussstrich ziehen
dreamless *113* traumlos
dried *104* Trocken-
to drift *86* treiben, zufällig kommen
drink driving *135* Trunkenheit am Steuer
to drop *49* fallen
to drown in *49* ertränken in
drug abuse *139* Drogenmissbrauch
drum *9* Trommel
drunk driving *(AE)* *142t* Trunkenheit am Steuer
dry cleaner's *66* chemische Reinigung
dryer *104* Trockner
due: to be due to *47* darauf zurückzuführen sein
duty *103* Zoll, Abgabe; *106* Pflicht, Aufgabe
dweller *69* Bewohner/in

E

earnings *101* Einkünfte
earth: Why on earth? *21* Warum um Himmels willen?
eastern *79* östlich
eating disorder *16* Essstörung
economy *80* Wirtschaft
effect *40* Auswirkung
efficient *66* effizient, leistungsfähig
effort *118* Bemühung, Anstrengung
either *58t* hier: beides; **not … either** *21* auch nicht
elderly *92* älter
e-learning *153* Lernen am Computer
election *74* (politische) Wahl
electricity *69* Elektrizität, Strom
elevator *(AE)* *37* Lift
embarrassed *17* verlegen
embarrassing *56* peinlich
to emerge *79* heraustreten, hervorkommen
emission *66* Emission, Ausstoß
emotional *116* emotional
to emphasize *62* betonen, hervorheben
employee *89* Arbeitnehmer/in, Beschäftigte/r
employer *8* Unternehmer, Arbeitgeber
employment *88* Arbeit, Beschäftigung, Beruf
to enable *129* (es) ermöglichen, in die Lage versetzen
to encourage *51t* anregen
encyclopedia *39* Lexikon, Enzyklopädie
enemy *124* Feind
energy *40* Energie
engine *69* Motor
engineer *69* Ingenieur/in, Techniker/in
enjoyable *36* angenehm
enquiry *106* Anfrage
to enter *71* hineingehen, -fahren
entertaining *56* unterhaltsam
entertainment *49* Unterhaltung
enthusiasm *107* Begeisterung (-sfähigkeit)
entire *131t* vollkommen, gänzlich
entry *39* Eintrag
environmental *66* Umwelt-
environmentalist *69* Umweltschützer/in
environmentally friendly *69* umweltfreundlich
epidemic *75* Epidemie
equal *12* Gleichberechtigte/r, Ebenbürtige/r
equipment *95* Ausrüstung
equivalent (of) *18* Entsprechung
to escape *49* flüchten
especially *22* besonders, insbesondere
essential *72* notwendig, wesentlich
to estimate *69* schätzen
estuary *121t* Mündung
ethnic *40* ethnisch
ethnicity *129* ethnische Zugehörigkeit
to evaluate *112* einschätzen, bewerten
event *43* Veranstaltung, Ereignis
evidence *17* Beweis, Beleg
to exaggerate *50* übertreiben
exam results *64* Examensnoten
exceptional *147* außergewöhnlich; *64* (Kurz-)Dialog
exchange *64* (Kurz-)Dialog; *133* Austausch
excited *65* aufgeregt, erregt
exciting *36* spannend, aufregend
exclusive *26* exklusiv
execution *136* Hinrichtung
exercise bike *11* Heimtrainer
exhaust *66* Auspuff(rohr)
exhausted *65* erschöpft
exhibition *38* Ausstellung
to exist *83* existieren
exotic *22* exotisch
to expand *46* expandieren, (sich) ausdehnen
to expect *7* erwarten
expectancy *153* Erwartung
expenses *106* Kosten, Ausgaben
experience *60* Erfahrung(en)
experienced *124* erfahren
explanation *52* Erklärung, Erläuterung
to exploit *56* be-, ausnutzen
to explore *40* erkunden
export sales *88* Exportverkäufe, Auslandsverkäufe
to express *42* ausdrücken
expression *7* Ausdruck
to extend *121t* ausweiten, ausbauen
extended *49* verlängert
extension *121t* Ausbau
extent *65* (Aus-)Maß, Umfang, Grad
extract *63* Auszug, Extrakt
extreme *113* Extrem
extremely *53* äußerst; *72* außerordentlich

F

fabulous *26* fabelhaft
to face *76* sich gegenübersehen, vor sich haben
to fail *49* versagen, scheitern; **to fail sb** *118t* jdn enttäuschen, jdn etw nicht geben können
failure *40* Versagen
fairly *131* ziemlich
fame *56* Ruhm
familiar *16* bekannt
fanatic *126* Fanatiker/in
to fancy *83* sich vorstellen
farewell *25* Abschied
farther *44* weiter
fascination *129* Faszination
fashion-conscious *26* modebewusst
fast-acting *136* schnell wirkend
fatty *18* fetthaltig, fettig
fear *12* Furcht
feasible *134* (praktisch) durchführbar, machbar
feature *28* Eigenschaft
to feature *35* eine Rolle spielen
federal *112* föderal(istisch)
fee *106* Gebühr
to feed *151t* ernähren
feminine *13* weiblich
feminist *136* Feministin
fence *134* Zaun
ferry *38* Fähre
fertilizer *150* Dünger
fictional *63* erfunden
field trial *151t* Experimente in der freien Natur
fifth; a fifth *81* Fünftel
figure *42, 81t* Zahl
filling station *33* Tankstelle
finance *40* Finanzen
financial *22* finanziell
first aider *13* Sanitäter
to fit *30* passen
fitted *76* eingebaut
fixed *28* befestigt
flavour *149* Geschmack
flexibility *66* Flexibilität
flick knife *140* Springmesser
to float *113* schweben
flood *75* Flut, Überschwemmung
to flood *131t* überschwemmen
floodlight *83* Flutlicht
flow chart *47* Flussdiagramm
fluctuation *153* Fluktuation
fluent *106* fließend, gewandt, flüssig
to flush *83* spülen
focus *35* Blickpunkt
to focus on *139* sich konzentrieren auf
to fold *113* verschränken, falten
follower *122* Anhänger
foot *120* Fuß; **to set foot in** *35* betreten
football *14* American Football (*BE:* Fußball)
forbidden *126* verboten
to force *57* zwingen
foreground *51* Vordergrund
forest *37* Wald
former *40* früher
formula *51t* Formel

fortunately *29* glücklicherweise
fortune *66* Vermögen
forum *49* Forum
fossil fuel *79* fossiler Brennstoff
foster family *124* Pflegefamilie
fraction *80* Bruch(teil)
frank *110* offen, ehrlich
fraud *135* Betrug, Unterschlagung
freedom *66* Freiheit
freelance *46* freiberuflich
freely *59* freimütig
freezer *20* Gefrierschrank
freezing *92* eiskalt, sehr kalt
frequency *29* Häufigkeit
frequent *44* häufig
fridge *21* Kühlschrank
fried *127* gebraten, geröstet
frightening *13* beängstigend, erschreckend
fringe benefits *85* zusätzliche Leistungen, freiwillige Sozialleistungen
frontier *110* Grenze
frustrated *65* frustriert
fuel *66* Kraftstoff
full-time *132* Vollzeit-
fumes *66* Abgase
fundamentalist *136* fundamentalistisch
fundraising *64* Wohltätigkeitsveranstaltung, Spendensammeln
further *15* weiter
fusion *79* Fusion, Verschmelzung

G

to gain *106* sammeln, erlangen
gambling *126* Glücksspiel
gas *68* Benzin, Treibstoff
gateway *38t* Tor, Pforte
gene *149* Gen
general *9* allgemein
generation *31* Generation
generous *89* großzügig
genetically-modified *146* genmanipuliert
genius *43* Genie
genre *58* Genre
gentle *36* freundlich
genuine *16* echt
geography *38t* Lage, Geographie
gesture *128* Geste(n), Gestik
to get a lot out of sth *7* viel davon haben
to get by *31* durchkommen
to get clear of *124* wegkommen von
to get drunk *18* sich betrinken
to get real *17* die Realität anerkennen
to get the green light *46* grünes Licht erhalten
to get used to *37* sich gewöhnen an
gigantic *114* gigantisch, riesig
glad *13* froh
glamorous *45* glamourös
global *79* global, weltweit
globalization *96* Globalisierung
to glow *28* leuchten
goal-oriented *90* ergebnisorientiert, zielorientiert
good-looking *18* gut aussehend
goods *64* Ware(n), Güter
government *66* Regierung
governor *134* Gouverneur/in
grade *14* Note
gradual *52* allmählich, nach und nach
grandad *89* Opa
greedy *16* gierig
greenhouse gas *83* Treibhausgas
greeting *38* Begrüßung
grid *23* Tabelle, Gitter
gridlock *66* Verkehrskollaps
to grin *16* lächeln, grinsen
gross profit *93* Bruttogewinn
grotesque *56* grotesk
guaranteed *99* garantiert
guard *134* Wache
to guess *44* raten
to guide *92* führen, leiten
guidebook *39* Reiseführer
guilty *16* schuldig
guy *12* Kerl, Typ

H

habitat *150* Lebensraum
to hack up *142t* zerstückeln
hairdresser *15* Friseur/in
ham *19* Schinken
to hand in *30* abgeben
to handle *103* umgehen mit, bearbeiten
to hang around *6* rumhängen
to happen *36* geschehen, passieren
hard sell *50* aggressive Verkaufstechnik
hardly *89* kaum
hardware *19* Hardware, Geräte
harmful *150* schädlich
harsh *126* scharf, harsch
haulier *69* Spediteur, Fuhrunternehmen
havoc: to play havoc *150* verheerende Schäden anrichten
heading *49* Überschrift
headquarters *105* Hauptsitz, Zentrale
headscarf *125* Kopftuch
healthcare *89* medizinische Versorgung
heating *73* Heizung
heavily-armed *139* schwer bewaffnet
heavyweight *43* Schwergewicht
hectare *101t* Hektar
hedge *123* Hecke
height *120* Höhe, Größe
hence *136* daher
herbicide *150* Unkrautvernichtungsmittel
herd *147* Herde
hereditary *145* erblich
heritage *115* Erbe, Herkunft
high *124* high, auf Drogen
hill *69* Hügel, Berg
hip *113* Hüfte
to hire sth *64* mieten
hold *12* Griff
to hold down *80t* niedrig halten
homeless: the homeless *7* die Obdachlosen
homosexual *127* Homosexuelle/r
honest *28* ehrlich
household *83* Haushalt
housemate *57* Mitbewohner/in
huge *37* gewaltig
hulk *12* Kerl wie ein Baum
Human Resources *48* Personal(abteilung)
humane *131t* human
to hunt *122* jagen
hurricane *55* Orkan, Wirbelsturm
to hurt *99* wehtun, hier: negativ beinflussen
hybrid *69* hybrid
hydroelectric *79* hydroelektrisch
hydrogen *69* Wasserstoff

I

ice-hockey *13* Eishockey
ID *91t* Ausweis
ideal *65* ideal
to identify *100* herausfinden
identity *59* Identität
idiom *67* Idiom, Redewendung
idiomatic *67* idiomatisch
illegal *67* verboten, illegal
to illustrate *51, 90* darstellen, illustrieren, veranschaulichen
imagination *51* Fantasie
immediate *51t* umgehend, sofort
immigrant *39* Einwanderer/Einwanderin
to immigrate *41* einwandern
immigration *133* Einwanderung
impact *66* (Aus-)Wirkung, Einfluss
to imply *151* andeuten, implizieren
to impose *141* auferlegen, erlassen
to impress *12* imponieren
impression *13* Eindruck
imprisonment *138* Haft, Gefängnis(strafe)

to improve *66* verbessern, besser werden
impulsive *113* impulsiv
incidence *139* Vorkommen, Häufigkeitsrate
incident *128* Vorfall, Ereignis
to include *43* einschließen, einbeziehen
including *40* einschließlich, inbegriffen, darunter
income *42* Einkommen
increase *42* Anstieg, Steigerung
to increase *31* ansteigen, zunehmen
increasing *13* zunehmend
independent *85* unabhängig
indirectness *92* Indirektheit
industrial *79* industriell
industry *41* Industrie
infection *147* Entzündung
to influence *50* beinflussen
informative *41* informativ
ingredient *146* Zutat, Bestandteil
injection *136* Spritze, Injektion
to injure *12* verletzen
injury *13* Verletzung
innovative *48* innovativ
input *118t* hier: Aufwendung, Hingabe
to inquire *134* fragen, sich erkundigen
insane *137* geisteskrank
to install *101t* installieren
instance: for instance *126* zum Beispiel
instead of *8* statt, anstatt (von)
instructor *85* Lehrer/in, Ausbilder/in
insulation *76* Isolierung
insurance *73* Versicherung
to integrate *111* sich integrieren
intense *36* intensiv
to interact *149* sich gegenseitig beeinflussen
interactive *55* interaktiv
interference *110* Einmischung
intermarriage *129* Mischehe
intermission *43* (Werbe-)Pause
intern *106* Praktikant/in, Volontär/in
internship *106* Volontariat
to interrupt *113* unterbrechen
to interview *31* interviewen
to introduce *148* einführen
to invent *40* erfinden
invention *43* Erfindung
to invest *89* investieren
to involve *106* einschließen, beinhalten
involvement *122* Beteiligung, Engagement
ironing *15* Bügeln
irregular *85* unregelmäßig
irresponsible *29* unverantwortlich
island *40* Insel
isolated *114* isoliert
issue *70* Frage, Thema, Anliegen
IT *88t* Informationstechnologie
IT officer *88t* EDV-Techniker/in
IT technician *85* Informationstechniker/in

J

jar *19* (Einmach)Glas
jet-colored *129* pechschwarz
job-related *31* beruflich
to join *51t* beitreten, sich anmelden
to joke: Are you joking? *7* Ist das dein Ernst?
journalist *76* Journalist/in
journey *46* Reise, Fahrt
to jump start *68* etwas auf die Sprünge helfen
junction *78* Kreuzung
junior *44* untergeordnet
justice *138* Gerechtigkeit

K

to keep: How have you been keeping? *94* Wie geht es dir?
to keep in touch with *28* in Verbindung bleiben
kid *62* Kind
knee *113* Knie
to knock down *121t* abreißen
knowledge *19* Wissen
kWh *83* Kilowattstunde

L

label *26* Label, Marke
labelling *147* Kennzeichnung
labour *93* Arbeit
labour market *133* Arbeitsmarkt
lake *38t* (Binnen-)See
landline *109* Festnetz(leitung)
lane *73* (Fahr-)Spur
large-scale *42* in großer Zahl
latest *55* neueste, letzte
to launch *46* einführen, starten
law-abiding *131t* gesetzestreu
lawyer *112* (Rechts-)Anwalt/Anwältin
leader *79* Führer/in
leading *51t* führend
leaflet *45* Broschüre, Flugblatt
league *83* Liga
to lean on *118t* sich lehnen an
least: at least *15* mindestens
legal *57* legal
legible *57* leserlich
leisure *153* Freizeit
leisure centre *15* Freizeitzentrum
length *44* Länge, Dauer
lesson: to teach sb a lesson *13* jdm eine Lektion erteilen
lethal *136* tödlich
letter of appointment *91t* Bewerbungsschreiben
level *79* Niveau, Stand
liar *142t* Lügner/in
liberal *137* Liberale/r
library *55* Bücherei, Bibliothek
licence *106* Führerschein
to lie *60* lügen
lifestyle *76* Lebensstil
lift: to give a lift *24* mit dem Auto mitnehmen
to lighten up *49* aufheitern
to limit *72* limitieren, begrenzen, auf etw beschränken
limited *51t* beschränkt, begrenzt
limitless *131t* grenzenlos, uneingeschränkt
to link *27* verbinden
listener *98* Zuhörer/in
literally *118t* buchstäblich
lively *49* lebhaft
living expenses *22* Lebenshaltungskosten
loads *30* eine Menge
loaf *19* (Laib) Brot
lobby *150* Lobby, Interessengruppe
location *69* (Stand-)Ort, Position
logging *119* Abholzung
logical *57* logisch
long-running *56* mit langer Laufzeit
to look round *7* sich umsehen
loophole *146* Schlupfloch
to loosen *126* lockern
to lose control over *16* die Beherrschung verlieren
loved one *138* Angehörige/r, Nahestehende/r
lovely *26* hübsch
low-cost *89* Niedriglohn-
low-energy *76* Niedrigenergie-, Spar-
low-lying *79* tief gelegen
luck *114* Glück
lucky: to be lucky *8* Glück haben
luggage *19* Gepäck
lunchtime *15* Mittagspause
lung *147* Lunge

M

machinery *78* Maschine(n), Gerät
madness *55* Wahnsinn
magical *40* magisch
mail-order catalogue *26* Versandhauskatalog
mains *83* (Strom-)Netz
mainstream *119* vorherrschend(e Meinung)
to maintain *72* unterhalten, warten
major *72* groß, größer

to make up *12* bilden
to make up for ***81t*** ausgleichen
mammal *147* Säugetier
to manage *11* zurechtkommen, fertig werden (mit), (es) schaffen
manipulation *149* Manipulation, Veränderung
man-made *41* von Menschenhand
manner *103* Art (und Weise)
to manufacture *69* herstellen, produzieren
march *119* (Protest-)Marsch
marital status *108* Familienstand
mark *9* Note
to mark *68* bedeuten, bezeichnen
marketing *88* Marketing, Vermarktung
massive *136* massiv, enorm
mast *151* Mast
mat *12* Matte
mate *10* Kumpel
materialist *127* Materialist/in
maternity leave *89* Mutterschaftsurlaub
matter *76* Sache, Ding, Angelegenheit; **What's the matter with ...?** *18* Was ist los mit ...?; **as a matter of fact** ***91t*** um genau zu sein
to matter *87* von Bedeutung sein
maximum *93* maximal
meantime: in the meantime *26* inzwischen
media hype ***151t*** Medienrummel
medical *17* medizinisch
medium *59* Medium
to melt *79* schmelzen
melting pot *40* Schmelztiegel
membership ***51t*** Mitgliedschaft
mental *17* mental
to mention *51* erwähnen, aufzählen; **don't mention it** *31* gern geschehen
merciless *139* unbarmherzig
message *51* Aussage, Botschaft
to mess up ***88t*** es verderben, es verpeilen
microchip *95* Mikrochip
micro-organism *149* Mikroorganismus
microphone *137* Mikrophon
microwave *54* Mikrowelle
Middle Ages *49* Mittelalter
middlemen *99* Zwischenhändler
migration *111* Wanderung(sbewegung)
mile *67* Meile
to mind: Do you mind if ...? ***109t*** Haben Sie etwas dagegen, wenn ...?
minister *66* Minister/in
minor ***118t*** geringfügig
minority *130* Minderheit
miscarriage *147* Fehlgeburt
miserable *127* kläglich
misleading *110* irreführend
to miss out on ***118t*** verpassen
missing *13* fehlend
misunderstanding *32* Missverständnis
mixture *75* Mischung
monitor *73* Monitor
monotonous *126* monoton
monthly *69* monatlich
moral *57* moralisch
moreover *79* außerdem, zudem
motherly ***118t*** mütterlich
motive *143* Motiv, Beweggrund
motor *69* Motor
motorway *67* Autobahn
move: on the move *65* unterwegs
movement *69* Bewegung
movies *6* Kino
mule *149* Maultier, -esel
multiculturalism *125* Multikulturalismus
multiracial *129* ethnisch gemischt
murder *136* Mord
muscle *12* Muskel
mushroom *127* Pilz
musician *115* Musiker/in
mustard *19* Senf
myth ***118t*** Legende

N

nail polish ***118t*** Nagellack
nanny ***131t*** Kindermädchen
nasty *12* gemein
Native American *131* Indianer/in, indianisch
naturalized *133* eingebürgert
navel-line *123* tiefer Ausschnitt (bis zum Nabel)
necessarily: not necessarily *8* nicht unbedingt
neckline *123* Ausschnitt
need: in need *55* bedürftig; **to meet needs** *76* Bedürfnisse decken
needle *124* Nadel
negotiation *106* Verhandlung
nepotism *139* Vetternwirtschaft
nervous *65* nervös
nervous breakdown *117* Nervenzusammenbruch
net *6* Internet
netiquette *62* Netiquette, Umgangsformen (im Internet)
to network *7* vernetzen
neutral *129* neutral
newly *40* kürzlich
newsletter *55* Rundschreiben, (Info-)Blatt
next door *12* nebenan
nickname *140* Spitzname
nightmare *37* Albtraum
non-governmental organization *122* Nichtregierungsorganisation
nonsense *114* Unsinn
noon *43* mittags
Nordic *129* nordisch
novel *39* Roman
now and then *29* ab und zu
nuclear *79* Atom-
nucleus *147* Kern
numerical *93* numerisch, Zahlen-
nurse *119* Krankenschwester, -pfleger/in
nursery *66* Kindertagesstätte, Kita,
nutritional *149* Nähr-

O

to obey *150* befolgen
objection to *32* Ablehnung gegenüber
to obtain *143* erwerben
obviously *29* offensichtlich
occasional *28* gelegentlich
off: to be off ***91t*** losgehen
offence *103* Straftat, Vergehen; *140* Delikt
office block *114* Bürogebäude, -hochhaus
office-based *85* im Büro, bürogebunden
official *71* Beamter/Beamtin
offline *59* offline, nicht im Internet
to offload *99* weitergeben
offshore *96* ins/im Ausland
offspring *146* Nachkommen
old people's home *33* Seniorenheim
omission *147* Lücke
once in a while ***118t*** dann und wann
one-sided *50* einseitig
to operate *85* betreiben
opponent *13* Gegner/in
opportunity *96* Chance, Möglichkeit
to oppose *68* widersprechen
opposed: to be opposed to sth *136* gegen etw sein
to opt out *114* austreten, aussteigen
order *8* Reihenfolge
ordinary *11* gewöhnlich, normal
organ *147* Organ
organism *149* Organismus
original *78* original, ursprünglich
otherwise *17* sonst, ansonsten
ought to *58* sollte/n
out-dated *130* überholt, veraltet
outdoor clothing ***109t*** Wanderbekleidung
outdoors *85* draußen, im Freien
outfit *123* Kleidung, Outfit
outgoing *106* kontaktfreudig

to outline *87* umreißen, skizzieren
to outnumber *130* übertreffen
overall *83* allgemein
to overcome *18* überwinden
overdose *124* Überdosis
overly *118t* übermäßig
overnight *83* über Nacht
to override *73* ausschalten
over the top *62* übertrieben
overtime *96* Überstunden
to owe *79* verdanken, schulden
owner *69* Besitzer/in
oxygen *69* Sauerstoff

P

PA *47* persönliche/r Assistent/in
packaging *103* Verpacken
packet *16* Schachtel, Packung, Tüte
paid *85* bezahlt
painless *136* schmerzlos
paint *19* Farbe
panel *45* hier: Spalte, Fläche
to panic *21* in Panik geraten
paradise *127* Paradies
parcel *92* Paket
parentage *133* elterliche Abstammung
parking space *73* Parkplatz, Parklücke
particular *36* bestimmt, speziell, besonders
part-time job *7* Teilzeitjob
part-timer *34* Teilzeitarbeiter/in
to pass *49* weitergegeben werden
passenger *66* Fahrgast
passion *137* Leidenschaft, Emotion
paternity leave *89* Vaterschafts-urlaub
path *78* Pfad, Weg
patience *135* Geduld
pattern *143* Muster
paycheck *96* Gehalt(sscheck)
payment *104* Bezahlung
peace *105* Frieden
peer group *115* Gleichaltrige, Clique
pen *88t* Stift
penalty *11* Strafstoß
pension *139* Rente, Pension
percentage *80* Prozentsatz
perfect *57* vollkommen
performance *43* Vorstellung
performance-related pay *90* leistungsbezogene Bezahlung
period drama *43* Historiendrama
permanent *7* ständig, dauerhaft
perpetrator *143* Täter/in
perplexed *127* perplex, verblüfft
personal space *98* Distanzzone, Abstand zwischen Personen
personality *56* Persönlichkeit
personally *72* persönlich
perspective *36* Perspektive, Ansicht
to persuade *53, 71* überzeugen, überreden
pesticide *150* Schädlingsbekämpfungsmittel
petrol *8* Benzin
phenomenal *14* phänomenal
phrase *17* Wendung, Ausdruck
to pick fruit *22* Obst pflücken
to pick up *58t* abholen
picker *99* Pflücker/in
pirate *58* Pirat
to pitch *46* anbieten
pity: it's a pity *58* es ist schade
placement *49* (Produkt-)Werbung
planner *15* (Termin-)Kalender
play on words *51t* Wortspiel
pleasant *13* angenehm
plenty of *20* viel(e)
to plunge *123* (ab)stürzen, tief fallen
poem *123* Gedicht
point of view *58* Standpunkt, Ansicht
poisonous *149* giftig
police officer *19* Polizeibeamter/beamtin
policy *139* Politik, Linie
to polish *116* polieren, putzen
polite *62* höflich
pollution *66* (Umwelt)Verschmutzung
popular press *56* Boulevardpresse
population *133* Bevölkerung
pop-up ad *45* Internet-Anzeige
port *103* Hafen
to pose *129* posieren, darstellen
position *29* Stellung
to post *143* veröffentlichen, bekannt geben
potential *46, 151t* potentiell; Potenzial
pound *114* Pfund (Sterling)
poverty *80t* Armut
to power *80* antreiben
power station *69* Kraftwerk
powerful *119* mächtig, stark
ppm *79* Teile pro Million
practical *106* praktisch
to practise *11* üben
precarious *99* unsicher, prekär
precisely *13* genau
predictable *149* voraussagbar
premature *147* vorzeitig, frühzeitig
premiership *83* Bundesliga
premium *73* Prämie
to present *82* vorstellen, behandeln
presentation *52* Vorstellung, Präsentation
present: at present *10* gegenwärtig
pressure *88* Druck
pretty soon *37* sehr bald
to prevent *73, 79* verhindern, verhüten
previous *76* vorher(gehend)
priest *119* Priester/in, Geistliche/r
princess *12* Prinzessin
principle *136* Prinzip
prior *143* vorherig
prison *135* Gefängnis
prisoner *138* Häftling, Gefangene/r
privacy *66* Privatsphäre
private *13* privat, persönlich
probation *141* Bewährung
process *47* Prozess, Vorgang
producer *56* Produzent/in, Erzeuger
product placement *45* Schleichwerbung
production *69* Produktion, Herstellung
production rate *93* Produktionsrate
professional *83* Profi-
profile *56* Profil, Ansicht, Herkunft, Berufsbild, Porträt
profit *56* Profit, Gewinn
progress *76* Fortschritt/e
progression *143* Werdegang, Entwicklung
to promote *45* fördern
proper *22* richtig, geeignet, korrekt, ordentlich
property *135* Eigentum
proportion *121* Teil, Verhältnis
to prosecute *139* anklagen, strafrechtlich verfolgen
prospect *89* Aussicht
prosperity *105* Wohlstand
prostitute *127* Prostituierte/r
proud *13* stolz
to prove *42* beweisen
to provide *106* (an)bieten, sorgen für, zur Verfügung stellen
provider *59* Anbieter
psychiatric *118* psychiatrisch
psychological *56* psychologisch
psychology *56* Psychologie
pub *10* Kneipe
public *55* öffentlich
public school *12* staatliche Schule
publicity *85* Öffentlichkeitsarbeit
to publish *63, 154* veröffentlichen, herausgeben
to pull oneself together *17* sich zusammenreißen
to pull on the same rope *111* an einem Strang ziehen
punctuation *62* Zeichensetzung, Interpunktion
punishment *29* Strafe, Bestrafung
purchase *26* (Ein-) Kauf
pure *26* rein

purpose *83* Zweck, Ziel
to push up *88t* ausbauen, hochtreiben
pushy *26* aufdringlich
to put down *88t* anzahlen
to put forward *58* vorbringen, zur Diskussion stellen
to put on weight *16* zunehmen
to put sth in perspective *82* etwas ins rechte Licht rücken, etw relativieren
puzzled *142t* verdutzt

Q

qualification *8* Qualifikation, Ausbildung
quality *26* Qualität
quantity *20* Menge, Quantität
query *106* Frage, Rückfrage
questionnaire *30* Fragebogen
queue *19* (Warte-)Schlange
quota system *134* Quotensystem
quotation *35* Zitat

R

to race *69* sich ein Wettrennen liefern
rack *32* Ständer
radar *73* Radar
radiation *151* Strahlung
to raise *51t, 55* wecken; sammeln
range *62* Reihe, Spektrum
to rank *73* einstufen, -ordnen
ransom *135* Lösegeld
rape *139* Vergewaltigung
rapid *52* rapide, schnell
rare *9* selten
raw material *50* Rohstoff
to react *55* reagieren
reality *65* Wirklichkeit
reality TV *56* Reality TV
really something *37* toll, beeindruckend
reasonable *85* vernünftig
reborn *96* wiedergeboren
to recap *121t* rekapitulieren, zusammenfassen
receipt *104* Eingang, Erhalt
to receive *38* empfangen
recently *33* kürzlich, neulich
receptionist *85* Empfangsdame, -chef
to recognize *49* erkennen
recommendation *112* Empfehlung
to recommend *110* empfehlen
to record *15* aufzeichnen
recovery *40* Erholung
Red Cross *7* Rotes Kreuz
to redevelop *96* erneuern, neu entwickeln
to reduce *66* reduzieren, verringern
reduction *71* Verringerung, Senkung
redundant *86* arbeitslos
to refer to *8* sich beziehen auf
referee *108* Referenzgeber/in
reference *106* Zeugnis
referendum *114* Volksentscheid
to reflect *129* widerspiegeln
reformed *137* gebessert
refugee *55* Flüchtling
to refuse *16* ablehnen, sich weigern, widerstehen
regarding *108* bezüglich, betreffend
to register *139* registrieren
registered *121* registriert, eingetragen
registration papers *142t* Papiere, Zulassung
to reintroduce *138* wieder einführen
to reject *105* ablehnen
rejected *116* abgelehnt
to relate to *100* sich beziehen auf
to relate to sb/sth *68* sich beziehen auf
relationship *38* Verhältnis
relatively *110* verhältnismäßig
relaxed *65* entspannt, locker
relevant *57* relevant, wichtig
reliability *132* Zuverlässigkeit
reliable *28* zuverlässig
to rely on *99* angewiesen sein auf, sich verlassen auf
to remain *52* bleiben
remark *57* Bemerkung
remorse *137* Reue
renewable *69* erneuerbar
to rent *38t* mieten
to repay *28* zurückzahlen
repentant *137* reuig, reumütig
repetitive *90* monoton
to replace *8* ersetzen
reply *92* Antwort, Erwiderung, Reaktion
report *76* Bericht, Reportage
to report *68* melden, berichten
repugnant *136* widerlich
request *107* Bitte, Aufforderung, Wunsch
to request *78* anfordern, bitten (um)
to require *13* erfordern
required *51* erforderlich; **to be required to** *96* müssen
requirement *12* Erfordernis
to rescue *96* retten
research *19* Forschung
researcher *59* Forscher/in
to resist *140* Widerstand leisten gegen, sich etw widersetzen
resort *85* Erholungsort
resource *89* Reserve, Ressource
respondent *129* Befragte/r
responsibility *88* Verantwortung, Verantwortlichkeit
result *71* Resultat, Ergebnis
retailer *29* Einzelhändler/in
to retire *117* in Rente/Pension gehen
retired *89* pensioniert, im Ruhestand
retribution *138* Vergeltung
return *74* (hin und) zurück
reunion *59* Treffen, Wiedersehen
to reveal *123* enthüllen, zeigen
revelation *146* Enthüllung
revision *94* Wiederholung
revolution *79* Revolution
to reward *131t* belohnen
to rewrite *78* umschreiben, neu schreiben
ride *38t* Tour, Fahrt, Flug
ridiculous *123* lächerlich
rise *80t* Anstieg
risk: at risk *59* gefährdet
risk-taker *113* Mensch mit Risikobereitschaft
rival *12* Gegner/in, Rivale, -lin
to rival *13* konkurrieren
road network *72* Straßennetz
road: to go down a road *16* etwas erleben
roadside *73* (am) Straßenrand
robbery *139* Raub, Überfall
role *15* Rolle
role model *115* Vorbild
Roman *56* Römer/in
room: to have room *20* Platz haben
rope *119* Seil, Tau
rotten *139* korrupt
roughly *36* ungefähr
route *67* Route, Strecke, Weg
routine *85* Routine, Ablauf
routinely *136* routinemäßig
row *28* Reihe
rowdy *127* laut, randalierend
to rub *118t* reiben
to rule *136* entscheiden
to run out of *76* ausgehen
to run up debts *26* sich verschulden, Schulden anhäufen
runner-up *121* Zweite/r
runway *121t* Landebahn
rural *36* ländlich
rush hour *69* Hauptverkehrszeit, Berufsverkehr

S

to sack *96* entlassen, feuern
sacking *103* Entlassung(en)
safety *73* Sicherheit
sake: for sb's sake *131t* um jds willen
salary *85* Gehalt, Lohn
sale *29* Schlussverkauf
sales *26* Verkaufs-
sales figures *54* Verkaufszahlen
salesman *65* Verkäufer
salesperson *85* Verkaufsmitarbeiter/in, Verkäufer/in
sari *125* Sari (Kleidungsstück)
satellite *69* Satellit
satire *58* Satire
to satirize *51* satirisch darstellen
satnav *69* Satellitennavigation, Navi
saving *66* Einsparung, Ersparnis
to scan *36* überfliegen, absuchen
scandal *103* Skandal
scandalous *144* skandalös
scarcity *111* Knappheit
scary *37* unheimlich, beängstigend
sceptical *28* skeptisch
school-leaver *25* Schulabgänger/in
schoolwork *7* Hausaufgaben
schoolyard *118t* Schulhof
sci-fi *58* Science-Fiction, wissenschaftlich-utopisch
to score a goal *8* ein Tor erzielen
to scream *16* schreien
screen *43* Bildschirm
to screen *56* ausstrahlen
to seal off *134* absperren, abriegeln
seaside *85* Bade-, Strand-, See-
seasonal *85* Saison-
secondary *83* Zweit-
second-hand *27* gebraucht
secret *16* geheim
secretarial course *86* Sekretariatskurs
sector *106* Sektor, Bereich
secure *64* sicher
security *153* Sicherheit
security check *38t* Sicherheitskontrolle
seed *139* Samen(korn)
to seek *99* suchen
segregation *129* Rassentrennung
seldom *9* selten
to select *93* auswählen
self-confident *113* selbstsicher, -bewusst
selfish *111* egoistisch
senior *37* Schüler/in im letzten Schuljahr
sensation *43* Sensation
sense *40* Sinn, Gefühl
sense: to make no sense *59* nicht sinnvoll sein
sensible *31* vernünftig
sensitive *98* empfindlich
sensor *73* Sensor, Messgerät
separate *146* getrennt
sequence *35* Episode, Sequenz
series *56* Serie
to serve *11* servieren
service *44* (Bus-/Zug-)Verbindung
session *12* Treffen, Termin
set: to be set in *75* spielen in
to set to work *12* ans Werk gehen
to set up *47* begründen
setting *128* Szenerie, Schauplatz
several *25* mehrere, einige
severe *79* ernst, schwer, stark
shade *119* Schattierung
to shake *98* schütteln
shareholder *99* Aktionär/in
sharp *52* rasch, schnell, stark
sheet *79* Platte, Decke
shelf *31* Regal
shelf life *149* Haltbarkeit
shelf-stacker *33* Regalauffüller/in
to shine *40* glänzen
to ship *131t* verschiffen, transportieren
shiver *12* Zittern
shocked *65* schockiert
shoplifter *29* Ladendieb/in
shoplifting *29* Ladendiebstahl
shopping mall *38* Einkaufszentrum
shopping trolley *26* Einkaufswagen
shore *40* Ufer
shortlisted *48* in der engeren Wahl
showroom *68* Austellungsraum, Verkaufsraum
to shrink *130* schrumpfen, zurückgehen
to shut up *62* den Mund halten
sight *43* Sehenswürdigkeit
signal *73* Signal
silk *26* Seide
similarity *63* Ähnlichkeit
since *31* seit
single-issue politics *120* Interessenpolitik
to sink *16* sinken
to sit back *30* sich zurückhalten, sich zurücklehnen
site *26* Website
skill *7* Fähigkeit, Geschick
skint *88t* pleite
skyline *37* Silhouette
skyscraper *37* Wolkenkratzer
slave *96* Sklave/Sklavin
sleepy *41* müde
to slide *139* (ab)rutschen, (ab) sacken
slight *52* leicht
slot *47* Termin
smash *43* Kassenschlager
to smooth *113* glatt streichen, glätten
to snap *143* ausflippen, ausrasten
to snort *124* sniffen, schnupfen
social life *30* Sozialkontakte
social services *117* Sozialamt, Sozialdienste
social worker *124* Sozialarbeiter/in
society *63* (die) Gesellschaft
soft drink *64* alkoholfreies Getränk
soft sell *50* zurückhaltende Verkaufstechnik
software *19* Software, Programme
solar *76* Sonnen-, Solar-
solar heating *88t* Solarheizung
solicitor *119* (Rechts-)Anwalt/Anwältin
solution *72* Lösung
to solve *102* lösen
somehow *76* irgendwie
song: for a song *43* spottbillig
to sort *32* sortieren
to sound *73* ausgelöst werden, ertönen
source *69* Quelle
sovereignty *111* Souveränität, Unabhängigkeit
spare part *151t* Ersatzteil
special offer *18* Sonderangebot
specialist *104* speziell, Fach-
to specialize in *106* sich spezialisieren auf
species *149* Art(en)
speech bubble *6* Sprechblase
speeding *142* Geschwindigkeitsüberschreitung
spelling *62* Rechtschreibung
spine: to form the spine of *43* das Rückgrat bilden
sponsor *46* Sponsor/in
to sponsor *48* finanziell unterstützen
sponsorship *45* finanzielle Unterstützung
spread *153* Verteilung
to spread *49* (sich) verbreiten
spy *58* Spion/in, Spionage-
stability *111* Stabilität
stabilization *79* Stabilisierung
stadium *83* Stadion
staff *26* Personal, Angestellte, Mitarbeiter/innen
stamp *154* Briefmarke
to stand for sth *51* für etw stehen
standard *143* Standard-, Normal-
standard of living *81t* Lebensstandard
standby *83* Bereitschaft, Ruhezustand
to stare *126* starren
to starve yourself *17* hungern

state *36* (Bundes-)Staat
statement *13* Aussage
statistical *52* statistisch
to stay up *30* aufbleiben
steady *52* stetig, fest, regelmäßig
steel-frame *40* Stahlträger
stereotype *12* Klischee
stitch *139* Stich
to stock *146* führen, anbieten
stock control *86* Lagersteuerung, Lagerkontrolle
stomach *113* Magen
to store *150* lagern, aufbewahren
stranger *59* Fremde/r
to strap *137* anschnallen, festbinden
strength *76* Kraft, Stärke
to strengthen *41* stärken
stressful *47* stressig, anstrengend
to stretch out *113* ausstrecken
stretcher *12* Trage
structure *41* Gebäude, Struktur, Aufbau
stuck: to be stuck *37* feststecken
studio *95* Studio
stuff *7* Zeug
to stuff *16* stopfen
stupid *83* dumm
sub-contractor *99* Subunternehmer
sub-heading *39* Untertitel
to subject *136* unterwerfen, aussetzen
to subsidize *72* subventionieren
subsidized *89* subventioniert
substance *149* Substanz, Stoff
suburb *66* Vorort, Außenbezirk
successful *47* erfolgreich
to suffer *7* leiden
sufferer *17* Leidende/r
suffragette *119* Frauenrechtlerin
to suggest *48* vorschlagen, andeuten
suggestion *64* Vorschlag
suitable *8* passend, geeignet
to summarize *121t* zusammenfassen
supervision *147* Überwachung
superweed *151t* hoch resistentes Unkraut
supply *48* Lieferung
to supply *48* liefern
supply chain *99* Versorgungskette
support *88t* Hilfe, Unterstützung
to support *68* unterstützen
supporter *148* Anhänger/in
Supreme Court *136* Oberster Gerichtshof
surely *66* sicherlich
to surf *9* surfen
surging *152* (Preis:) anziehend, steigend
surprised *65* überrascht, erstaunt
surprising *82* überraschend
surveillance *63* Überwachung
survey *6* Umfrage
to survive *56* überleben
suspended sentence *141* (Freiheits-)Strafe auf Bewährung
sustainable *102* nachhaltig
SUV *68* Geländewagen (mit Vierradantrieb)
to swallow *127* (ver)schlucken
to swap *15* tauschen
sweater *76* Pullover
sweetie *12* Liebling, Schatz
switch *78* Schalter
to switch off *28* abschalten
sympathetic *17* mitfühlend, verständnisvoll
sympathy *119* Mitgefühl, Mitleid

T

tailback *66* Autoschlange
to take off *24* starten
take on *110* Einstellung zu
to take over *40* übernehmen
talent *14* Talent
tap *83* (Wasser-)Hahn
target *80t* Ziel(vorgaben), Soll(zahlen)
task *17* Aufgabe
tax *66* Steuer
taxpayer *40* Steuerzahler/in
teammate *12* Mannschaftskamerad/in
technique *51t* Methode, (Arbeits-) Technik
temper *126* Beherrschung
temporary *85* zeitlich befristet
to tend *143* dazu neigen
tendency *149* Tendenz
term *63* Ausdruck
terms *89* Bedingungen, Konditionen: **to come to terms with** *118t* zurechtkommen mit
terrible *49* schrecklich, furchtbar
terrified *65* erschrocken
terrorist *40* Terrorist/in
to test *7* prüfen
to text *30* SMS schicken, simsen
text message *6* SMS
textile *96* Textil-
thanks to *79* dank
theme *31* Thema
theoretical *107* theoretisch
thief *59* Dieb/in
though *80t* doch, jedoch
thought bubble *51* Denkblase
threat *111* Bedrohung, Drohung
thrill *26* Spannung
to throw out *56* hinauswerfen
to throw up *16* (sich) erbrechen
to tick *129* ankreuzen
tidal *79* Gezeiten-
tie *126* Krawatte, Schlips
tight *38t* knapp, eng
time: from time to time *29* von Zeit zu Zeit; **in no time** *16* im Handumdrehen
timeline *77* Zeitachse, -leiste
time off *21* Freizeit
time out *22* Freizeit
time-consuming *149* zeitraubend
times *8* mal
timetable *154* Zeitplan, Fahrplan
tingling *16* kribbelnd, prickelnd
tiring *118* anstrengend, ermüdend
toilet *83* Toilette
toilet pan *16* Kloschüssel
tolerance *139* Toleranz
tolerant *139* tolerant
to tolerate *131t* tolerieren
tonne *76* Tonne
tooth *83* Zahn
top: over the top *61* übertrieben
tourism *106* Tourismus, Fremdenverkehr
toxic *150* giftig, toxisch
tradition *40* Tradition
traditional *69* traditionell
traffic jam *66* (Verkehrs-)Stau
transmission *96* Übertragung
transplant *149* Transplantation
transport *65* Verkehr(smittel)
travel agency *32* Reisebüro
travel insurance *89* Reiseversicherung
treatment *17* Behandlung
treaty *105* Vertrag
to tremble *126* zittern
tremendous *129* gewaltig
trend *52* Trend
to trick *135* betrügen, hereinlegen
to trigger *149* auslösen
trivial *135* trivial, geringfügig
trouble *56* Schwierigkeiten, Ärger
troubled: to be troubled *136* beunruhigt sein
trunk *(AE)* *142t* Kofferraum
to trust *98* vertrauen
to try on *11* anprobieren
tub *16* Becher
tube *19* Tube
tuition *33* Unterricht
turbine *76* Turbine, Rad
turn: to take it in turns *33* sich abwechseln; **to turn down** *76* herunterregeln
turnaround *139* Kehrtwendung, Umschwung
to turn one's back on sb/sth *82* jdm/etwas den Rücken kehren
twice *79* zweimal, doppelt
to twist *12* (ver)drehen
typical *109* typisch
tyre *111* Reifen

U

ultimate *118t* ultimativ
unavailable *72* nicht verfügbar
unblinking *12* unbewegt
uncanny *137* ungeheuer, unheimlich
unclear *129* unklar
uncool *22* uncool
uncountable *19* nicht zählbar
uncultivated *150* brachliegend
undemocratic *110* undemokratisch
to underline *62* unterstreichen
underlined *8* unterstrichen
undernourished *152* Unterernährte/r
understandable *21* verständlich
unelected *110* nicht gewählt
unemployment *40* Arbeitslosigkeit
unfit *143* ungeeignet
uniformity *129* Gleichmäßigkeit
unintentional *151* unabsichtlich
union *89* Gewerkschaft
to unite *112* vereinigen
unless *69* wenn nicht
unluckily *29* unglücklicherweise
unnecessary *62* unnötig
unpaid *107* unbezahlt
unreliable *76* unzuverlässig
unspecified *20* unbestimmt
unusual *59* ungewöhnlich
up: to be up for *58t* bereit sein für, Lust haben auf
to upgrade *86* erweitern, verbessern
upmarket *68* anspruchsvoll, exklusiv
upset *65* bestürzt, entsetzt
urban *36* städtisch
urgent *48* dringend, eilig
user *59* Anwender/in, Benutzer/in

V

valid *134* gültig
valley *78* Tal
valuable *7* wertvoll
value *28* Wert
variety *40* Vielfalt
various *65* verschieden
to vary *45* variieren
vast *147* riesig, ungeheuer
vehicle papers *134* Wagenpapiere
verdict *141* Urteil, Beurteilung
verse *123* Vers, Strophe
victim *135* Opfer
victory *136* Sieg
view *81* Ansicht
violence *119* Gewalt
violent *7* gewalttätig
viral *49* viral, Virus-
virtual *26* virtuell
virtually *134* praktisch, nahezu
visa *24* Visum
vision *79* Vision, Vorausschau
visual *103* visuell, optisch
vocational *87* in der beruflichen Ausbildung, beruflich, Berufs-
voluntary *7* freiwillig
to vomit *16* erbrechen
to vote *56* abstimmen, wählen
voter *105* Wähler/in

W

wage *131t* Lohn
wages *88* Lohn, Löhne
to wait in line *43* anstehen
waiter *17* Kellner, Ober
wardrobe *26* Kleiderschrank, Garderobe
warehouse *140* Lager(halle)
warming *80* Erwärmung
warmth *98* Wärme
warning *141* Verwarnung, Warnung, Aufforderung
warrior *12* Krieger
washing powder *116* Waschpulver
waste *69* Abfall
wasteful *49* verschwenderisch
to watch out *24* aufpassen
waterfall *37* Wasserfall
wave *40* Welle
weakness *99* Schwäche
weapon *143* Waffe
weatherman *24* Meteorologe
to weed out *139* aussondern, -merzen
weekday *9* Wochentag
welfare *153* Fürsorge, Soziales
whatever *58* was (auch) immer
white-collar *89* Schreibtisch-, Büro-
whopping *83* gewaltig
widening *111* Erweiterung
willing: to be willing *139* bereit/gewillt sein
wise *79* weise, klug
within *40* innerhalb
to wonder *56* sich fragen, sich wundern
word of mouth *49* Mundpropaganda
to work out *51t* trainieren
workforce *89* Belegschaft
workplace *86* Arbeitsplatz
worldwide *43* weltweit
worried: to be worried *59* befürchten; *78* besorgt
worse *113* schlechter, schlimmer
worth of *83* im Wert von
worthwhile *7* der Mühe wert
wound *118t* Wunde
to wrestle *12* ringen
wrestler *13* Ringer/in
wrinkly *83* runzlig

XYZ

to yell *37* schreien
yield *149* Ertrag
Yours faithfully *106* Mit freundlichen Grüßen
zero *69* Null
zone *69* Zone, Bereich

Geographical names

Abilene ['æbəli:n] *Abilene*
Africa ['afrɪkə] *Afrika*
Alexandria [ˌælɪg'zɑ:ndriə] *Alexandria*
America [ə'merɪkə] *Amerika*
Antarctic [ænt'ɑ:ktɪk] *die Antarktis*
Arizona [ærɪ'zəʊnə] *Arizona*
Asia ['eɪʃə] *Asien*
Atlanta [ət'læntə] *Atlanta*
Austin [ˌtɪm 'ɒstɪn] *Austin*
Australia [ɒ'streɪliə] *Australien*
Austria ['ɒstriə] *Österreich*
Bangalore [ˌbæŋgə'lɔ:] *Bangalore*
Belgium ['beldʒəm] *Belgien*
Bengal [ˌben'gɔ:l] *Bengalen*
Big Apple [ˌbɪd 'æpl] *Spitzname für New York*
Brazil [brə'zɪl] *Brasilien*
Bristol ['brɪstl] *Bristol*
Britain ['brɪtn] *Großbritannien*
Broadway ['brɔ:dweɪ] *Broadway (Straßenname)*
Bronx [brɒŋks] *Bronx*
Brooklyn ['brʊklɪn] *Brooklyn*
Brussels ['brʌslz] *Brüssel*
Bulgaria [bʌl'geəriə] *Bulgarien*
California [ˌkælə'fɔ:niə] *Kalifornien*
Canada ['kænədə] *Kanada*
Cape Town ['keɪptaʊn] *Kapstadt*
(the) Caribbean [ðə ˌkærə'bi:ən] *(die) Karibik*
Central America [ˌsentrəl ə'merɪkə] *Mittelamerika*
Chicago [ʃɪ'kɑ:gəʊ] *Chicago*
China ['tʃaɪnə] *China*
Cologne [kə'ləʊn] *Köln*
Colorado [ˌkɒlə'rɑ:dəʊ] *Colorado*
Dublin ['dʌblɪn] *Dublin*
East Asia [ˌi:st 'eɪʃə] *Ostasien*
East River [ˌi:st 'rɪvə] *East River*
eastern Europe [ˌi:stən 'jʊərəp] *Osteuropa*
Eighth Ave [ˌeɪtθ 'ævənju:] *Eighth Ave (Straßenname)*
England ['ɪŋglənd] *England*
Europe ['jʊərəp] *Europa*
Finland ['fɪnlənd] *Finnland*
Florida ['flɒrɪdə] *Florida*
France [frɑ:ns] *Frankreich*
Galax ['gæləks] *Galax*
Georgia ['dʒɔ:dʒə] *Georgia*
Germany ['dʒɜ:məni] *Deutschland*
Greenland ['gri:nlənd] *Grönland*
Guatemala [ˌgwɑ:tə'mɑ:lə] *Guatemala*
Harlem ['hɑ:ləm] *Harlem*
Holland ['hɒlənd] *Holland*
Houston ['hju:stən] *Houston*
Hudson River [ˌhʌdsn 'rɪvə] *Hudson River*
Hull [hʌl] *Hull*
Illinois [ˌɪlə'nɔɪ] *Illinois*
India ['ɪndiə] *Indien*
Indonesia [ˌɪndəʊ'ni:ziə] *Indonesien*
Iran [ɪ'rɑ:n] *Iran*
Ireland ['aɪələnd] *Irland*
Italy ['ɪtəli] *Italien*
Kings Street [ˌkɪŋz 'stri:t] *Kings Street (Straßenname)*
Latin America [ˌlætɪn ə'merɪkə] *Lateinamerika*
Littleton ['lɪtltən] *Littleton*
London ['lʌndən] *London*
Los Angeles [lɒs 'ændʒəli:z] *Los Angeles*
Luxemburg ['lʌksəmbɜ:g] *Luxemburg*
Manchester ['mæntʃɪstə] *Manchester*
Manhattan [mæn'hætn] *Manhattan*
(the) Mediterranean [ðə ˌmedɪtə'reɪniən] *Mittelmeer*
Miami [maɪ'æmi] *Miami*
Morocco [mə'rɒkəʊ] *Marokko*
(the) Netherlands [ðə 'neðələndz] *die Niederlande*
New Orleans [ˌnju: ɔ:'li:əns] *New Orleans*
New York (NY) [ˌnju: 'jɔ:k] *New York*
New York Bay [ˌnju: jɔ:k 'beɪ] *New Yorker Bucht*
New York City [ˌnju: jɔ:k 'sɪti] *New York City*
New Zealand [ˌnju: 'zi:lənd] *Neuseeland*
Norfolk ['nɔ:fək] *Norfolk*
North America [ˌnɔ:θ ə'merɪkə] *Nordamerika*
Norway ['nɔ:weɪ] *Norwegen*
Norwich ['nɒrɪdʒ] *Norwich*
Oak Street [ˌəʊk 'stri:t] *Oak Street (Straßenname)*
Oregon ['ɒrɪgən] *Oregon*
Oxford ['ɒksfəd] *Oxford*
Paris ['pærɪs] *Paris*
Perryton ['perɪtən] *Perryton*
(the) Philippines [ðə 'fɪləpi:nz] *die Philippinen*
Phoenix ['fi:nɪks] *Phoenix*
Queens [kwi:nz] *Queens*
Richmond ['rɪtʃmənd] *Richmond*
Rio Grande [ˌri:əʊ 'grænd] *Rio Grande*
Rome [rəʊm] *Rom*
Route 66 [ˌru:t ˌsɪksti 'sɪks] *Route 66 (Straßenverbindung zur US-amerikanischen Westküste)*
Russia ['rʌʃə] *Russland*

San Bernando [sæn bə'nændəʊ]	*San Bernando*
San Diego [ˌsæn di'eɪgəʊ]	*San Diego*
San Francisco [ˌsæn frən'sɪskəʊ]	*San Francisco*
Seattle [si'ætl]	*Seattle*
Shanghai [ˌʃæŋ'haɪ]	*Shanghai*
Shropshire ['ʃrɒpʃə]	*Shropshire*
Silver Creek [ˌsɪlvə 'kriːk]	*Silver Creek*
South Africa [saʊθ 'æfrɪkə]	*Südafrika*
South America [ˌsaʊθ ə'merɪkə]	*Südamerika*
Stafford ['stæfəd]	*Stafford*
Staten Island [ˌstætn 'aɪlənd]	*Staten Island*
Strasbourg ['stræzbɜːg]	*Straßburg*
Sweden ['swiːdn]	*Schweden*
Swindon ['swɪndən]	*Swindon*
Texas ['teksəs]	*Texas*
Tokyo ['təʊkiəʊ]	*Tokio*
Tucson ['tuːsɒn]	*Tucson*
Turkey ['tɜːki]	*Türkei*
Tuusula ['tuːsulɑ]	*Tuusula*
(the) UK [ðə ˌjuː 'keɪ]	*(das) Vereinigte Königreich*
(the) USA [ðə ˌjuː es 'eɪ]	*(die) Vereinigten Staaten von Amerika*
Vermont [və'mɒnt]	*Vermont*
Virginia [və'dʒɪniə]	*Virginia*
Wales [weɪlz]	*Wales*
Washington D.C. ['wɒʃɪŋtən ˌdiː 'siː]	*Washington D.C.*

Irregular verbs

be	was/were	been	*sein*
beat	beat	beaten	*schlagen, besiegen*
become	became	become	*werden*
begin	began	begun	*anfangen, beginnen*
bend	bent	bent	*(sich) beugen*
blow	blew	blown	*wehen, blasen, ziehen*
break	broke	broken	*brechen*
breed	bred	bred	*sich vermehren, sich ausbreiten*
bring	brought	brought	*(mit)bringen*
build	built	built	*bauen*
burn	burnt/burned	burnt/burned	*(ver)brennen*
buy	bought	bought	*kaufen*
catch	caught	caught	*fangen, fassen, erreichen*
choose	chose	chosen	*(aus)wählen*
come	came	come	*kommen*
cost	cost	cost	*kosten*
cross-breed	cross-bred	cross-bred	*kreuzen*
cut	cut	cut	*schneiden*
deal	dealt	dealt	*versetzen, verteilen*
dig	dug	dug	*graben*
do	did	done	*tun, machen*
draw	drew	drawn	*zeichnen*
dream	dreamt/dreamed	dreamt/dreamed	*träumen*
drink	drank	drunk	*trinken*
drive	drove	driven	*fahren*
eat	ate	eaten	*essen*
fall	fell	fallen	*fallen*
feed	fed	fed	*füttern, ernähren*
feel	felt	felt	*(sich) fühlen, empfinden*
fight	fought	fought	*kämpfen*
find	found	found	*finden*
fit	fit/fitted	fit/fitted	*passen, entsprechen, anbringen*
fly	flew	flown	*fliegen*
forbid	forbade	forbidden	*verbieten*
forget	forgot	forgotten	*vergessen*
get	got	got (*AE* gotten)	*bekommen*
give	gave	given	*geben*
go	went	gone	*gehen, fahren*
grow	grew	grown	*wachsen*
hang	hung	hung	*hängen*
have	had	had	*haben*
hear	heard	heard	*hören*
hide	hid	hidden	*(sich) verstecken*
hit	hit	hit	*schlagen*
hold	held	held	*halten, festhalten*

hurt	hurt	hurt	*verletzen*
keep	kept	kept	*behalten*
know	knew	known	*kennen, wissen*
lay	laid	laid	*legen*
lead	led	led	*führen*
lean	leant/leaned	leant/leaned	*sich lehnen, sich beugen*
learn	learnt/learned	learnt/learned	*lernen*
leave	left	left	*abfahren, verlassen, weggehen*
let	let	let	*lassen*
lie	lay	lain	*liegen*
light	lit	lit	*anzünden, beleuchten*
lose	lost	lost	*verlieren*
make	made	made	*machen*
mean	meant	meant	*meinen, bedeuten*
meet	met	met	*treffen*
overcome	overcame	overcome	*überwinden, überwältigen*
override	overrode	overridden	*sich hinwegsetzen über*
panic	panicked	panicked	*in Panik geraten*
pay	paid	paid	*bezahlen*
put	put	put	*setzen, stellen, legen*
quit	quit/quitted	quit/quitted	*verlassen, aufhören*
read	read	read	*lesen*
repay	repaid	repaid	*zurückzahlen*
rewrite	rewrote	rewritten	*umschreiben*
ride	rode	ridden	*reiten, fahren*
ring	rang	rung	*anrufen, läuten*
rise	rose	risen	*(an)steigen*
run	ran	run	*laufen, rennen*
say	said	said	*sagen*
see	saw	seen	*sehen*
seek	sought	sought	*suchen*
sell	sold	sold	*verkaufen*
send	sent	sent	*senden, schicken*
set	set	set	*setzen, stellen*
shake	shook	shaken	*schütteln*
shine	shone	shone	*scheinen, glänzen*
show	showed	shown	*zeigen*
shrink	shrank	shrunk	*schrumpfen, zurückgehen*
shut	shut	shut	*schließen*
sing	sang	sung	*singen*
sink	sank	sunk	*sinken*
sit	sat	sat	*sitzen*
sleep	slept	slept	*schlafen*
slide	slid	slid	*(ab)rutschen, (ab)sacken*
smell	smelt/smelled	smelt/smelled	*riechen*
speak	spoke	spoken	*sprechen*

spell	spelt/ spelled	spelt/ spelled	*buchstabieren*	tell	told	told	*sagen, erzählen*
spend	spent	spent	*ausgeben, verbringen*	think	thought	thought	*denken*
spread	spread	spread	*(sich) verbreiten*	throw	threw	thrown	*werfen*
stand	stood	stood	*stehen*	under-stand	under-stood	under-stood	*verstehen*
steal	stole	stolen	*stehlen*	wake	woke	woken	*aufwachen, aufwecken*
swim	swam	swum	*schwimmen*	wear	wore	worn	*tragen*
take	took	taken	*nehmen*	win	won	won	*gewinnen*
teach	taught	taught	*unterrichten, beibringen*	write	wrote	written	*schreiben*

Quellenverzeichnis

Titel: Fotofinder: A1PIX; DLR; istockphoto; Fotofinder: Karlheinz Oster

RF photos:
Alamy: S. 6/2/E. Audras, S. 3/Itani, S. 7/4/IS503; S. 16/T. Kroeger, S. 46/moodboard, S. 52/K. Brofsky, S. 77/2/J. Pelaez, S. 85/2/BananaStock, S. 85/4/EV107, S. 85/5/R. McVay, S. 85/6/IS147, S. 89/2/J. Hollingsworth, S. 89/3/Bananastock, S. 95/3/WidStock, S. 105/3/Big Cheese Special, S. 96/1/J. Woodhouse, S. 96/5/SomosGroup1, S. 106/Niehoff, S. 110/K. Glubish, S. 111/1/IS945, S. 111/2/rubberball, S. 111/3/Radius images, S. 111/4/J. Hollingsworth, S. 116/2/BananaStock, S. 116/3/IS732, S. 120/1/Shoosh, S. 123/indykb, S. 140/2/Photodisc, S. 140/3/S. Marcus;
Corbis: S. 14/moodboard, S. 17/1;
Comstock: S.17/2;
Istock: S. 6/1/3; S7/1/2, S. 37/2, S. 68/2; S. 141;
Maly, V.: S. 95/2, S. 99/1/2;
Masterfile: S. 114;
Shutterstock: S. 22/1/2, S. 26/1/2, S. 35/2/3/4/6, S. 50/1-5, S. 66/1/3/4/5, S. 67, S. 73, S. 77/1, S. 82, S. 90/1/2, S. 95/1, S. 96/1/3, S. 99/3, S. 105/1, S. 115/2-8, S. 138, S. 145/4/6, S. 151;

RM photos:
Actionpress: S. 145/7;
Advertising Archives: S. 45/1/2/3/5, S. 53;
Alamy: S. 30/1/P. Cutler, S30/2/J. West, S. 35/5/BLimages, S. 37/1/D. Frates, S40/P. Bennett, S. 66/2/Travelshots, S. 71/Kiedrowski, S. 72/JoeFox, S76/1/G. Williams, S. 76/3/J. Moers, S. 76/4/Caro, S. 89/4/zoonar.com, S. 94/Pixland0907, S. 116/1/ClassicStock, S. 124/acestock, S. 127/1/dbtravel, S. 139/1/H. Threlfall, S. 139/2/D. Grossman, S. 140/1/T. McGuire, S. 140/4/H. Westheim, S. 145/2/acestock, S. 146/A. Segre, S. 151/2/Nick Gregory;
Cinetext: S. 58, S. 75/1; Condé Nast Publications: S. 129/Allure Cover;
Corbis: S. 12/1/Emely, S. 12/2/Duomo, S. 89/1, S. 96/3/E.Jansson;
Fotofinder: S. 16/2/Andreas Buck, S. 26/Fotoagtur Magics/P. Schatz, S. 30/Weisflog, S. 76/2/
GettyImages: S. 128/AFP;
Greenpeace: S. 148/2;
ImageSource, S. 85/1/A1Pix, S. 85/3/Matthias Stolt, S. 86/Mediacolors, S. 105/2/F1online, S. 115/tranistArchiv/T. Roetting, S. 120/2/Caro/Teschner;
PictureAlliance: S. 35/7, S. 56/1/GMTV, S. 56/2/J. Ryan, S. 75/2/3/4, S. 105/4/R. Hirschberger, S. 105/5/dpa, S. 119/1/PA, S119/2/L. Ruymen, S. 121/EPA, S. 122/2/dpa, S127/2, S. 129/2/A. Teich, S. 129/3/I. West, S. 131/1/L. Stringer, S131/2/G. Caddick, S. 136/P. Buck, S. 145/1/EPA, S. 145/5/ P. Kneffel;
Mondolithic Studios: S. 81/Kenn Brown;
Reuters: S. 102/2/Fabrizio Bensch, S. 122/1/Ho New;
Ullstein-Bild: S. 137;

Cartoons
cartoonStock.com: S. 61, 65, 68/1, 102;
Martyn Ford, LGP, Brighton: S. 92; The Cartoonist Group: S. 132; Punch Ltd: S. 135; Mark Parisi, offthemark.com: S. 51/1; Mike Ramirez, Creators Syndicate: S. 152; Klaus Stuttmann: S. 111/5

Textquellen
S. 59: Adapted and abridged from *Things you wouldn't tell your mother* by Alison George, New Scientist, 16.09.06, p. 50
S. 63: Extract from *1984* by George Orwell, London 2004
S. 73: Adapted from *Zero emissions, zero deaths, total choice*, Sunday Times, 19.06.05
S. 102: Abridged From *The World in 2011* by David Cameron, The Economist, 22.11.10
S. 102: Abridged From *Schwere Krawalle bei Großdemo*, stern.de, 02.06.07
S. 122: Abridged From *Neptune's Navy* by Raffi Khatchadourian, The New Yorker, 05.11.07
S. 122: Abridged From *Mappschiedsparty gipfelt in Ausschreitungen*, dapd.de, 28.03.11
S. 123: *Dress Sense* by David Kitchen,Collins Study & Revision Guide, Stage 4, Collins Educational, HarperCollins, London 1998
S. 126/127: Hanif Kureishi, *Love in a Blue Time*, Faber and Faber, 1997
S. 132: Adapted from *Foreign Workers Help Business Survive* by Amanda Crawford, whsv.com, 08.04.11
S. 136: Based on *http://en.wikipedia.org/wiki/Karla_Faye_Tucker*
S. 146/147: Abridged from *British supermarkets call for a boycott of 'cloned' meat and milk*, Daily Mail 10.01.07

European Union